Teaching, Learning and the Curriculum in Secondary Schools

The Open University *Flexible* Postgraduate Certificate in Education

The readers and the companion volumes in the *flexible* PGCE series are:

Aspects of Teaching and Learning in Secondary Schools: Perspectives on practice

Teaching, Learning and the Curriculum in Secondary Schools: A reader

Aspects of Teaching Secondary Mathematics: Perspectives on practice

Teaching Mathematics in Secondary Schools: A reader

Aspects of Teaching Secondary Science: Perspectives on practice

Teaching Science in Secondary Schools: A reader

Aspects of Teaching Secondary Modern Foreign Languages: Perspectives on practice

Teaching Modern Foreign Languages in Secondary Schools: A reader

Aspects of Teaching Secondary Geography: Perspectives on practice

Teaching Geography in Secondary Schools: A reader

Aspects of Teaching Secondary Design and Technology: Perspectives on practice

Teaching Design and Technology in, Secondary Schools: A reader

Aspects of Teaching Secondary Music: Perspectives on practice

Teaching Music in Secondary Schools: A reader

All of these subjects are part of the Open University's initial teacher education course, the *flexible* PGCE, and constitute part of an integrated course designed to develop critical understanding. The set books, reflecting a wide range of perspectives, and discussing the complex issues that surround teaching and learning in the twenty-first century, will appeal to both beginning and experienced teachers, to mentors, tutors, advisers and other teacher educators.

If you would like to receive a *flexible* PGCE prospectus please write to the Course Reservations Centre at The Call Centre, The Open University, Milton Keynes MK7 6ZS. Other information about programmes of professional development in education is available from the same address.

Teaching, Learning and the Curriculum in Secondary Schools
A reader

The articles which make up this reader provide both overview and analysis of the central issues in secondary education. Focused closely upon what it means to teach and learn in the modern secondary classroom, *Teaching, Learning and the Curriculum in Secondary Schools* provides invaluable insight into the development of secondary education today. It is an ideal introduction to the task of teachers in secondary schools.

Issues covered by this book include:

- The new agenda around teaching and learning
- Effective pedagogy
- The teacher–student relationship
- Teaching, learning and the digital age
- Grouping by ability
- Managing curriculum change
- Assessment
- Equal opportunities and educational change

The *Teaching in Secondary Schools* series brings together collections of articles by highly experienced educators that focus on the issues surrounding the teaching of National Curriculum subjects. They are invaluable resources for those studying to become teachers, and for newly qualified teachers and more experienced practitioners, particularly those mentoring students and NQTs. The companion volume to this book is *Aspects of Teaching and Learning in Secondary Schools: Perspectives on practice*.

Bob Moon is Professor of Education and Director of the Centre for Research and Development in Teacher Education at The Open University. **Ann Shelton Mayes** is Director of Initial Teacher Training Strategy at the Open University's Faculty of Education and Language Studies. **Steven Hutchinson** is Director of Secondary Initial Teacher Training at The Open University.

Set book for the Open University *flexible* PGCE courses.

Teaching, Learning and the Curriculum in Secondary Schools

A reader

Edited by Bob Moon
Ann Shelton Mayes
and Steven Hutchinson

RoutledgeFalmer
Taylor & Francis Group

LONDON AND NEW YORK

The Open
University

First published 2002
by RoutledgeFalmer
2 Park Square, Milton Park, Abingdon, Oxon, OX14 4RN

Simultaneously published in the USA and Canada
by RoutledgeFalmer
270 Madison Avenue, New York, NY 10016

RoutledgeFalmer is an imprint of the Taylor & Francis Group

Reprinted 2004, 2005

© 2002 Compilation, original and editorial matter,
The Open University

Typeset in Goudy by Bookcraft Ltd, Stroud, Gloucestershire
Printed and bound in Great Britain by MPG Books Ltd, Bodmin

British Library Cataloguing in Publication Data
A catalogue record for this book is available from the British Library

Library of Congress Cataloging in Publication Data
A catalog record has been requested

ISBN 0–415–26066–3 (hbk)

ISBN 0–415–26067–1 (pbk)

Contents

Illustrations

Figures

Tables

Abbreviations

DfEE   Department for Education and Employment
        (now Department for Education and Skills, DfES)
ERA   Education Reform Act
GCE   General Certificate of Education
GCSE   General Certificate of Secondary Education
GNVQ   General National Vocational Qualification
NVQ   National Vocational Qualification
QCA   Qualifications and Curriculum Authority

Note
In the chapters which have previously been published elsewhere an ellipsis denotes omitted material, while an ellipsis in square brackets […] indicates that a paragraph or more has been omitted.

Sources

Where a chapter in this book is based on or is a reprint or revision of material previously published elsewhere, details are given below, with grateful acknowledgements to the original publishers. In some cases chapter titles are different to the original title of publication; in such cases the original title is given below.

Chapter 1   This chapter was originally published in Banks, F. and Shelton Mayes, A. (eds) (2001) *Early Professional Development for Teachers*, David Fulton Publishers, London.

Chapter 2   This is an edited version of a chapter originally published in Bruner, J. *The Culture of Education*, pp. 13–43, Cambridge, Mass.: Harvard University Press, © 1996 by the President and Fellows of Harvard College. Reprinted by permission of the original publisher. This chapter was originally titled *Culture, Mind and Education*.

Chapter 3   This is an edited version of a chapter originally published in Moon, B. and Shelton Mayes, A. (eds) (1994) *Teaching and Learning in the Secondary School*, Routledge, London.

Chapter 4   This is an edited version of a chapter originally published in Moon, B. and Shelton Mayes, A. (eds) (1994) *Teaching and Learning in the Secondary School*, pp. 50–6, Routledge, London.

Chapter 5   This is an edited version of an article originally published in *Education Researcher* 29 (1), ©American Educational Research Association (2000), Washington.

Chapter 6   This is an edited version of a report originally published by the DfEE (2000).

Chapter 7   This is an edited version of a chapter originally published in Mortimore, P. (ed.) (1999) *Understanding Pedagogy and its Impact on Learning*, Paul Chapman, London. Reprinted by permission of Paul Chapman Publishing. This chapter was originally titled *The Common Strands of Pedagogy and Their Implications*.

Chapter 8   This is an edited version of a chapter originally published in Leach, J. and Moon, B. (eds) (1999) *Learners and Pedagogy*, Paul Chapman, London. Reprinted by permission of Paul Chapman Publishing.

Chapter 9   This is an edited version of an article originally published in *Educational Review* 51 (3), Carfax Publishing, Taylor & Francis Ltd, Basingstoke (1999) http://www.tandf.co.uk.

Chapter 10   This is an edited version of an article originally published in *The*

British Journal of Sociology of Education 20 (4), Carfax Publishing, Taylor & Francis Ltd, Basingstoke (1999) http://www.tandf.co.uk.

Chapter 11   This chapter was originally published in Pring, R. and Walford, G. (eds) (1997) *Affirming the Comprehensive Ideal*, pp. 137–47, Falmer Press, London.

Chapter 12   This chapter was originally published in Moon, B. and Shelton Mayes, A. (eds) (1994) *Teaching and Learning in the Secondary School*, Routledge, London.

Chapter 13   This is an edited version of a chapter originally published in Moon, B., Brown, S. and Ben-Peretz, M. (eds) (2000) *Routledge International Companion to Education*, Routledge, London.

Chapter 15   This chapter was originally published in the *Education Journal* (January 1999) EPC Publishing, Hove.

Chapter 16   This chapter was originally published in Moon, B., Brown, S. and Ben-Peretz, M. (eds) (2000) *Routledge International Companion to Education*, Routledge, London.

Chapter 18   This is an edited version of a chapter in Moon, B. and Shelton Mayes, A. (eds) (1994) *Teaching and Learning in the Secondary School*, Routledge, London.

Chapter 19   This is an edited version of a chapter originally published in Fullan, M. (2001) *The New Meaning of Educational Change*, 3rd edn, Routledge Falmer. The chapter was originally titled *Planning, Doing and Coping with Change*.

Chapter 20   This chapter was originally published in Moon, B. and Shelton Mayes, A. (eds) (1994) *Teaching and Learning in the Secondary School*, Routledge, London.

Chapter 21   This chapter was originally published in Moon, B. and Shelton Mayes, A. (eds) (1994) *Teaching and Learning in the Secondary School*, Routledge, London.

Chapter 22   This chapter was originally published in Mortimore, P. (1998) *The Road to Improvement: Reflections on school effectiveness*, pp. 113–35, Swets and Zietlinger, Lisse. Reprinted with permission of the original publisher.

Chapter 24   This article was originally published in *Education Review* 11 (2), Carfax Publishing, Taylor & Francis Ltd, Basingstoke (1997) http://www.tandf.co.uk.

Chapter 25   This chapter was originally published in Beck, J. and Earl, M. (eds) (1999) *Key Issues in Secondary Education*, Cassell, London. Reprinted with permission of Continuum International Publishing Group Ltd, the Tower Building, 11 York Road, London, England.

Chapter 26   This chapter was originally published in Best, R., Lang, P., Lodge, C., and Watkins, C. (eds) (2000) *Pastoral Care and Personal-Social Education*, Cassell, London. Reprinted with permission of Continuum International Publishing Group Ltd, the Tower Building, 11 York Road, London, England.

Chapter 27   This is an edited version of a chapter originally published in Munn, P., Lloyd, G., and Cullen, M. (eds) (2000) *Alternatives to Exclusion in School*, Paul Chapman, London. Reprinted by permission of Paul Chapman Publishing. This chapter was originally titled *Policy Matters (on Exclusion from Schools)*.

Foreword

The nature and form of initial teacher education and training are issues that lie at the heart of the teaching profession. They are inextricably linked to the standing and identity that society attributes to teachers and are seen as being one of the main planks in the push to raise standards in schools and to improve the quality of education in them. The initial teacher education curriculum therefore requires careful definition. How can it best contribute to the development of the range of skills, knowledge and understanding that makes up the complex, multi-faceted, multi-skilled and people-centred process of teaching?

There are, of course, external, government-defined requirements for initial teacher training courses. These specify, amongst other things, the length of time a student spends in school, the subject knowledge requirements beginning teachers are expected to demonstrate or the ICT skills that are needed. These requirements, however, do not in themselves constitute the initial training curriculum. They are only one of the many, if sometimes competing, components that make up the broad spectrum of a teacher's professional knowledge that underpins initial teacher education courses.

Certainly today's teachers need to be highly skilled in literacy, numeracy and ICT, in classroom methods and management. In addition, however, they also need to be well grounded in the critical dialogue of teaching. They need to be encouraged to be creative and innovative and to appreciate that teaching is a complex and problematic activity. This is a view of teaching that is shared with partner schools within the Open University Training Schools Network. As such it has informed the planning and development of the Open University's initial teacher training programme and the *flexible* PGCE.

All of the *flexible* PGCE courses have a series of connected and complementary readers. The *Teaching in Secondary Schools* series pulls together a range of new thinking about teaching and learning in particular subjects. Key debates and differing perspectives are presented, and evidence from research and practice is explored, inviting the reader to question the accepted orthodoxy, suggesting ways of enriching the present curriculum and offering new thoughts on classroom learning. These readers are accompanied by the series *Perspectives on practice*. Here, the focus is on the application of these developments to educational/subject policy and the classroom, and on the illustration of teaching skills, knowledge and understanding in a variety of school contexts. Both series include newly commissioned work.

This series from RoutledgeFalmer, in supporting the Open University's *flexible* PGCE, also includes two key texts that explore the wider educational background. These companion publications, *Teaching, Learning and the Curriculum in Secondary Schools: A reader* and *Aspects of Teaching and Learning in Secondary Schools: Perspectives on practice*, explore a contemporary view of developments in secondary education with the aim of providing analysis and insights for those participating in initial teacher training education courses.

Hilary Bourdillon – Director ITT Strategy
Steven Hutchinson – Director ITT Secondary
The Open University
September 2001

Preface

In 2002 The Open University introduced a new programme for the education and training of secondary school teachers. This reader was compiled as a resource for students participating in this programme. A wide range of sources has been drawn on – books, journal articles, occasional papers and some newly commissioned chapters. The selection is made with the particular needs of Open University courses in mind. We hope, however, that it will be of value for others who are similarly involved in the preparation of teachers. The selection can be used and interpreted in a variety of ways. We hope, as well, that the reader will be of interest and value more widely to those involved in the important ongoing task of improving and reforming secondary education. We would like to acknowledge and express our thanks to the range of contributors, and to Mike Bird for his essential support in preparing this reader.

Bob Moon
Ann Shelton Mayes
Steve Hutchinson

Introduction
The context of secondary schooling

Bob Moon

Secondary education in the UK is undergoing significant transformation. A quest for diversity and specialization, an urgency about raising standards of student attainment and new approaches to bringing the academic and vocational into stronger alignment are characteristics of this process. This is not a new phenomenon. Secondary schools have been under the spotlight for most of the twentieth century, particularly in the period following the 1944 Education Act that established the structures for compulsory secondary schooling.

Between 1944 and the early 1970s powerful and opposing ideological forces fought out a battle over the merits and demerits of the tripartite system of separate grammar, technical and secondary modern schools that had been planned in the 1944 Education Act. In that period those who favoured a more comprehensive approach to secondary schooling gradually gained the upper hand. The abolition of the 11+ examination and then, in the early 1980s, the introduction of the common 16+ General Certificate of Secondary Education (GCSE) examination were both symbolic of the change. Comprehensivizsation happened over different timescales across the country and strong local conditions of control have meant that in some areas (Kent, Buckinghamshire and Northern Ireland, for example) selective systems of schooling were retained into the present century. The large majority of maintained secondary schools, however, had become comprehensive by the early 1980s. Almost immediately, however, major political concerns began to be articulated about the performance and effectiveness of secondary schools, particularly in England and Wales. This was manifest in the first part of the 1980s by a national project, the Technical and Vocational Education Initiative (TVEI) which aimed to inject practical, relevant and vocationally orientated courses into the curriculum. It was run from the Department of Employment rather than Education.

In 1988, concerned about the variations and quality of the secondary curriculum, the then Conservative government introduced into England and Wales a national curriculum. Northern Ireland followed shortly. TVEI funding ceased, although some of the associated development work was incorporated into a national systems of vocational qualifications (NVQs).

The Labour government elected in 1997 focused primarily on raising standards in primary schools. The introduction of national literacy and numeracy strategies, for example, aimed significantly to improve attainment in these basic areas. The second Labour government, re-elected in 2001, moved the focus to secondary schooling with a similar agenda in terms of literacy and numeracy and with a strong determination to diversify the system through the funding of schools specializing in different aspects of the curriculum.

These shifts and changes in policy represent, of course, a complex interplay of political, ideological and economic forces. Over the last twenty years political activity, especially from central government, has increased enormously. The status and power of education ministers have grown in equal measure.

The political interest in schooling, however, is also related to changing patterns of employment and economic development. The more knowledge-based forms of industry and commerce that emerged in the latter part of the twentieth century require a workforce significantly more educated than appeared necessary at the time of the 1944 Education Act. Although the link between education and economic productivity is a complex one, some form of relationship clearly exists. Successive governments, therefore, have placed the improvement of education high on the political agenda.

The development of secondary schooling, however, is more than the story of the changes in governmental policies, important as this may be. While the subjects of the secondary curriculum may have titles similar to those used fifty or a hundred years ago, the nature of the processes and content that make up the subject has undergone important change. Mathematics and Science, for example, have increasingly adapted more investigational or experimental exploratory approaches than was traditionally the case. English, while still developing verbal and written skills, has brought out the relationship between literature and social issues in new approaches to the subject. Inevitably in many, if not all, subject areas the changes have been a matter of considerable controversy. When the National Curriculum was being written the types of literature in English, the forms of music in Music and the content chosen for History all caused impassioned debates in schools and in the media. Differences of views around more general issues also exist. How pupils should be grouped (streams, sets or mixed attainment), for example, continues to be a source of lively debate.

Over the last fifty years secondary schools have also come increasingly to accept a social as well as an academic role in society. Personal tutors, guidance and counselling systems and forms of personal and social education have all come to have increasing significance in the life of the school. Secondary schools have been in the front line of institutions that have faced the challenge of society's changing attitudes to issues such as ethnicity, gender or disability.

Important work in the 1980s and 1990s, continuing today, has attempted to look at political and pedagogic issues in seeking to understand the change process, particularly in ways that relate to effectiveness and improvement. No universal formula has, or is likely, to emerge but some key issues including leadership and clarity of planning can be identified. The quality of teachers is also crucial, particularly the building of shared values about the purposes and processes of teaching and learning and school organization.

This reader is aimed particularly at those preparing to become teachers, and at newly qualified practitioners, in secondary schools. It brings together a range of resources that provide varied viewpoints on key areas:

- learners and learning
- teachers and teaching
- classrooms
- curriculum
- schools.

The reader touches on the formal agenda associated with national policies, but also considers the range of debates that occur in parallel with that. It does not provide a complete coverage of the issues and challenges facing contemporary secondary schools. It does aim, however, to be a representative collection that addresses the major concerns of the day.

Anyone looking back at the significant moments of change for secondary schools will often discern high levels of optimism, even excitement, about the possibilities of reform. Over time, given changing social and economic conditions, disappointment can set in. Great expectations were set for the tripartite system of schooling in the 1940s. Similar aspirations were associated with the early development of comprehensive schools. Attempts are now being made to renew a sense of vision around secondary schooling. Teachers have a key role to play. A knowledge of the forces that have shaped and are shaping secondary education is essential to a productive engagement in the processes of change and reform.

Section 1

Learners and learning

1 Learning perspectives on the teachers' task

Bob Moon

Down through the centuries people have wondered about the nature of human learning. What is the relationship between the physical object we know to be our brains and the rich, informational and emotional world we know to be our mind? By what process of evolution did humankind develop capacities for thought? How did our mental strategies for dealing with the usual and the unusual evolve?

Creating the conditions for learning, observing learning, and assessing learning is the key task of teachers. Yet learning is a misty territory. At the beginning of the twenty-first century we are still unsure quite how our minds work, or how the physical and mental processes within ourselves and between ourselves and the outside world create the conditions for learning. Numerous theories exist. At different periods in history particular ideas have often gained ascendancy but no one view of learning has ever gained universal approval.

Despite the uncertainties about how it happens, the process of learning is a wonderful thing to behold. Two- or three-year-old children have minds far more complex than the most sophisticated computers. Their language recognition skills far outstrip the most advanced voice recognition technologies and appear likely to do so for a long time yet.

The challenge for formal teaching is how to transpose the extraordinary human capacity for learning, particularly in the young, to those artificial worlds we have created in schools and classrooms. I say artificial because much of our learning, and certainly all our early learning, occurs in far less structured places than schools. We are all voracious learners. It is estimated that the average adult has understanding of 75,000 words (Gopnick *et al.* 1999), with the foundation for that vocabulary laid well before the years of formal schooling begins.

Learning is full of paradoxes. How come our linguistic skill at the age of five and the linguistic uncertainty, even embarrassment, in another language at the age of ten or twenty? By what means does a sight or smell conjure up memories that have lain dormant for decades or more? While there are theories about these sorts of phenomena, no one has definitive answers.

A few years ago Brazilian psychologists became intrigued by the numerical abilities of children who lived on the streets (Carraher *et al.* 1985). These children, street traders by day and night, were found to have very high level mental computational skills, particularly when working with rapidly changing exchange rates. Yet in school their mathematics performance, especially in written exercise, was poor. Learning was clearly taking place, but not the sort schools expected or wanted, and certainly not using the rules and routines of school mathematics. Learning, therefore, is also influenced by context. Most people, from personal experience, will remember a time when they became passionately interested in some topic. Music, fashion, fishing or football might be examples from our teenage world. Learning about these things, fired by strong motivation, was almost effortless. What a contrast with some of the subjects we struggled with at school.

Controversies about learning have also been dominated by the nature–nurture debate. How much capability are we born with? How much do we acquire through our own efforts? There is now, however, a strong consensus that our intelligence and capacity for learning grows and develops given the right environment. Yes, there are some components that nature seems to provide. The ratio of nature to nurture, however, is unclear, not the least because learning covers such a huge array of contents and contexts.

A great deal of evidence now shows intelligences to be a multi-faceted and pliable concept, more flexible than suggested by pre-war psychologists who argued the case for fixed IQs. Yet the idea of 'born not made' is a strong one in the popular imagination.

The American psychologist, Howard Gardner, is an influential figure who has challenged the idea of a single and measurable intelligence. In a series of books he has argued the case for what he terms 'multiple intelligences'. Our minds, he suggests, are more complex than a singular notion of intelligence suggests. Gardner (1983) suggests at least seven types of intelligence that require different forms of encouragement and support:

- logical mathematical
- linguistic
- spatial
- bodily-kinaesthetic
- musical
- interpersonal
- intrapersonal.

Schooling, he argues, has tended to emphasize some forms of intelligence more than others and this is highly restrictive of full educational development. Gardner, mostly in the USA, has had the courage to put his ideas into practice (see Gardner 1993) in seeking new forms of curriculum and school organization that fosters the broad range of intelligences. It is too soon to pass judgement on the outcome of these experiments. There are, however, those who question the conceptual basis. John White, for example, in a critique (White 1998), suggests that Gardner conflates ideas of physical and mental growth and he sees Gardner's own cultural context and values as heavily influencing a determination of intelligences that are claimed as universal.

In a similar way psychologists have increasingly focused on the way in which learning is very dependent on the situation in which it takes place. The phrase 'situated learning' is now used extensively by those working in this field. While not directly critiquing Gardner they point out the problems of theories that treat knowing as the manipulation of symbols inside the mind of the individual and learning as the acquisition of knowledge and skills that can then be applied across a range of contexts (Putnam and Borko 2000).

We are so accustomed to thinking of learning in individual terms that this can be quite a difficult concept to grasp. Essentially the argument is that learning always means engaging with some sort of other (outside ourselves) situation. This might be a book (with all the cultural associations that has for use) or a group of other learners in an impressively equipped science laboratory. You cannot think of learning without embracing a situation. Teachers, therefore, need to understand the significance of the contexts of learning every bit as much as they think about the organization of knowledge or the receptivity of individual learners. In this context learning is a social process and the role of all the 'others' is crucial to effective learning.

There are some straightforward examples of how this works. Most people have had the experience of formulating an idea and hypothesis and then discovered that the first time they verbalize it to others it seems lacklustre and inadequate. The old adage 'the best way to learn is to teach' has some resonance here. Repeated verbalization of ideas and concepts certainly can enhance learning and hence the vital role accorded to language in our understandings of teaching and learning, hence, over the past few decades, the interest in encouraging learners to articulate their ideas in pairs or groups, a mode of learning that worries some who would prefer a classroom with serried, silent ranks of children.

There is also another dimension to situated learning which goes under the term 'distributed'. This term emphasizes the way that in most parts of everyday life learning and human action is hardly ever 'wholly individual'. Most of the time we work with tools and others to create joint learning communities. This goes back to the very first social human activities. The first time a flint or tree branch was used to supplement our individual prowess was the moment our learning became distributed across tools. The first groupings-together to solve problems in our environment (hunting, fishing, agriculture) represented a distribution of learning across others. Often both tools and others work together in a learning environment.

Traditional school contexts often focus on individualistic learning. Learning with others and using tools (calculators, for example) may even be discouraged.

This is an interesting debate that continues. Over the last few decades, however, a professional consensus among psychologists and social psychologists has emerged that brings into question the notion of any overarching intelligence that embraces all human activity, including the range of activities played out in schools. Equally any idea that our capacities are limited at birth is now seen as flying in the face of all the evidence. Brain research, for example, is now demonstrating that our brains evolve and grow throughout most of our life, even if the early years, in establishing a conceptual understanding of the world, are particularly crucial. A consensus is also emerging that questions the dominance of highly individualistic approaches to understanding learning.

Implicit and explicit models of how our minds work do, however, have a strong influence on theories about how we learn. Numerous theories have been advanced and significant schools of thought exist that argue passionately for one approach rather than another. I have mentioned the work on multiple intelligence and situated learning. Etienne Wenger has usefully summarized the pedagogical focus of four psychological theories of learning (Wenger 1998). The terms described often appear in the professional dialogue around teaching and learning:

- *Behaviourist* theories focus on behaviour modification via stimulus-response pairs and selective reinforcement. Their pedagogical focus is on control and adaptive response. Because they completely ignore issues of meaning, their usefulness lies in cases where addressing issues of social meaning is made impossible or is not relevant, such as automatisms, severe social dysfunctionality, or animal training (Skinner 1974).
- *Cognitive* theories focus on internal cognitive structures and view learning as transformations in these cognitive structures. Their pedagogical focus is on the processing and transmission of information through communication, explanation, recombination, contrast, inference, and problem-solving. They are useful for designing sequences of conceptual material that build upon existing information structures (Anderson 1983: Wenger 1987: Hutchins 1995).
- *Constructivist* theories focus on the processes by which learners build their own mental structures when interacting with an environment. Their pedagogical focus is task-oriented. They favour hands-on, self-directed activities oriented toward design and discovery. They are useful for structuring learning environments, such as simulated worlds, so as to afford the construction of certain conceptual structures through engagement in self-directed tasks (Piaget 1954: Papert 1980).
- *Social learning* theories take social interactions into account, but still from a primarily psychological perspective. They place the emphasis on interpersonal relations involving imitation and modelling, and thus focus on the study of cognitive processes by which observation can become a source of learning. They are useful for understanding the detailed information-processing mechanisms by which social interactions affect behaviour (Bandura 1977).

Wenger goes on to suggest that some theories are moving away from the traditional exclusively psychological approach. One perspective he cites, highly relevant to the world of schools, is that of organizational theories. These concern themselves with the way individuals learn in organization contexts and with the ways in which organizations can be said to learn as organizations. The pedagogical focus is on organizational systems, structures and politics and on institutional forms of memory (see Argyris and Schon 1978: Brown and Duguid 1991). Teachers joining a school, for example, can spend a considerable time coming to grips with the collective memory that is particular to any institution and that is crucial to their learning. In fact everything we say here about learning in general applies as much to teacher learning as it does to children.

Wenger himself takes a social perspective. In a number of influential publications, particularly the book co-written with Jean Lave (Lave and Wenger 1991), he has argued that learning is a process of participation in communities of practice, participation that is at first legitimately peripheral but that increases gradually in engagement and complexity. The situation or context is crucial. It follows:

- For *individuals*, it means that learning is an issue of engaging in and contributing to the practices of their communities.
- For *communities*, it means that learning is an issue of refining their practice and ensuring new generations of members.
- For *organizations*, it means that learning is an issue of sustaining the interconnected communities of practice through which an organization knows what it knows and thus becomes effective and valuable as an organization.

Theories about learning have often become linked to social and political attitudes. Behaviourist ideas, for example, have been associated with more rigid, even totalitarian ways of organizing society. Constructivist ideas have been linked to progressive, child-centred forms of organizing teaching and learning. Protagonists for learning theories have, on occasions, brought to the debate the fervour associated with supporting a football team or a political party. Given the uncertainties in the field the wise teacher will draw eclectically from the range of insights provided by a range of ideas.

Jerome Bruner, another very influential figure over the last few decades, takes such a view. In the introduction to the essay (Bruner 1996) that is reprinted in Chapter 2, he groups contemporary ideas about learning into two categories.

The first he terms the computational: the belief that you can devise a formal way of presenting any and all functioning systems that manage the flow of information. This is done in a way that produces foreseeable, systematic outcomes. In one manifestation this became what is termed artificial intelligence, the capability of systems outside the human mind to replicate our mental processes.

The second Bruner terms culturalism, which takes its inspiration from the evolutionary fact that mind could not exist save for culture. For Bruner the culturalist conception sees mind as both constituted by, and realized in, the use of human culture. He sees the rules common to all information systems (the computational conception) as not covering the messy, ambiguous and context-sensitive processes of 'meaning making', as he terms it, that most of us experience in most learning situations.

Bruner makes it clear that these two approaches are not necessarily in direct contradiction. Although he doubts that the computationalists will ever tame the messy or the ambiguous, he sees their efforts as interesting in shedding light on the divide between meaning making and information processing.

Why are these ideas about learning significant for teachers? There is plenty of evidence to suggest that the ideas we carry in our heads, implicit or explicit, about the nature of intelligence or the way the mind works, strongly influence the models of teaching that we adopt. A flexible, non-determinist perspective on learning might make us optimistic and ambitious for learners, even the struggling ones. An appreciation of the social context of learning will make us appreciate that a range of variables needs taking account of in developing teaching and learning strategies. Acknowledging the importance of building on prior knowledge challenges the perception of the mind as a *tabula rasa* or blank slate upon which the imprint of learning can be made.

Such theories do not always offer the easiest way forward for teachers. We have all experienced the teacher who starts the year with a 'clean sheet' approach to the new class. Often this is with the best of motives in not wasting previous experience, successful or otherwise, to influence expectations. But the approach has limitations. Most of us learn by making connections with our previous knowledge. We have all experienced the inspirational moment when 'things become clear' (going 'meta', as Bruner terms it) as the new frame of reference clicks in with our established ideas and understandings. The challenge for the teacher is orchestrating that over time, and mostly with twenty or thirty different pupils.

The importance of thinking about 'how pupils learn' lies in the way it will begin to influence patterns and styles of pedagogic practice. On a lesson-by-lesson basis it is not necessarily going to be in the forefront of teachers' minds. But as they reflect on the planning and implementation of their teaching, theories of learning can be influential in a wide range of ways.

Anyone working as a teacher has a unique opportunity to observe and enquire about the process of learning. It is at the core of professional activity and in the decades to come new ideas, insights and empirical evidence will become available that may make existing theories appear naïve or simplistic. Keeping abreast of ideas about learning, I am suggesting, is a significant part of the professional knowledge that needs to be updated, refined and questioned throughout a teaching career. I conclude with a quotation from a review by an American educationalist, Alison Gopnick (Gopnick 1999), who is optimistic about the way knowledge about mind may develop in the immediate future:

> The history of education in the twenty-first century may turn out to be like the history of medicine in the nineteenth century. Both medicine and education have great moral urgency. Passing on what we know to our children is, after all, one of the few ways we have of genuinely defying death; medicine just postpones it. Both medicine and education invoke knowledge to justify their authority. Doctors have always justified their practices by claiming that they understand how our bodies work. Educators have always justified theirs by claiming that they understand how our children's minds work. But for most of history those claims were based on scarcely any systematic research. At best, they were pragmatic generalizations, the outcome of a long process of empirical tinkering.
>
> During the last 150 years we have gradually begun to integrate real biological science into our medical practice. This has been one of the great scientific success stories. Surely even the most adamant postmodern critics of science believe that vaccinating babies is not just an exercise in patriarchal control. But our new biological knowledge has also told us that organisms and their illnesses are individual, variable, and complicated. And biology itself can't determine what kind of medicine is worth having, and how much we're willing to pay for it.
>
> A similar story could unfold in education. In the last thirty years, we have begun to develop a science of children's minds. This new research might be the

equivalent of the scientific physiology that has transformed medicine. But it is unlikely to lead to some simple educational panacea. In fact, helping our children to be both smart and wise is likely to be just as difficult, as complicated and demanding, though just as valuable, as helping them to be healthy.

References

Anderson, J. R. (1983) *The Architecture of Cognition*, Cambridge, (MA): Harvard University Press.

Argyris, C. and Schon, D. A. (1978) *Organisation Learning: A Theory of Action Perspective*, Reading, (MA): Addison-Wesley.

Bandura, A. (1977) *Social Learning Theory*. Englewood Cliffs, (NJ): Prentice-Hall.

Brown, J. S. and Duguid, P. (1991) 'Organizational learning and communication of practice: towards a unified view of working, learning and innovation', *Organisation Science* 2: 40–57.

Bruner, J. (1996) *The Culture of Education*, London: Harvard University Press.

Carraher, T., Carraher, D.W. and Schliema, A.C. (1985) 'Mathematics in the streets and in schools', *British Journal of Developmental Psychology*, 3: 21–9.

Gardner, H. (1983) *Frames of Mind*, New York: Basic Books.

Gardner, H. (1993) *Multiple Intelligences: The Theory in Practice*, New York: Basic Books.

Gopnick, A., Meltzoff, A.N. and Kuhl, P.K. (1999) *The Scientist in the Crib: Minds, Brains and How Children Learn*, New York: William Morrow.

Hutchins, E. (1995) *Cognition in the Wild*, Cambridge, (MA): MIT Press.

Lave, J. and Wenger, E. (1991) *Situated learning: legitimate peripheral participation*, Cambridge: Cambridge University Press.

Papert, S. (1980) *Mindstorm*, New York: Basic Books.

Piaget, J. (1954) *The Construction of Reality in the Child*, New York: Basic Books.

Putnam, R.T. and Borko, H. (2000) 'What do new views of knowledge and thinking have to say about research on teacher learning?', *Educational Researcher*, 291: 4–15.

Skinner, B. F. (1974) *About Behaviourism*, New York: Knopf.

Wenger, E. (1998) *Communities of Practice: Learning, Measuring, and Identity*, Cambridge: Cambridge University Press.

White, J. (1998) *Do Howard Gardner's multiple intelligences add up?*, London: London Institute of Education series, Perspectives on Education Policy.

2   Tenets to understand a cultural perspective on learning

Jerome Bruner

Let me set out some tenets that guide a psycho-cultural approach to education. In doing so I shall commute back and forth between questions about the nature of mind and about the nature of culture, for a theory of education necessarily lies at the intersect between them. We shall, in consequence, constantly be inquiring about the interaction between the powers of individual minds and the means by which the culture aids or thwarts their realization. And this will inevitably involve us in a never-ending assessment of the fit between what any particular culture deems essential for a good, or useful, or worthwhile way of life, and how individuals adapt to these demands as they impinge on their lives. We shall be particularly mindful of the resources that a culture provides in making this fit possible. These are all matters that relate directly to how a culture or society manages its system of education, for education is a major embodiment of a culture's way of life, not just a preparation for it.

Here, then, are the tenets and some of their consequences for education.

1 The perspectival tenet

First, about meaning making. The meaning of any fact, proposition, or encounter is relative to the perspective or frame of reference in terms of which it is construed. A treaty that legitimizes the building of the Panama Canal, for example, is an episode in the history of North American imperialism. It is also a monumental step in the history of inter-ocean transportation, as well as a landmark in man's effort to shape nature to his own convenience at whatever cost. To understand well what something 'means' requires some awareness of the alternative meanings that can be attached to the matter under scrutiny, whether one agrees with them or not.

Understanding something in one way does not preclude understanding it in other ways. Understanding in any one particular way is only 'right' or 'wrong' from the particular perspective in terms of which it is pursued. But the 'rightness' of particular interpretations, while dependent on perspective, also reflects rules of evidence, consistency, and coherence. Not everything goes. There are inherent criteria of rightness, and the possibility of alternative interpretations does not license all of them equally. A perspectival view of meaning making does *not* preclude common sense or 'logic'. Something that happens a century after an event cannot be taken as a 'cause' or 'condition' of that event. I shall return to this issue of common sense, logic, and reason in a later tenet.

Interpretations of meaning reflect not only the idiosyncratic histories of individuals, but also the culture's canonical ways of constructing reality. Nothing is 'culture free', but neither are individuals simply mirrors of their culture. It is the interaction between them that both gives a communal cast to individual thought and imposes a certain unpredictable richness on any culture's way of life, thought, or feeling. There are, as it were, 'official' versions of all of these – 'Frenchmen are realistic', for example – and some of them are even inscribed in the law or in widely accepted kinship practices. And of course, they are also portrayed (often ambiguously and even problematically) in a culture's literature and its folk theories.

Life in culture is, then, an interplay between the versions of the world that people form under its institutional sway and the versions of it that are products of their individual histories. It rarely conforms to anything resembling a cookbook of recipes or formulas, for it is a universal of all cultures that they contain factional or institutional interests. [...]

An 'official' educational enterprise presumably cultivates beliefs, skills, and feelings in order to transmit and explicate its sponsoring culture's ways of interpreting the natural and social worlds. And as we shall see later, it also plays a key role in helping the young construct and maintain a concept of Self. In carrying out that function, it inevitably courts risk by 'sponsoring', however implicitly, a certain version of the world. Or it runs the risk of offending some interests by openly examining views that might be taken as like the culture's canonically tabooed ones. That is the price of educating the young in societies whose canonical interpretations of the world are multivocal or ambiguous. But an educational enterprise that fails to take the risks involved becomes stagnant and eventually alienating.

It follows from this, then, that effective education is always in jeopardy either in the culture at large or with constituencies more dedicated to maintaining a *status quo* than to fostering flexibility. The corollary of this is that when education narrows its scope of interpretive inquiry, it reduces a culture's power to adapt to change. And in the contemporary world, change is the norm.

In a word, the perspectival tenet highlights the interpretive, meaning-making side of human thought while, at the same time, recognizing the inherent risks of discord that may result from cultivating this deeply human side of mental life. It is this double-facing, Janus-like aspect of education that makes it either a somewhat dangerous pursuit or a rather drearily routine one.

2 The constraints tenet

The forms of meaning making accessible to human beings in any culture are constrained in two crucial ways. The first inheres in the nature of human mental functioning itself. Our evolution as a species has specialized us into certain characteristic ways of knowing, thinking, feeling, and perceiving. We cannot, even given our most imaginative efforts, construct a concept of Self that does not impute some causal influence of prior mental states on later ones. We cannot seem to accept a version of our own mental lives that denies that what we thought before affects what we think now. We are obliged to experience ourselves as invariant across circumstances and continuous across time. Moreover, to pick up a theme that will concern us later, we need to conceive of ourselves as 'agents' impelled by self-generated intentions. And we see others in the same way. In answer to those who deny this version of selfhood on philosophical or 'scientific' grounds, we reply simply, 'But that's how it is: can't you *see?*' All this despite the fact that there have always been rhetorically compelling philosophers (or, in more recent centuries, psychologists) who have denied this 'folk psychological' view and even called it mischievous.

Indeed, we even institutionalize these so-called folk beliefs. Our legal system takes it as a given and constructs a *corpus juris* based upon notions like 'voluntary consent', 'responsibility', and the rest. It does not matter whether 'selfhood' can be proved scientifically or whether it is merely a 'fiction' of folk psychology. We simply take it as in the 'nature of human nature'. Never mind what critics say. 'Common sense' asserts it to be so. To be sure, we bend slightly for the critics. The law, typically, meets its critics by enunciating 'principled exceptions' – as in the extension and clarification of the *mens rea* doctrine.

Such intrinsic constraints on our capacities to interpret are by no means limited only to subjective concepts like 'selfhood'. They even limit our ways of conceiving of such presumably impersonal, 'objective' matters as time, space, and causality. [...]

But while they may reflect the evolution of the human mind, these constraints should not be taken as man's *fixed* native endowment. They may be common to the species, but they also reflect how we represent the world through language and folk theories. And they are not immutable. Euclid, after all, finally altered our way of conceiving of, even looking at, space. And in time, doubtless, Einstein will have done the same. Indeed, the very predispositions that we take to be 'innate' most often require shaping by exposure to some communally shared notational system, like language. Despite our presumably native endowment, we seem to have what Vygotsky called a Zone of Proximal Development, a capacity to recognize ways beyond that endowment. The famous slave-boy in Plato's *Meno* was indeed capable of certain 'mathematical' insights (at least in response to the questions posed by the masterful Socrates). Would his insights have been possible without the queries of Socrates?

The educational implications that follow from the foregoing are both massive and subtle. If pedagogy is to empower human beings to go beyond their 'native' predispositions, it must transmit the 'toolkit' the culture has developed for doing so. It is a commonplace that any math major in a halfway decent modern university can do more mathematics than, say, Leibniz, who 'invented' the calculus – that we stand on the shoulders of the giants who preceded us. Obviously, not everybody benefits equally from instruction in the culture's toolkit. But it hardly follows that we should instruct only those with the most conspicuous talent to benefit from such instruction. That is a political or economic decision that should never be allowed to take on the status of an evolutionary principle. Decisions to cultivate 'trained incompetencies' will concern us presently.

I mentioned *two* constraints on human mental activity at the start of this discussion. The second comprises those constraints imposed by the symbolic systems accessible to human minds generally – limits imposed, say, by the very nature of language – but more particularly, constraints imposed by the different languages and notational systems accessible to different cultures. The latter is usually called the Whorf-Sapir hypothesis – that thought is shaped by the language in which it is formulated and/or expressed.

As for the 'limits of language', not much can be said with any certainty – or with much clarity. It has never been clear whether our ability to entertain certain notions inheres in the nature of our minds or in the symbolic systems upon which mind relies in carrying out its mental operations. Is it in mind or in language that it is 'necessary' that something cannot be both A and not-A? Or is it 'in the world' – except for the part of the world covered by quantum theory? Is it in the structure of natural language that the world divides into subjects and predicates, or is this a reflection of how human attention works naturally? [...]

But as the greatest linguist of our century, Roman Jakobson, long ago noted, the *metalinguistic* gift, the capacity to 'turn around' on our language to examine and transcend its limits, is within everybody's reach. There is little reason to believe that anybody, even the speech-disabled, cannot be helped to explore more deeply the nature and uses of his language. Indeed, the spread of literacy may itself have increased linguistic awareness just by virtue of externalizing, decontextualizing, and making more permanent 'what was said', as David Olson has recently argued.

The pedagogical implications of the foregoing are strikingly obvious. Since the limits of our inherent mental predispositions can be transcended by having recourse to more powerful symbolic systems, one function of education is to equip human beings with the needed symbolic systems for doing so. And if the limits imposed by the languages we use are expanded by increasing our 'linguistic awareness', then another function of pedagogy is to cultivate such awareness. We may not succeed in transcending all the limits imposed in either case, but we can surely accept the more modest goal of improving thereby the human capacity for construing meanings and constructing realities. In sum, then, 'thinking about thinking' has to be a principal ingredient of any empowering practice of education.

3 The constructivism tenet

This tenet has already been implied in all that has gone before. But it is worth making explicit. The 'reality' that we impute to the 'worlds' we inhabit is a constructed one. To paraphrase Nelson Goodman, 'reality is made, not found'. Reality construction is the product of meaning making shaped by traditions and by a culture's toolkit of ways of thought. In this sense, education must be conceived as aiding young humans in learning to use the tools of meaning making and reality construction, better to adapt to the world in which they find themselves and to help in the process of changing it as required. In this sense, it can even be conceived as akin to helping people become better architects and better builders.

4 The interactional tenet

Passing on knowledge and skill, like any human exchange, involves a subcommunity in interaction. At the minimum, it involves a 'teacher' and a 'learner' – or if not a teacher in flesh and blood, then a vicarious one like a book, or film, or display, or a 'responsive' computer.

It is principally through interacting with others that children find out what the culture is about and how it conceives of the world. Unlike any other species, human beings deliberately teach each other in settings outside the ones in which the knowledge being taught will be used. Nowhere else in the animal kingdom is such deliberate ' teaching' found – save scrappily among higher primates. To be sure, many indigenous cultures do not practice as deliberate or decontextualized a form of teaching as we do. But 'telling' and 'showing' are as humanly universal as speaking.

It is customary to say that this specialization rests upon the gift of language. But perhaps more to the point, it also rests upon our astonishingly well developed talent for 'intersubjectivity' – the human ability to understand the minds of others, whether through gesture, or other means. It is not just words that make this possible, but our capacity to grasp the role of the settings in which words, acts, and gestures occur. We are the intersubjective species *par excellence*. It is this that permits us to 'negotiate' meanings when words go astray.

Our Western pedagogical tradition hardly does justice to the importance of intersubjectivity in transmitting culture. Indeed, it often clings to a preference for a degree of explicitness that seems to ignore it. So teaching is fitted into a mold in which a single, presumably omniscient teacher explicitly tells or shows presumably unknowing learners something they presumably know nothing about. Even when we tamper with this model, as with 'question periods' and the like, we still remain loyal to its unspoken precepts. I believe that one of the most important gifts that a cultural psychology can give to education is a reformulation of this impoverished conception. For only a very small part of educating takes place on such a one-way street – and it is probably one of the least successful parts.

So back to the innocent but fundamental question: how best to conceive of a subcommunity that specializes in learning among its members? One obvious answer would be that it is a place where, among other things, learners help each other learn, each according to her abilities. And this, of course, need not exclude the presence of somebody serving in the role of teacher. It simply implies that the teacher does not play that role as a monopoly, that learners 'scaffold' for each other as well. The antithesis is the 'transmission' model first described, often further exaggerated by an emphasis on transmitting 'subject matter'. But in most matters of achieving mastery, we also want learners to gain good judgment, to become self-reliant, to work well with each other. And such competencies do not flourish under a one-way 'transmission' regimen. Indeed, the very institutionalization of schooling may get in the way of creating a subcommunity of learners who bootstrap each other.

Consider the more 'mutual' community for a moment. Typically, it models ways of doing or knowing, provides opportunity for emulation, offers running commentary, provides 'scaffolding' for novices, and even provides a good context for teaching deliberately. It even makes possible that form of job-related division of labor one finds in effective work groups: some serving *pro tem* as 'memories' for the others, or as record keepers of 'where things have got up to now', or as encouragers or cautioners. The point is for those in the group to help each other get the lay of the land and the hang of the job.

One of the most radical proposals to have emerged from the cultural-psychological approach to education is that the classroom be reconceived as just such a subcommunity of mutual learners, with the teacher orchestrating the proceedings. Note that, contrary to traditional critics, such subcommunities do not reduce the teacher's role nor his or her 'authority'. Rather, the teacher takes on the additional function of encouraging others to share it. Just as the omniscient narrator has disappeared from modern fiction, so will the omniscient teacher disappear from the classroom of the future.

There is obviously no single formula that follows from the cultural psychological approach to interactive, intersubjective pedagogy. For one thing, the practices adopted will vary with subject: poetry and mathematics doubtless require different approaches. Its sole precept is that where human beings are concerned, learning (whatever else it may be) is an interactive process in which people learn from each other, and not just by showing and telling. It is surely in the nature of human cultures to form such communities of mutual learners. Even if we are the only species that 'teaches deliberately' and 'out of the context of use', this does not mean that we should convert this evolutionary step into a fetish.

5 The externalization tenet

A French cultural psychologist, Ignace Meyerson, first enunciated an idea that today, a quarter-century after his death, now seems both obvious and brimming with educational implications. Briefly, his view was that the main function of all collective cultural activity is to produce 'works' – *oeuvres*, as he called them, works that, as it were, achieve an existence of their own. In the grand sense, these include the arts and sciences of a culture, institutional structures such as its laws and its markets, even its 'history' conceived as a canonical version of the past. But there are minor oeuvres as well: those 'works' of smaller groupings that give pride, identity, and a sense of continuity to those who participate, however obliquely, in their making. These may be 'inspirational' – for example, our school soccer team won the county championship six years ago, or our famous Bronx High School of Science has 'produced' three Nobel Laureates. Oeuvres are often touchingly local, modest, yet equally identity-bestowing, such as this remark by a 10-year-old student: 'Look at *this* thing we're working on if you want to see how *we* handle oil spills.'

The benefits of 'externalizing' such joint products into oeuvres have too long been overlooked. First on the list, obviously, is that collective oeuvres produce and sustain group solidarity. They help *make* a community, and communities of mutual learners are no exception. But just as important, they promote a sense of the division of labor that goes into producing a product: Todd is our real computer wonk, Jeff's terrific at making graphics, Alice and David are our 'word geniuses', Maddalena is fantastic at explaining things that puzzle some of the rest of us. One group we will examine in later discussions even devised a way to highlight these 'group works' by instituting a weekly session to hear and discuss a report on the class's performance for the week. The report, presented by a 'class ethnographer' (usually one of the teaching assistants), highlights *overall* rather than individual progress; it produces 'metacognition' on the class's oeuvre and usually leads to lively discussion. […]

I can see one other benefit from externalizing mental work into a more palpable oeuvre, one that we psychologists have tended to ignore. Externalization produces a *record* of our mental efforts, one that is 'outside us' rather than vaguely 'in memory'. It is somewhat like producing a draft, a rough sketch, a 'mock-up'. 'It' takes over our attention as something that, in its own right, needs a transitional paragraph, or a less frontal perspective there, or a better 'introduction'. 'It' relieves us in some measure from the always difficult task of 'thinking about our own thoughts' while often accomplishing the same end. 'It' embodies our thoughts and intentions in a form more accessible to reflective efforts. The process of thought and its product become interwoven, like Picasso's countless sketches and drawings in reconceiving Velásquez's *Las Meninas*. There is a Latin motto, *scientia dependit in mores*: knowledge works its way into habits. It might easily be retranslated as 'thinking works its way into its products'. [...]

Externalizing, in a word, rescues cognitive activity from implicitness, making it more public, negotiable, and 'solidary'. At the same time, it makes it more accessible to subsequent reflection and metacognition. Probably the greatest milestone in the history of externalization was literacy, putting thought and memory 'out there' on clay tablets or paper. Computers and e-mail may represent another step forward. But there are doubtless myriad ways in which jointly negotiated thought can be communally externalized as oeuvres – and many ways in which they can be put to use in schools.

6 The instrumentalism tenet

Education, however conducted in whatever culture, always has consequences in the later lives of those who undergo it. Everybody knows this; nobody doubts it. We also know that these consequences are instrumental in the lives of individuals, and even know that, in a less immediately personal sense, they are instrumental to the culture and its various institutions (the latter are discussed in the following tenet). Education, however gratuitous or decorative it may seem or profess to be, provides skills, ways of thinking, feeling, and speaking, that later may be traded for 'distinctions' in the institutionalized 'markets' of a society. In this deeper sense, then, education is never neutral, never without social and economic consequences. However much it may be claimed to the contrary, education is always political in this broader sense.

There are two pervasive considerations that need to be taken into account in pursuing the implications of these hard-edged facts. One has to do with *talent*; the other with *opportunity*. And while the two are by no means unrelated, they need to be discussed separately first. ...

About talent, it is by now obvious that it is more multifaceted than any single score, like an IQ test, could possibly reveal. Not only are there many ways of using mind, many ways of knowing and constructing meanings, but they serve many functions in different situations. These ways of using mind are enabled, indeed often brought into being, by learning to master what I earlier described as a culture's 'toolkit' of symbolic systems and speech registers. There is thinking and meaning making for intimate situations different in kind from what one uses in the impersonal setting of a shop or office.

Some people seem to have great aptitude in using certain powers of mind and their supporting registers, others less. Howard Gardner has made a good case for certain of these aptitudes (he calls them 'frames of mind') having an innate and universal basis – like the ability to deal with quantitative relations, or with linguistic subtleties, or with skilled movement of the body in dance, or with sensing the feelings of others. And he is engaged in constructing curriculums for fostering these differing aptitudes.

Beyond the issue of differing native aptitudes, however, it is also the case that different cultures place different emphasis upon the skilled use of different modes of thought and different registers. Not everybody is supposed to be numerate, but if you occupy the role of engineer, you're something of a queer duck if you're not. But everybody is supposed to be passingly competent in managing interpersonal relations. Different cultures distribute these skills differently. The French even have an expression that refers to the 'shape' of one's trained capabilities, 'professional deformation' in literal translation. And these very rapidly get 'typed' and consolidated through training and schooling: girls used to be considered more 'sensitive' to poetry, were given more experience in it, and more often than not *became* more sensitive. But this is a harmless example of the kinds of considerations that affect the *opportunity* young people have for developing the skills and ways of thinking that they will later trade for distinctions and rewards in the larger society.

There are many uglier features of opportunity that blight lives far more profoundly. Racism, social-class entitlements, and prejudice, all of them amplified by the forms of poverty they create, have powerful effects on how much and how we educate the young. Indeed, even the so-called innate talents of children from 'socially tainted' backgrounds are altered before they ever get to school – in ghettos, barrios, and those other settings of poverty, despair, and defiance that seem to suppress and divert the mental powers of the young who 'grow up' in them. ...

Schools have always been highly selective with respect to the uses of mind they cultivate – which uses are to be considered 'basic', which 'frills', which the school's responsibility and which the responsibility of others, which for girls and which for boys, which for working-class children and which for 'swells'. Some of this selectivity was doubtless based on considered notions about what the society required or what the individual needed to get along. Much of it was a spillover of folk or social class tradition. Even the more recent and seemingly obvious objective of equipping all with 'basic literacy' is premised on moral-political grounds, however pragmatically those grounds may be justified. School curriculums and classroom 'climates' always reflect inarticulate cultural values as well as explicit plans; and these values are never far removed from considerations of social class, gender, and the prerogatives of social power. [...]

Surely one of the major educational tenets of a cultural psychology is that the school can never be considered as culturally 'free standing'. *What* it teaches, what modes of thought and what 'speech registers' it actually cultivates in its pupils, cannot be isolated from how the school is situated in the lives and culture of its students. For a school's curriculum is not only *about* 'subjects'. The chief subject matter of school, viewed culturally, is school itself. That is how most students experience it, and it determines what meaning they make of it.

This, of course, is what I mean by the 'situatedness' of school and school learning.
[...]

None of this is new. What does the cultural psychologist have to say about such matters? Certainly one general thing: education does not stand alone, and it cannot be designed as if it did. It exists in a culture. And culture, whatever else it is, is also about power, distinctions, and rewards. We have, in the laudable interest of protecting freedom of thought and instruction, officially buffered schools against political pressures. School is 'above' politics. In some important sense, this is surely true – but it is a threadbare truth. Increasingly, we see something quite different. For, as it were, the secret is out. Even the so-called man in the street knows that how one equips minds matters mightily later in our post-industrial, technological era. The public, to be sure, has a rather unformed sense of this – and certainly the press does. But they are aware. The *New York Times* carried as front-page news in the spring of 1995 that achievement levels had gone up in the city's schools; and Dublin's *Irish Times* in the summer of that same year carried on its front page the news that Irish students had scored 'above the average' in a comparative study of reading ability in European schools.

Why not, then, treat education for what it is? It has always been 'political', though cryptically so in more settled, less aware times. There has now been a revolution in public awareness. But it has not been accompanied by a comparable revolution in our ways of taking this awareness into account in the forging of educational policies and practices. All of which is not to propose that we 'politicize' education, but simply that we recognize that it is already politicized and that its political side needs finally to be taken into account more explicitly, not simply as though it were 'public protest'. I will return to this issue in more detail later in this chapter.

7 The institutional tenet

My seventh tenet is that as education in the developed world becomes institutionalized, it behaves as institutions do and often must, and suffers certain problems common to all institutions. What distinguishes it from others is its special role in preparing the young to take a more active part in other institutions of the culture. Let us explore now what this implies.

Cultures are not simply collections of people sharing a common language and historical tradition. They are composed of institutions that specify more concretely what roles people play and what status and respect these are accorded – though the culture at large expresses its way of life through institutions as well. Cultures can also be conceived as elaborate exchange systems, with media of exchange as varied as respect, goods, loyalty, and services. Exchange systems become focalized and legitimized in institutions which provide buildings, stipends, titles, and the rest. They are further legitimized by a complex symbolic apparatus of myths, statutes, precedents, ways of talking and thinking, and even uniforms. Institutions impose their 'will' through coercion, sometimes implicit as in incentives and disincentives, sometimes explicit as in restriction backed by the power of the state, such as the disbarring of a lawyer or the refusal of credit to a defaulting merchant.

Institutions do the culture's serious business. But for all that, they do so through an unpredictable mix of coercion and voluntarism. I say 'unpredictable' because it remains perpetually unclear both to participants in a culture and to those who observe it from 'outside' when and how the power of enforcement will be brought to bear by those delegated or otherwise thought privileged to use it. So if it can be said that a culture's institutions do 'serious business', it can equally be said that it is often ambiguous and uncertain business. [...]

Institutions, as Pierre Bourdieu has suggested, provide the 'markets' where people 'trade' their acquired skills, knowledge, and ways of constructing meanings for distinctions or privileges. Institutions often compete in getting their 'distinctions' prized above those of others, but the competition must never be 'winner take all', for institutions are mutually dependent upon each other. Lawyers and businessmen need each other as much as patients and doctors do. So, as in Diderot's delightful *Jacques le fataliste et son maître*, bargaining for distinction becomes a subtle game, often a source of sly humor. The struggle for distinction seems to be a feature of all cultures.

While all this may at first seem remote from schools and the process of education, the remoteness is an illusion. Education is up to its elbows in the struggle for distinctions. The very expressions *primary*, *secondary*, and *tertiary* are metaphors for it. It has even been argued recently that the 'new' bourgeoisie in France after the Revolution used the schools as one of their principal tools for 'turning around' the system of prestige and distinction previously dominated by the aristocracy and gentry of the *ancien régime*. Indeed, the very concept of a meritocracy is precisely an expression of the new power that schools are expected to exercise in fixing the distribution of distinctions in contemporary bureaucratic society. [...]

It is astonishing how little systematic study is devoted to the institutional 'anthropology' of schooling, given the complexity of its situatedness and its exposure to the changing social and economic climate. Its relation to the family, to the economy, to religious institutions, even to the labor market, is only vaguely understood. [...]

I must conclude this discussion of 'institutionalization' on a more homely note. Improving education requires teachers who understand and are committed to the improvements envisioned. So banal a point would scarcely be worth mentioning were it not so easily overlooked by many efforts at educational reform. We need to equip teachers with the necessary background training to take an effective part in reform. The people who run them make institutions. However thoughtful our educational plans may become, they must include a crucial place for teachers. For, ultimately, that is where the action is.

8 The tenet of identity and self-esteem

I have put this tenet late in the list. For it is so pervasive as to implicate virtually all that has gone before. Perhaps the single most universal thing about human experience is the phenomenon of 'Self', and we know that education is crucial to its formation. Education should be conducted with that fact in mind.

We know 'Self' from our own inner experience, and we recognize others as selves. Indeed, more than one distinguished scholar has argued that self-awareness requires as its necessary condition the recognition of the Other as a self. Though there are universals of selfhood – and we will consider two of them in a moment – different cultures both shape it differently and set its limits in varying ways. Some emphasize autonomy and individuality, some affiliation, some link it closely to a person's position in a divine or secular social order, some link it to individual effort or even to luck. Since schooling is one of life's earliest institutional involvements outside the family, it is not surprising that it plays a critical role in the shaping of Self. But I think this will be clearer if we first examine two aspects of selfhood that are regarded as universal.

The first is *agency*. Selfhood, most students of the subject believe, derives from the sense that one can initiate and carry out activities on one's own. Whether this is 'really' so or simply a folk belief, as radical behaviorists would have us believe, is beyond the scope of this inquiry. I shall simply take it as so. People experience themselves as agents. But then too, any vertebrate distinguishes between a branch *it* has shaken and one that has shaken *it*. So there must be something more to selfhood than the recognition of simple sensorimotor agentivity. What characterizes human selfhood is the construction of a conceptual system that organizes, as it were, a 'record' of agentive encounters with the world, a record that is related to the past (that is, 'autobiographical memory', so-called) but that is also extrapolated into the future – self with history and with possibility. It is a 'possible self' that regulates aspiration, confidence, optimism, and their opposites. While this 'constructed' self-system is inner, private, and suffused with affect, it also extends outward to the things and activities and places with which we become 'ego-involved' – William James's 'extended self'. Schools and school learning are among the earliest of those places and activities.

But just as important as the inner psychodynamics of selfhood are the ways in which a culture institutionalizes it. All natural languages, for example, make obligatory grammatical distinctions between agentive and patientive forms: *I hit him; he hit me.* And even the simplest narratives are built around, indeed depend upon, an agent-Self as a protagonist with his or her own goals operating in a recognizable cultural setting. There is a moral aspect to selfhood as well, expressed simply by such ubiquitous phenomena as 'blaming yourself' or 'blaming another' for acts committed or outcomes that result from our acts. At a more evolved level, all legal systems specify (and legitimize) some notion of *responsibility* by which Self is endowed with obligation in regard to some broader cultural authority – confirming 'officially' that we, our Selves, are presumed to be agents in control of our own actions.

Since agency implies not only the capacity for initiating, but also for completing our acts, it also implies *skill* or *know-how*. Success and failure are principal nutrients in the development of selfhood. Yet we may not be the final arbiters of success and failure, which are often defined from 'outside' according to culturally specified criteria. And school is where the child first encounters such criteria – often as if applied arbitrarily. School judges the child's performance, and the child responds by evaluating himself or herself in turn.

Which brings us to a second ubiquitous feature of selfhood: *evaluation*. Not only do we experience Self as agentive, we evaluate our efficacy in bringing off what we hoped for or were asked to do. Self increasingly takes on the flavor of these valuations. I call this mix of agentive efficacy and self-evaluation 'self-esteem'. It combines our sense of what we believe ourselves to be (or even hope to be) capable of and what we fear is beyond us.

How self-esteem is experienced (or how it is expressed) varies, of course, with the ways of one's culture. Low self-esteem sometimes manifests itself in guilt about intentions, sometimes simply in shame for having been 'found out', sometimes it is accompanied by depression, even to the point of suicide, sometimes by defiant anger. In some cultures, particularly those that emphasize achievement, high self-esteem increases level of aspiration; in others it leads to status display and standing pat. There may even be an individual temperamental component in how people deal with threatened self-esteem – whether one blames oneself, others, or circumstances.

Only two things can be said for certain and in general: the management of self-esteem is never simple and never settled, and its state is affected powerfully by the availability of supports provided from outside. These supports are hardly mysterious or exotic. They include such homely resorts as a second chance, honor for a good if unsuccessful try, but above all the chance for discourse that permits one to find out why or how things didn't work out as planned. It is no secret that school is often rough on children's self-esteem, and we are beginning to know something about their vulnerability in this area. Ideally, of course, school is supposed to provide a setting where our performance has fewer esteem-threatening consequences than in the 'real world', presumably in the interest of encouraging the learner to 'try things out'. [...]

Any system of education, any theory of pedagogy, any 'grand national policy' that diminishes the school's role in nurturing its pupils' self-esteem fails at one of its primary functions. The deeper problem – from a cultural-psychological point of view, but in workaday common sense as well – is how to cope with the erosion of this function under modern urban conditions. Though I shall touch on some specific efforts to cope with these problems in later chapters, one point can certainly be made clear in this opening chapter. Schools do not simply equip kids with skills and self-esteem or not. They are in competition with other parts of society that can do this, but with deplorable consequences for the society. America manages to alienate enough black ghetto boys to land nearly a third of them in jail before they reach the age of thirty.

More positively, if agency and esteem are central to the construction of a concept of Self, then the ordinary practices of school need to be examined with a view to what contribution they make to these two crucial ingredients of personhood. Surely the 'community of learners' approach mentioned earlier contributes to both. But equally, the granting of more responsibility in setting and achieving goals in all aspects of a school's activities could also contribute – everything from maintenance of a school's physical plant to a share in decisions about academic and extracurricular projects to be undertaken. Such a conception, earlier so dear to the progressive tradition in education, is also in the image of the constitutional principle that (in a democracy) rights and responsibilities are two sides of the same coin. If, as I noted at the outset, school is an entry into the culture and not just a preparation for it, then we must constantly reassess what school does to the young student's conception of his own powers (his sense of agency) and his sensed chances of being able to cope with the world both in school and after (his self-esteem). In many democratic cultures, I think, we have become so preoccupied with the more formal criteria of 'performance' and with the bureaucratic demands of education as an institution that we have neglected this personal side of education.

9 The narrative tenet

I want finally to leapfrog over the issue of school 'subjects' and curriculums in order to deal with a more general matter: the mode of thinking and feeling that helps children (indeed, people generally) create a version of the world in which, psychologically, they can envisage a place for themselves – a personal world. I believe that story making, narrative, is what is needed for that, and I want to discuss it briefly in this final tenet.

I still hold firmly to the views expressed in my earlier work about subject-matter teaching: the importance of giving the learner a sense of the generative structure of a subject discipline, the value of a 'spiral curriculum', the crucial role of self-generated discovery in learning a subject matter, and so forth. The issue I want to address now has to do more directly with the issue of how growing children create meanings from school experience that they can relate to their lives in a culture. So let me turn to narrative as a mode of thought and as a vehicle of meaning making,

I shall begin with some basics. There appear to be two broad ways in which human beings organize and manage their knowledge of the world, indeed structure even their immediate experience: one seems more specialized for treating of physical 'things', the other for treating of people and their plights. These are conventionally known as *logical-scientific* thinking and *narrative* thinking. Their universality suggests that they have their roots in the human genome or that they are (to revert to an earlier tenet) givens in the nature of language. They have varied modes of expression in different cultures, which also cultivate them differently. No culture is without both of them, though different cultures privilege them differently.

It has been the convention of most schools to treat the arts of narrative-song, drama, fiction, theater, whatever – as more 'decoration' than necessity, something with which to grace leisure, sometimes even as something morally exemplary. Despite that, we frame the accounts of our cultural origins and our most cherished beliefs in story form, and it is not just the 'content' of these stories that grips us, but their narrative artifice. Our immediate experience, what happened yesterday or the day before, is framed in the same storied way. Even more striking, we represent our lives (to ourselves as well as to others) in the form of narrative. It is not surprising that psychoanalysts now recognize that personhood implicates narrative, 'neurosis' being a reflection of either an insufficient, incomplete, or inappropriate story about oneself. Recall that, when Peter Pan asks Wendy to return to Never Never Land with him, he gives as his reason that she could teach the Lost Boys there how to tell stories. If they knew how to tell them, the Lost Boys might be able to grow up.

The importance of narrative for the cohesion of a culture is as great, very likely, as it is in structuring an individual life. Take law as an illustration. Without a sense of the common trouble narratives that the law translates into its common law writs, it becomes arid. And those 'trouble narratives' appear again in mythic literature and contemporary novels, better contained in that form than in reasoned and logically coherent propositions. It seems evident, then, that skill in narrative construction and narrative understanding is crucial to constructing our lives and a 'place' for ourselves in the possible world we will encounter.

It has always been tacitly assumed that narrative skill comes 'naturally', that it does not have to be taught. But a closer look shows this not to be true at all. We know now, for example, that it goes through definite stages, is severely impaired in brain damage of certain kinds, fares poorly under stress, and ends up in literalism in one social community while becoming fanciful in a neighboring one with a different tradition. Observe law students or young lawyers preparing their final arguments for litigation or mock court and it will quickly be plain that some people have the knack more than others – they have simply learned how to make a story believable and worth thinking about.

Feeling at home in the world, knowing how to place oneself into self-descriptive stories, is surely not made easier by the enormous increase in migration in the modern world. It is not easy, however multicultural your intentions, to help a ten-year-old create a story that includes him in the world beyond his family and neighborhood, having been transplanted from Vietnam to the San Fernando Valley, from Algeria to Lyons, from Anatolia to Dresden. If school, his *pied-à-terre* outside the family, can't help him, there are alienated countercultures that can.

None of us knows as much as we should about how to create narrative sensibility. Two commonplaces seem to have stood the rest of time. The first is that a child should 'know', have a 'feel' for, the myths, histories, folktales, conventional stories of his or her culture (or cultures). They frame and nourish an identity. The second commonplace urges imagination through fiction. Finding a place in the world, for all that it implicates the immediacy of home, mate, job, and friends, is ultimately an act of imagination. So, for the culturally transplanted, there is the imaginative challenge of the fiction and 'quasi-fiction' that takes him or her into the world of possibilities – as in the novels of a Maxine Hong Kingston or the poems of a Maya Angelou. And for any schoolboy pondering how it all came about, there is a Simon Schama narratively restoring the human plights to the 'dead certainties' of the past, to use his telling phrase.

Obviously, if narrative is to be made an instrument of mind on behalf of meaning making, it requires work on our part – reading it, making it, analyzing it, understanding its craft, sensing its uses, discussing it. These are matters much better understood today than a generation ago.

All of which is not intended to undervalue the importance of logical-scientific thinking. Its value is so implicit in our highly technological culture that its inclusion in school curriculums is taken for granted. While its teaching may still be in need of improvement, it has become strikingly better since the curriculum reform movements of the 1950s and 1960s. But it is no secret that for many of the young now in school, 'science' has come to seem 'inhuman' and 'uncaring' and 'off-putting' – despite the first-class efforts of science and mathematics teachers and their associations. Indeed, the image of science as a human and cultural undertaking might itself be improved if it were also conceived as a history of human beings overcoming received ideas – whether Lavoisier overcoming the dogma of phlogiston, Darwin rethinking respectable creationism, or Freud daring to look under the smug surface of our self-satisfaction. We may have erred in divorcing science from the narrative of culture.

10 To conclude

A summary is hardly necessary. A system of education must help those growing up in a culture find an identity within that culture. Without it, they stumble in their effort after meaning. It is only in the narrative mode that one can construct an identity and find a place in one's culture. Schools must cultivate it, nurture it, cease taking it for granted. There are many projects now in the making, not only in literature but also in history and social studies, that are following up interesting leads in this field. […]

3 Ability, intelligence and attainment in secondary schools

Bob Moon and Jill Bourne

In this chapter I raise questions about the commonsense concept of ability, to trace its origins, and to look at the implications for teachers today. What do we mean to talk about a child's ability? The dictionary defines ability as cleverness, talent or mental power. When we speak of a child's ability are we describing some kind of inborn intelligence, a genetic inheritance? How do teachers know how to assess a child's ability? Can children be labelled bright or slow? Why is it that the newer models of assessment avoid the term ability and choose instead to focus on attainment? Of course, the fact that we have such words as ability or intelligence, as with the unicorn, does not mean that such things have to exist. But while the terms may not be real they can, and do, create labels that have a significant impact on how people see themselves and how they are seen by others.

As with most commonsense concepts, there is a history behind what has come to be such a natural way of talking about children. When mass schooling was first introduced in the nineteenth century, 'ignorance' seems to have been conceived of in moral terms as the result of sloth or laziness (Birchenough 1914). However, education was not equally open to everyone. There was a different form of differentiation among children, one based not on inborn mental characteristics, but in terms of social hierarchy. Children were educated to take up 'their place' in society. Jacqueline Rose (1984) has shown how, in the nineteenth century, a different form of language education was marked out for different social groups: classics for the wealthy, English literature for the middle classes, basic literacy and 'clear expression' for the poor. Thomas Crabbe wrote of the way education was becoming a social device to mark out social groups and to control the new industrialized society: 'For every class we have a school assigned, rules for all ranks and food for every mind' (cited in Birchenough 1914: 5). One mid-nineteenth century education report (The Taunton Commission) on secondary schooling proposal explicitly proposed a grade system of schools to reflect the three grades of society, each with its own curriculum. First-grade schools were to prepare children for universities, and their curriculum should be that of the classics, elements of political economy, modern languages, mathematics and natural science. Second-grade schools were to prepare pupils for professions, business and the army and should have a curriculum of Latin, mathematics, science and a modern language. Third-grade schools were for those who would be artisans who should enjoy a curriculum of basic subjects plus inorganic chemistry, practical geometry and drawing. Secondary schooling was deemed unsuitable for the working classes.

Over the twentieth century, however, explicit control over different types of knowledges for different classes, and indeed, gender groups, was gradually relaxed, as intellectual 'ability' or 'intelligences' became naturalized as a biological construct. The influence of Darwin's evolutionary theory, in the context of the heyday of British imperialism, brought about the popularity of 'eugenic' theories of generically superior types, providing 'scientific' explanations for the dominance of men over women, of the upper and middle classes over the poor, or white over black groups. Poverty was taken as a sign of inferiority, wealth a sign of strength. These ideas evolved in the first part of the century into the science of psychometry. The idea was that intelligence, usually conceived of as innate, could be measured. Such measurements were seen to have predictive qualities about what a child or person (the army was an extensive test bed for intelligence research at that time) was likely to achieve later in life and, therefore, what form of education was best suited to them. The g-factor, as it is known, or general intelligence (measured by IQ tests), was of great significance in the middle years of the last century. Given its close affiliation to concepts of class (and gender and ethnicity), its resonance with taken-for-granted assumptions also permeated public consciousness. The quotes that follow, from the Spens Report which prepared the ground for the post-war tripartite system of education, and from Cyril Burt, one of the psychological witnesses that Spens relied on, exemplify the perceptions of the time.

> Intellectual development during childhood appears to progress as if it were governed by a single central factor, usually known as 'general intelligence, which may be broadly described as innate all round ability'. It appears to enter into everything which the child attempts to think, or say, or do, and seems on the whole to be the most important factor in determining his work in the classroom. Our psychological witnesses assured us that it can be measured approximately by means of intelligence tests... The average child is said to attain the effective limit of development in general intelligence between the ages of 16 and 18... Since the ratio of each child's mental age to his chronological age remains approximately the same, while his chronological age increases, the mental differences between one child and another will grow larger and larger and will reach a maximum during adolescence. It is accordingly evident that different children from the age of 11, if justice is to be done to their varying capacities, requires types of education varying in certain important respects ...
>
> (Spens Report on Secondary Education 1938: 357–81)

> ... about 1 in 20 of the candidates [for the 11+] were rejected and subsequently did better (or were ultimately judged capable of doing better) than an equal number who had been accepted... The important point, however, is this: none of the 'errors' were bad errors; the majority were confined to borderline cases.
>
> (Cyril Burt, Black Paper Two: 18)

In elementary schools early in the last century, children worked through each 'standard', the majority moving up to the next 'standard' as they passed the annual examinations, others repeating the year (a familiar system today in other parts of the world). But the schools were also given the function of discovering individual children who show promise of exceptional capacity, to send them on scholarships to fee-paying secondary schools, previously used only by middle-class children. The concept of 'bright' and 'slow' children seemed an unquestioned assumption, with psychological theories suggesting the direct dependence of attainment of mental abilities.

This was shown strikingly in the 1920s and 1930s when a number of important national reports argued for the introduction of psychological tests to assess a child's suitability for the different types of secondary schooling that were proposed. Harry Torrance (1981) shows how different reports legitimized the notion of general intelligence and fitted this to a form of structurally differentiated school provision very similar to that advanced by Thomas Crabbe.

A large part of the growth in testing, and particularly intelligence testing, can be traced to the national imperative to apportion pupils to schools. This was seen as the progressive direction education should take, and was influenced by ideas that had spread from North America. Individualization, and the measurement of intelligences, was seen as a crucial feature in the development of the new method and the fair society.

The technology of IQ testing made the new system of selective schools, introduced by the 1944 Education Act, seem fair. There were, after all, only a limited number of places at universities and in higher education, yet compulsory, free education was for all. By the 1950s, nearly all schools which were big enough were streamed. Children went to secondary schools that matched their apparently innate abilities and were not only differentiated between schools, but also within them, segregated into different streams. The system spread down into the junior and infant schools. A survey of those junior schools large enough to be able to stream was carried out by Brian Jackson (1964). It showed that 96 per cent were streamed, and that 74 per cent streamed the children by the age of seven years. So, children's life chances were usually fixed by the age of seven years, as there was very little transfer between streams (Plowden 1967). Brian Simon (1971) concluded:

> the school system appeared to be (as indeed it was) run on the assumption that children could never ever rise above themselves and that their level of achievement was wholly determined by an IQ.

We can see, therefore, that the post-Second World War history of secondary schooling has been dominated by the debate about ability and many of the assumptions about ability are still alive today.

> While ABC 1s can conceptualise, C2s and Ds often cannot. They can relate only to things they can see and feel. They absorb their information and often views from television and tabloids. We have to talk to them in a way they understand.
> (Leaked Tory party election proposals by former minister John Maples, reprinted in the *Financial Times*, 21 November 1994: 10)

The idea of general ability or intelligence, however, has come under increasing challenge. Research on the brain has shown that the relationship between brain and mind is far more complex than can be measured by sample scores. Research on brain activity indicates that different functioning aspects of the brain are significant for different types of activity. We know from research on brain damage that an accident does not necessarily impede all our mental functions and appears on occasions to be very specific indeed. All this brings into question the claim that overall ability either exists or is measurable. Other perspectives also inform this debate. Given the wide purposes of education, reflected for example in the aims of most schools, it is unlikely that any one of us would claim high ability across all facets of human endeavour. The most talented university mathematician is rarely equally talented in the personal, practical or physical domains of our existence. Talking of a child as able/less able therefore in a broad general sense seems inevitably inaccurate.

Just as we see the use of ability in a generic sense as problematic, so it follows that 'mixed ability' used in a similar way is also conceptually confusing. There are parts of the world where streaming or setting is not used in secondary schools. Japan is one example. Japanese teachers, however, do not talk about their mixed-ability classes. The Western concept of predetermined ability does not exist, nor, therefore, mixed ability.

Secondary schools today, in organizational terms, reflect more sophisticated concepts of ability than existed in the period of the 11 + or the A, B and C streams. There might be quite rigid attainment setting in mathematics but none at all in drama or physical education. Increasingly, teachers refer to attainment in a subject (he or she is a high attainer in maths and science) rather than general references to an able/average/less able child. In the professional culture of secondary schools elements of a deterministic terminology exist even if actual grouping practice has moved away from it.

The question of attainment grouping and setting is a hotly debated one in many schools. Quite what this involves is relative, however, to factors such as school size and socio-economic context. A small rural secondary school with just two forms of entry would not be able to set as finely as a ten-form entry school. The nature of the sets in a five-form entry school in a socially and financially advantaged community would be very different from a similar sized school in a poorer, disadvantaged neighbourhood. Political and professional debates about ability grouping often miss these important distinctions.

There have, over the years, been a number of studies that have investigated different forms of grouping by ability in schools. While to some it may appear self-evident that grouping by attainment in subjects is the best approach, there is conflicting empirical evidence as to whether it necessarily leads to higher standards.

A number of major research reports have failed to show any particular advantage, in terms of academic attainment, for either streamed or mixed-ability forms of grouping. One well-known study (Newbold 1977) reported research in a large comprehensive school that had been divided into two 'halls', one streamed and one not. The finding was that:

> variations in academic performance which occur at the end of the first two
> years are generally not attributable to differences in methods of ability

grouping ... with common overall objectives the system of organisation is of less importance for academic standards, if indeed it is important at all, than the other substantial variables which exist.

(Newbold 1977: 178)

The study, whilst not detecting academic benefits for either form of organization, did see social effects which could be taken to support the principle of heterogeneous ability grouping as a means of achieving increased social integration.

More recently in 1998 the National Foundation for Educational Research carried out a major review of evidence about streaming, setting and grouping by ability (Sukhnandan and Lee 1998). Some of the key findings, taken from a summary of the review (see www.nfer.ac.uk) are set out below:

- From the findings of studies and meta-analyses in this area it is possible to argue that streaming and setting, compared with mixed-ability teaching, have no significant effect on pupil achievement – either in terms of overall average achievement or in terms of the average achievement of pupils of high, middle or low ability. This remains valid for pupils at both the primary and secondary level, and across all subject areas.
- In contrast, the more limited research on within-class grouping suggests that, compared with other forms of ability grouping, it has a beneficial effect for pupils of all abilities especially in subjects such as mathematics, science and modern languages.
- Streaming and setting, compared with within-class grouping and mixed-ability teaching, have been found to have a detrimental effect on the attitudes and self-esteem of pupils of middle and low ability. This has been associated with a decrease in levels of achievement for these pupils, and thus the creation of a vicious circle.
- Low-ability pupils who are grouped homogeneously, compared with those who are in mixed-ability groups, are less likely to participate in school activities, exhibit lower expectations, experience more disciplinary problems and have higher levels of absenteeism and non-completion.
- Research indicates that grouping pupils by ability reinforces the segregation of pupils in terms of social class, gender, race and age (season of birth). As a result, low-ability classes/groups tend to contain a disproportionately large number of pupils from working-class backgrounds, boys, pupils from ethnic minorities and summer-born children.
- Following the Education Reform Act of 1988, there has been a shift, within British schools, towards increased grouping by ability. This shift has occurred as a result of growing disillusionment with mixed-ability teaching, the introduction of the National Curriculum and its assessments and the move towards a market-led education system: developments which have led to a shift in educational values away from issues of equality and back to the pursuit of excellence.
- The return to ability grouping has brought with it many of the limitations traditionally associated with it. Researchers have therefore argued that systems of

ability grouping should be implemented with greater selectivity and flexibility than they have been in the past. Researchers have also advocated greater investigation into the use of alternative forms of grouping.

The evidence from this review suggests that when taking decisions about which system(s) of pupil grouping to implement, individual schools need to take account of the needs of: their pupils, staff, parents and community; their local context, and developments at the national level. Systems of ability grouping should be evaluated and monitored to ensure that they are working effectively and are not implemented in ways that discriminate against certain groups of pupils.

A similar review carried out by the Scottish Council for Educational Research (Harlen and Malcolm 1997) covered much of the same ground and came to similar conclusions.

In the USA during the same period a major review of the literature published in the Harvard Educational Review (Mosteller *et al.* 1996) found that the findings were equivocal when comparing the relative merits of classes grouped by ability with those that were not.

All the evidence, therefore, points to the need for being tentative about advocacy of any one approach to groupings in school. I have argued in this chapter that the simple, even commonsense, notions of ability need to be challenged. In looking at transposing any concept of ability or attainment into school organization a range of factors needs to be taken account of. Apparent gains in terms of teaching efficiency and increased pupil attainment need to be weighed against the way that some forms of grouping appear to discriminate against certain groups of pupils.

In the well-ordered school of the future, pupils may well move in and out of a variety of forms of grouping within, as well as between, the school years. Their capacity to utilize, alone and with others, new interactive forms of technology may also challenge some of the models of organization that have become familiar in secondary schools.

References

Birchenough, C. (1914) *History of Elementary Education in England and Wales*, London: University Tutorial Press.

Harlen, W. and Malcolm, H. (1997) *Setting and Streaming: A Research Review*, Scottish Council for Research in Education.

Jackson, B. (1964) *Streaming: an education system in miniature*, London: RKP.

Mosteller, F., Light, R. and Sacher, A. (1996) 'Sustained inquiry in education: lessons from skill grouping and class size', *Harvard Educational Review*, 66(4): 797–842.

Newbold, B. (1977) *Ability Grouping: The Banbury Enquiry*, Windsor: NFER/Nelson.

Plowden Report (1967) *Children and their Primary Schools*, London: HMSO.

Rose, J. (1984) *The Case of 'Peter Pan' or the Impossibility of Children's Fiction*, London: Macmillan.

Simon, B. (1971) *Intelligence Psychology Education*, London: Lawrence and Wishart.

Sukhnandan, L. and Lee, B. (1998) *Streaming, Setting and Grouping by Ability: a Review of the Literature*, Slough: NFER.

Torrance, H. (1981) 'The origins and development of mental testing in England and Wales and the USA', *Journal of Sociology of Education*, 2(1).

4 How children learn
Implications for practice

Neville Bennett and Elisabeth Dunne

How children learn

[...] The topic of how children learn is a complex one, and no attempt is made here to provide a full and critical exposition. The aim of this chapter is to capture the essence of learning by identifying core issues, and by considering the ideas of the different theorists in the debate.

The first point to note is that what children learn in the classroom will depend to a large extent on what they already know. Irrespective of their age, children will have some knowledge and some conception of the classroom topic they are faced with, which they have acquired from books, television, talking to parents and friends, visits to places of interest, previous work in school, and so on. However, these conceptions, or schemata as they are generally called, are likely to be incomplete, hazy or even plain wrong. They are, nevertheless, the children's current ideas, which they use to make sense of everyday experiences. In other words, children do not come to any lesson empty-headed; they come with partial schemata. For example, a top junior teacher we observed recently asked her class, 'What are clouds made of?' The responses were many and varied. Some thought they were made of smoke, some had fuzzy notions about them being made over the sea, but they were unclear of the process. On the other hand, another child, the son of a local meteorologist, was able to talk about evaporation and had a clear schema of the water cycle. There was, then, tremendous variation in the schemas held by the children in that class. The teacher's job there, as in any classroom, was to find effective ways of modifying, extending or elaborating the children's schemata. Indeed, we can define learning in these terms as the extension, modification or elaboration of existing cognitive schemas.

That children have different schemata is, of course, one reason for the stress on individualization of learning. But this should not be taken too far. Ideas or schemata are often shared, and this is not surprising. Children who come from the same school catchment area will, for example, have shared experiences in their local environment as well as in their school; another powerful shared experience is that of television.

So, children have schemata which are differentially complete or correct, some of which are shared. But how do their schemata change in school? Teachers offer knowledge in the form of telling, demonstrating and explaining, and pupils work on different kinds of tasks or activities designed to allow the practice, development or generation of a wide range of knowledge and understanding. Most importantly, it is the child who makes sense of these inputs, by constructing links with their prior knowledge. It is assumed that the construction of links is an active intellectual process involving the generation, checking and restructuring of ideas in the light of those already held. Construction of meaning is a continuous process and this view of learning is often referred to as 'constructivist'.

There is little argument among theorists that learning involves the construction of knowledge through experience. Arguments occur in relation to the conditions under which such learning is optimized – should learning be individual or social? Bruner and Haste (1987) capture this argument well when contrasting children as 'social beings' and 'lone scientists':

> A quiet revolution has taken place in developmental psychology in the last decade. It is not only that we have begun to think again of the child as a social being – one who plays and talks with others, learns through interactions with parents and teachers – but because we have come once more to appreciate that through such social life, the child acquires a framework for interpreting experience, and learning how to negotiate meaning in a manner congruent with the requirements of the culture. 'Making sense' is a social process; it is an activity that is always situated within a cultural and historical context.

> Before that, we had fallen into the habit of thinking of the child as an 'active scientist', constructing hypotheses about the world, reflecting upon experience, interacting with the physical environment and formulating increasingly complex structures of thought. But this active, constructing child had been conceived as a rather isolated being, working alone at her problem-solving. Increasingly, we see now that, given an appropriate, shared social context, the child seems more competent as an intelligent social operator than she is as a 'lone scientist' coping with a world of unknowns.

This support for the child as a social being rather than as a lone scientist constitutes an attack on Piaget's views of learning, which assume that genuine intellectual competence is a manifestation of a child's largely unassisted activities. Bruner (1986) stresses far more the importance of the social setting in learning.

> I have come increasingly to recognise that most learning in most settings is a communal activity, a sharing of the culture. It is not just that the child must make his knowledge his own, but that he must make it his own in a community of those who share his sense of belonging to a culture.

This leads him to emphasize the role of negotiating and sharing in children's classroom learning, and in this he has been influenced by the work of Vygotsky. Vygotsky (1978) assigned a much greater significance to the social environment than Piaget:

Learning awakens a variety of internal developmental processes, that are able to operate only when the child is interacting with people in his environment and in co-operation with his peers.

Social interaction is thus assigned a central role in facilitating learning. For Vygotsky, a child's potential for learning is revealed and indeed is often realized in interactions with more knowledgeable others. These 'more knowledgeable others' can be anybody – peers, siblings, the teacher, parents, grandparents, and so on.

One of Vygotsky's main contributions to our understanding of learning is his concept of the 'zone of proximal development', which refers to the gap between what an individual can do alone and unaided, and what can be achieved with the help of more knowledgeable others – 'What a child can do today in co-operation, tomorrow he will be able to do on his own' (Vygotsky 1962). For him, the foundation of learning and development is co-operatively achieved success, and the basis of that success is language and communication. 'Children solve practical tasks with the help of their speech, as well as with their eyes and their hands' (Vygotsky 1962). Through speech to themselves (inner speech) and others, children begin to organize their experiences into thought.

The belief that talk is central to learning is not new. In 1972 Britton wrote:

> We have seen that talk is a major instrument of learning in infancy; that the infant *learns by talking* and that *he learns to talk by talking* ... they must practise language in the sense in which a doctor 'practises'... and not in the sense in which a juggler 'practises' a new trick before he performs it.

The Bullock Report (1975) devoted itself entirely to language, and welcomed the growth of interest in oral language, 'for we cannot emphasise too strongly our conviction of its importance in the education of the child'. It was argued that all schools ought to have, as a priority objective, a commitment to the speech needs of their pupils.

The National Association for the Teachers of English (NATE) neatly encapsulated the argument when stating that:

> One of the major functions of language that concerns teachers is its use for learning: for trying to put new ideas into words, for testing out one's thinking on other people, for fitting together new ideas with old ones and so on, which all need to be done to bring about new understanding. These functions suggest active uses of language by the pupil, as opposed to passive reception.

The status of talk in the classroom was reinforced in the 1980s through the focus on oracy by the Assessment of Performance Unit (APU). From their survey of 11-year-olds, they reported that gains in mastery of spoken language may have beneficial effects on pupils' learning capabilities:

> The experience of expressing and shaping ideas through talk as well as writing,

and of collaborating to discuss problems or topics, help to develop a critical and exploratory attitude towards knowledge and concepts.

They concluded that 'pupils' performances could be substantially improved if they were given regular opportunities in the classroom to use their speaking and listening skills over a range of purposes, in a relaxed atmosphere' (APU 1986).

Following this, the authors of the English National Curriculum recommended a separate language component for speaking and listening, thus demonstrating their belief in oracy:

> Our inclusion of speaking and listening as a separate profile component in our recommendations is a reflection of our conviction that these skills are of central importance to children's development.
>
> (National Curriculum Council 1989)

Hence, a constructivist view of learning perceives children as intellectually active learners already holding ideas or schemata which they use to make sense of their everyday experiences. Learning in classrooms involves the extension, elaboration or modification of their schemata. This process is one by which learners actively make sense of the world by constructing meanings. Learning is optimized in settings where social interaction, particularly between a learner and more knowledgeable others, is encouraged, and where co-operatively achieved success is a major aim. The medium for this success is talk, which is now widely accepted as a means of promoting pupils' understandings and of evaluating their progress.

Implications for practice

That pupils bring schemas of their own to bear on any given topic, and that some of these will be shared and others idiosyncratic, has to be taken into account by teachers in their planning of classroom tasks. To take these schemas adequately into account necessitates a clear understanding of what they are; that is, it requires the teacher to take on the role of diagnostician (Bennett *et al.* 1984). A useful metaphor for gaining access to children's conceptions is that of creating 'a window into the child's mind'. To open the curtains of that window often needs far more than a rudimentary look at a child's work. It demands a sophisticated combination of observation and careful questioning and this is likely to need a great deal of time.

Judging an appropriate level for a task or activity is clearly critical to the development of learning. In this context, the notion of the 'zone of proximal development' is again important; Vygotsky believed that optimal learning is that which involves the acquisition of cognitive skills slightly beyond the child's independent grasp. A similar concept is that of 'match' between task and child, about which Her Majesty's Inspectorate (HMI) have been much concerned over the past decade. Their definition, put crudely, is that tasks should be planned which are neither too difficult nor too easy for the child (HMI 1978, 1983, 1985; see also, Bennett and Desforges 1988). Despite 'match' or 'appropriateness' being differently defined by

Vygotsky and HMI, their relationship to diagnosis is the same. Without adequate diagnosis of children's competences or understandings, it is unlikely that teacher judgements of appropriate tasks will be accurate.

Having made decisions about content, teachers then present tasks to pupils. In whatever mode this is done (demonstration, discussion, experiment, etc.), pupils' construction of meanings will be facilitated by clear statements of purpose, and information about how the task fits into work previously done and its relation to that which will be tackled in the future.

The view that learning is optimized through talk in co-operative settings has implications for presentation, as well as for classroom management. The nature of the teacher's talk needs to be carefully considered, as does the kind of classroom setting which allows for peer tutoring and co-operative working between pupils.

The most explicit advice on this aspect of classroom practice is to be found in the NCC guidance on the English curriculum, particularly that on speaking and listening (NCC 1989). Here the guidance prescribes classrooms where children feel sufficiently encouraged and secure to be able to express and explore their thoughts, feelings and emotions; where teachers encourage talk which is genuinely tentative and explanatory, while demonstrating that talk is a rigorous activity. Drawing clearly from constructivist ideas, the guidance argues that children should be able to make connections between what they already know and new experiences and ideas, and that the main vehicle for this will be their own talk. Teachers are also asked to reflect on their own questioning strategies. For example, in talking with children the teacher should ensure that questions are genuinely open-ended, that children have problems to solve without a subtly indicated, expected answer, and that they are encouraged to speculate, hypothesize, predict and test out ideas with each other and with the teacher. The emphasis should be on language being used, not to communicate what is known, but as an instrument of learning. 'It is time for children to think aloud, to grapple with ideas and to clarify thoughts.' The guidance argues that once children have developed new understandings they will need to reflect and exchange ideas and views with other pupils and the teacher in order to consolidate their learning. Such talk does, of course, also indicate to the teacher the state of the child's understanding; that is, it is an aid to diagnosis.

This guidance appears to be attempting to create what Edwards and Mercer (1987) describe as a framework for shared understanding with children, based on joint knowledge and action. This framework acts as a 'scaffold':

> for children's mental explanations, a cognitive climbing-frame – built by children with their Vygotskyan teacher – which structures activity more systematically than the discovery sand-pit of the Piagetian classroom. Talk between teachers and children helps build the scaffolding. Children's activity, even 'discovery', in the absence of such a communicative framework may, in cognitive terms, lead nowhere.

Current practice

Having considered current perspectives on how children learn, and the implications of these perspectives for classroom practice, the critical question now to be

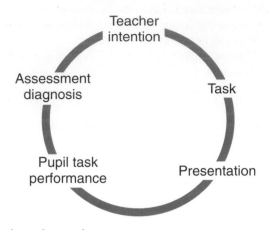

Figure 4.1   A simple teaching cycle

considered is, 'How does current teaching measure up?' The aim here is not to provide a complete description of present-day primary practice and analyse its strengths and weaknesses – that would need a book in itself. Rather, we will concentrate on those aspects of teaching identified in the last section: eliciting and diagnosing children's conceptions, provision and presentation of appropriate learning activities, co-operation and grouping, and the nature of classroom talk.

The use of a simple diagram of a teaching cycle allows these aspects, and their inter-relationships, to be examined. In Figure 4.1, the cycle begins with the teacher planning and preparing tasks and activities for children which are then presented in some way (e.g. through discussion, an experiment, a television programme, etc.). The children then engage with their work within a classroom management system set up by the teacher (e.g. individuals working on individual tasks; mixed-ability groups in an integrated day arrangement; the whole class working in small co-operative groups on the same technology task, etc.). Once this work has been completed, it would be expected that teachers would assess or diagnose it, using that information to feed back to pupils, and to feed forward to inform their next round of planning.

References

Assessment and Performance Unit (1986) *Speaking and Listening, Assessment at Age 11*, Windsor: NFER-Nelson.

Bennett, N. and Desforges, C. (1988) 'Matching classroom tasks to students' attainments', *Elementary School Journal*, 88: 221–34.

Bennett, N., Desforges, C., Cockburn, A. and Wilkinson, B. (1984) *The Quality of Pupil Learning Experiences*, London: Erlbaum.

Britton, J. (1970) *Language and Learning* (1972 edition), Harmondsworth: Penguin Books.

Bruner, J. (1986) *Actual Minds, Possible Worlds*, Cambridge (MA): Harvard University Press.

Bruner, J. and Haste, H. (1987) *Making Sense*, London: Methuen.

Bullock Report (1975) A *Language for Life*, London: HMSO.

Edwards, D. and Mercer, N. (1987) *Common Knowledge: The Development of Understanding in the Classroom*, London: Methuen.

Her Majesty's Inspectorate (1978) *Primary Education in England*, London: HMSO.

Her Majesty's Inspectorate (1983) *9–13 Middle Schools: An Illustrative Survey*, London: HMSO.

Her Majesty's Inspectorate (1985) *Education 8–12 in Combined and Middle Schools*, London: HMSO.

National Curriculum Council (1989) *English in the National Curriculum Key Stage One*, York: NCC.

Vygotsky, L.S. (1962) *Thought and Language*, Cambridge (MA): MIT Press.

Vygotsky, L.S. (1978) *Mind and Society: The Development of Higher Psychological Processes*, Cambridge (MA): Harvard University Press.

5   What do new views of knowledge and thinking have to say about research on teacher learning?

Ralph T. Putnam and Hilda Borko

The education and research communities are abuzz with new (or at least re-discovered) ideas about the nature of cognition and learning. Terms like 'situated cognition', 'distributed cognition', and 'communities of practice' fill the air. ... Some have argued that the shifts in world view that these discussions represent are even more fundamental than the now-historical shift from behaviorist to cognitive views of learning (Shuell 1986).

These new ideas about the nature of knowledge, thinking, and learning – which are becoming known as the 'situative perspective' (Greeno 1997: Greeno *et al.* 1996) – are interacting with, and sometimes fueling, current reform movements in education. Most discussions of these ideas and their implications for educational practice have been cast primarily in terms of students. Scholars and policy makers have considered, for example, how to help students develop deep understandings of subject matter, situate students' learning in meaningful contexts, and create learning communities in which teachers and students engage in rich discourse about important ideas. ...

Less attention has been paid to teachers – either to their roles in creating learning experiences consistent with the reform agenda or to how they themselves learn new ways of teaching. In this chapter we focus on the latter. Our purpose in considering teachers' learning is twofold. First, we use these ideas about the nature of learning and knowing as lenses for understanding recent research on teacher learning. Second, we explore new issues about teacher learning and teacher education that this perspective brings to light. We begin with a brief overview of three conceptual themes that are central to the situative perspective – that cognition is (a) situated in particular physical and social contexts; (b) social in nature; and (c) distributed across the individual, other persons, and tools.

Cognition as situated

Early cognitive theories typically treated knowing as the manipulation of symbols inside the mind of the individual, and learning as the acquisition of knowledge and skills thought to be useful in a wide variety of settings (Greeno *et al.* 1996). Situative theorists challenge this assumption of a cognitive core independent of context and intention (Brown *et al.* 1989: Greeno and The Middle School Through Applications Project Group 1998: Lave and Wenger 1991). They posit, instead, that the physical and social contexts in which an activity takes place are an integral part of the activity, and that the activity is an integral part of the learning that takes place within it. How a person learns a particular set of knowledge and skills, and the situation in which a person learns, become a fundamental part of what is learned. Further, whereas traditional cognitive perspectives focus on the individual as the basic unit of analysis, situative perspectives focus on interactive systems that include individuals as participants, interacting with each other as well as materials and representational systems (Cobb and Bowers 1999: Greeno 1997).

A focus on the situated nature of cognition suggests the importance of *authentic activities* in classrooms. J. S. Brown and colleagues (1989) defined authentic activities as the 'ordinary practices of a culture' (p. 34) – activities that are similar to what actual practitioners do. They claimed that 'school activities', which do not share contextual features with related out-of-school tasks, typically fail to support transfer to these out-of-school settings. A. Brown and colleagues (1993) offered a different definition of authentic classroom activities – derived from the role of formal education in children's lives. If we consider the goal of education to be preparing students to be lifelong intentional learners, then activities are authentic if they serve that goal. Authentic activities foster the kinds of thinking and problem-solving skills that are important in out-of-school settings, whether or not the activities themselves mirror what practitioners do. Our discussion of authentic activities for teacher learning adopts a position similar to that of A. Brown and colleagues; that is, we consider the kinds of thinking and problem-solving skills fostered by an activity to be the key criterion for authenticity.

Cognition as social

Dissatisfied with overly individualistic accounts of learning and knowing, psychologists and educators are recognizing that the role of others in the learning process goes beyond providing stimulation and encouragement for individual construction of knowledge (Resnick 1991). Rather, interactions with the people in one's environment are major determinants of both what is learned and how learning takes place. This *sociocentric* view (Soltis 1981) of knowledge and learning holds that what we take as knowledge and how we think and express ideas are the products of the interactions of groups of people over time. Individuals participate in numerous *discourse communities* (Fish 1980: Michaels and O'Connor 1990: Resnick 1991), ranging from scholarly disciplines such as science or history, to groups of people sharing a common interest, to particular classrooms. These discourse communities provide the cognitive tools – ideas, theories, and concepts – that individuals appropriate as their own through their personal efforts to make sense of experiences. The process of learning, too, is social. Indeed, some scholars have conceptualized learning as coming to know how to participate in the discourse and practices of a particular community (e.g. Cobb 1994: Lave and Wenger 1991). From this perspective, learning is as much a matter of enculturation into a community's ways of thinking and dispositions as it is a result of explicit instruction in specific concepts, skills, and procedures (Driver *et al.* 1994: Resnick 1988: Schoenfeld 1992). It is important to note that this learning is not a unidirectional phenomenon; the community, too, changes through the ideas and ways of thinking its new members bring to the discourse.

One important idea emerging from a social perspective is that a central goal of schooling is to enculturate students into various discourse communities, equipping them with competence in using the concepts and the forms of reasoning and argument that characterize those communities (Lampert 1990: Michaels and O'Connor 1990: Resnick 1988). This perspective leads to the question of what kinds of discourse communities to establish in classrooms. In parallel to their position on authentic activities, some scholars argue that classroom communities should be modeled after disciplinary communities of mathematicians, scientists, historians, and so on (J. S. Brown *et al.* 1989). Others argue that – rather than preparing students to participate in the professional cultures of mathematicians and historians – 'schools should be communities where students learn to learn' (A. Brown *et al.* 1993: 190). Their assumption is that by participating in activities designed to question and extend their own knowledge in various domains, students will become enculturated into ways of learning that will continue for the rest of their lives. In either case, the discourse communities being envisioned are significantly different from those traditionally found in public school classrooms.

Cognition as distributed

Rather than considering cognition solely as a property of individuals, situative theorists posit that it is distributed or 'stretched over' (Lave 1988) the individual, other persons, and various artifacts such as physical and symbolic tools (Salomon 1993a). For example, Hutchins (1990, 1991) described the navigation of a US Navy ship, where the knowledge for successfully piloting the ship was distributed throughout the entire navigational system. Six people with three different job descriptions and using several sophisticated cognitive tools were involved in piloting the ship out of the harbor. The distribution of cognition across people and tools made it possible for the crew to accomplish cognitive tasks beyond the capabilities of any individual member (Hutchins 1990).

School learning environments typically do not emphasize such sharing of learning and cognitive performance, focusing instead on the importance of individual competencies. But, as Resnick (1987) wrote, 'as long as school focuses mainly on individual forms of competence, on tool-free performance, and on decontextualized skills, educating people to be good learners in school settings alone may not be sufficient to help them become strong out-of-school learners' (p.18). Pea (1993) made a similar point: 'Socially scaffolded and externally mediated, artifact-supported cognition is so predominant in out-of-school settings that its disavowal in the classroom is detrimental to the transfer of learning beyond the classroom' (p. 75). Admittedly there are disadvantages to incorporating tool-aided cognition and socially shared cognitive activities in classrooms; it seems clear, however, that to prepare students for successful participation in society, schools must achieve a better balance between activities that incorporate ideas of distributed cognition and those that stress only individual competence.

These three themes – learning and knowing as situated, social, and distributed – are fairly recent arrivals on the educational research scene in North America, although they have roots in the thinking of educators and psychologists as early as the late nineteenth century (e.g. Dewey 1896: Vygotsky, 1934/1962). Greeno and colleagues (1996) wove these themes together in characterizing the situative perspective:

> Success in cognitive functions such as reasoning, remembering, and perceiving is understood as an achievement of a system, with contributions of the individuals who participate, along with tools and artifacts. This means that thinking is situated in a particular context of intentions, social partners, and tools.
>
> (p. 20)

As well as providing new perspectives on teaching and learning in K–12 classrooms, the situative approach has important implications for research on the learning of preservice and inservice teachers. In the remainder of this article, we consider these implications. We focus on three issues: (a) where to situate teachers' learning experiences, (b) the nature of discourse communities for teaching and teacher learning, and (c) the importance of tools in teachers' work. (For a more comprehensive discussion of the three themes and their implications for classroom practices and teacher education, see Putnam and Borko 1997.)

Where should teachers' learning be situated?

Teacher educators have long struggled with how to create learning experiences powerful enough to transform teachers' classroom practice. Teachers, both experienced and novice, often complain that learning experiences outside the classroom are too removed from the day-to-day work of teaching to have a meaningful impact. At first glance, the idea that teachers' knowledge is situated in classroom practice lends support to this complaint, seeming to imply that most or all learning experiences for teachers should take place in actual classrooms. But the situative perspective holds that all knowledge is (by definition) situated. The question is not whether knowledge and learning are situated, but in what contexts they are situated. For some purposes, in fact, situating learning experiences for teachers outside of the classroom may be important – indeed essential – for powerful learning.

The situative perspective thus focuses researchers' attention on how various settings for teachers' learning give rise to different kinds of knowing. We examine here some of the approaches that researchers and teacher educators have taken to help teachers learn and change in powerful ways, focusing on the kinds of knowing each approach addresses. We begin by considering professional development experiences for practicing teachers.

Learning experiences for practicing teachers

One approach to staff development is to ground teachers' learning experiences in their own practice by conducting activities at school sites, with a large component taking pla3ce in individual teachers' classrooms. The University of Colorado

Assessment Project (Borko *et al.* 1997: Shepard *et al.* 1996) provides an example of this approach. The project's purpose was to help teachers design and implement classroom-based performance assessments compatible with their instructional goals in mathematics and literacy. As one component, a member of the research/staff development team worked with children in the classrooms of some participating teachers, observed their mathematical activities, and then shared her insights about their mathematical understandings with the teachers. Teachers reported that these conversations helped them to understand what to look for when observing students and to incorporate classroom-based observations of student performances into their assessment practices (Borko *et al.* 1997).

Another approach is to have teachers bring experiences from their classrooms to staff development activities, for example through ongoing workshops focused on instructional practices. In the UC Assessment Project (Borko *et al.* 1997), one particularly effective approach to situating learning occurred when members of the staff development/research team introduced materials and activities in a workshop session, the teachers attempted to enact these ideas in their classrooms, and the group discussed their experiences in a subsequent workshop session. Richardson and Anders's (1994) practical argument approach to staff development provides another example. These researchers structured discussions with participating elementary teachers to examine their practical arguments – the rationales, empirical support, and situational contexts that served as the basis for their instructional actions – often using videotapes of the teachers' classrooms as springboards for discussion.

These approaches offer some obvious strengths when viewed from a situative perspective. The learning of teachers is intertwined with their ongoing practice, making it likely that what they learn will indeed influence and support their teaching practice in meaningful ways. But there are also some problems. One is the issue of scalability: having researchers or staff developers spend significant amounts of time working alongside teachers is not practical on a widespread basis – at least not given the current social and economic structure of our schools. A second problem is that, even if it were possible in a practical sense to ground much of teachers' learning in their ongoing classroom practice, there are arguments for not always doing so. If the goal is to help teachers think in new ways, for example, it may be important to have them experience learning in different settings. The situative perspective helps us see that much of what we do and think is intertwined with the particular contexts in which we act. The classroom is a powerful environment for shaping and constraining how practicing teachers think and act. Many of their patterns of thought and action have become automatic – resistant to reflection or change. Engaging in learning experiences away from this setting may be necessary to help teachers 'break set' – to experience things in new ways.

For example, pervading many current educational reform documents is the argument that 'school' versions of mathematics, science, literature, and other subject matters are limited – that they overemphasize routine, rote aspects of the subject over the more powerful and generative aspects of the discipline. Students and teachers, reformers argue, need opportunities to think of mathematics or science or writing in new ways. It may be difficult, however, for teachers to experience these disciplines in new ways in the context of their own classrooms – the pull of the existing classroom environment and culture is simply too strong. Teachers may need the opportunity to experience these and other content domains in a new and different context. […]

Conclusion

In this chapter we set out to consider what the situative perspective on cognition – that knowing and learning are situated in physical and social contexts, social in nature, and distributed … – might offer those of us seeking to understand and improve teacher learning. As we pointed out earlier, these ideas are not entirely new. The fundamental issues about what it means to know and learn addressed by the situative perspective have engaged scholars for a long time. […]

Labaree (1998) argued … that this sort of continual revisiting of fundamental issues is endemic to the field of education. Unlike the *hard* sciences, whose hallmark is replicable, agreed-upon knowledge, education and other *soft* knowledge fields deal with the inherent unpredictability of human action and values. As a result, the quest for knowledge about education and learning leaves scholars

> feeling as though they are perpetually struggling to move ahead but getting nowhere. If Sisyphus were a scholar, his field would be education. At the end of long and distinguished careers, senior educational researchers are likely to find that they are still working on the same questions that confronted them at the beginning. And the new generation of researchers they have trained will be taking up these questions as well, reconstructing the very foundations of the field over which their mentors labored during their entire careers.
>
> (p. 9)

[…] Given the enduring nature of these questions and the debates surrounding them, what is to be gained by considering teacher knowledge and teacher learning from a situative perspective? Can this perspective help us think about teaching and teacher learning more productively? We believe it can – that the language and conceptual tools of social, situated, and distributed cognition provide powerful lenses for examining teaching, teacher learning, and the practices of teacher education (both preservice and inservice) in new ways.

For example, these ideas about cognition have helped us, in our own work, to see more clearly the strengths and limitations of various practices and settings for teacher learning. But this clarity comes only when we look closely at these concepts and their nuances. By starting with the assumption that all knowledge is situated in contexts, we were able to provide support for the general argument that teachers' learning should be grounded in some aspect of their teaching practice. Only by pushing beyond this general idea, however, to examine more closely the question of where to situate teachers' learning, were we able to identify specific advantages and limitations of the various contexts within which teachers' learning might be meaningfully situated: their own classrooms, group settings where participants' teaching is the focus of discussion, and settings emphasizing teachers' learning of subject matter. Similarly, ideas about the social and distributed nature of cognition help us think in new ways about the role of technological tools in creating new types of discourse communities for teachers, including unresolved issues regarding the guidance and support needed to ensure that conversations within these communities are educationally meaningful and worthwhile. [...]

References

Borko, H., Mayfield, V., Marion, S., Flexer, R. and Cumbo, K. (1997) 'Teachers' developing ideas and practices about mathematics performance assessment: Successes, stumbling blocks, and implications for professional development', *Teaching and Teacher Education, 13,* 259–78.

Brown, A., Ash, D., Rutherford, M., Nakagawa, K., Gordon, A. and Campione, J.C. (1993) 'Distributed expertise in the classroom' in G. Salomon (ed.) *Distributed cognitions: Psychological and educational considerations* 188–228, Cambridge: Cambridge University Press.

Brown, J.S., Collins, A. and Duguid, P. (1989) 'Situated cognition and the culture of learning', *Educational Researcher* 18(l): 32–42.

Cobb, P. (1994). 'Where is the mind? Constructivist and sociocultural perspectives on mathematical development', *Educational Researcher, 23*(7):13–19.

Cobb, P. and Bowers, J.S. (1999) 'Cognitive and situated learning perspectives in theory and practice', *Educational Researcher* 28(2): 4–15.

Dewey, J. (1896) 'The reflex arc concept in psychology', *Psychological Review,* 3: 356–70.

Driver, R., Asoko, H., Leach, J., Mortimer, E. and Scott, P. (1994) 'Constructing scientific knowledge in the classroom', *Educational Researcher* 23(7): 5–12

Fish, S. (1980) *Is there a text in this class? The authority of interpretive communities,* Cambridge (MA): Harvard University Press.

Greeno, J.G. (1997) 'On claims that answer the wrong questions', *Educational Researcher,* 26(1): 5–17.

Greeno, J.G., Collings, A.M. and Resnick, L.B. (1996) 'Cognition and learning' in D. Berliner and R. Calfee (eds, *Handbook of educational psychology* 15–16, New York: Macmillan.

Greeno, J.G., and the Middle School Through Applications Project Group (1998) 'The situativity of knowing, learning and research', *American Psychologist,* 53: 5–26.

Hutchins, E. (1990) 'The technology of team navigation' in J. Galegher, R.E. Kraut and C. Egido (eds) *Intellectual teamwork: Social and technological foundations of cooperative work* 191–120, Hillsdale, NJ: Erlbaum.

Hutchins. E. (1991) 'The social organization of distributed cognition' in L.B. Resnick, J.M. Levine and S.D. Teasley (eds) *Perspectives on socially shared cognition* 283–307, Washington, DC: American Psychological Association.

Labaree, D.F. (1998) 'Educational researchers: Living with a lesser form of knowledge', *Educational Researcher.* 27(8): 4–12.

Lampert, M. (1990) 'When the problem is not the question and the solution is not the answer: Mathematical knowing and teaching', *American Educational Research Journal,* 27: 29–63.

Lave, J. (1988) *Cognition in practice: Mind, mathematics and culture in everyday life,* Cambridge: Cambridge University Press.

Lave, J. and Wenger, E. (1991) *Situated learning: Legitimate peripheral participation,* Cambridge: Cambridge University Press.

Michaels, S. and O'Connor, M.C. (1990) *Literacy as reasoning within multiple discourses: Implications for policy and educational reform*, paper presented at the Council of Chief State School Officers 1990 Summer Institute: 'Restructuring Learning,' Literacies Institute, Educational Development Center, Newton, MA.

Pea, R. (1993) 'Practices of distributed intelligence and designs for education' in G. Salomon (ed.) *Distributed cognitions: Psychological and educational considerations* 47–87, New York: Cambridge University Press.

Putnam, R.T. and Borko, H. (1997) 'Teacher learning: Implications of new views of cognition' in B.J. Biddle, T.L. Good and I.F. Goodson (eds) *International handbook of teachers and teaching* (Vol. II: 1223–96), Dordrecht: Kluwer.

Resnick, L.B. (1987) 'Learning in school and out', *Educational Researcher*, 16(9): 13–20.

Resnick, L.B. (1988) 'Treating mathematics as an ill-structured discipline' in R.I. Charles and E.A. Silver (eds), *Research agenda for mathematics education: Vol. 3. The teaching and assessing of mathematical problem solving* 32–60, Hillsdale, NJ: Erlbaum.

Resnick, L.B. (1991) 'Shared cognition: Thinking as social practice' in L.B. Resnick, J.M. Levine and S.D. Teasley (eds) *Perspectives on socially shared cognition* 1–20, Washington, DC: American Psychological Association.

Richardson, V. and Anders, P. (1994) 'The study of teacher change' in V. Richardson (ed.) *A theory of teacher change and the practice of staff development. A case in reading instruction*, 159–180, New York: Teachers College Press.

Salomon, G. (ed.) (1993a) *Distributed cognitions: Psychology and educational considerations*, Cambridge: Cambridge University Press.

Schoenfeld, A.H. (1992) 'Learning to think mathematically: Problem solving, metacognition, and sense making in mathematics' in D. Grouws (ed.) *Handbook for research on mathematics teaching and learning* 334–70, New York: Macmillan.

Shepard, L.A., Flexer, R.J., Hiebert, E.H., Marion, S.F., Mayfield, V. and Weston, T.J. (1996) 'Effects of introducing classroom performance assessments on student learning', *Educational Measurement: Issues and Practice*, 15(3): 7–18.

Shuell, T.J. (1986) 'Cognitive conceptions of learning', *Review of Educational Research*, 56: 411–36.

Soltis, J.F. (1981) 'Education and the concept of knowledge' in J.F. Soltis (ed.) *Philosophy and education* 95–113, Chicago: National Society for the Study of Education.

Vygotsky, L.S. (1962) *Thought and Language* (Eugenia Hanfmann and Gertrude Vakar, ed. and trans.), Cambridge (MA): MIT Press. (Original work published in Russian in 1934.)

Section 2

Teachers and teaching

6   Teacher effectiveness

Hay McBer Report

A good teacher ...
is kind
is generous
listens to you
encourages you
has faith in you
keeps confidences
likes teaching children
likes teaching their subject
takes time to explain things
helps you when you're stuck
tells you how you are doing
allows you to have your say
doesn't give up on you
cares for your opinion
makes you feel clever
treats people equally
stands up for you
makes allowances
tells the truth
is forgiving.

(descriptions by 12-year-olds)

Three factors

This chapter ... is intended to be of practical use to teachers and headteachers who are interested in what we found to be important in effective teaching.

Our research confirms much that is already known about the attributes of effective teaching. It also adds some new dimensions that demonstrate the extent to which effective teachers make a difference for their pupils. We found three main factors within teachers' control that significantly influence pupil progress:

- professional characteristics
- teaching skills
- classroom climate.

Each provides distinctive and complementary ways that teachers can understand the contribution they make. None can be relied on alone to deliver value-added teaching.

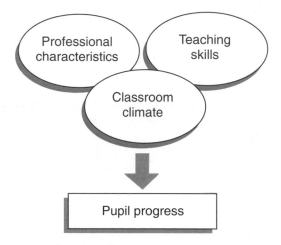

Figure 6.1   The measures of teacher effectiveness

The three factors are different in nature. Two of them – professional characteristics and teaching skills – are factors which relate to what a teacher brings to the job. The professional characteristics are the ongoing patterns of behaviour that combine to drive the things we typically do. Amongst those things are the 'micro-behaviours' covered by teaching skills. Whilst teaching skills can be learned, sustaining these behaviours over the course of a career will depend on the deeper seated nature of professional characteristics. Classroom climate, on the other hand, is an output measure. It allows teachers to understand how the pupils in their class feel about nine dimensions of climate created by the teacher that influence their motivation to learn.

So, for example, a teacher may have – amongst other things – the professional characteristic of *holding people accountable*, which is the drive and ability to set clear expectations and parameters and to hold others accountable for performance. Such a pattern of behaviour could make it more natural for this teacher to exhibit teaching skills like providing opportunities for students to take responsibility for their own learning, or correcting bad behaviour immediately. And the impact of these teaching skills, regularly exhibited, might be that pupils feel that there is a higher degree of order in their class, or that there is the emotional support needed to try new things.

It should be noted, however, that this is only an example. In other circumstances, with different pupils, in a different context, other approaches might have been more effective. There is, in other words, a multiplicity of ways in which particular patterns of characteristics determine how a teacher chooses which approach to use from a repertoire of established techniques in order to influence how pupils feel.

All competent teachers know their subjects. They know the appropriate teaching methods for their subjects and curriculum areas and the ways pupils learn. More effective teachers make the most of their professional knowledge in two linked ways. One is the extent to which they deploy appropriate teaching skills consistently and effectively in the course of all their lessons – the sorts of teaching strategies and techniques that can be observed when they are at work in the classroom, and which underpin the national numeracy and literacy strategies. The other is the range and intensity of the professional characteristics they exhibit – ongoing patterns of behaviour which make them effective.

Pupil progress results from the successful application of subject knowledge and subject teaching methods, using a combination of appropriate teaching skills and professional characteristics. Professional characteristics can be assessed, and good teaching practice can be observed.

Classroom climate provides another tool for measuring the impact created by a combination of the teacher's skills, knowledge and professional characteristics. Climate is a measure of the collective perceptions of pupils regarding those dimensions of the classroom environment that have a direct impact on their capacity and motivation to learn.

Taken in combination, these three factors provide valuable tools for teachers to enhance the progress of their pupils.

On the other hand, we found that biometric data (i.e. information about a teacher's age and teaching experience, additional responsibilities, qualifications, career history and so on) did not allow us to predict his or her effectiveness as a teacher. Effective and outstanding teachers came from diverse backgrounds. Our data did not show that school context could be used to predict pupil progress. Effective and outstanding teachers teach in all kinds of schools and school contexts. This means that using biometric data to predict a teacher's effectiveness could well lead to the exclusion of some potentially outstanding teachers. This finding is also consistent with the notion that pupil progress outcomes are affected more by teachers' skills and professional characteristics than by factors such as their sex, qualifications or experience.

We used start-of-year and end-of-year pupil attainment data to underpin our assessment of relative effectiveness based on value added. Using this knowledge and the outcomes from our research described below, we have been able to model the impact teachers have on the classroom climate, how that climate affects pupil progress and what aspects of teaching skills and behavioural characteristics had most impact on climate.

Our findings suggest that, taken together, teaching skills, professional characteristics and classroom climate will predict well over 30 per cent of the variance in pupil progress. This is very important for teachers because it gives them a framework for assessing how they achieve their results and for identifying the priorities for improvement.

So we show that teachers really do make a difference. Within their classrooms, effective teachers create learning environments which foster pupil progress by deploying their teaching skills as well as a wide range of professional characteristics. Outstanding teachers create an excellent classroom climate and achieve superior pupil progress largely by displaying more professional characteristics at higher levels of sophistication within a very structured learning environment.

Teaching skills

Teaching skills are those 'micro-behaviours' that the effective teacher constantly exhibits when teaching a class. They include behaviours like:

- involving all pupils in the lesson
- using differentiation appropriately to challenge all pupils in the class
- using a variety of activities or learning methods
- applying teaching methods appropriate to the National Curriculum objectives
- using a variety of questioning techniques to probe pupils' knowledge and understanding.

The 35 behaviours we looked for are based on research conducted by Professor David Reynolds and other colleagues. They are clustered under the seven Ofsted inspection headings for ease of use.

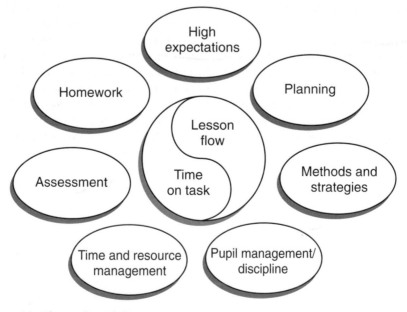

Figure 6.2 The teaching skills

In addition to the micro-behaviours under the seven inspection headings, teaching skills can be observed in terms of the way the lesson is structured and flows, and the number of pupils who are on task through the course of the lesson.

In primary schools the outstanding teachers scored higher on average in four out of the seven clusters: *high expectations, time and resource management, assessment,* and *homework.* In secondary schools there was stronger differentiation covering all clusters, but it was particularly evident in *high expectations, planning,* and *homework.*

Our lesson observations revealed that, in classes run by effective teachers, pupils are clear about what they are doing and why they are doing it. They can see the links with their earlier learning and have some ideas about how it could be developed further. The pupils want to know more. They understand what is good about their work and how it can be improved. They feel secure in an interesting and challenging learning environment. And they support one another and know when and where to go for help. The research shows the criticality of the teacher in the pupil learning process. The effective teachers whom we observed and studied were very actively involved with their pupils at all times. Many of the activities were teacher-led. They created maximum opportunities to learn and no time was wasted. The environment was very purposeful and businesslike. But at the same time there was always a great deal of interaction between teacher and pupils.

One factor that led to this purposeful learning environment was the range of effective teaching skills and techniques deployed by the teacher in the classroom. The following paragraphs describe these skills and techniques in detail.

Effective teachers set *high expectations* for the pupils and communicate them directly to the pupils. They challenge and inspire pupils, expecting the most from them, so as to deepen their knowledge and understanding. The most effective teachers determine the appropriateness of objectives for pupils by some form of differentiation. At its lowest level, this means expecting different outcomes from pupils of varying ability. At a more sophisticated level teachers know and use an extensive repertoire of means of differentiation – so that they are able to cope with the needs of more and less able pupils. But within these parameters effective teachers are relentless in their pursuit of a standard of excellence to be achieved by all pupils, and in holding fast to this ambition. These expectations are high, clear and consistent.

Key questions

1   Does the teacher encourage high standards of

- effort?
- accuracy?
- presentation?

2   Does the teacher use differentiation appropriately to challenge all pupils in the class?

3   Does the teacher vary motivational strategies for different individuals?

4   Does the teacher provide opportunities for students to take responsibility for their own learning?
5   Does the teacher draw on pupil experiences or ideas relevant to the lesson?

Effective teachers are good at *planning*, setting a clear framework and objectives for each lesson. The effective teacher is very systematic in the preparation for, and execution, of each lesson. The lesson planning is done in the context of the broader curriculum and longer-term plans. It is a very structured approach beginning with a review of previous lessons, and an overview of the objectives of the lesson linked to previous lessons and, where appropriate, the last homework assignment. Where homework is set (normally in secondary schools and for older primary pupils), the teacher often spends 5–10 minutes reviewing what pupils have learnt from it.

The effective teacher communicates the lesson content to be covered and the key activities for the duration of the lesson. Material is presented in small steps, with opportunities for pupils to practise after each step. Each activity is preceded by clear and detailed instructions. But the planning also takes into account the differing needs of pupils, including those with specific learning difficulties. For pupils, there is clarity of what they are doing, where they are going and how they will know when they have achieved the objectives of the lesson.

Effective teachers create the time to review lesson objectives and learning outcomes at the end of each lesson. Some teachers employ a Tactical Lesson Planning approach which describes both the content of lesson and the learning objectives, and the methods to be employed. But the focus of the planning activity is on pupil learning outcomes.

In some schools, particularly special schools, the highly effective teachers involve support staff in the preparation of the curriculum/lesson plans, and outline to them the role they are expected to play.

Key questions

1   Does the teacher communicate a clear plan and objectives for the lesson at the start of the lesson?
2   Does the teacher have the necessary materials and resources ready for the class?
3   Does the teacher link lesson objectives to the National Curriculum?
4   Does the teacher review what pupils have learned at the end of the lesson?

Effective teachers employ a *variety of teaching strategies* and techniques to engage pupils and to keep them on task. In our observations we saw effective teachers doing a great deal of active teaching. Many of the activities were led by the teacher. The teachers presented information to the pupils with a high degree of clarity and enthusiasm and, when giving basic instruction, the lessons proceeded at a brisk pace. Nevertheless, there was, in the majority of the classes, a range of teaching approaches and activities designed to keep the pupils fully engaged.

Individual work and small group activities were regularly employed as ways of reinforcing pupil learning through practice and reflection. However, it was evident that when the effective teachers were not actively leading the instructions they were always on the move, monitoring pupils' focus and understanding of materials. Content and presentation were varied to suit the needs of the class and the nature of learning objectives.

So what we saw effective teachers doing was a great deal of direct instruction to whole classes, interspersed with individual and small-group work. But the active style of teaching does not result in passive pupils. Rather, there is a great deal of interaction between teacher and pupils. Effective teachers ask a lot of questions and involve the pupils in class discussion. In this way the pupils are actively engaged in the lesson, and the teacher is able to monitor pupils' understanding and challenge their thinking by skilful questioning. It is evident that effective teachers employ a sophisticated questioning approach – ranging from asking many brief questions on main and supplementary points to multiple questioning of individuals to provide greater understanding and challenge.

Key questions

1   Does the teacher involve all pupils in the lesson?
2   Does the teacher use a variety of activities/learning methods?
3   Does the teacher apply teaching methods appropriate to the National Curriculum objectives?
4   Does the teacher use a variety of questioning techniques to probe pupils' knowledge and understanding?
5   Does the teacher encourage pupils to use a variety of problem-solving techniques?
6   Does the teacher give clear instructions and explanations?
7   Does practical activity have a clear purpose in improving pupils' understanding or achievement?
8   Does the teacher listen and respond to pupils?

Effective teachers have a clear strategy for pupil management. A sense of order prevails in the classroom. Pupils feel safe and secure. This pupil management strategy is a means to an end: allowing maximum time for pupils to be focused on task, and thus maximizing the learning opportunity. Effective teachers establish and communicate clear boundaries for pupil behaviour. They exercise authority clearly and fairly from the outset, and in their styles of presentation and engagement they hold the pupils' attention. Inappropriate behaviour is 'nipped in the bud' with immediate direct action from the teacher. Some effective teachers employ a 'catch them being good' policy whereby pupil behaviour which is appropriate and on task is recognized and reinforced by praise. One outstanding teacher referred to the importance of the 'lighthouse effect' – being fully aware of everything that is going on in the classroom and having 360° vision.

In those schools where there was a likelihood of a high incidence of pupil misbehaviour, the effective teachers employed a very structured behavioural approach to each lesson, e.g. standing at the door to greet pupils; commanding attention at the beginning of the lesson; taking action on latecomers; taking direct and immediate action on inappropriate behaviours. The most effective teachers had a longer-term strategy of getting to know the pupils with behavioural problems. In other words the highly effective teacher is able to create an environment in which all pupils can learn by employing direct means of pupil management to ensure that disruption to pupil learning is minimized and pupils feel safe and secure.

Key questions

1   Does the teacher keep the pupils on task throughout the lesson?
2   Does the teacher correct bad behaviour immediately?
3   Does the teacher praise good achievement and effort?
4   Does the teacher treat different children fairly?
5   Does the teacher manage non-pupils (support teachers/staff) well?

Effective teachers *manage time and resources* wisely. The effective management of pupils, time, resources and support promotes good behaviour and effective learning. Effective teachers achieve the management of the class by having a clear structure for each lesson, making full use of planned time, using a brisk pace and allocating his/her time fairly amongst pupils. The effective teachers start their lessons on time and finish crisply with a succinct review of learning.

Where they are able to do so, pupils are encouraged to manage their own time well and to achieve what is required in the time available. The classrooms are effective learning environments in which activities run smoothly, transitions are brief, and little time is lost in getting organized or dealing with disruptions. In our observations we found that highly effective teachers managed to get well over 90 per cent of the pupils focused on task over the course of a lesson.

In those schools where support and/or parental help was available, the effective teachers involved helpers in the lesson planning stage and in the execution of the lessons. In some instances, support staff were trained in aspects of pupil management, reading support and computer skills.

Key questions

1   Does the teacher structure the lesson to use the time available well?
2   Does the lesson last for the planned time?
3   Are appropriate learning resources used to enhance pupils' opportunities?
4   Does the teacher use an appropriate pace?
5   Does the teacher allocate his/her time fairly amongst pupils?

It is evident that effective teachers employ a range of *assessment* methods and techniques to monitor pupils' understanding of lessons and work. These could be tests, competitions, questioning or regular marking of written work. The effective teachers look for gains in learning, gaps in knowledge and areas of misunderstanding through their day-to-day work with pupils. Also, effective teachers encourage pupils to judge the success of their own work and to set themselves targets for improvement. They also offer critical and supportive feedback to pupils.

Key questions

1   Does the teacher focus on

- understanding and meaning?
- factual memory?
- skills mastery?
- applications in real-life settings?

2   Does the teacher use tests, competitions, etc. to assess understanding?
3   Does the teacher recognize misconceptions and clear them up?
4   Is there evidence of pupils' written work having been marked or otherwise assessed?
5   Does the teacher encourage pupils to do better next time?

An important part of the assessment process is the regular setting and marking of homework, particularly in secondary schools. The effective teachers ensure that homework is integrated with class work, is tailored to individual needs and is regularly and constructively marked.

Key questions

1   Is homework set either to consolidate or extend the coverage of the lesson?
2   Is homework which had been set previously followed up in the lesson?
3   Does the teacher explain what learning objectives pupils will gain from homework?

Overall effective teachers had well over 90 per cent of the pupils on task through the lesson, and their lessons flowed naturally to achieve an appropriate balance between

- whole class interactive
- whole class lecture
- individual work
- collaborative group work
- classroom management

and

- testing or assessment.

The full observation schedule used in our research has since been adapted by the DfEE as a standard observation tool which has been offered to all schools as part of the new performance management arrangements.

Professional characteristics

Professional characteristics are deep-seated patterns of behaviour which outstanding teachers display more often, in more circumstances and to a greater degree of intensity than effective colleagues. They are how the teacher does the job, and have to do with self-image and values; traits, or the way the teacher habitually approaches situations; and, at the deepest level, the motivation that drives performance.

From the in-depth interviews (behavioural event interviews) with the teachers in our sample we found that 16 characteristics contribute to effective teaching. Strength in five clusters is required. Certain different combinations of characteristics within these clusters can be equally effective. This is not a static 'one-size-fits-all' picture. Effective teachers show distinctive combinations of characteristics that create success for their pupils.

The characteristics and the descriptions of different levels for each characteristic were not part of a pre-existing model. They are defined by the data we collected from teachers. [...]

The particular characteristics that emerge from our research represent what teachers actually do over time, both in the classroom and outside it, to deliver results. We looked for a description of the combinations of characteristics (an 'algorithm') which would enable us to sort our sample with around 80 per cent accuracy between outstanding and typical.

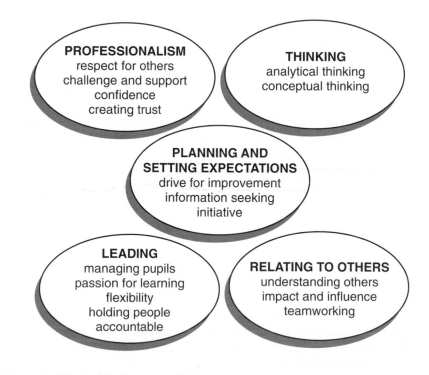

Figure 6.3 The model of professional characteristics

And we looked for algorithms which would accurately describe effective performance at the threshold, at main professional grade, at AST, and in shared leadership positions.

The AST algorithm accurately sorts outstanding and typical performers 72 per cent of the time in a small sample. The threshold algorithm accurately sorts 86 per cent of the time. The main professional grade algorithm is designed to allow all effective teachers to pass, and over 80 per cent of the total sample would do this. We did not see evidence of particular middle manager patterns in primary schools, but we were able to arrive at an algorithm for secondary heads of department which accurately sorted 78 per cent of the time. The shape of this middle manager model was very similar to the shared leadership model developed in a parallel research project investigating the characteristics of deputy headteachers and newly-appointed heads.

It was not evident from our research that it would be possible or appropriate to differentiate between subjects, phases, or within professional levels (e.g. threshold).

The professional characteristics fall into five clusters: professionalism, thinking, planning and setting expectations, leading, and relating to others. Effective teachers need to have some strengths in each of them. On the following pages we describe the characteristics cluster by cluster.

Professionalism

The driver for teachers is a core of strongly held and enacted values which, taken together, are a powerful basis for *professionalism*. There are four characteristics which describe this cluster or group of characteristics.

Respect for others underpins everything the effective teacher does, and is expressed in a constant concern that everyone should treat pupils and all members of the school community with respect. Effective teachers explicitly value others, and value the diversity in the school community, and retain their respect of others even when sorely tried. Outstanding teachers take a number of steps over time to create a feeling of community in the class or in the school. Effective teachers also provide *challenge and support* – a 'tough caring' where they not only cater for pupils' needs for physical and psychological safety but, crucially, repeatedly express positive expectations and build pupils' self-esteem and belief that they can succeed, as learners and in life. Threshold and outstanding teachers do everything in their power to ensure all pupils get the best deal possible from their education.

Effective teachers show *confidence* in most situations, expressing optimism about their own abilities and making an active contribution in meetings. Over time this confidence grows, so that a teacher sees him or herself as a fully rounded professional, able to succeed in most circumstances. Effective teachers take a full part in moving the school forward and improving its effectiveness, drawing on their experience to help shape policies and procedures.

They have emotional resilience in dealing with challenging pupils and situations where, because they have a range of professional skills and have already experienced similar challenges, they are able to keep calm. This ability is fuelled by a conviction about the importance and value of what they are doing as highly effective practitioners in shaping the future of their pupils. They identify with the job and see the challenge of an increasingly 'front line' role as part of the territory. The very best go even further, rising to stretching challenges and expressing a belief that they will succeed against the odds.

Effective teachers are consistent and fair, *creating trust* with their pupils because they honour their commitments. They are genuine, and generate the atmosphere where pupils can venture to be themselves, express themselves and not be afraid of making mistakes – an important starting point for learning. They are a dependable point of reference in what, for many pupils, is a turbulent world. As they progress in the profession, increasingly they live up to their professional beliefs.

These characteristics, taken together, result in an underlying concern for pupils and their achievement. Effective teachers are quite evidently there to support their pupils, and their sense of vocation is at the heart of the model of effective teaching.

Characteristic definitions

Respect for others   The underlying belief that individuals matter and deserve respect.
Challenge and support   A commitment to do everything possible for each pupil and enable all pupils to be successful.
Confidence   The belief in one's ability to be effective and to take on challenges.
Creating trust   Being consistent and fair. Keeping one's word.

Thinking

The *thinking* that effective teachers bring to the job is characterized by *analytical thinking* – the drive to ask why, to see cause and effect and think ahead to implications; and *conceptual thinking* – the ability to see patterns in behaviour and situations and, at the level of outstanding teaching, to adapt creatively and apply concepts, ideas and best practice. Effective teachers plan individual lessons, units and programmes of work soundly based on data and evidence-led assessment of pupils, and evaluation of results. They attend to what is actually happening and have a logical, systematic approach to the job, looking after the details in order to achieve success for all pupils. Outstanding teachers are able to analyse many more variables in a complex situation, and have the ability to trace many possible causes and effects.

Characteristic definitions

Analytical thinking   The ability to think logically, break things down, and recognize cause and effect.
Conceptual thinking   The ability to see patterns and links, even when there is a lot of detail.

Planning and setting expectations

By adopting a professional approach, teachers' energy can be channelled into *planning and setting expectations*, targeting the key elements which will make the most difference to their pupils, and the results they are able to achieve. Teaching is a demanding role and the pace of change rapid. Effective teachers are committed to meeting the needs of all pupils and to including everyone in the class. This means carefully prioritizing and targeting their efforts so that all pupils get their fair share of attention and everyone achieves good results. There are three characteristics which group together in this cluster of the model.

In terms of *drive for improvement*, all effective teachers want not only to do a good job but also to set and measure achievement against an internal standard of excellence. Threshold teachers seek to do everything they can to improve the attainment of their pupils, to make the school itself more effective in raising achievement, and to reflect on and improve their own professional practice. Outstanding teachers continuously set and meet ambitious targets for themselves and their pupils. They refer regularly to visible, quantifiable and tangible measures; and they focus on whether they and the school really are making a difference and adding value to pupils.

Information seeking works with this drive for results. All effective teachers ask questions to get a first-hand understanding of what is going on. At threshold level teachers dig deeper to find out more about their pupils and their classes, so they can set differentiated programmes of work, and targets that start from an understanding of prior attainment and potential performance. Outstanding teachers continually gather information from wider and more varied sources and use their own systems progressively to do so.

All effective teachers use their *initiative* to seize immediate opportunities and sort out problems before they escalate, and are able to act decisively in a crisis situation. Pupils in their classes will be aware of the 'lighthouse effect', the habitual scanning by which effective teachers appear to pick up everything that is going on. Threshold and outstanding teachers show a stronger ability to think and act ahead, to seize a future opportunity or to anticipate and address future problems: for example, to enrich the curriculum or to bring additional resources into the school.

Characteristic definitions

Drive for improvement   Relentless energy for setting and meeting challenging targets, for pupils and the school.
Information seeking   A drive to find out more and get to the heart of things; intellectual curiosity.
Initiative   The drive to act now to anticipate and pre-empt events.

Leading

In terms of delivery of effective teaching and learning, teachers take a role in *leading* others. There are four characteristics in this cluster of the model.

In their drive to motivate and provide clear direction to pupils, all effective teachers are adept at *managing pupils*. They get pupils on task, clearly stating learning objectives at the beginning of a lesson and recapping at the end, and giving clear instructions about tasks. They keep pupils informed about how the lesson fits into the overall programme of work, and provide feedback to pupils about their progress. Threshold teachers are more consistently able to make every lesson effective and remove any barriers to the effective working of the class and groups within it. Outstanding teachers go further, going out of their way to get extra materials or extra resources they need. Many of them are able consistently to enthuse pupils in their classes and achieve full involvement, creating a positive, upbeat atmosphere to secure the results planned.

All teachers demonstrate a *passion for learning* by providing a stimulating classroom environment, giving demonstrations, checking understanding and providing whole-class, group and individual practice in using and applying skills and knowledge. They consistently differentiate teaching and learning when it is appropriate to do so, to help all pupils learn and to tailor opportunities to practise, embed and extend new learning to each pupil. Outstanding teachers are able to go further in the extent to which they are consistently able to support all pupils in their classes to think for themselves, and to deepen their understanding of a subject or a skill.

Effective teachers show a high degree of *flexibility*. Not only are they open to new approaches and able to adapt procedures to meet the demands of a situation, but they are also flexible in the classroom and outside. At threshold level, when they need to change direction they do so fluently. If they are not getting through to a pupil or a class they approach things from another angle, accessing a wide repertoire of teaching techniques and methods to do so. They are also able to deviate from and return to a lesson plan, to take advantage of an unexpected occurrence or to pursue something in which pupils show particular interest.

Because effective teachers are determined that pupils will achieve good results, they are committed to *holding people accountable* – both pupils and others with whom they work in the school. They set clear expectations of behaviour and for performance, and contract with pupils on these, setting clear boundaries for what is acceptable. In this way they provide a clear framework, routines and security in which work can take place. Teachers at threshold level go further, in that they constantly keep pupils and others up to the mark and get them to do what they had undertaken to do. Outstanding teachers consistently and successfully confront poor performance, taking timely and decisive action to ensure performance recovery.

Characteristic definitions

Managing pupils   The drive and the ability to provide clear direction to pupils, and to enthuse and motivate them.
Passion for learning   The drive and the ability to support pupils in their learning, and to help them become confident and independent learners.
Flexibility   The ability and willingness to adapt to the needs of a situation and change tactics.

Holding people accountable   The drive and the ability to set clear expectations and parameters and to hold others accountable for performance.

Relating to others

Underpinning their leadership role, effective teachers are good at *relating to others*. In this cluster there are three characteristics. Effective teachers have strengths in *understanding others*, working out the significance of the behaviour of pupils and others, even when this is not overtly expressed. Outstanding and threshold teachers have a deep insight into the reasons for the ongoing behaviour of others: why pupils and others act the way they do. They have an insight into what will motivate others, or what may be obstructing learning.

It also means they can use their ability to *impact and influence* pupils to perform. All effective teachers use several different logical arguments to persuade. At threshold level, teachers are able consistently to calculate what will appeal to pupils – and others – so that learning can be vivid, memorable and fun. Outstanding teachers go further in their use of indirect influence, with and through others, to bring about positive educational outcomes. This, together with their own deep understanding of and enthusiasm for their subject or specialism, works as a strong influencing factor on pupils and how they engage with learning.

Finally, all effective teachers are good at *teamworking*. Not only do they provide help and support to colleagues, but they also seek and value their ideas and input. Outstanding teachers are active in building team spirit and the 'feel good' factor, so that people in the school feel part of the team, identify with it, and are proud of what it is doing to support pupils in achieving their full potential, as learners and in life.

7 What do we know about effective pedagogy?

Judith Ireson, Peter Mortimore and Susan Hallam

... One of Vygotsky's ideas, subsequently developed by Wertsch (1985), was that cultures assist development by enabling members of society to appropriate and use a range of tools. For Vygotsky, tools were both physical objects (such as hammers) and conceptual systems or ways of thinking. Could this be extended to include pedagogic tools? Marton and Booth (1997) have argued that one of the most important ways in which we, as humans, differ from other animals is in how we explicitly and deliberately teach our children and each other. Alongside this is our ability to learn deliberately and to take conscious control of our own learning. Our knowledge and thinking about the complex and challenging process of teaching may provide us with powerful cultural tools to enhance learning in the next generations. These tools may be the key to our culture's survival.

So how can we respond to the Vygotskian idea of cultural tools, place them within a pedagogical framework, and make generalizations? ...

Six key ideas

1 The term pedagogy is seldom clearly defined

Pedagogy has been seen by many within and outside the teaching profession as a somewhat vague concept. Even amongst continental educationalists – where the term is much more commonly used – it is seldom clearly defined and, as a result, is used fairly generally. Yet it could offer those involved with teaching a useful conceptual framework with which to examine their own professional practice and those outside of this group a way to understand the often complex approaches that are needed. Further, the time for a consideration of pedagogy is ripe. The technological revolution currently underway on the one hand demands and yet also offers an opportunity for a reappraisal and evaluation of current pedagogical practice with a view to examining its appropriateness for the needs of the future – with or without assistance from information and communications technology.

2 There is no pedagogical panacea

Different learners at different ages and stages require different methods of teaching in order to achieve optimum learning of different kinds. There is no simple recipe for effective teaching in any phase of education. Teachers need to develop a full repertoire of skills and techniques designed to achieve different types of learning outcome. This process takes time and involves training, practice and reflection. It is ongoing throughout the careers of teachers whichever phase of education they work in and is optimized where teachers are in a supportive environment and can adopt a mastery approach to their own learning. Allowance needs to be made for this in the demands made on teachers' working lives.

3 Teachers are important

Whatever the age or stage of learners, it is clear that teachers are crucially important. They need to devote themselves to the needs of their students but must be aware they cannot do the learning for them. As so many of the authors have stressed, teaching is a highly sophisticated activity in which thousands of judgements are made in the course of a single day. Teachers – in their attempts to promote learning – have to provide information, challenge their learners to find information themselves, assess understanding, measure skills and provide formative feedback. Most of all, they have to inspire in their learners the desire to learn and reinforce their self-confidence. They will achieve this more readily if they have high self-esteem themselves and are regarded as members of a respected profession rather than one that faces constant criticism.

4 Context matters

The arenas for learning, whether kindergarten, schoolroom, lecture hall, workplace or other 'life' setting, bring with them sets of expectations about learning and behaviour. Transferability of learning from one setting to another does not happen automatically. Learners have to develop the skills of boundary crossing. Such skills are enormously important to the ability to succeed in modern life. But for some young learners, feelings of powerlessness and of being a captive audience can get in the way and can inhibit learning.

For teachers, this often means that issues of power and control become mixed up with pedagogical concerns. Control can become the first priority, learning the second. Pedagogy may be selected to facilitate control and not necessarily be the best teaching strategy for the desired learning outcome. If pupils have to be wooed to learn – and punished if they refuse to conform to the norms of the school – what hope is there of enlisting them as active learners at school or in their future lives? And what hope is there of them benefiting from the natural learning that appears to occur in other aspects of life? Commentators sometimes juxtapose the ease of 'real-life' learning with the difficulties of school learning. But this misses the point that, for young pupils, it is school rather than the worlds of pop music, premier league football or super models that is the 'real world'. These other worlds may exist but for most pupils will be unattainable. Yet young people seem to learn about these worlds very easily. Is this because the concepts are relatively simple or because motivation is strong? The evidence would suggest the latter (Morris et al. 1985). The compliance expected of school pupils (for very good institutional reasons) can act as a barrier to effective learning. This, as we have seen, is very different to the position of the adult learner who has much greater personal power and is generally in a learning environment because they wish to be there. The increasing trend for workplace learning may mean, however, that some adults lose the voluntarism that has been an important part of the adult learning tradition.

5 There are some general pedagogic principles

Some pedagogical principles for teachers can be formulated, though only at a very general level. From the literature searches undertaken by various authors it appears to be beneficial if teachers:

- are clear about their aims and share them with learners
- plan, organize and manage their teaching effectively
- try to formulate the highest expectations about the potential capabilities of learners and their level of progress
- endeavour to provide positive formative feedback to all their students
- recognize the distinctiveness of individual learners within a general context of inclusivity
- provide learning tasks which will challenge and interest and which are aligned to appropriate assessment procedures
- seek to relate academic learning to other forms of learning and promote 'boundary crossing' skills
- make explicit the rules and, at times, the hidden conventions of all learning institutions so that all learners become aware of ways in which they will be judged
- include an understanding of metacognition in their objectives so that all learners can benefit from this knowledge and – as they advance through their learning careers – take increasing responsibility for their own learning
- motivate and enthuse learners.

6 Teachers are learners too

Finally, as so many of the authors have argued, it is important that the teacher remains a learner. Not only is our knowledge about the world growing at an increasingly rapid pace, but our knowledge of how learning takes place is also developing. It is imperative that teachers – with their many skills and experiences – continue to increase their own capabilities. Governments cannot do this for teachers – no matter how much they may want to do so. The teaching profession, itself, must set about becoming a learning profession. [...]

Key pedagogical isssues

There remain a number of key pedagogical issues about which we know very little. The following five examples illustrate the point.

Whether it is equally beneficial to teach those who find learning easy with those who find it difficult

This argument lies at the heart of controversies about inclusion, selection, streaming and setting. The evidence for and against integration or segregation of different sorts of learners is often contradictory. At present, segregation of learners increases through the primary and secondary phases of education. In the post-compulsory phases, selection segregates learners but learners, themselves, also select courses and exercise some control over their learning. As with so many policy issues, the question cannot be considered without taking account of the aims of education. What does society wish to achieve through its system of education? With a clear set of aims established, educators and those involved in research may then address how they might best be achieved. Controversy arises where discussions about educational and institutional structures are undertaken without relation to the purposes for which they are intended. For instance, evidence from accumulated research on streaming has indicated that it tends to increase the gap in achievement between those in the bottom and top sets and has a detrimental effect on the self-esteem of those in the lower sets. If society requires a small proportion of well educated individuals and a greater mass of unskilled labour then it may be the best way of achieving this end. If, on the other hand, a society is required where everyone has high levels of skill then it is unlikely that streaming will be the appropriate means to attain this aim.

How much the adoption of particular assessment techniques influences the pedagogy chosen by teachers and the strategies adopted by learners

In 1979, Elton and Laurillard argued persuasively on the basis of their research that assessment is the driving force in determining teaching and learning strategies. The American literature similarly asserts that 'teaching to test' and 'learning for test' are common reactions to formal assessment. Where test data are taken as a measure of teachers' accountability, the more 'high stakes' the process becomes and the more likely it is that a 'backwash' effect will be discerned (Biggs and Moore 1993). If learning is driven by assessment then to achieve the desired learning outcomes requires that the assessment procedures reflect precisely the aims of the pedagogy. In the UK, national testing throughout the school years is still in its infancy and opportunities to target it specifically on higher order attainments are often defeated by the need to produce reliable – and hence defensible – measures. This also influences students' behaviour. Not surprisingly, some adopt strategies solely to get through tests and examinations regardless of whether such strategies involve any real changes in understanding.

How much the features of a disadvantaged life (poorer housing,
health care, diet and emotional stress caused by relative poverty)
impact on the pedagogy of schools and colleges

There is mounting evidence that, in a competitive education system, socio-economic disadvantage has a negative impact on the learning of pupils. However, as Mortimore and Whitty (1997) point out, data do not yet exist which could document the amount of improvement that particularly effective schools are able to endow on disadvantaged pupils. Whether learners who experience material or economic disadvantage would benefit from a different – perhaps more structured – pedagogy is yet to be researched. Entry to higher education is also influenced by social class with the lower classes being under-represented. In further and higher education, increasingly students are taking paid employment to support themselves, particularly where financial help is not available from their families. Where long hours are worked this can have detrimental effects on studying (Hodgson and Spours 1998). Economic disadvantage has effects which continue beyond the school years. The question for society is whether educational aims should encompass the promotion of equity of opportunity and if so how this aim might be achieved.

How much ICT should change traditional approaches to pedagogy

ICT offers an opportunity to transform the pedagogy traditionally adopted in formal learning situations … . In higher education, the Teaching and Learning Technology Programme has generated a number of multi-media and interactive packages and simulations designed to extend the quality of teaching. There are interactive educational programmes available for schools and for individual learners to use on PCs at home. Many relate to the National Curriculum, Key Stage tests or national examinations at 16 or 18. Schools are also making increasing use of the internet and available software in a range of subject domains. Despite the increased availability of ICT, the question remains as to the extent to which ICT can and should replace more traditional forms of teaching. Is a scenario likely in the foreseeable future where most learning takes place individually through interactive learning packages, and institutions of learning as we know them, for instance schools, colleges, universities, disappear?

Whether it is equally beneficial to both parties to teach girls and boys
together and if so in what phases of education

There are advocates of the idea that it is best to educate girls and boys separately in secondary schools. Because girls develop physically, emotionally and intellectually at a different pace to boys, arguments are made that progress for both would be better if their education was undertaken separately. The evidence to support these arguments is inconclusive at the moment and there are many possible confounding factors. There is also the question of why segregation should be in adolescence and not in other phases of education. Are there particular concerns about the education of adolescents that are distinct from learners of other ages? A fruitful approach might be to consider the common and distinct needs of boys and girls and how these might be met within a broadly co-educational environment. In addition, the personal and social development needs of young people must be considered alongside their academic attainment.

[...]

References

Biggs, J.B. and Moore, P.J. (1993) *The Process of Learning*, New York: Prentice Hall.

Elton, L.R. and Laurillard, D. (1979) 'Trends in research on student learning', *Studies in Higher Education*, 4: 87–102.

Hodgson, A. and Spours, K. (1998) 'Pushed too far', *Times Educational Supplement*, December 11.

Marton, F. and Booth, S. (1997) *Learning and Awareness*, Mahwah, N.J: Lawrence Erlbaum.

Morris, P.E., Tweedy, M. and Gruneberg, M. M. (1985) 'Interest, knowledge and the memorising of soccer scores', *British Journal of Psychology*, 76: 415–25.

Mortimore, P. and Whitty, J. (1997) *Can School Improvement Overcome the Effects of Disadvantage?* London: Institute of Education.

Wertsch, J.V. (1985) *Vygotsky and the Social Formation of Mind*, Cambridge: Cambridge University Press.

8 New understandings of teachers' pedagogic knowledge

Frank Banks, Jenny Leach and Bob Moon

Introduction

How significant is content or subject knowledge for creative and effective teaching? What links can be made between a teacher's knowledge and the associated pedagogic strategies and practices to ensure successful learning? How important is the updating of a teacher's knowledge base? What form should this take?

These questions illustrate a theme in teacher education that is increasingly catching the attention of policy-makers. In England and Wales, for example, in the 1990s some regulatory requirements were placed on the first degree required for entry to a postgraduate teacher training course. Secondary teachers were required to have at least two years of their first degree in the subject they wished to teach. More recent legislation (DfEE 1998) statutorily requires that all entrants to the teaching profession demonstrate very detailed requirements relating to a specialist subject both at primary and secondary level.

The question of content, subject or disciplinary knowledge can also easily become embroiled in some of the petulant political rhetoric around education. In the USA, as in other countries, there is a continuous polemic associated with the place of disciplines in school reform. Advocacy of this importance has become linked to a particular political stance as the debate surrounding Bloom's *The Closing of the American Mind* (1987), a polemic against the contemporary curriculum of the universities, illustrated. In England and Wales a traditionalist subject-based approach to the National Curriculum attracted widespread opposition (Haviland 1988). In the 1990s the debate continued, again with a sometimes confusing mixture of political, epistemological and pedagogic interpretations. The frequent revisions to the National Curriculum in England and Wales since 1987 and the recently increasingly vigorous debate about how to teach it have been indicative of this.

The relationship between knowledge and pedagogy is, however, an important one and needs further exploration. Does a degree in archaeology provide a basis for teaching contemporary history? Is the high-flying physicist able to teach adequately the biology of a general science course? Can a primary teacher successfully work across the whole of the primary curriculum even though his or her subject expertise may lie in one or two areas? Does the phrase 'the best way to learn is to teach' really underpin the teaching role?

In this chapter we want to explore these issues, to describe some of the debates and research taking place, to suggest a reconceptualization of the field and to set out some preliminary research with preservice students using the model identified. The aim is to stimulate debate around an important area, not least in providing a stronger theoretical framework against which policy and regulatory proposals can be described, analysed and critiqued.

The subject knowledge debate

In debating these questions we have formulated a distinction between the terms knowledge, school knowledge and pedagogy. Our focus, therefore, is on the defini-tions and inter-relations of these three concerns for teacher education. We acknowl-edge the wider concerns that influence and constrain the manifestations of each within the development of teacher knowledge and expertise. We are sympathetic, for example, to Walter Doyle's (1983: 377) assertion that he 'continues to be impressed by the extent to which classroom factors push the curriculum around'. The concern here, however, is with a specific focus on the relation of knowledge to pedagogy.

In seeking a stronger theoretical foundation to this work we have been working with three clusters of ideas: the curriculum-orientated work of Shulman (1986), the cognitive approach of Gardner (1983: 1991) and the inter-related tradition of didactics and pedagogy in continental Europe (Verret 1975: Chevellard 1991). Having identified key areas of professional knowledge, we have also considered how a teacher's professional development is also centrally formed by the 'community of practice' of schools and subject communities. We review each of these ideas in turn.

The curriculum perspective

Since the mid-1980s there has been a growing body of research into the complex relationship between subject knowledge and pedagogy (Shulman 1986: Shulman and Sykes 1986: Wilson *et al.* 1987: MacNamara 1991). Shulman's original work in this field has been an obvious starting point, arising from the pertinent question: 'How does the successful college student transform his or her expertise into the subject matter form that high school students can comprehend?' (Shulman 1986: 5). His conceptual framework is based on the now well-known distinction between *subject content knowledge, curricular knowledge* and the category of *pedagogic content knowledge*. This complex analysis has spawned a plethora of subject-specific research (e.g. Leinhardt and Smith 1985: Wilson and Wineberg 1988: Grossman *et al.* 1989: McDiarmid *et al.* 1989).

Whilst our exploration of professional knowledge has acknowledged Shulman's anal-ysis as an important and fruitful starting point, it has offered only partial insight into the complex nature of subject expertise for teaching. We are critical in particular of Shulman's implicit emphasis on professional knowledge as a static body of content somehow lodged in the mind of the teacher. Shulman's work, we would argue, is informed by an essentially objectivist epistemology. In this tradition academic scholars search for ultimate truths, whilst teachers 'merely seek to make that privileged representation accessible to ordinary mortals' (McKewan and Bull 1991). Pedagogical content knowledge as defined by Shulman (1986: 6) requires the subject specialist to know 'the most useful forms of analogues, illustrations, examples, explanations, and demonstrations – in a word, the ways of representing and formulating the subject in order to make it comprehensible to others'. From this perspective, Shulman's work leans on a theory of cognition that views knowledge as a contained, fixed and external body of information but also on a teacher-centred pedagogy which focuses primarily on the skills and knowledge that the teacher possesses, rather than on the process of learning:

> The key to distinguishing the knowledge base of teaching lies at the intersection of content and pedagogy, in the capacity of *a teacher to transform the content knowledge he/she possesses* into forms that are pedagogically powerful and yet adaptive to the variations in ability and background presented by the students.
> (Shulman 1987: 15)

The learner perspective

Gardner's (1983) work by contrast provides us with a perspective on professional knowledge which is rooted in a fundamental reconceptualization of knowledge and intelligence. His theory of multiple intelligences, centrally informed by the sociocultural psychology of Bruner (1986: 1996), encourages a perspective on pedagogy that places emphasis on student understanding. The focus shifts from teachers' knowledge to learners' understandings, from techniques to purposes. The five entry points which Gardner (1991) proposes for approaching any key concept – narrational, logical-quantitative, foundation, experiential and aesthetic – do not simply represent a rich and varied way of mediating a subject. Rather they emphasize the process of pedagogy and a practice which seeks to promote the highest level of understanding possible (Gardner and Boix-Mansilla 1994). At the same time, Gardner's work places discipline and domain at the core of pedagogy. Drawing extensively from Dewey, he argues that understanding through disciplinary knowledge is indispensable:

> Organised subject matter represents the ripe fruitage of experiences … it does not represent perfection or infallible vision: but it is the best at command to further new experiences which may, in some respects at least, surpass the achievements embodied in existing knowledge and works of art
> (ibid.: 198)

Gardner's espousal of disciplinary knowledge has, in earlier exchanges, been criticized. Gardner, says Egan (1992: 403), seems to offer progressive programmes to achieve traditionalist aims, and he goes on (ibid.: 405) to argue that Gardner's solution

> appears to assume that effective human thinking is properly more disciplined, more coherent and more consistent than seems to me to be the case. This is not an argument on behalf of greater in-discipline, incoherence and inconsistency

but a speculation that human thinking operates very effectively with a considerable degree of those characteristics, and that attempting to reduce them to greater conformity with what seems like rules of disciplinary understanding – whose provisionalness and unclarity should not he underestimated – will more likely reduce our humanity or enhance it.

He further states:

> the danger of letting disciplinary understanding call the educational tune was, for Dewey, no less than an attack on democracy itself. It inevitably lead to an aristocracy, or meritocracy, and so to the kinds of social divisions America was founded to prevent.
>
> (ibid.)

Gardner (1992) is quick to retort and, in return, also quotes extensively from Dewey to back up his claim for the pre-eminence of understanding through disciplinary knowledge in reforming teaching and schooling:

> Organised subject matter represents the ripe fruitage of experiences ... it does not represent perfection or infallible vision: but it is the best at command to further new experiences which may, in some respects at least, surpass the achievements embodied in existing knowledge and works of art.

Gardner's work has been critical in challenging views of cognition based on the concept of 'intelligence', and his work is central to an endeavour to challenge widely held notions of ability as fixed and unchanging (see Gardner 1983). His espousal of disciplines and exploration of curriculums which are rooted in, but which move beyond, disciplines into 'generative themes' has given rise to some important work (Project Zero – Sizer 1992, Gardner 1983). However, it has little epistemological analytical underpinning.

The pedagogical perspective

For this we have turned to the work of Verret (1975) and Chevellard (1991). The concept of didactic transposition, a process by which subject knowledge is transformed into school knowledge, an analytical category in its own right, permits us both to understand and question the process by which disciplinary transformations take place. The range of historical examples in Verret's work also provides for the social and ideological dimensions of the construction of knowledge. *La transposition didactique* of Chevellard is defined as a process of change, alteration and restructuring which the subject matter must undergo if it is to become teachable and accessible to novices or children. As this work is less known and less accessible to English-speaking discourse we will give a little more space to explanation. Verret's original thesis was that school knowledge, in the way it grows out of any general body of knowledge, is inevitably codified, partial, formalized and ritualized.

Learning in that context is assumed to be programmable, defined in the form of a text, syllabus or national curriculum, with a conception of learning that implies a beginning and an end, an initial state and a final state. Verret argues that knowledge in general cannot be sequenced in the same way as school knowledge and that generally learning is far from being linear. Such a model, he suggests, in ways that predate Gardner, lacks cognitive validity as it does not take into account the schemes, constructed representations and personal constructs of the learner.

Verret's thesis is illustrated by a range of historical examples. He describes, for instance, the transformation of literature and divinatory magic into the scholastic forms of Confucian schooling and of Christian metaphysics into school and university philosophy. He looks in detail at the version of Latin that was constructed for the French schools of the seventeenth century and the way this evolved didactically in the centuries that follow.

For Chevellard, as with Verret, 'didactic objects', which we have termed school knowledge, are under constant interpretation and reinterpretation, a process which operates at a number of different levels. Didactic transformation of knowledge, therefore, becomes for Tochan and Munby (1993: 206–7):

> a progressive selection of relevant knowledge, a sequential transmission involving a past and a future, and a routine memory of evolutionary models of knowledge. Because didactics is a diachronic anticipation of contents to be taught it is essentially prepositional. It names teaching experience in prepositional networks and so involves a mediation of time.

The process of didactics is carefully distinguished from pedagogy (ibid.):

> Some research on novice teaching suggests that they have abilities to plan but encounter problems during immediate interactions. They seem to identify their role as a mainly didactic one. Their way of organising time has no flexibility: it is not synchronic… Though action research and reflection reveals the existence of basic principles underlying practical classroom experience, no matter what rules might be inferred, pedagogy still remains an adventure.

Understanding teachers' pedagogic knowledge

Figure 8.1 represents in diagrammatic form our synthesis of the inter-relation of subject knowledge, school knowledge and pedagogic knowledge, our starting point for conceptualizing teacher-professional knowledge. Shulman's category of subject content knowledge we have retained, but we denote it simply as *subject knowledge*. In doing so we wish to emphasize the dynamic, process-driven nature of subject knowledge which encompasses essential questions, issues and phenomena drawn from the natural and human world, methods of inquiry, networks of concepts, theoretical frameworks, techniques for acquiring and verifying findings … symbol systems, vocabularies and mental models (Gardner 1994). *School knowledge*, we suggest, is an analytic category in its own right, subsuming the curricular knowledge of Shulman.

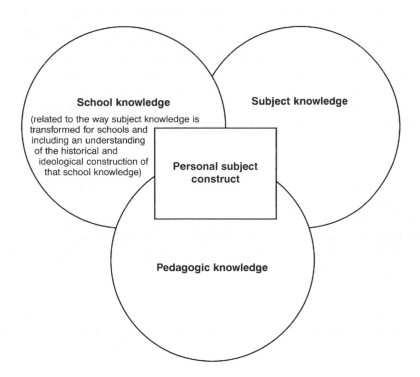

Figure 8.1 Teachers' professional knowledge

We have, therefore, split the category of pedagogic content knowledge as defined by Shulman to gain a greater hold on this important epistemological construct. By 'school knowledge' we do not mean a knowledge of the school context. Rather we view it as the transposition of subject knowledge referred to above,

Our third category which we call *pedagogic knowledge* we see as going beyond the generic set of beliefs and practices that inform teaching and learning. Although these exist, and rightly form an important part of the development of teacher expertise, they are insufficient, we would argue, unless integrated into an understanding of the crucial relationship between subject knowledge and school knowledge.

One might initially see 'school knowledge' as being intermediary between subject knowledge (knowledge of technology as practised by different types of technologists, for example) and pedagogic knowledge as used by teachers ('the most powerful analogies, illustrations, example, explanations and demonstrations'). This would be to underplay the dynamic relationship between the categories of knowledge implied by the diagram. For example, a teacher's subject knowledge is transformed by his or her own pedagogy in practice and by the resources which form part of his or her school knowledge, It is the active interaction of subject knowledge, school knowledge and pedagogical understanding and experience that brings teacher professional knowledge into being.

Lying at the heart of this dynamic process are the *personal constructs* of the teacher, a complex amalgam of past knowledge, experiences of learning, a personal view of what constitutes 'good' teaching and belief in the purposes of the subject. These all underpin a teacher's professional knowledge and hold good for any teacher. A student teacher needs to question his or her personal beliefs about his or her subject as he or she works out a rationale for classroom practice. But so must those teachers who, although more expert, have experienced profound changes of what contributes to 'school knowledge' during their career.

The model in use

This model has been discussed with a number of professionals groups in the UK and in other parts of the world such as Spain, The Netherlands, Sweden and South Africa (Banks *et al.* 1996: Leach and Banks 1996: Moon and Banks 1996: Banks 1997). These professionals have been different groups of school teachers of design and technology and of English, teacher educators and researchers. The reaction to the model across this spectrum of professional expertise has been remarkably similar. We have noticed the following points:

- The different aspects of teacher knowledge are recognized by all these groups as being meaningful. Teachers, in particular, are excited by the categories and value the model as a way of easily articulating what they know and are able to do. The model has a spin-off for mentoring and initial teacher education, facilitating explicit discussion about the nature of professional knowledge.
- School knowledge is often misunderstood as knowledge of the context for teaching. This illustrates the importance of this category in framing the teacher's role.
- The model can be interpreted at different levels. Some see it as a tool for categorizing personal understanding. Others see it as being useful for planning in-service development for a group of teachers.

Figure 8.2 illustrates the way in which the model was developed by one group of English teachers. They recognized a strong distinction between 'English' as conceived, for example, by university and college courses and 'school English'. In most schools much of the English literature studied involves knowledge of authors, themes and styles (texts written for children or teenagers, or deemed suitable for the younger reader) distinctively different from literature studied in universities and colleges. And few English courses at degree level currently incorporate knowledge about the reading process, but this is a statutory part of school 'English' in the UK.

We would argue that the development of professional knowledge is a dynamic process. It depends on the interaction of the elements we have identified, but is brought into existence by the learning context itself – learners, setting, activity and communication as well as context in its broadest sense.

[...]

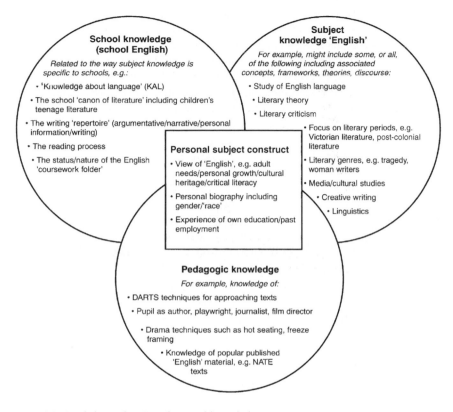

Figure 8.2 English teachers' professional knowledge

Conclusion

In this chapter we have argued for a reconceptualization of the relationship between knowledge and pedagogy and offer a framework through which this can be achieved. We accept the limitations of any diagrammatic representation and have already, in a number of presentations, been pushed to develop a three-dimensional configuration! The aim at this stage, however, is to stimulate further debate and research. Finding a place for 'subject' is important in primary and secondary schools as well as in the 'secret garden' curriculum of further and higher education. The analysis we suggest is every bit as significant for the university lecturer as the nursery school teacher.

In teacher education it is critical that these issues are fully explored. A model of practice must evolve that acknowledges the importance of subject knowledge within the curriculum as much as the processes or pedagogies of teaching. To do this is not necessarily to reassert some traditionalist subject-centred view of the curriculum, or to adopt solely a secondary or tertiary perspective: it is rather to say that 'subject' is important.

The model points to the need for greater sophistication in the curriculum-building process that creates particular forms of school knowledge. The analysis of *la transposition didactique* (the use of transposition rather than transformation is significant) points up some of the clumsiness that goes on in building curriculum at a national level. The jockeying for space and the internal feuds of subject communities that have been associated with the building of the National Curriculum in England and Wales give scant regard to the epistemological and methodological issues raised by Verret and Chevellard. The boundary between knowledge and school knowledge, however, is more than the framing of a national curriculum. It is part of the web and weave of a teacher's daily work – whether the recollection of a metaphor or the building of a whole scheme of work, the transposition of knowledge is a continuous process. Again we need to look more deeply into the issues raised. Does the English teacher who sat at the feet of Leavis thirty years ago teach differently, create different forms of learning from a younger colleague with Derrida or Foucault as a model? Does the technology teacher with a three-dimensional design background offer his or her pupils substantially different insights into product development from the one who studied mechanical engineering? Do the primary teachers who are mathematicians, scientists or musicians bring particular advantages to their class or particular attributes to their teaching? Our knowledge in these areas is limited and needs to he extended.

The central argument of this chapter is, thus, that the interfaces between knowledge, school knowledge (i.e. that selection from the broader fields of knowledge that constitutes the school curriculum), pedagogic knowledge and personal construct are crucial areas of inquiry. The surprisingly separate worlds of curriculum and teaching studies, we contend, need to be brought together in any reconceptualization of practice.

We contend that teacher education also bears a major responsibility for formulating theoretical frameworks which will encourage both understanding and evaluation of pedagogic practices. Teacher education must provide, we would argue, ongoing challenge to the educational bureaucracies which seek rather to define teachers primarily as technicians or pedagogical clerks, incapable of making important policy or curriculum decisions (Giroux 1988). Our experience of using this model with teachers gives us optimism that it is a helpful and meaningful tool to assist in the articulation of teacher professional knowledge.

References

Banks, F. (1997) *Assessing Technology Teacher Professional Knowledge*, proceedings of the PATT-8 Conference, Scheveningen, Netherlands, April.

Banks, F., Leach, J. and Moon, B. (1996) 'Knowledge, school knowledge and pedagogy: reconceptualising curricula and defining a research agenda', paper presented at ECER '96 Conference, Seville, Spain, September.

Bloom, A. (1987) *The Closing of the American Mind*, Harmondsworth: Penguin.

Bruner, J.S. (1986) *Actual Minds, Possible Worlds*, Harvard University Press, London.

Bruner, J.S. (1996) *The Culture of Education*, Cambridge, Mass.: Harvard University Press.

Chaucer, G. (1957) 'Canterbury tales' in F.N. Robinson (ed.) *The Complete Works of Geoffrey Chaucer*, London: Oxford University Press.

Chevellard, Y. (1991) *La Transposition Didactique: du savoir savant au savoir enseigné*, Paris: La Pensée Sauvage.

DfEE (1998) *Circular 4/98: Teaching: High Status, High Standards*, London: DfEE.

Doyle (1983) 'Academic Work', *Review of Educational Research*, 53(2): 159–99.

Egan, K. (1992) 'An Exchange', *Teachers' College Record*, 94(2).

Egan, K. (1992) 'A review of' *The Unschooled Mind, Teachers' College Record*, 94(2): 397–413.

Gardner, H. (1983) *Frames of Mind: The Theory of Multiple Intelligences*, New York: Basic Books.

Gardner, H. (1991) *The Unschooled Mind*, New York: Basic Books.

Gardner, H. (1992) A Response, *Teachers' College Record*, 94(2).

Gardner, H. and Boix-Mansilla, V. (1994) 'Teaching for understanding in the disciplines and beyond', *Teachers' College Record*, 96(2): 198–218.

Giroux, H.A. (1988) *Teachers as Intellectuals: Towards a Critical Pedagogy of Learning*, New York: Bergin & Garvey Publications, Inc.

Grossman, P.L., Wilson, S.M. and Shulman, L.S. (1989) 'Teachers of substance: subject matter knowledge for teaching' in M.C. Reynolds (ed.) *Knowledge Base for the Beginning Teacher*, Oxford: Pergamon Press.

Haviland, J. (1988) *Take Care, Mr Baker*, London: Fourth Estate.

Lawler, S. (1988) *Correct Case*, London: Centre for Policy Studies.

Leach, J. and Banks, F. (1996) 'Investigating the developing 'teacher professional knowledge' of student teachers', paper presented at the BERA Conference, Lancaster, September.

Leinhardt, G. and Smith, D. (1985) 'Expertise in mathematical instruction: subject matter knowledge', *Journal of Educational Psychology*, 77(3): 247–71.

MacNamara, D. (1991) 'Subject knowledge and its application: problems and possibilities for teacher educators', *Journal of Education for Teaching*, 17(2): 113 –28.

McDiarmid, G., Ball, D.J. and Anderson, C.W. (1989) 'Why staying one chapter ahead doesn't really work: subject specific pedagogy' in M.C. Reynolds (ed.) *Knowledge Base for the Beginning Teacher*, Oxford: Pergamon Press.

McKewan, H. and Bull, B. (1991) 'The pedagogic nature of subject matter knowledge', *American Educational Research Journal*, 28(2): 319–34.

Moon, B. and Banks, F. (1996) 'Secondary school teachers' development: reconceptualising knowledge and pedagogy', paper presented at the Association for Teacher Education in Europe (ATEE) Conference, Glasgow, September.

Shulman, L.S. (1986) 'Those who understand: knowledge growth in teaching', *Educational Research Review*, 57(1): 4–14.

Shulman, L.S. (1987) 'Knowledge and teaching: foundations of the new reform', *Harvard Educational Review*, 57: 1–22.

Shulman, L.S. and Sykes, G. (1986) *A National Board for Teaching? In Search of a Bold Standard. A Report for the Task Force on Teaching as a Profession*, New York: Carnegie Corporation.

Sizer, T.R. (1992) *Horace's School*, New York: Houghton Mifflin.

Tochan, F., and Munby, H. (1993) Novice and expert teachers time epistemology: a wave function from didactics to pedagogy. *Teacher and Teacher Education*, 9(2): 205–18.

Verret, M. (1975) *Le temps des études*, Paris: Librarie Honoré Champion.

Wilson, S.M., Shulman, L.S. and Richert, A. (1987) '150 different ways of knowing: representations of knowledge in teaching' in J. Calderhead (ed.) *Exploring Teacher Thinking*, Eastbourne: Holt, Rhinehart & Winston.

Wilson, S.M. and Wineberg, S.S. (1988) 'Peering at history through different lenses: the role of the disciplinary perspectives in teaching history', *Harvard Educational Review*, 89(4): 527–39.

9 'He's such a nice man, but he's so boring, you have to really make a conscious effort to learn':

The views of Gemma, Daniel and their contemporaries on teacher quality and effectiveness

M. Younger and M. Warrington

This chapter is based upon research into the gender gap at GCSE in a number of selective and comprehensive schools in eastern England, and contrasts girls' and boys' perspectives on 'good' teachers. It discusses the extent to which girls are willing to take more responsibility for their own learning than are boys, and considers how boys expect teachers to take greater responsibility for generating enjoyment and motivation in lessons. Contrasting attitudes to group work and classroom management issues are discussed, and significant differences are identified in girls' and boys' perspectives about teacher quality and effectiveness.

In the course of the last decade, the underachieving boy has emerged in many countries of the western world as a source of anxiety and concern (Teese *et al.* 1995: Gordon 1996: Yates 1997: Arnot *et al.* 1998). In England and Wales, despite the fact that the levels of academic achievement of both girls and boys at the end of compulsory schooling has increased significantly during this time (David 1996: Warrington and Younger 1999), the main concern has been with the gender gap, with the disparity of achievements between girls and boys, as evidenced in end of Key Stage testing and in GCSE examinations (Gipps 1996: Weiner *et al.* 1997). Explanations for supposed male underachievement have been sought in a wide range of social and psychological factors (Mac an Ghaill 1994: Harris *et al.* 1995: Rudduck *et al.* 1995: Bleach 1996: Head 1996: Jackson and Salisbury 1996: Younger and Warrington 1996: QCA 1998), focusing on policies and practices within schools, on student attitude and image, on changing employment opportunities in the post-modern society and on motivation and self-esteem. Attention has also been directed to the role of the teacher, to teacher-girl/boy interactions within the classroom (Stanworth 1981: Byrne 1993: Clark and Trafford 1995: Burton 1996: Younger *et al.* 1999) and to characteristics of 'good lessons' (Barber 1996: Barker 1997). As the debate has intensified, so there has been a concern, too, to listen to the student perspective, to become more alert to the student voice (Nieto 1994: Rudduck *et al.* 1995), to generate teaching-learning strategies which take account of student reaction and response.

It is within these contexts that this paper aims to contrast girls' and boys' perspectives on 'good' teachers and on the nature of the teaching–learning context established by such teachers. It focuses on aspects of research carried out in contrasting schools, selective and comprehensive, independent and state, in eastern England over a 3-year period and draws largely upon information elicited from focus group interviews with Year 11 students, where students were interviewed in small, single-sex groups ... .

Discussion within the focus groups revealed that in some aspects of teaching there was little difference between girls' and boys' perceptions of a good teacher. Good lessons were commonly characterized as enjoyable, fun ... and interesting ... with ... groups of boys ... (mainly from the middle and low-ability groups) seeing good lessons as those in practical subjects such as physical education or science (Barker 1997). Students of both sexes appreciated enthusiasm, subject knowledge and a willingness of teachers to go beyond the syllabus. These were valued by the students, who themselves were fired by the teachers' enthusiasm.

> You can tell just by the way he talks that he is, he's just obsessed with his subject, he lives history. He could be Stalin's best mate, he just knows everything there is to know about him.
>
> (Girl)

Good personal relationships between students and teachers were stressed:

> They talk to you on a level and don't take advantage of the authority they have over you... They talk to you about normal things, not just about school. And in the corridor, they'll come up to us and talk to us as a friend sometimes.
>
> (Boy)

> He actually talks to you like a friend, so you can communicate with him properly, and you don't feel so left out. He's all right. He makes you feel comfortable and relaxed, and not all tensed up. He talks to you in the corridor as well.
>
> (Girl)

Students also responded to teachers who showed their commitment to the class and to individuals, who offered extra help and who were sensitive to the needs of the individual.

A vitally important factor in facilitating learning and identifying a good lesson, mentioned by students of all abilities and schools, was student involvement and participation. This might take place through group work (cited more often by girls), through discussion involving students and teachers (cited more often by boys) or through students asking the teacher questions. Not surprisingly, a variety of activities in carefully structured lessons was identified by ... boys and girls ... as one way in which learning could be positively facilitated. Both girls and boys stressed, however, that variety did not necessarily need to occur in each lesson: one group of boys said that sometimes their English teacher dictated notes and that this was helpful because you had the most important points for revision; it was acceptable as part of a varied curriculum. The main thing was that there was variety between lessons in the same subject. Didactic teaching methods were criticized, especially by those in selective schools ... . Students in selective schools complained about teachers who just stood at the front talking or reading from a book and a number of groups expressed dislike of long periods of time spent copying off the board or out of books:

> When someone just reads from a book you lose your concentration if they've got a really monotonous voice which goes on and on and on. It gets really boring. Or just writing on the board all lesson, and you just sit there taking notes and you end up writing, but you're not taking it in. It's really boring, so you just switch off.
>
> (Girl)

Some of the selective school students, girls and boys, were critical of the amount of dictation they had, saying that it was impossible to think about what they were taking down and preferring to make their own notes. In some respects, it could be argued that this emphasis on transmission approaches to teaching is generated by the content-heavy nature of GCSE syllabuses in many subjects, such that in some schools it becomes the students' main teaching experience, but it is likely to become counter-productive and in some contexts to generate only apparent learning (Quicke and Winter 1993: Harris *et al.* 1995) … .

The personal and professional qualities of a good teacher have been well documented (see, for example, Barber 1996: Clark and Trafford 1996: Barker 1997) and the above findings will not be surprising. What is of particular interest in the context of the differential achievement of girls and boys, however, is the way in which girls' and boys' perceptions of quality teachers show some significant differences. This was particularly evident when boys and girls spoke of the importance of teaching styles. Boys in selective schools said that good lessons were where they learnt a great deal and ten groups of boys … , compared with four groups of girls, stressed the need for teachers to explain work well: they wanted to know exactly what the were doing. When talking about poor lessons, nine groups of boys cited the failure of teachers to explain work properly. Once the work was explained, boys seemed more likely to want to get on with it, with seven groups (no groups of girls) wanting teachers to let them work at their own pace:

> He lays down clearly what's to be done, and he lets you get on with it. He tells us exactly what he wants to be done, but he's not on your back all the time.
>
> (Boy)

Variety of teaching style within the lesson, clearly structured achievable targets and tasks, and an energetic and caring teaching style were all valued by both girls and boys, but the boys in particular put a great deal of emphasis on the teacher's role in generating enjoyment in a particular subject: it was the teacher who determined whether it was a good lesson or not. Boys in both selective and comprehensive schools saw the role of the teacher as crucial in whether they got on well in the subject and worked hard. There was some recognition that the students had a role to play in whether a lesson went well, but the emphasis was on the teacher motivating the students, rather than any idea of self-motivation:

If the teachers made the subjects enjoyable I would work harder.

(Boy)

If he asks you to do a homework or something or revise for a test, if you get on with a teacher and you've got respect for him, you want to impress him or her.

(Boy)

Girls were much more inclined to take responsibility upon themselves (Head 1996), acknowledging that their own liking for various subjects affected the way in which they responded in lessons and accepting that the students themselves crucially affected the teaching-learning situation. A 'middle-ability' girl in a comprehensive school, for example, explained how she did not like mathematics lessons because she was unable to do the subject. This inability to understand mathematics was attributed entirely, to herself: she did not feel that a different teacher would be able to help her or that the subject was poorly presented to her. The student's role in a good lesson was also acknowledged by another girls' group:

It's got a lot to do with you. I mean, if you decide that you don't like a particular subject, you're not prone to really try in it, whereas if you like another one you're going to really try and do well in it, and concentrate more in the lesson.

(Girl)

These views, expressed by girls we interviewed, link centrally to attribution theory (Dweck 1986), with girls blaming themselves for their own lack of achievement. Despite the fact that much of the curriculum and the pedagogy of secondary schools is beyond the control or influence of students, many girls apparently attribute their own lack of success to themselves, although this is not always so, as Bowler (1997) clearly demonstrates within the context of secondary mathematics:

(the girls) were unable to improve their situation, *not because* they were disillusioned by their own inadequacies, but because they, were powerless to change the pedagogical traditions of their institution.

(Bowler 1997: 302; our italics)

This contrast in girl-boy attitude and responsibility for learning is succinctly summarized by Head (1996):

Males tend to develop a defence mechanism of attributing success to their own efforts and failure to external factors. Girls show the reverse tendency. The pedagogic implication is that girls may sink into... 'learned helplessness' in which the perception of failure inhibits subsequent performance. By contrast boys have to learn to take responsibility for their poor work.

(p. 63)

Linked to this was the contrasting motivation of girls and boys (Mac an Ghaill

1994: Barber 1996: Warrington and Younger 1996). There was widespread agreement amongst the boys' groups that they were more willing to participate and learn
if the teacher was friendly and relaxed and if the lessons were fun and interesting,
but where this was not the case, many said they only worked if they were made to or
if it was assessed work. It was almost as if they were doing the work for the teacher's
benefit, rather than for their own benefit. Only one boys' group spoke of the failure
of students to participate as spoiling a good lesson. Girls across schools and ability
groups were more intrinsically motivated, clearer of their own targets and aims and
more aware of what was needed if they were to achieve those goals.

Boys, more than girls, appeared to value a relaxed, informal atmosphere in the
classroom ... . Particularly important in both types of school was being able to talk
and both sexes raised this, though this was mentioned more often by girls, and
having to sit in silence in some lessons was identified as a problem by a third of girls'
groups. Although it was appreciated that silence was sometimes necessary, they felt
strongly that being able to talk about the work with the people sitting near them
was helpful and contributed to their learning ... . It is clear that student–student
talk and discussion is still not valued highly as an effective teaching–learning
strategy ... .

Both girls and boys welcomed the opportunity to work in groups ... . Group
work changed the focus of the classroom, giving a different emphasis to the role
of the teacher (from director of learning to facilitator of learning), and allowed
the students opportunities to express themselves and to develop ideas more fully
than in other contexts (Battersby and Younger 1993). Some students spoke of
feeling more confident and less isolated and suggested that they were more
likely to take an active part in the lesson. Boys, in particular, found it helpful to
work in mixed groups:

> They [girls] might help us get on and express things better. They also sort of
> keep it a bit more sensible ... boys sometimes lose it a bit, if you know what I
> mean. The girls keep it under control, they don't let us talk about other things.
>
> (Boy)

Some boys credited girls with having a wider perspective on issues, with seeing
issues from different angles:

> *Jane Eyre* we thought was rubbish, but the girls enjoyed it a lot more, and then
> we could get contrasting views from that; more of a balance; whereas with
> things like *Macbeth*, I think it went down generally better as a boys' book and so
> working together, you get the benefit of different views.
>
> (Boy)

Equally, some girls enjoyed the stimulation of working with people with different ideas:

> I think I work better, especially in drama, because boys have different views on
> how to put something across, and girls have ideas too to pull it together. It's

different than if you're just working with girls, you know. It's totally different, so sometimes we do that, but a lot of the time it's just girls together and boys together.

(Girl)

[...]

There were differences of opinion, however, about the composition of groups ... . Grammar school students, especially girls, often said they liked working in groups, because you could bounce ideas off each other, which helped to work things out, but girls generally preferred single-sex groupings. Mixed groups did not always work well and there was evidence, in both comprehensive and selective schools, of group work contexts where both girls and boys acknowledged that girls were ignored in mixed groups and where boys' off-task and sexist behaviour on occasions disrupted learning:

It's like in drama, I'm being put with two boys who I don't really like that much, and they're annoying me and stuff. So whenever they annoy me, I get told off for it ... Sometimes they're really immature and that, and they just don't do the work, and whenever you tell them, the teacher thinks that you're the one who's provoking it. But you're not.

(Girl)

You feel more confident if you've just got girls in a group. You feel more confident than with boys because they sort of moan at you, or take the mickey, or things like that.

(Girl)

Many girls preferred the security of working with friends, usually other girls. They frequently talked about feeling more comfortable with friends and being able to concentrate on the subject instead of trying to prove yourself; with 'strangers' there was the need to tread more carefully, working out what everyone was trying to do, almost exploring the hidden agenda of others.

Group work is hardly a panacea, therefore, but on occasions it can provide a context for student learning where performance may be improved simply because students have the opportunity to talk, to explore ideas and resources with each other (Phelan *et al.* 1992), to justify their own views and opinions and to take account of those of other students. Within this context, however, the composition of the group is crucial if opportunities for learning are to be maximized, and here the perspectives of girls and boys showed marked differences.

Running alongside the plea for informality in the classroom, however, was a recognition that too much talking and disruptive behaviour was counter-productive, but control over behaviour was seen, particularly by boys, as the teacher's responsibility. In none of the groups was self-discipline mentioned; rather, it seemed to be the case that many students felt it legitimate to misbehave if the teacher allowed it:

She just sits there, and she doesn't do anything. She says, 'Can you be quiet please?', and she just sits down, and everyone keeps talking because they say there's no point: if you keep talking she's not going to do anything anyway. It's just not a good way of dealing with the lesson.

(Boy)

This emphasis on the teacher's classroom management was stressed especially in the comprehensive schools where all but one of the girls' groups raised the issue as a matter which concerned them ... . Some of the girls talked about the way in which the level of disruption in some classes affected their ability to concentrate, and they felt that it was crucial that every teacher was able to exert the necessary amount of discipline. Often it was just a small group of male students who were particularly disruptive (Lee 1996: Kenway *et al.* 1998) and had a disproportionate effect on the learning of the rest of the class.

It's a small group but it's always being disrupted and we don't really learn anything. We're hoping to do GCSE but there are so many people mucking around in the lesson the teacher can't control them, so it's not very good, and we're learning hardly anything.

(Boy)

Whilst controlling the class was evidently an important issue, a number of groups ... said the teachers should not be 'too strict'. Students stressed that control was not achieved through shouting but through gaining the respect of the students.

The teacher who gets respect from the students will be listened to, and the way they get respect is not by being strict and always working with the rules. As long as you pay the same amount of respect to them, they'll make it more interesting for you. We've got teachers who are trying to teach without getting communication sorted out first.

(Boy)

When you get to this stage in your schooling, you feel as if you deserve a little bit of respect from the teachers. When they're saying, 'Right, sit down, shut up and get on with your work. That's final', you tend to say 'Sod you mate, we're not interested'. If they treat you more as adults, we'd probably act like adults. Rather than a robot that's just there to learn.

(Girl)

Equal numbers of boys' and girls' groups ... wanted to be able to ask for help when necessary; they wanted the teachers to be willing to go over things and to be able to ask questions without being made to feel stupid or humiliated. This was especially the case with the lower achieving students, who sometimes felt patronized if they asked questions or that the teachers showed impatience with them:

He just doesn't want you to ask questions. Some teachers in the school think that if you can't do it, you shouldn't be in this school. It's a grammar school, you should be able to do it.

(Girl)

You just have to try and do your best with what you think you have to do. He just says, 'Oh, you've done it wrong', and doesn't give you any help to try and correct it. You just have to try and do it again.

(Boy)

A good lesson, according to one group of girls, was:

Where you feel you're allowed to ask questions without feeling kind of nervous and afraid to ask, and if you ask, people aren't going to kind of mock you about it and stuff.

(Girl)

It was boys, however, who consistently spoke of the need for encouragement, with no girls' groups … explicitly mentioning this. Some students were concerned that some teachers focused too much on what was wrong, rather than what was right with their work, and were reluctant to give praise. This emphasis on the importance of praise is crucial (Head 1996: Slater 1996: Place 1997: Warrington and Younger 1999); some students, particularly boys, spoke of the tensions between wanting to do well and being quite proud when you do, but not wanting to be seen to be doing well. In such contexts, certificates of merit and commendation schemes for academic work were seen to have little credibility and public praise was counter-productive. However, private praise and encouragement are important, and much valued by many students; they enabled the self-esteem of students, particularly of disaffected boys, to be nurtured and enhanced and helped to establish an accepting and supportive classroom environment:

We need to do all that we can in schools to praise and offer all our children opportunities for personal success and a real sense of achievement. We need to teach all our children that everyone can learn to succeed.

(Slater 1996: 24)

Boys, particularly, liked teachers who talked to them about things other than work and who were on their wavelength and they particularly appreciated rapport with younger male members of staff, talking to them about shared interests such as football or music. Yet this very rapport was sometimes resented by girls, who felt that teachers should not be too friendly with their students, especially when younger male teachers appeared to condone laddish behaviour. A good sense of humour and a willingness to 'have a laugh' or share a joke were also seen as necessary attributes for a good teacher by more groups of boys … than girls … , but the way in which students were treated (with respect, fairness and equality) was cited as important by both sexes in each type of school. Students preferred teachers to be approachable, helpful and friendly and were critical of those who were unpredictable in their moods. Like Clark and Trafford (1996), we found that the sex of the teacher was seen to be important in very few contexts; personality, relationships, a sense of fun, an ability to appreciate the pressures the students were under, were all cited as much more important characteristics of the good teacher.

It was an interest in the students as individuals which was seen as crucially important:

> We had an English teacher, a really good teacher, and she showed that she was worried about us: we weren't just people running around trying to make their job worthwhile. We were people, so that was much better.
>
> (Boy)

Some students, in contrast, believed that some teachers were only interested in what results the class as a whole achieved and were not bothered about those who were less good at their subject. In the selective schools some girls felt that there was sometimes more pressure put on students to get straight A grades, but there were other students who, although they did their best, were not capable of such high levels of achievement and yet were constantly reminded that they should do well because they were at a grammar school. Those at the lower end of the grammar schools sometimes felt that their achievements counted for little; such students would probably have been high achievers in the context of some of the comprehensives. In one of the comprehensives, the girls thought that some teachers were only interested in those who were likely to get a grade C or above and focused their attention on those students.

In each of these selective and comprehensive schools, then, we encountered aspects of teaching which appealed both to girls and to boys and characteristics of good teaching with which many students concurred. Equally, however, we found significant differences related to girls' and boys' willingness (or otherwise) to take responsibility for learning, differing reactions to group work, contrasting responses to classroom management and self-discipline, and different attitudes to praise and encouragement. In all of the interviews we carried out, however, students appreciated the pressures teachers and school were under and realized the need for an emphasis on results and achievement; but the good teacher was interested in them as individuals, was aware of some of their interests and their extra-curricular achievements and helped support them in times of stress. With Nieto (1994), we found that students placed high value on teachers who were imaginative, energetic and generous of time and energy: they also praised teachers

> ... who were interesting, creative and caring ... one student spoke movingly of a teacher who has 'always been there for me; she keeps me on my toes; when I start getting down, she peps me up and I get on my feet'.
>
> (p. 406)

Good teachers recognized the achievements of all students and gave them encouragement; good teachers brought their subject alive, believed in the importance of the subject and could communicate it to the students. In sum, in this most demanding of professions, a good teacher

... is not unfair to anyone. The lesson's always interesting and he makes it funny, and we always seem to do more work than we actually think we're doing, and we learn a lot as well.

(Boy)

... doesn't treat anyone unequally. He tries to give the class a good go, and we get on really well with him. He knows his stuff. He knows your weaknesses and strengths, and he'll sit down and talk to you the whole lesson to explain something. He'll go round and you learn more then. He's a very good teacher.

(Girl)

[...]

References

Arnot, M., Gray, J., James, M. and Rudduck, J. (1998) *Recent Research on Gender and Educational Performance*, London: Ofsted.

Barber, M. (1996) *The Learning Game: arguments for an education revolution*, London: Victor Gollancz.

Barker, B. (1997) 'Girls' world or anxious times: what's really happening at school in the gender war?', *Educational Review*, 49: 221–8.

Battersby, J. and Younger, M. (1993) *The Assessment of Groupwork at GCSE*, WJEC, Cardiff.

Bleach, K. (1996) *What Difference Does It Make? An investigation of factors influencing motivation and performance of year 8 boys in a West Midlands comprehensive school*, Wolverhampton: University of Wolverhampton Education Research Unit.

Bowler, J. (1997) 'Reclaiming school mathematics: the girls fight back', *Gender and Education*, 9: 285–305.

Burton, L. (1996) 'A socially just pedagogy for the teaching of mathematics' in P.F. Murphy and C.V. Gipps (eds) *Equity in the Classroom: towards effective pedagogy for girls and boys*, 136–145, London: Falmer Press.

Byrne, E. (1993) *Women and Science: the Snark syndrome*, London: Falmer Press.

Clark, A. and Trafford, J. (1995) 'Boys and modern languages: an investigation of the discrepancy in attitudes and performance between boys and girls in modern languages', *Gender and Education*, 7: 315–25.

Clark, A. and Trafford, J. (1996) 'Return to gender: boys' and girls' attitudes and achievements', *Language Learning Journal*. 14: 40–9.

David, M. (1996) *Targeting Underachievement: boys or girls*, London: London Centre for Education and Research on Gender.

Dweck, C.S. (1986) 'Motivational processes affecting learning', *American Psychologist*, 41: 1040–8.

Gipps, C. (1996) 'Introduction' in P.F. Murphy and C.V. Gipps (eds) *Equity in the Classroom: towards effective pedagogy for girls and boys*, 1–6, London: Falmer Press.

Gordon, T. (1996) 'Citizenship, difference and marginality in schools: spatial and embodied aspects of gender construction' in P.F. Murphy and C.V. Gipps (eds) *Equity in the Classroom: towards effective pedagogy for girls and boys*, 34–45, London: Falmer Press.

Harris, S., Wallace, G. and Rudduck, J. (1995) ' "It's not just that I haven't learnt much. It's just that I don't really understand what I'm doing": metacognition and secondary school students', *Research papers in Education*, 10: 254–71.

Head, J. (1996) 'Gender identity and cognitive style' in P.F. Murphy and C.V. Gipps (eds) *Equity in the Classroom: towards effective pedagogy for girls and boys*, 59–69, London: Falmer Press.

Jackson, D. and Salisbury, J. (1996) 'Why should secondary schools take working with boys seriously?', *Gender and Education*, 8: 103–15.

Kenway, I., Willis, S., Blackmore, J. and Rennie, L. (1998) *Answering Back: girls, boys and feminism in schools*, London: Routledge.

Lee, A. (1996) *Gender, Literacy, Curriculum: rewriting school geography*, London: Taylor & Francis.

Mac an Ghaill, M. (1994) *The Making of Men: masculinities, sexualities and schooling*, Buckingham: Open University Press.

Nieto, S. (1994) 'Lessons from students: creating a chance to dream', *Harvard Educational Review*, 64: 392–426.

Phelan, P., Davidson, A.L. and Caso, H.T. (1992) 'Speaking up: students' perspectives at school', *Phi Delta Kappan*, 73: 695–704.

Place, J.D. (1997) 'Boys will be boys: boys and under-achievement in modern foreign languages', *Language Learning Journal*, 16: 3–10.

Qualifications and Curriculum Authority (1998) *Can Do Better: raising boys' achievements in English*, London: QCA.

Quicke, J. and Winter, C. (1993) 'Teaching the language of learning: towards a metacognitive approach to pupil empowerment', paper presented to the *BERA Conference*, Liverpool.

Rudduck, J., Chaplain, R. and Wallace, G. (1995) *School Improvement: what can pupils tell us?*, London: David Fulton.

Slater, A. (1996) 'The lost boys', *Managing Schools Today*, January: 24–6.

Stanworth, M. (1981) *Gender and Schooling: a study of sexual inequalities in the classroom*, London: Hutchinson.

Teese, R., Davies, M., Charlton, M. and Polesel, J. (1995) *Who Wins at School? Boys and girls in Australian secondary education*, Melbourne: Department of Education Policy and Management, University of Melbourne.

Warrington, M. and Younger, M. (1996) 'Goals, expectations and motivation: gender differences in achievement at GCSE', *Curriculum*, 17(2): 80–93.

Warrington, M. and Younger, M. (1999) 'Perspectives on the gender gap in English secondary schools', *Research Papers in Education*, 14: 51–77.

Weiner, G., Arnot, M. and David, M. (1997) 'Is the future female? Female success, male disadvantage and changing gender patterns in education' in A.H. Halsey, H. Lauder, P. Brown and A. Stuart Wells (eds) *Education: culture, economy and society*, 620–30, Oxford: OUP.

Yates, L. (1997) 'Gender equity and the boys debate: what sort of challenge is it?', *British Journal of Sociology of Education*, 18: 337–47.

Younger, M. and Warrington, M. (1996) 'Differential achievement of girls and boys at GCSE: some observations from the perspective of one school', *British Journal of Sociology of Education*, 17: 299–314.

Younger, M., Warrington, M. and Williams, J. (1999) 'The Gender Gap and Classroom Interactions: reality and rhetoric?', *British Journal of Sociology of Education*, 20: 327–43.

10 The teacher–student relationship in secondary school

Insights from excluded students

Eva Pomeroy

Introduction

Exclusion from school has received much attention in recent years as a result of evidence indicating a significant rise in the number of exclusions (BCC 1995: DfEE 1995: The *Guardian* 1996: Ofsted 1996: *Times Educational Supplement* 1997). Although there has been considerable commentary on the issue of exclusion by the media, government and educational researchers, very little of that commentary has been derived from the views of the young people directly affected. Recently, the Commission for Racial Equality published a 'good practice' guide to exclusion (1997). One of their many suggestions was that pupils be involved in decision-making, particularly with respect to behaviour standards. The teachers in the study found that pupil involvement was key to co-operation and good discipline, while the young people said that being involved increased their motivation and made them feel part of the school (p. 6). Clearly, the involvement of students had a positive effect for students themselves, teachers, classrooms and schools.

This chapter is derived from an in-depth study of the views and experiences of a relatively small group of secondary school students (33), all of whom have been permanently excluded from school. The study recognizes the inherent value of the views of students. As the recipients of policy-in-practice, they possess a knowledge of the educational system which is not necessarily known to teachers, parents or policy-makers. In order to understand fully an educational phenomenon such as exclusion, it is important to construct this understanding from all relevant perspectives. Too often, the viewpoint of the student remains unheard. The students in this study have had a unique, if unenviable, school experience. Upon leaving school, these young people lost whatever voice, however small, they had when they were members of the institution. Rudduck *et al.* (1996) comment on the importance of capturing the views of such students.

> ... the voices of *all* pupils should be listened to and not just those who are more academically and socially confident, for it is the less effective learners who are most likely to be able to explore aspects of the system that constrain commitment and progress; these are the voices least likely to be heard and yet most important to be heard.
>
> (Rudduck *et al.* 1996: 177)

The accounts that follow tell us as much about school processes and how they operate for some students as they do about the young people themselves. Student views are not the only perspective; however, students form one very important 'stake-holder' group in the educational system. As identified by Rudduck *et al.* (1996), the views of those students disaffected from school are particularly useful as they reveal the ways in which the educational system operates so as to create difficulty for some of its students.

The excluded students' views included in this chapter are derived from semi-structured interviews that covered all aspects of the school experience leading to their exclusion. The three key factors identified as problematic by the interviewees are relationships with teachers, relationships with peers at school and factors outside of school (e.g. home life, involvement in criminal activity). Overall, relationships with teachers was the most salient and consistently described feature of the interviewees' experience of school. It was the topic that tended to take up more interview time than any other.

Considered too are the interviewees' views on desirable and undesirable teacher qualities, discipline, and the social structure of school, paying particular attention to excluded students' perceptions of hierarchy. In the final section, these areas are integrated and form the basis of an ideal model of teacher–student relationships. The model identifies alternative patterns of teacher–student interaction, founded on an alternative set of power relationships to those that presently exist in schools. By building the model on excluded students' accounts of lived experiences, it both highlights the strengths that exist in many student–teacher relationships and identifies significant aspects of those relationships that impede these students' ability to engage in school in a positive manner.

Youth perspectives in educational research

In recent years there has been an increasing interest in students' perspectives on school. As the interest in student perspectives increases, so does the breadth of our understanding about the school experience. Writings by Rudduck *et al.* (1996), Nieto (1994) and Cooper and McIntrye (1993) shed light on students' views on learning and the conditions in school which either help or hinder it. Blatchford (1996), Chaplain (1996) and de Pear and Garner (1996) consider students' perceptions of themselves as learners. Other work focuses more on the social-interpersonal aspects of schooling, including relationships with peers and relationships with teachers (Woods 1990: Crozier and Antiss 1995: John 1996: Cullingford and Morrison 1995, 1997). Another area of research is that which concentrates on particular areas of concern in education, such as truancy and exclusion (Bealing 1990: Cohen and Hughes 1994: Kinder *et al.* 1997). Much of the work cited here is descriptive in nature, aiming to represent accurately the views of young people. This has been an important development given that student perspectives have been so under-represented in educational research. As the number of studies into students' perspectives on school increases, however, we must re-examine the purpose of youth perspectives research.

Research into young people's perceptions of their school experiences must move beyond case-specific description in order to increase its relevance and utility.

Progress has been made towards this end. Some researchers have used the knowledge gained through young people to challenge existing concepts within the educational system. For example, on the basis of their data, Cullingford and Morrison (1995) review the accepted concept of bullying and begin to re-conceptualize the phenomenon. Similarly, Crozier and Antiss (1995) use their data on girls' perceptions of disruption in school to challenge the commonly-held definitions of disruptive behaviour. These authors re-conceptualize aspects of the educational experience on the basis of the views of those most directly affected – students. By considering the implications of their data on a conceptual, systemic level, the authors provide findings which are more widely applicable. It is this quality of understanding about students' perceptions and experiences that can serve as a foundation for change in education. [...]

Student perspectives on relationships with teachers

Student–teacher relationships are a key feature of school life. Wallace (1996), in her study of secondary school students, found that teachers' various approaches to subject teaching were less important to students than the interactive relationships established with students (p 36). Garner (1995), commenting on his study of disruptive boys, states

> Teachers, rather than curriculum, are the substantive opinion-formers [in relation to the boys' experience of school]
>
> (p. 28)

In this study, students' relationships with teachers also surfaced as one of the most salient features of the educational experience. [...]

Teacher qualities

Research over the past decade has enabled us to understand better the characteristics and behaviour of teachers whom students like or dislike. Much of this research has focused on young people who experience difficulty at school. Often it is undesirable qualities and interactions which are more prevalent in the students' accounts. Hardly surprisingly, students often cite public humiliation, especially shouting, as one of the most negative teacher–student interactions (White and Brockington 1983: Woods 1990: Chaplain 1996: John 1996: Rudduck *et al.* 1996). In this study, teacher behaviour patterns that were found to be antagonistic and humiliating included shouting, telling students to 'shut up', responding sarcastically, putting young people down and name-calling. These actions were often perceived to communicate a message to the students that they are not valued as students and, often, that they are not liked as individuals.

Students also experience difficulty when they feel they are not afforded enough attention by teachers. This is particularly true of young people outside mainstream school speaking of their school experience (Lloyd-Smith 1984: John 1996: de Pear 1997). In this study, the most consistent and common grievance is that teachers do not listen to students. There seem to be two bases upon which teachers' 'not listening' is deemed inappropriate. The first is students' sense that their point of view is not valued enough to be heard.

Danni: When I went to talk to 'em, like if I got into trouble, they wouldn't hear my side of the story. They'd take other people's side of the story, but they just wouldn't listen.

The second basis upon which 'not listening' is deemed inappropriate is when it is interpreted as teachers failing to meet young people's social and emotional needs.

Sarah: … [peers] just used to like, mess about with me and that used to get me really annoyed, and then I'd get into trouble, and then, when I'd tell the teacher that I was annoyed, they wouldn't listen to me, and tell me to shut up and sit down. And that's when I started arguing with the teachers.

Teachers' failure to intervene in student conflict was also raised by Crozier and Antiss (1995) in their study of girls' perceptions of disruption. They comment: 'The girls were emphatic about the power of words to hurt and claimed that teachers did not take the problem seriously or do anything about it' (p. 42). Either teachers do not recognize the significance of these interactions to students or there is an inconsistency between teachers' perceptions of their role *vis à vis* student relations and students' perceptions of the teachers' role.

Another problematic feature of teacher–student interactions arising in the literature is behaviour that discriminates on racial grounds (Phelan *et al.* 1994: John 1996: Wright *et al.* 1998). Six of the interviewees in this study reported incidents of racism from teachers. Three of the young people mentioned teacher comments that were racist either in terminology or inference. The other three raised the issue of differential treatment on the basis of race. The topic of racism in schools was not an explicit part of the interview structure. It was raised by these interviewees as a salient feature of their school experience. Perhaps, if the questioning had been more explicit, more incidents such as these may have been reported. Interestingly, three of the young people who reported racist incidents are African-Caribbean, one is of mixed parentage, one Asian and one white-European. It is beyond the scope of this paper to explore the complex and subtle nature of racism in schools. Within this study, the accounts of some interviewees show how racist teacher behaviour, actual or perceived, has unquestionably had a negative impact on their sense of self and self-value.

Almost all the interviewees experienced some negative interactions with teachers. However, the majority also spoke of the positive qualities possessed by some teachers. It is well documented that students like those teachers who take time to talk with and listen to students (Woods 1990: Cooper 1992: Nieto 1994). It is also important that teachers are able to understand and relate to their students (Gannaway 1984: SooHoo 1993: Howe 1995). Finally, a friendly approach and sense of humour were important in establishing and fostering relationships (Gannaway 1984: Garner 1995: Chaplain 1996). The ability of teachers to establish positive relationships is of the utmost importance to the interviewees in this study. The qualities summarized in the research cited above all apply to the young people in the sample.

Eva: So what was good about Mr Knight?
Yaz: I just used to get on with him, if I had any problems, then I'd tell him.
Eva: Right.
Yaz: … and if I used to walk past him in the school, he [would], he'd stop me, 'Where you going, what you up to now?' And just to make sure that I weren't doing nothing wrong.
Eva: Right.
Yaz: He was a fun teacher and some days if I was really ill and I didn't wanna go home, I just wanted to stay in school for a bit, he'd say, 'Well, go and sit in my office then'…
Nathan: She's funny [Centre Head]. She makes me laugh … [—] it's talking about … I swear I talk to some of the teachers here about mad stuff that I wouldn't talk about with mad teachers [at school] because they couldn't be assed.

These quotations highlight the points made by the sample as a whole. Unlike the teacher qualities that students disliked which often left them feeling undervalued, the comments above describe teachers who actively made efforts to establish relationships with students. The interviewees respond most positively to those teachers who they perceived as breaking out of a more distant teacher–student relationship model to establish a certain type of friendship with the students. This fulfils students' need for teachers to take on a pastoral role in their interactions with students, clearly demonstrating care and concern.

Another important quality in teachers is their ability to educate – that is, to impart skills and knowledge to their students. It is well documented in the literature that students appreciate teachers who make an effort to teach in an interesting and effective way (White and Brockington 1983: Woods 1990: Nieto 1994: Wallace 1996). Although there was greater variability amongst this sample in their desire to learn than their desire to be related to in an appropriate manner, the ability to teach subjects remained important to many of the young people.

Nahim: She was like, she used to be real good at drawing, and she used to give you lots of good tips, she used to always talk to you, never used to shout. And she never used to shout at the class and they never used to talk … They used to just get on with the work. 'Cause like, she used to give us things to do, and you know like she, uh, you're happy that you're doing it.

Failure to teach in an interesting manner often met with criticism. The following account is from a student who was given the assignment: 'Design a safe park for children'.

Nathan: … I built a park five times. He used to come in every lesson and say, 'Carry on with your park', then he'd go away and we didn't have a park. We smashed it up every lesson.

Equally important to teaching ability is the willingness to provide students with the help and attention they need in order to learn. Again, this point is often raised by young people in alternative provision settings as they reflect on their mainstream school experience (Colville and Craig 1995: Sinclair and Taylor 1995: de Pear 1997). Although there were examples of teachers offering appropriate help, the more common experience within this sample is that of the student who was unable to elicit the help seen as necessary.

Michael: Well, when I go up and talk to her, I go, 'Can you explain this?', and that, she'll go, 'Explain what? You've been doing it all, like, all term. This is what you've been taught'. And I don't understand what I'm doing …

Although comments like this one reflect the students' perception of their teachers as not responding to their needs, they also suggest that the students believe learning to be a valuable activity and that the teachers' failure to facilitate learning is largely what is being criticized. It is well documented that the vast majority of young people wish to learn and succeed in school (Lloyd and Smith 1984: Woods 1990: Rudduck *et al.* 1996: de Pear 1997). Woods (1990) comments: 'Even the apparently most anarchic pupils may want to work' (p. 21). It is not surprising then that teachers' failure to teach effectively is seen as problematic.

By examining the teacher qualities raised by the students, a profile of a good teacher emerges. For the students interviewed, a good teacher is primarily one who is able to establish meaningful relationships with students. Many authors have commented on the importance of relationships with teachers to students' experience of school. Wallace (1996) notes that it was the perception of the teachers as being friendly and 'liking' students that was paramount (p. 29). The perception of teachers as caring about their students has a direct relation to the students' perceived ability to engage in work and learn. Gannaway (1984) summarizes the view of one of his interviewees as follows:

John then remarked that it was the teacher that makes all the difference to a lesson and the rest of the class seemed to agree with this. It was said that a good teacher is *one who understands the pupils*.

Somewhat more emphatically, one of SooHoo's (1993) student researchers makes a similar point:

If they (the teachers) have an attitude, I don't know how they expect us to learn.

(p. 391)

Thus, the teacher's management of relationships with students directly affects students' perceptions of the teacher's ability to teach.

Discipline

Discipline is identified as a central aspect of teacher–student relations. Unsurprisingly, interactions of a disciplinary nature were a common feature of the interviewees' experience. Interestingly, several of the interviewees commented that their teachers should have been more strict than they were.

Eva: Oh, right. So you could like swear at teachers …
Shelly: Well, you couldn't, but that lot, they did, but they [teachers] hardly done nothing about it.
Eva: Right, right. And what do you think they should have done?
Shelly: They should have given better punishment or sommat like that.
Sarah: … I think I needed to have more strict teachers. Like, if I'd have had, like, stricter teachers teaching, then I probably would have got on better at the school. 'Cause, like, I behave for them. But like, teachers who like, can't control ya, I had quite a few of them. And, um, I just didn't get on.

The call for more vigilant disciplinary action is not unique to this study. Bealing (1990) asked a group of students with a record of truanting from school what could be done about truancy. Their suggestions included taking registers to each lesson, cross-checking attendance with tutors, spot-checking the toilets for students absent from lessons, and phoning the students' homes at the earliest sign of trouble (p. 29). Although the expressed need for increased disciplinary action partly reflects the young people's reluctance to assume responsibility for the behaviour of themselves or their peers, it also reflects their understanding of the role of the teachers in the school. Clearly, the young people feel that teachers are responsible for the monitoring and ultimate control of student behaviour.

Given that the young people seem to view discipline as an important aspect of the teachers' role, what is the nature of the discipline they advocate? It is clear that some forms of discipline are definitely not seen as acceptable, such as shouting or belittling students in the presence of peers. When the interviewees call for teachers to be more strict, they seem to describe a particular kind of disciplinary practice. One of the characteristics of this practice is that sanctions are both fair and appropriate for the misdemeanour.

Tuscar: … when I was in PE, I didn't really get shouted at, except when I was throwing the ball over the fence and that, on purpose. Like, things what, like, that you know you're doing wrong, [the teacher should] just shout at you then.
Michael: … 'Cause you think of a good way, what it needs putting to. Say, like, if I kick somebody, do something in that area.
Eva: Right.

Michael: Rounders, or if I kick something, do something, give me some kind of
punishment to do with … not going out and kicking people again.
Eva: Right.
Michael: So that would mean stopping in at break and not going out for dinner.

One part of fair discipline is the importance of gaining all sides of a story.

Eva: … how do you think the teachers should be with students?
Gary: Listen to both sides of the story and then put them together and then
come to a conclusion. Like to both of ya because, like in that school I've
just been expelled from, they always just sort of put it down to one person
and goes, 'Ah, like, we'll chuck him out'. Just like that, 'cause they ain't
really bothered, I don't think. It's just one more student to them.

The way in which discipline is applied is also important to the interviewees. Both the
tone and the wording are significant. In the following comments, the young people
provide concrete examples of disciplinary interaction which they feel is appropriate.

Kirsty: Helped ya, not like shouting, shouting at ya, being more polite to ya, being
there when you need to talk to em. Um, like, you like a warning like, to get
your earrings out like, 'Don't wear 'em tomorrow'. But put it the right way,
like, 'You shouldn't do this, you should do this'. Like, as time going on
teachers like shouting out in the classroom, what work I do, 'Get them
earrings out NOW! DO IT NOW, or you're going home', and all this. 'I don't
care', I thought, I wouldn't get my earrings out, so send me home.
Leon: Like, do this, do that, don't do this. They said that as well [in the Centre],
but in a politer way. Like they explained. That sort.
Eva: Does that make a difference, explaining?
Leon: Mm-hmm, it does. It makes a lot of difference. Saying in a friendly kind of
way – it depends how you say it.

The interviewees acknowledge the need for disciplinary action to be taken by
teachers. Ideally, discipline would be fair, take into account all relevant perspectives and provide appropriate sanctions. It would also be delivered in a manner
which involved discussion and avoided shouting.
    The students also highlighted another aspect of good disciplinary action:
preventative intervention.

Nahim: Next day go in late, they used to keep track of anybody that missed out lots
of days, they used to phone your house up and used to find out why you
never come.
Eva: Right.
Nahim: Hillcrest, never went there for about two months, and they didn't have
the phone number or anything, they wasn't organized. 'Cause everyone
used to mess around, they used to say.

Eva: Right.

Nahim: What's the point?

Eva: So do you think they should have phoned home?

Nahim: I wouldn't have got kicked out if they would have phoned home to my parents.

Lorraine: ... like Mr Jennings [Centre teacher] yesterday, phoned me mom, 'cause I never went to [a regular placement assisting in a primary school]. He phoned my mom, and he could see if there's anything wrong. Like is there any problems at home, that's what he asked my mom. And then he could see. In Marchant's Hall they didn't see, they didn't see nothing.

Eva: And you feel that that what Mr Jennings did is what teachers should do?

Lorraine: Yeah, they should do that.

In both of these cases, the early link with home was seen as a central feature of preventative disciplinary action. Other interviewees noted the ability of some teachers to recognize potentially volatile situations in school and intervene before any serious disruption took place.

Perry: ... say the mood I felt in before I go on the playground, I would have end up hitting someone, you know what I'm saying? So what I used to do is I used to go and see Mr Reid. He used to put me on the computers all dinner time, like. Didn't have to – used to go out of his way. Open the computer cupboard, know what I mean? Didn't have to do that, didn't have to come out of his lunch, come and open the computer cupboard and then come after his lunch and close it, but he knew, man, he did it for me, you know what I'm saying?

Yaz: But, Mr Knight would always be able to calm me down, and just say things what would calm me down. 'There's no point in doing that cause you know what Miss Dover's like, she won't let you straight in straight away', or, 'If you do that, then you've got this to...'. He just used to speak to me properly.

Richard: Like it was bad in year seven, and year eight got all right, in year nine was okay, 'cause I had, in year nine I used to just, I had this year tutor called Miss Dixon.

Eva: Mm, hmm.

Richard: She was saying, she always used to tell when I came in of a morning, and afternoon, she always used to tell if I was in a mood, and she used to sit down and listen. 'Sit over here and read a book' or something like that ...

In each of these cases the teacher is described as recognizing a state of volatility for the young person. This recognition suggests that there are certain circumstances that can lead to a predictable pattern of interactions resulting in the student 'getting into trouble'. Given that the pattern is predictable, the skill required by the teacher is to recognize the pattern at its preliminary stages and intervene appropriately. The intervention itself does not reflect what we often think of as disciplinary action. In two of the cases, the students are offered alternative activities to divert them from potential conflict with peers. In the third case, the teacher speaks to the student on a one-to-one basis reminding her of the reality of the situation and the consequences of particular lines of action. Here, interviewees are suggesting a discipline dynamic which diverges from the traditional model. It requires the teachers both to know the students on a personal basis and to care for them. The relationship is essential to good disciplinary practice.

Clearly, the young people in this study feel that effective discipline is necessary in schools. What is deemed effective by the interviewees does not always reflect more traditional notions of discipline. There are three central features to the disciplinary action advocated by the young people. The first is that it is fair, the second is that it is delivered in a respectful manner, and the third, that it is seen to be motivated by a concern for the well-being of the students.

Hierarchy

All of the interactions described thus far take place within the social system of school. Understanding the way in which young people comprehend this system helps us to contextualize their perceptions. It also helps us to gain insight into the nature of the system itself.

In school, the framework which underlies the young people's interpretation of events and interactions, within a social system, is the framework of hierarchy. Interactions are seen to take place between individuals who hold different positions within a hierarchy. Most clearly, the young people interviewed perceive themselves as occupying the lowest position in the hierarchy while teachers assume the highest position. The interviewees identify a hierarchical imbalance in the teacher–student relationship and clearly identify that teachers possess an unequal and greater share of power.

Tuscar: … Just that I don't like teachers, and it's like they think that they're higher than you. Like just 'cause they like try and teach me how to work and that, think like they're higher than you, and things like that, so.

Tonya: … You can't make a person talk to you like dirt and you're talking to them like they're Queen and King.

Yvonne: … And then he started, he started shouting at me, telling me that I'm wasting [his time] … And I just said, 'Sir, why you shouting at me?', 'cause I mean he just starts shouting. I says, 'There's no need to shout' and then he got even more angry, 'cause I told him there's no need to shout, and told me if I carried on, I'm going to have to go home. I says, 'But, why, I just told you not to shout at me. But if I turned round and started shouting at you first, right, you'd call me rude. So why is there any difference? It's just a age group. If you want respect off me, you've got to give it back.'

Teachers are seen to hold a privileged position within a hierarchy. There was also a sense, for many young people, that certain students were higher in the school hierarchy than themselves. Several of the interviewees felt that they and some of their peers maintained the lowest positions in the hierarchy, while other students enjoyed a more preferential status in relation to the teachers.

Eva: I mean, is there, did they give any of the kids respect?
Kirsty: Some yeah, who they liked. People who work at the subject, who was the brightest in the class, and like that.
Eva: And so what was different in the, in the higher groups?
Nahim: Teachers were quite serious, some teachers [I] used to have them for some lessons, and they used to really care, but in the higher groups.
Eva: Right.
Nahim: They used to care a lot. They only liked people that would be clever. And people that don't know that much, they don't like 'em at all.

Inter-relationships in the school are framed by a hierarchy of worth. The hierarchy, as understood by the interviewees, consists of teachers at the top, themselves at the bottom, and 'more able' or 'better behaved' students between themselves and the teachers. The criteria for determining one's position in the hierarchy are entirely teacher- and school-defined. The recognized dimensions of importance are ability and/or knowledge, and behaviour. Interestingly, there were only a few of the interviewees who criticized the behaviour of students assumed to hold higher positions in the hierarchy. It is the differential treatment teachers demonstrate that is subject to criticism.

The hierarchical relationship, at least that aspect which concerns teachers and students on the lowest tier, is often compared to the parent–child relationship at home. Compared to the private realm of home, the behaviour of teachers is then deemed inappropriate either because it assumes the role reserved for parents or because it extends the boundaries of appropriate treatment as established by families.

Tuscar: Yeah. It's like that, I don't think anyone should shout at anyone, like done wrong or not …
Eva: What would be a better way then?
Tuscar: I dunno, do what they wanted, but start shouting at everybody and that. It's like, like if anyone should shout it's parents, so, that's what I think anyway.

Flattening the hierarchy and rejecting particular behaviours which reflect the power imbalance seemed to hold some significance for the young people. Often this was expressed through the use of adult–child constructs. Finding themselves chronologically between the two, the interviewees aspire to the former and reject treatment deemed appropriate for the latter. This arose most often when the interviewees were comparing their previous school to their present Centre.

Sarah: Um, they don't treat you like little kids, they treat you like you're an adult. And um, they're just polite, and things like that, so.
Eva: So how is it, how can teachers treat you like a little kid?
Sarah: That's the point, used to tell you to shut up, and used to say stupid things to you, like do your work and behave yourself, and stop messing about. Stop doing this and stop doing that. Here, like they don't say things like that. Like, I don't play up here, so.

Yaz: … I feel like an adult myself when I'm here, cause that's how the teachers teach you when you're here.

The use of adult–child constructs further shapes our understanding of hierarchy as a framework. The interviewees view the treatment afforded to them, at the lowest tier of the hierarchy, as treatment suitable for children: lack of autonomy, responsibility and, most importantly, respect. Acquiring these qualities is associated with gaining adult status. In school, this status was reserved for teachers and possibly some students. Moving up the hierarchy, to attain a more adult status seemed unachievable at school; however, many interviewees felt this status was achieved in Centres. It is not that the interviewees assume a higher position in the hierarchy at the Centres, but rather that the nature of the Centre social system is qualitatively different. The interviewees did not understand the Centres in terms of hierarchy. One of the effects of this is that a different set of teacher–student interactions emerged.

Discussion

The excluded students' ideal model of teacher–student relationships

The analysis of the interviewees' accounts of both mainstream and Centre experiences provides the basis for the construction of an ideal model of the teacher–student relationship. It is important to the interviewees that they feel cared for; however, the *in loco parentis* model of care is not seen as appropriate. These students, in their final years of schooling, do not express a wish for teachers to act as surrogate parents during school hours. Rather, they seem to want a unique relationship in which their non-child status is recognized and responded to accordingly while, at the same time, their pastoral needs are met. The defining feature of the ideal teacher–student model which enables teachers to communicate 'caring', without inadvertently 'parenting', is dialogue. Repeatedly interviewees mention certain teachers who *knew* them, who would *talk to* and *explain things* to them, and who would *listen*. Knowing students in this way implies that the teachers have an ability to assume the students' perspective. The fact that the students' value teachers explaining things suggests that they are interested in understanding the perspective of the teachers insofar as that perspective offers guidance about behaviour. Mutual perspective-recognition forms the foundation of the ideal teacher–student relationship. Respectful interactions communicating the teacher's belief in the students' worth are also a key feature of the ideal model of teacher–student relationships.

Rudduck *et al.* (1996) in their conclusion comment that '… the conditions of learning in the majority of secondary schools do not adequately take account of the maturity of young people, nor of the tensions and pressures that they experience …' (p. 173). In advocating the above model, the interviewees are demonstrating their capacity to interact on a more adult level. They both recognize and value teachers' roles as educators and providers of pastoral care. In challenging the present model of teacher–student relationships, they are not calling for teachers to cease either teaching or taking responsibility for discipline. Rather, they challenge the ways in which these responsibilities can be carried out. In this model, respect for individuals mediates teachers' actions in fulfilling their professional responsibilities. Teacher and student interact on an almost adult-to-adult level.

There is one aspect of the young people's accounts, however, which contradicts their desire to interact in a more adult-like fashion. This is the question of who takes responsibility for behaviour. The interviewees expressed a desire for teachers to speak to them 'proper' and 'kind', to treat them like adults rather than young children, and generally to recognize their ability to interact in a mature way. At the same time many of the comments imply that the young people feel teachers should take responsibility for the behaviour of their peers and themselves. This was clearly demonstrated when the interviewees called for the teachers to be more strict. Some young people want the teachers to take responsibility for physically keeping other students away, either particular individuals or the entire student body by isolating the interviewee.

Dana: … Could have just put me in a classroom on me own. I would have been happy.

Like most of the interviewees who experienced difficulty relating to peers, Dana felt the teachers could resolve her behaviour issues by preventing social interaction. Other interviewees wanted teachers to prevent them from misbehaving by offering diversionary activities such as using the computer or reading a book. The call for teachers to play a greater role in controlling student behaviour seems to jeopardize the development of the ideal model of teacher–student relationships discussed above. Rarely do the interviewees comment on the role of their behaviour in conflicts, or express a concern about the 'rightness' or 'wrongness' of their actions. It is easy to see how this reluctance to assume responsibility for actions could lock students and teachers into interactions where the students are, indeed, treated like 'babies'. Why is it, then, that the interviewees perceive the responsibility for their own behaviour to lie with teachers? The suggestion here is that the current system, as it is in operation, serves to infantalize young adults.

Power and the teacher–student relationship

We have seen that hierarchy is understood by the interviewees to be the organizing principle that structures the formal social system at school. Teachers are perceived to hold the majority of the power in this system. This works for and against students. Certainly, the interviewees recognize that, by virtue of their position, teachers have many unique responsibilities. The students in this study identify these primarily as the responsibilities to teach, to maintain control and to provide pastoral care. The last responsibility held particular salience to the young people excluded from school. More specifically, they identified pastoral care as establishing meaningful relationships, intervening in peer conflict, preventing disruption, offering guidance, and generally showing concern for the well-being of the student. When these responsibilities are met, teachers' power is seen to be exercised appropriately: that is, to influence and shape positive experiences of school.

However, this power is also seen as having worked against the students in the study. The interviewees perceive themselves as disadvantaged when teachers use their power wrongly. We have seen examples of teacher–student interactions that are perceived to humiliate, de-value and disempower the young people interviewed. We have also seen a distinct absence of dialogue between teachers and students around key concerns, such as behaviour and discipline. Within the social hierarchy at school, as experienced by these students, it seems that a grossly disproportionate share of power is allocated to teachers with very little left for those students at the bottom of the hierarchy. In such conditions, students' capacity to practise mature, responsible, adult-like interactions is not explored. This may not be the case for all students. It has been argued that students in the higher academic streams are afforded greater status within the school (Hargreaves 1967: Lacey 1970). It is likely that these students, by virtue of their status, enjoy more power in the formal school system, and greater freedom of movement and behaviour as a result. The students in this study, however, are low-status. The majority consider themselves to be at the bottom of the school hierarchy. They have been identified as either low-achieving, poorly behaved or both, and have not been offered opportunities to share power and exercise control over their educational experience in a more adult-like manner. The default position for the interviewees to assume, then, is that of the child: dependent, lacking power, and not to be held responsible for their actions.

Alternative relationships and models of power-sharing could exist. Cummins (1994), studying literacy programmes, identifies two distinct understandings of relations of power. The first is coercive relationships: the exercise of power by the dominant group to the detriment of a subordinate group. This approach assumes that power exists in a fixed quantity. It defines the subordinate group as inferior, necessarily making the dominant group superior, in order to justify a greater share of power. The second model is that of collaborative relations of power. Here, power is not fixed, but can be generated by interpersonal relations; it is something created in the relationship and shared among participants (p. 299). Integral to this approach is the need to 'view students as cultural resource persons and to *listen* to their *self*-expression' (p. 322). Arguably, the disempowering, infantalizing practices outlined above are more indicative of coercive relations of power. Furthermore, the model developed from the interviewees' perspectives, with its emphasis on dialogue and consultation, is congruent with Cummins' notion of collaborative relationships of power.

The differences that exist between the interviewees' descriptions of their negative experiences at school and their ideal model of teacher–student relations are considered here to be the differences between the way things are and the way they could be. Unsurprisingly, the school experiences of many of the excluded students in this study have been predominantly negative. In part, the interviewees' model of ideal teacher–student relations is based on changing the features of the existing set of relations that have been identified by the students as problematic. That is, discarding behaviour viewed as antagonistic and increasing the amount of teacher behaviour perceived as caring and helpful. However, the model has also been built upon interviewees' positive experiences – some in the mainstream and many more in the Centres. Thus, the ideal model of teacher–student relations based on the views of a group of students excluded from school is not an unrealistic goal. Already many of these students, who may be amongst those most disaffected from school, have experienced collaborative relations of power with teachers and valued these experiences. Particularly in the Centres, the interviewees report feeling respected as individuals and learners, cared for as young people and valued. Relations of this type tend to have occurred too late in interviewees' academic careers – after their permanent exclusion from mainstream school. The proposed model of teacher–student relations, based on the interviewees' accounts and views, can be read as an appeal for change. This appeal is driven by the often negative experiences of excluded students, but is also informed by what these students consider to be teachers' 'good practice'. […]

References

BCC (Birmingham City Council) (1995) 'Education and Director of Social Services, Joint Report of Chief', *Exclusions – The Interim Report of a Working Party*, Birmingham: BCC.

Bealing, V. (1990) 'Inside information: pupil perceptions of absenteeism in the Secondary School', *Maladjustment and Therapeutic Education*, 8(1): 19–33.

Blatchford, P. (1996) 'Pupils' views on school work and school from 7–16 years', *Research Papers in Education*, 11(3): 263–88.

Chaplain, R. (1996) 'Making a strategic withdrawal: disengagement and self-worth protection in male pupils' in J. Rudduck, R. Chaplin and G. Wallace (eds) *School Improvement: what can pupils tell us?* London: David Fulton.

Cohen, R. and Hughes, M. (1994) *School's Out: the family perspective on school exclusion*, London: Family Service Unit and Barnardo's.

Colville-Craig, D. (1995) 'Exploring pupils' perceptions of their experience in secure accommodation' in M. Lloyd-Smith and R. Davies (eds) *On the Margins: the educational experiences of 'problem' pupils*, Stoke: Trentham.

Commission For Racial Equality (1997) *Exclusion from school and Racial Equality: a good practice guide*, London: CRE.

Cooper, P. (1992) 'Exploring pupils' perceptions of the effects of residential schooling on children with emotional and behavioural difficulties', *Therapeutic Care and Education*, 1 (Spring): 22–34.

Cooper, P. and McIntyre, D. (1993) 'Commonality in teachers' and pupils' perceptions of effective classroom learning', *British Journal of Educational Psychology*, 63: 381–99.

Crozier, J. and Antiss, J. (1995) 'Out of the spotlight: girls' experience of disruption' in M. Lloyd-Smith and R. Davies (eds) *On the margins: the educational experience of 'problem' pupils*, Stoke: Trentham.

Cullingford, C. and Morrison, J. (1995) 'Bullying as a formative influence: the relationship between the experience of school and criminality', *British Educational Research Journal*, 21 (5): 547–60.

Cullingford, C. and Morrison, J. (1997) 'Peer pressure within and outside school', *British Educational Research Journal*, 23 (1): 61–80.

Cummins, J. (1994) 'From coercive to collaborative relations of power in teaching literary' in B. Ferman, R.M. Weber and A. Ramirez (eds) *Literacy Across Languages and Cultures*, New York State: University of New York Press.

de Pear, S. (1997) 'Excluded pupils' views of their educational needs and experiences', *Support for Learning* 12(1): 19–22.

de Pear, S. and Garner, P. (1996) 'Tales from the exclusion zone: the views of teachers and pupils' in E. Blyth and J. Milner (eds) *Exclusion from School*, London: Routledge.

DfEE (1995) *Final Report to the Department for Education: National Survey of Local Education Authorities' Policies and Procedures for the Identification of and Provision for Children who are Out of School by Reason of Exclusion or Otherwise,* Canterbury: Canterbury Christ Church College.

Gannaway, H. (1984) 'Making sense of school' in M. Hammersley and P. Woods (eds) *Life in School: the sociology of pupil culture,* Buckingham: Open University.

Garner, P. (1995) 'Schools by scoundrels: the views of "disruptive" pupils in mainstream schools in England and the United States' in M. Lloyd-Smith and J. Davis (eds) *On the Margins: the educational experience of 'problem' pupils,* Stoke: Trentham.

Guardian (1996) 'Rate of expulsions rising despite Shephard's claim', *Guardian,* 22 November: 6.

Hargreaves, D.H. (1967) *Social Relations in a Secondary School,* London: Routledge and Kegan Paul.

Howe, T. (1995) 'Former pupils' reflections on residential special provision' in M. Lloyd-Smith and J. Davies (eds) *On the Margins: the educational experience of 'problem' pupils,* Stoke: Trentham.

John, P. (1996) 'Damaged goods? An interpretation of excluded pupils' perceptions of schooling' in E. Blyth and J. Milner (eds) *Exclusion from School,* London: Routledge.

Kinder, K., Wilkin, A. and Wakefield, A. (1997) *Exclusion: who needs it?* Slough: NFER.

Lacey, C. (1970) *Hightown Grammar,* Manchester: Manchester University Press.

Lloyd-Smith, M. (ed.) (1984) *Disrupted Schooling,* London: John Murray.

Lloyd-Smith, M. and Davies, R. (eds) (1995) *On the Margins: the educational experience of 'problem' pupils,* Stoke: Trentham.

Nieto, S. (1994) 'Lessons from students on creating a chance to dream', *Harvard Educational Review,* 64(4): 392–426.

Ofsted (1996) *Exclusions from Secondary School 1995/96,* London: Ofsted.

Phelan, P., Cao, H. and Davidson, A. (1994) 'Navigating the psychosocial pressures of adolescence: the voices and experiences of High School youth', *American Educational Research Journal* 31(2): 415–47.

Rudduck, J., Chaplain, R. and Wallace, G. (eds) (1996) *School Improvement: what can pupils tell us?* London: David Fulton.

Sinclair-Taylor, A. (1995) 'A "Dunce's Place": pupils' perceptions of the role of a special unit' in M. Lloyd-Smith and R. Davies (eds) *On the Margins: the educational experience of 'problem' pupils,* Stoke: Trentham.

SooHoo, S. (1993) 'Students as partners in research and restructuring schools', *The Educational Forum,* 57: 386–92.

Times Educational Supplement (1997) 'Exclusions "spiral out of control"', *Times Educational Supplement,* 26 September: 25.

Wallace, G. (1996) 'Relating to teachers' in J. Rudduck, R. Chaplain and G. Wallace (eds) *School Improvement: what can pupils tell us?* London: David Fulton.

White, R. and Brockington, D. (1983) *Tales Out of School: consumers' views of British education,* London: Routledge and Kegan Paul.

Willis, P. (1977) *Learning to Labour: how working class kids get working class jobs,* Westmead: Saxon House.

Woods, P. (1990) *The Happiest Days?: how pupils cope with school,* London: Falmer Press.

Wright, C., Weeks, D., Mcglaughlin, A. and Webb, D. (1998) 'Masculinised discourse within education and the constitution of black male identities amongst African-Caribbean youth', *British Journal of Sociology of Education* 19(1): 75–87.

11 Teachers for the comprehensive idea

Ted Wragg

Teachers in comprehensive schools are asked to play many roles in our society. Not the least of these is the traditional one as 'keeper of the runes', bearer of what our civilization knows and has acquired over countless generations. Were that the only assignment teachers had to fulfil, then life would be more straightforward, but there are many others as well. In this contribution to the debate about the comprehensive secondary school, I want to analyze some of these roles. I shall do that, however, in the context of looking at the future, for without a vision of the future, as well as an awareness of the past, education would be unfounded, detached from the sub- and superstructures that hold it in place. Some of the ideas put forward in the first part of this analysis are described in greater detail elsewhere (Wragg 1997).

As medical treatments improve it becomes highly likely that children born in the late twentieth and early twenty-first century will live to be 90, 100 or more. The term 'future' can mean a very long time indeed. Some pupils may even survive until the twenty-second century. There can be a very long 'lead time' in education, and some payoffs may not occur for decades. If education is society's investment in its own posterity, then a long- rather than a short-term strategy is essential.

There have been numerous predictions about life in the twenty-first century, some gloomy, others more hopeful. Indeed, the same data can be quoted to support either a pessimistic or an optimistic vision of what is to come. Forecasts that job opportunities may diminish can be used to predict boredom and street riots, or to welcome the release of people from dangerous and demeaning employment. The benevolence or malevolence of those in positions of power can determine the climate within which education flourishes or languishes. The support, or lack of it, from ordinary citizens and their children can be greatly influential on the success of schools. In the end the quality and character of the teachers in any comprehensive school will exert a critical effect, even against the odds.

Even intelligent guesswork about present and past trends and where they might eventually lead can go disastrously astray, so it would be a mistake to base a whole education system entirely on a single conjecture. It is hazardous enough predicting next year's events on the basis of what is happening this year, let alone what will happen in the next millennium. Small wonder that the great oracles have often spoken in ambiguous terms. I propose to deal here, therefore, with a range of possibilities that seem to be worth considering, and see what the implications would be were they to materialize, though none of the following messages is offered with any certainty.

Education for an uncertain future

Will pupils who leave comprehensive schools find employment in future? The jobs that people hold do not consume the whole of their life, but they are an important part of it. Until fairly recently many men, if they lived long enough, worked for some fifty or so years before entering retirement, while women tended to work in paid employment for fewer years, or did not return to their previous career after giving birth to children. Changes in work patterns have been dramatic in the last third of the twentieth century, but it is not entirely clear where these changes are leading.

A series of industrial revolutions in the nineteenth century saw masses of people move out of rural areas and into cities, as they left agriculture to seek work in factories. In early Victorian Britain about a third of the population worked on the land. Today about 2 per cent of the workforce is employed in agriculture, a remarkable transformation in the landscape of working life. Several significant changes have taken place during the last three decades of the twentieth century, but the eventual outcome of these post-industrial revolutions remains clouded. The disappearance of millions of jobs in the manufacturing industry has not led to a single type of employer emerging to absorb those displaced during the labour-shedding process.

What was notable about these huge losses of traditional forms of employment was that the vast majority of posts that disappeared were unskilled, semi-skilled or barely skilled. Graduate employment also suffered, but the biggest decline was in areas where machines were brought in to perform the numerous tasks that had previously been carried out by armies of worker ants. Firms that used to employ dozens of girl school leavers to fill cardboard boxes with their products, and dozens of boy school leavers to load them onto lorries, replaced the girls with automated packing machines and the boys with a couple of fork lift truck operators. As in other countries our society began to put an enormous premium on skill, and for those without it the prospects became bleak.

Unemployment gradually appeared to be endemic rather than cyclical. Recessions earlier in the century had been followed by boom times. Workers dropped to a three-day week, or lost their jobs, only to regain exactly the same posts later, often with bonus and overtime payments, as the economy moved into a higher gear. When the cycle stopped it was partly because, in the new automated economy, no employer was going to get rid of two fork lift trucks and two drivers in order to employ twenty people with large biceps. Yet even in areas of high unemployment, there were vacancies. Unfortunately the vacancies did not always match the talents and skills of the jobless. It was of little consolation to the dispossessed coal miner or steel worker to see a job advert asking for someone to repair video recorders or computers.

Retraining became an important matter. Those who had no skills to sell, or whose skills had become outmoded, needed to acquire fresh human capital in order to become employable. There were even examples of people who did retrain and obtain another post, only to experience redundancy in their newly found career.

Serial retraining became a significant feature of their lives. It was not confined to the unskilled or those who worked in traditional craft trades in manufacturing industry.

In the case of office work, secretaries had to acquire the skills of word processing and other forms of information technology. Surgeons had to learn transplant surgery, the use of immuno-suppressive drugs, laser technology. Headteachers were pressed to turn into financial, marketing and resource management experts. Trade union officials, previously regarded as wage negotiators, found themselves increasingly involved in advising their workmates about compensation for accidents, or the workings of an industrial tribunal for those who had lost their jobs, so they needed higher reading competence in order to cope with the literature on health and safety at work, or employment protection. Some forms of knowledge and skill seemed to have a very short life before becoming obsolete. Few employees escaped the remorseless march of novelty and innovation.

There were other significant changes. New technology meant that certain kinds of activity could be done in the home, or in a remote satellite location at a distance from the main centre of production. Publishing, journalism, garment manufacture, design work, telephone sales, consultancy, all of these could, given the right equipment, be carried out as easily in someone's attic as in a noisy and crowded office or factory. The shift to much more part-time employment meant that women in particular often took jobs that required part of the day, rather than the whole of it. Many people moved to part-time employment as an element of an early retirement package. Hutton (1995) estimated the number of British part-time workers in the late twentieth century to be in excess of five million, of whom 80 per cent were women.

Part-time working and phased retirement liberated parts of the day and week for recreation or leisure, or for more time with family and friends. At its worst, however, part-timers and home workers were exploited, paid low wages, denied the same safety and employment protection rights as full-timers. Since some 70 per cent of all new part-time jobs were for sixteen hours a week or less (ibid.), this meant that the holders of them had no right to appeal against unfair dismissal or to redundancy payments. Much time had to be expended, by those who would have preferred a full-time post, trying to stitch together several part-time jobs, a practice which became known as 'portfolio' employment. Numerous families dropped to a lower standard of living because the male adult had lost his full-time job and the female adult had only been able to obtain a part-time post.

The new opportunities for employment that did emerge were often in service and support industries. Alongside smaller numbers of the big employers of labour, there sprang up numerous small and medium-sized businesses. Unfortunately a number of these did not succeed and bankruptcies increased as several small concerns ceased training. This added to the problems of those seeking work, as small firms closed and some failed entrepreneurs returned to being employees of someone else.

There are several important messages for comprehensive schools from this analysis of work trends. They include the following:

(a)   as the numbers of unskilled and semi-skilled jobs decline, a much higher level of knowledge and skill will be necessary, from those wishing to enter or remain in employment

(b)   if there are to be more jobs in service and support, leisure and recreation, rather than in factories, then social skills may become more valued

(c)   people may have to retrain significantly, several times in their adult lives, perhaps every five to seven years, so flexibility and willingness to continue learning are important

(d)   as more people take part-time jobs, or work from their own home or in a place remote from their employer's headquarters, qualities such as independence, resourcefulness and adaptability may be highly valued

(e)   people will need to know their rights and entitlements, as well as their obligations to others, if they are to play a full part in society, and not be exploited by the unscrupulous.

Home and family life may also continue to change. Those that have full-time jobs often worker longer hours than they did in earlier times. Others are frustrated that their talents and aspirations cannot find expression. Some people have too little to do, while others have too much. The increase in working hours is explained by a number of factors. It is partly because of what Handy (1994) called the $\frac{1}{2} \times 2 \times 3$ formula. Productivity and profit are increased if half the previous workforce are paid twice their salary, to obtain three times as much output. The unemployed or under-occupied may pursue income-generating 'hobbies', like vegetable growing, collecting (buying and selling artefacts), decorating, or car repair.

Home and family life now require greater knowledge and skill than in former times. Families run into debt if they are unable to manage their own finances. Some fall victim to 'loan sharks' and others who prey on the ill-educated, paying vast amounts of interest on small loans which leave them in thrall for years. The predators in society exploit those whose rudimentary levels of numeracy, literacy or oral competence mean they are unable to calculate percentages, read legalistic agreements, or argue with articulate and persuasive usurers. Citizens unable to compose a letter, attend and speak at a public meeting, or combine with others to lobby decision-makers, may find their child is unable to obtain the school place of his or her choice. All of these combine to exert considerable pressure on both primary and secondary schools to extract the maximum benefit from the eleven years of compulsory schooling.

The four ages

There have been and continue to be significant changes during what are sometimes called the four ages. The first age is the age of full-time education and training, the second age the period of working life, the third age the years of healthy retirement, and the fourth age represents the time of infirmity. Since the nineteenth century, when large numbers of people never even reached the later ages, the transformation has been dramatic. Children in school today, for example, may find that it is their third, rather than their second, age which occupies the greatest number of years.

These four ages have transformed dramatically. The first age has become longer. For much of the nineteenth century children were not required to attend school at all, and in many cases commenced employment at the age of ten or earlier. The twentieth century saw a significant lengthening of the first age as, in the United Kingdom, the school leaving age was fixed at 14 following the First World War, at 15 after the Second World War, and at 16 in the 1970s. Subsequently the advent of higher unemployment produced a variety of youth training schemes, first of a few months and later lasting one and eventually two years. This effectively lengthened the first age from less than a decade in the nineteenth century to more like 18 years for the majority by the late twentieth century.

Evidence from earlier in the nineteenth century shows that girls, on average, entered the age of menarche, that is, started their periods, at about the age of 17. By the late twentieth century the average age of menarche was down to about 12½. In the nineteenth century, children left the first age physically immature and were still children for the first few years of their second age, when they commenced work. By the late twentieth century it was the exact opposite. They reached physical maturity only to find that they had to spend at least four, and possibly up to ten more years in the first age, unable to start in a job. Boys in particular often go through a period of aggression on reaching physical maturity, so teachers in comprehensive schools have had to contain and educate potentially aggressive young adults who, 100 years previously, would have been well into their second age and off school premises. What had been an external social problem in Victorian times had now become an internal school problem.

The second age has shortened at both ends. Children enter work later, and adults begin to leave it earlier. For many in Victorian times the second age was virtually their whole life, as killer diseases like typhoid and tuberculosis, the ravages of war, and deaths in childbirth robbed millions of their third and fourth age. It is difficult to say what the second age will become in future for those currently in school, as it may be that improved health in later years might lead to it lengthening once more, if people choose and have opportunities to work into their seventies. Present indications are that for many people it may not last more than thirty-five years.

By contrast the third age, the period of healthy retirement that was non-existent for most in the nineteenth century, when a mere 6 or so per cent of the population was over 60, is becoming dramatically longer, as the 60+ age group swells to a quarter or more of the population. Handy (1994) cites surveys showing that only a third of British adults over the age of 55 are still in paid employment, and in France and Italy the figures are 27 per cent and 11 per cent respectively. Many children currently in school may experience twenty, thirty or even forty years in the third age.

This particular social change has considerable implications for teachers in comprehensive schools, since children who are disenchanted with their schooling may be reluctant to take on fresh intellectual challenges in their third age. The evidence suggests that older people are perfectly capable of learning new knowledge and skills. Although they may need a little more time and slightly longer intervals between 'lessons', they can often draw on a wider range of strategies than are available to younger people with more limited experience. The Open University has thousands of students who graduate in their seventies and eighties.

Even during the fourth age, the time of infirmity, when the elderly may be confined indoors, most will be perfectly capable of continuing to learn something new, and continued mental activity in old age is often closely associated with better general health. According to 1990 census data, there are over 36,000 centenarians living in the United States. Hence the importance for the highly significant third age, and the not insignificant fourth age, of effective groundwork, particularly during the first age.

The many roles of the comprehensive school teacher

Traditionally teachers are *transmitters of knowledge*. They introduce their pupils to the knowledge, skills, values, attitudes and forms of behaviour that civilized societies have accumulated over several centuries. Millions of years passed before intelligent life worked out that water molecules consist of two atoms of hydrogen and one of oxygen. Teachers can transmit that information in seconds. However, the sheer amount of knowledge now available is awesome. It was dubious whether anyone could really absorb all of what was known even during times when 'Universal Man' was supposed to exist. In the eighteenth century writers like Goethe, who composed poetry, novels, plays, historical and philosophical works, and even a scientific treatise, were admired as complete scholars, yet they only knew a fraction of what had been discovered.

The quest for universal knowledge would be an impossibility in the late twentieth and early twenty-first centuries, as millions of books, articles, films, radio and television programmes, as well as ideas expressed in electronic media, are produced every year. Even with access to international databases containing millions of research findings in every imaginable field, it is inconceivable that anyone will personally know more than the tiniest portion of all knowledge available in their discipline or area of interest. The gathering of knowledge seems to be an activity which will, if anything, continue to quicken in future.

The consequences for teachers of this remorseless addition to the store of human knowledge are of several kinds. First of all, though we cannot teach everything, we have to teach something. Hence the interminable debates and discussions about the *content* of various subject curriculums. In a vast field like health education, for example, what should pupils study at the age of 11, 13 or 15? When can they best learn about the need for a healthy diet and exercise regime, or the effects on health of smoking, alcohol or drugs? Some may already have been exposed to these in their primary school. What information, skills, attitudes and forms of behaviour might pupils need to acquire? When might be too late and when too soon to study a particular topic?

The second consequence of the knowledge explosion is that if we cannot teach everything in school, and have to settle for a small proportion of what exists, then pupils have to know how to find out for themselves. The ability to track down vital information, abstract its essence, work out how to apply what we have learned often without external help, is a key element of independence of mind and action.

Most adults have to make numerous decisions on their own during the day, some trivial, like where to shop, others more profound, like what actions to take in their working or home life. This ability to explore, discover and then act, often with tenacity and imagination, is particularly crucial given the points made earlier about the length of adult life and the importance of the third age. Pupils need to experience many forms of teaching and learning if they are to be both autonomous and good team members in adult life, and it is a pity that the public debate about teaching styles has concentrated on a stereotyped division between 'traditional' and 'progressive' approaches. In the twenty-first century major social, as well as technological and scientific, problems are likely to be resolved by small or large teams of resourceful and flexible adults.

We live in a society that is rich in information, but information is not the same as knowledge. Information is 'out there'; knowledge is what is inside the brain, digested and understood. Indeed, children in particular, unable to chart a path through the dense mass, might despair if left to explore unaided. What is essential in this burgeoning expanse of information is people who can structure and track what is going on: in other words, *teachers as annotators* who can help to unravel and explain what might otherwise be an enormous bewildering maze. Other annotators include writers, publishers, broadcasters. In the future, as in the present, numerous sources of information will be available to pupils other than what their teachers choose to bring before them, and it will be important for them to develop the skill and resourcefulness not only to act on advice and help, but also to pursue their own pathways through what they are studying.

Alongside the many demands on comprehensive school teachers as repositories of subject expertise are numerous others. Some of these are social roles. For example, there are pupils who fail to attend school. Teachers have to try and ensure that they are present, even if children's parents condone their absence. *Teacher as jailer* is an assignment that ought not to exist in an ideal world, but the reality is that schools are also judged partly by truancy tables, so failure to keep in those who would rather be absent is seen as a dereliction of duty.

One prime strategy is to make sure that the work done is sufficiently interesting to ensure that pupils are keen to attend, but even the most dynamic and engaging of teachers may still find that some pupils are reluctant to come to school no matter what they do. Yet support services for teachers have been eroded as a consequence of large reductions in the budgets of local education authorities. In keeping with the 'tough talking' image that many politicians prefer, there are proposals for volunteers to report truants seen in shopping centres and elsewhere, rather than the hiring of more Education Welfare Officers, or home–school liaison teachers.

'I am a teacher, not a social worker' is a slogan that has been declaimed at teachers' conferences for many years. *Teacher as social worker* is a role that some teachers take on gladly, others reluctantly. Certainly few have been trained properly for it, even though they may teach children from families with severe problems. I asked one of my former students how she was enjoying her first year of teaching. It was fine in most respects, she explained, but she found the circumstances in which some pupils lived to be harrowing, and she regularly made breakfast in her laboratory for two pupils who never had much to eat at home. Running soup kitchens was something of which the Mafia proudly boasted, but the only decent meal that some children will get is their school lunch.

Indeed, *teacher as parent* is an interesting variant of this particular role. Teachers may find they are given confidential information by their pupils, or even asked for advice by those who have no one else to turn to. Many senior women teachers have at some time had a private conversation with a girl who either was, or thought she might be, pregnant. Teachers' own role as a parent might also be called into question, particularly in lessons to do with pastoral care, the teaching of literature and the humanities. Where their own children attend school, their attitudes towards teenage behaviour in their own family, the career choices their children make, can all be given scrutiny. In small communities it is especially difficult to detach personal life from professional life.

There is another important aspect of teacher as parent. Good parents fight for their children's rights, stand up for them, support them when they are down, treat them fairly, give them every chance. It is more difficult for teachers to generate equivalent effort for every single child in a large secondary school, but many do put themselves out to ensure justice, fairness and fair opportunities. This is what comprehensive education is supposed to stand for.

Teacher as hero is an image that appeals to young people before they start their career, determined to shed light wherever there is darkness, but to their dismay they soon see their profession depicted in the popular press as the Anti-Christ. Heroes are of many kinds. Some, like Hercules, show great physical prowess, personal skill and ingenuity. Others heroes are more reflective, producing great works of art, music and literature, writing inspirational treatises or making important scientific discoveries. Teachers are often only labelled 'heroes' in the public mind if they display courage when their children are in danger.

The daily job of educating the next generation is seen as more mundane and routine, unglamorous to the outside world. Perhaps those who work in public service should be resigned to being categorized in this low-key way. On the other hand many teachers fill out the concept of 'hero', albeit in a modest way, and few adults would not acknowledge a lifelong debt to at least one of their mentors, no small contribution to society. I was once talking to James Stone, or 'Joe' as he was known, the imaginative Chief Education Officer of Nottinghamshire in the 1970s, about the frustrations of trying to cope with the many difficulties in education. Hercules, I pointed out, found a quick solution to the problem of clearing out years of accumulated dung in the Augean stables by knocking a hole in each end and diverting a river through them. Joe reflected for a moment. 'The trouble is,' he mused, 'I'd never get planning permission.' It is increasingly difficult for teachers to be heroes amid shelves full of government regulations and syllabuses.

Just as pupils need to be able to work in teams as preparation for a complex future, so too do teachers. *Teachers as team players* is a vital part of comprehensive education, as most will belong to a subject team, a planning group, or an administrative unit. Harmonious rather than dissonant relationships are essential ingredients of successful teams. Learning to pool one's knowledge and skills as part of a greater whole is an important element of such spectacular global enterprises as the

American space programme, which involves the world's leading authorities on a variety of scientific, technical and human matters, combining their expertise to achieve what none of them could do individually. On a more modest scale team play is also a feature of the comprehensive school staffroom.

Teams need leadership, and it is not only the responsibility of the head to provide this. Many teachers will, at one time or another, offer leadership to their colleagues. The model I prefer is that of *teacher as Viennese orchestra conductor*. There is a tradition in Vienna, when playing Strauss in particular, for the conductor to join in, not merely wave a baton. Viennese conductors are themselves proficient musicians, usually violinists, so they often hold their instrument, wave their bow, and then, with evident enjoyment, play along with the orchestra during certain passages. Admittedly it must be difficult for double bass or tuba players, but leadership through participation and collaboration must be a better model than one based on conflict or a sense of superiority.

The formidable demands of these several roles mean that teachers need to rethink what they do. Skilful and sensitive appraisal can be an important part of this, but the Leverhulme Appraisal Project (Wragg *et al.* 1996) found that only half of the teachers in the sample said that they changed what they did as a result of appraisal. Many found there was not enough time for a proper analysis, few had experience of studying classroom processes in a systematic way, and over a quarter of teachers were only observed once instead of the minimum of two sessions that was required.

Lack of time and the conflicting demands of other priorities means that professional development can, if we are not careful, become crude and pragmatic. I have written elsewhere (Wragg 1994) about the need for dynamic practitioners in dynamic schools, reflecting judiciously and then improving what they do, and I reject entirely the mechanistic approach of some vocational qualifications which, at their worst, make for *teacher as YTS trainee*.

I was once served breakfast by a YTS trainee who had received what was known as 'training to standards'. Checklist duly completed he brought me a plate of bacon and eggs, cleared it away nicely when I had finished, and then served me the grapefruit. It reminded me of the television sketch in which Eric Morecambe is accused by André Previn of not playing the correct notes. 'I am playing the right notes,' he replies indignantly, 'but not necessarily in the right order.' Teachers lay down deep structures over a professional lifetime which determine how they teach. The crude competency approach which dominates the thinking of the Teacher Training Agency is completely inadequate for the complexities I have described.

One role which has become increasingly important in education is that of public relations officer, *teacher as Kenneth Baker* as it should be known, in honour of a Secretary of State who set the standard for attaching more importance to form and tone than to substance. Glossy brochures, advertising, image-making are all well established artefacts of the commercial world that have begun to intrude into education as part of the market model. Yet the commercial analogy hardly bears scrutiny. None of these things increases the numbers of pupils, in the way that advertising might increase sales. All of them sap teachers' time and energy away from their central purpose, and money is wasted on moving round a small number of pupils.

But the saddest role at present is that of *teacher as football manager*. This applies in particular to heads. Just as football managers are made to resign if their team has a bad run, irrespective of whether or not they have acted intelligently, so too teachers are scapegoated in the press and by politicians. Increasingly after an inspection by the Office for Standards in Education headteachers resign, not always justifiably. Many teachers now leave the profession early, some three-quarters quitting before they reach retirement age. Over 6,000 teachers now retire each year on health grounds, a threefold increase in eight years. In many cases it is a scandalous waste.

Like karaoke singers teachers may now find that the music moves on relentlessly whether or not they can mouth the words fast enough. If education is as important as society, the press, politicians and others always say it is, then the least we should be doing is supporting teachers in comprehensive schools. In the world of business and commerce it is regarded as good practice to make demands on workers, set targets, but then to provide the means by which the targets can be met, a two-sided contract. It should not be too much to ask for teachers in comprehensive schools, especially those working in the most difficult circumstances, to be given the same opportunities.

References

Handy, C. (1994) *The Empty Raincoat: Making Sense of the Future*, London: Hutchinson.
Hutton, W. (1995) *The State We're In*, London: Jonathan Cape.
Wragg, E.C. (1994) *An Introduction to Classroom Observation*, London: Routledge.
Wragg, E.C. (1997) *The Cubic Curriculum*, London: Routledge.
Wragg, E.C., Wikeley, F.J., Wragg, C.M. and Haynes, G.S. (1996) *Teacher Appraisal Observed*, London: Routledge.

Section 3

Classrooms

12 Life in classrooms

Philip Jackson

School is a place where tests are failed and passed, where amusing things happen, where new insights are stumbled upon, and skills acquired. But it is also a place in which people sit, and listen, and wait, and raise their hands, and pass out paper, and stand in line, and sharpen pencils. School is where we encounter both friends and foes, where imagination is unleashed and misunderstanding brought to ground. But it is also a place in which yawns are stifled and initials scratched on desktops, where milk money is collected and recess lines are formed. Both aspects of school life, the celebrated and the unnoticed, are familiar to all of us, but the latter, if only because of its characteristic neglect, seems to deserve more attention than it has received to date from those who are interested in education.

In order to appreciate the significance of trivial classroom events, it is necessary to consider the frequency of their occurrence, the standardization of the school environment, and the compulsory quality of daily attendance. We must recognize, in other words, that children are in school for a long time, that the settings in which they perform are highly uniform, and that they are there whether they want to be or not. Each of these three facts, although seemingly obvious, deserves some elaboration, for each contributes to our understanding of how students feel about and cope with their school experience.

The amount of time children spend in school can be described with a fair amount of quantitative precision, although the psychological significance of the numbers involved is another matter entirely. In the US, in most states, the school year legally comprises 180 days. A full session on each of those days usually lasts about six hours (with a break for lunch), beginning somewhere around nine o'clock in the morning and ending about three o'clock in the afternoon. Thus, if a student never misses a day during the year, he spends a little more than 1,000 hours under the care and tutelage of teachers. If he has attended kindergarten and was reasonably regular in his attendance during the grades, he will have logged a little more than 7,000 classroom hours by the time he is ready for junior high school.

The magnitude of 7,000 hours spread over six or seven years of a child's life is difficult to comprehend. On the one hand, when placed beside the total number of hours the child has lived during those years, it is not very great – slightly more than one-tenth of his life during the time in question, about one-third of his hours of sleep during that period. On the other hand, aside from sleeping and perhaps playing, there is no other activity that occupies as much of the child's time as that involved in attending school. Apart from the bedroom (where he has his eyes closed most of the time) there is no single enclosure in which he spends a longer time than he does in the classroom. From the age of six onward he is a more familiar sight to his teacher than to his father, and possibly even to his mother.

A classroom, like a church auditorium, is rarely seen as being anything other than that which it is. No one entering either place is likely to think that he is in a living room, or a grocery store, or a train station. Even if he entered at midnight or at some other time when the activities of the people would not give the function away, he would have no difficulty understanding what was *supposed* to go on there. Even devoid of people, a church is a church and a classroom, a classroom.

This is not to say, of course, that all classrooms are identical, any more than all churches are. Clearly there are differences, and sometimes very extreme ones, between any two settings. One has only to think of the wooden benches and planked floor of the early American classroom as compared with the plastic chairs and tile flooring in today's suburban schools. But the resemblance is still there despite the differences, and, more important, during any particular historical period the differences are not that great. Also, whether the student moves from first to sixth grade on floors of vinyl tile or oiled wood, whether he spends his days in front of a black blackboard or a green one, is not as important as the fact that the environment in which he spends these six or seven years is highly stable.

In their efforts to make their classrooms more homelike, elementary school teachers often spend considerable time fussing with the room's decorations. Bulletin boards are changed, new pictures are hung, and the seating arrangement is altered from circles to rows and back again. But these are surface adjustments at best, resembling the work of the inspired housewife who rearranges the living room furniture and changes the colour of the drapes in order to make the room more 'interesting'. School bulletin boards may be changed but they are never discarded, the seats may be rearranged but thirty of them are there to stay, the teacher's desk may have a new plant on it but there it sits, as ubiquitous as the roll-down maps, the drab olive wastebasket, and the pencil sharpener on the window ledge.

Even the odours of the classroom are fairly standardized. Schools may use different brands of wax and cleaning fluid, but they all seem to contain similar ingredients, a sort of universal smell which creates an aromatic background that permeates the entire building. Added to this, in each classroom, is the acrid scent of chalk dust and the faint hint of fresh wood from the pencil shavings. In some rooms, especially at lunch time, there is the familiar odour of orange peels and peanut butter sandwiches, a blend that mingles in the late afternoon (following recess) with the delicate pungency of children's perspiration. If a person stumbled into a classroom blindfolded, his nose alone, if he used it carefully, would tell him where he was.

All of these sights and smells become so familiar to students and teachers alike that they exist dimly, on the periphery of awareness. Only when the classroom is encountered under somewhat unusual circumstances does it appear, for a moment, a strange place filled with objects that command our attention. On these rare occasions when, for example, students return to school in the evening, or in the summer when the halls ring with the hammers of workmen, many features of the school environment that have merged into an undifferentiated background for its daily inhabitants suddenly stand out in sharp relief. This experience, which obviously occurs in contexts other than the classroom, can only happen in settings to which the viewer has become uncommonly habituated.

Not only is the classroom a relatively stable physical environment, it also provides a fairly constant social context. Behind the same old desks sit the same old students, in front of the familiar blackboard stands the familiar teacher. There are changes, to be sure – some students come and go during the year and on a few mornings the children are greeted at the door by a strange adult. But in most cases these events are sufficiently uncommon to create a flurry of excitement in the room. Moreover, in most elementary classrooms the social composition is not only stable, it is also physically arranged with considerable regularity. Each student has an assigned seat and, under normal circumstances, that is where he is to be found. The practice of assigning seats makes it possible for the teacher or a student to take attendance at a glance. A quick visual sweep is usually sufficient to determine who is there and who is not. The ease with which this procedure is accomplished reveals more eloquently than do words how accustomed each member of the class is to the presence of every other member.

An additional feature of the social atmosphere of elementary classrooms deserves at least passing comment. There is a social intimacy in schools that is unmatched elsewhere in our society. Buses and movie theatres may be more crowded than classrooms, but people rarely stay in such densely populated settings for extended periods of time and, while there, they usually are not expected to concentrate on work or to interact with each other. Even factory workers are not clustered as closely together as students in a standard classroom. Indeed, imagine what would happen if a factory the size of a typical elementary school contained three or four hundred adult workers. In all likelihood the unions would not allow it. Only in schools do thirty or more people spend several hours each day literally side by side. Once we leave the classroom we seldom again are required to have contact with so many people for so long a time.

A final aspect of the constancy experienced by young students involves the ritualistic and cyclic quality of the activities carried on in the classroom. The daily schedule, as an instance, is commonly divided into definite periods during which specific subjects are to be studied or specific activities engaged in. The content of the work surely changes from day to day and from week to week, and in this sense there is considerable variety amid the constancy. But spelling still comes after arithmetic on Tuesday morning, and when the teacher says, 'All right class, now take out your spellers', his announcement comes as no surprise to the students. Further, as they search in their desks for their spelling textbooks, the children may not know what new words will be included in the day's assignment, but they have a fairly clear idea of what the next twenty minutes of class time will entail.

Despite the diversity of subject matter content, the identifiable forms of classroom activity are not great in number. The labels: 'seatwork', 'group discussion', 'teacher demonstration', and 'question-and-answer period' (which would include work 'at the board') are sufficient to categorize most of the things that happen when class is in session. 'Audio-visual display', 'testing session', and 'games' might be added to the list, but in most elementary classrooms they occur rarely.

Each of these major activities is performed according to rather well-defined rules which the students are expected to understand and obey – for example, no loud talking during seatwork, do not interrupt someone else during discussion, keep your eyes on your own paper during tests, raise your hand if you have a question. Even in the early grades these rules are so well understood by the students (if not completely internalized) that the teacher has only to give very abbreviated signals ('Voices, class', 'Hands, please') when violations are perceived. In many classrooms a weekly time schedule is permanently posted so that everyone can tell at a glance what will happen next.

Thus, when our young student enters school in the morning he is entering an environment with which he has become exceptionally familiar through prolonged exposure. Moreover, it is a fairly stable environment – one in which the physical objects, social relations, and major activities remain much the same from day to day, week to week, and even, in certain respects, from year to year. Life there resembles life in other contexts in some ways, but not all. There is, in other words, a uniqueness to the student's world. School, like church and home, is someplace special. Look where you may, you will not find another place quite like it.

There is an important fact about a student's life that teachers and parents often prefer not to talk about, at least not in front of students. This is the fact that young people have to be in school, whether they want to be or not. In this regard students have something in common with the members of two other of our social institutions that have involuntary attendance: prisons and mental hospitals. The analogy, though dramatic, is not intended to be shocking, and certainly there is no comparison between the unpleasantness of life for inmates of our prisons and mental institutions, on the one hand, and the daily travails of a first or second grader, on the other. Yet the school child, like the incarcerated adult, is, in a sense, a prisoner. He too must come to grips with the inevitability of his experience. He too must develop strategies for dealing with the conflict that frequently arises between his natural desires and interests on the one hand and institutional expectations on the other. The thousands of hours spent in the highly stylized environment of the elementary classroom are not, in an ultimate sense, a matter of choice, even though some children might prefer school to play. Many seven-year-olds skip happily to school, and as parents and teachers we are glad they do, but we stand ready to enforce the attendance of those who are more reluctant. And our vigilance does not go unnoticed by children.

In sum, classrooms are special places. The things that happen there and the ways in which they happen combine to make these settings different from all others. This is not to say, of course, that there is no similarity between what goes on in school and the students' experiences elsewhere. Classrooms are indeed like homes and churches and hospital wards in many important respects. But not in all.

The things that make schools different from other places are not only the paraphernalia of learning and teaching and the educational content of the dialogues that take place there, although these are the features that are usually singled out when we try to portray what life in school is really like. It is true that nowhere else do we find blackboards and teachers and textbooks in such abundance and nowhere else is so much time spent on reading, writing, and arithmetic. But these obvious characteristics do not constitute all that is unique about this environment. There are other features, much less obvious though equally omnipresent, that help to make up 'the facts of life', as it were, to which students must adapt. From the standpoint of understanding the impact of school life on the student some features of the classroom that are not immediately visible are fully as important as those that are.

The characteristics of school life to which we now turn our attention are not commonly mentioned by students, at least not directly, nor are they apparent to the casual observer. Yet they are as real, in a sense, as the unfinished portrait of Washington that hangs above the cloakroom door. They comprise three facts of life with which even the youngest student must learn to deal and may be introduced by the key words: *crowds*, *praise*, and *power*.

Learning to live in a classroom involves, among other things, learning to live in a crowd. This simple truth has already been mentioned, but it requires greater elaboration. Most of the things that are done in school are done with others, or at least in the presence of others, and this fact has profound implications for determining the quality of a student's life.

Of equal importance is the fact that schools are, basically, evaluative settings. The very young student may be temporarily fooled by tests that are presented as games, but it doesn't take long before he begins to see through the subterfuge and comes to realize that school, after all, is a serious business. It is not only what you do there but what others think of what you do that is important. Adaptation to school life requires the student to become used to living under the constant condition of having his words and deeds evaluated by others.

School is also a place in which the division between the weak and the powerful is clearly drawn. This may sound like a harsh way to describe the separation between teachers and students, but it serves to emphasize a fact that is often overlooked, or touched upon gingerly at best. Teachers are indeed more powerful than students, in the sense of having greater responsibility for giving shape to classroom events, and this sharp difference in authority is another feature of school life with which students must learn how to deal.

In three major ways then – as members of crowds, as potential recipients of praise or reproof, and as pawns of institutional authorities – students are confronted with aspects of reality that at least during their childhood years are relatively confined to the hours spent in classrooms. Admittedly, similar conditions are encountered in other environments. Students, when they are not performing as such, must often find themselves lodged within larger groups, serving as targets of praise or reproof, and being bossed around or guided by persons in positions of higher authority. But these kinds of experience are particularly frequent while school is in session and it is likely during this time that adaptive strategies having relevance for other contexts and other life periods are developed.

13 Has classroom teaching served its day?

Donald McIntyre

Introduction: What is teaching?

Teaching is a relatively easy concept to define: teaching is acting so as deliberately and directly to facilitate learning. While *what* is done to achieve the purpose of teaching may be almost infinitely diverse, it is the purpose of these activities, not the activities themselves, which is definite. Similarly, teaching of important kinds is undertaken in many different contexts and by many people in diverse roles. The concept of teaching has no implications for *where* or *by whom* teaching is done. It is only the purpose of the activity, that of facilitating learning, that is crucial to the definition.

This definition of teaching is of course a crude one, which might properly be the subject of various elaborations and qualifications. Yet the central truth that it offers is of much more then semantic importance, since it emphasizes the point that, in a world where the importance of learning is beyond debate, nothing can be taken for granted about the importance of any kind of teaching, except its purpose of facilitating learning. Answers to the question of what kind of teaching is needed or is useful must always be contingent on answers to other questions, primarily about what will best facilitate the kinds of learning that we most want.

We have become accustomed to having various institutions designed for the facilitation of learning, and it is a matter of judgement as to whether it will be helpful to go back to first principles to question the value of any of these institutions. Two such institutions which each have a history of at least two or three millennia are those of *professional teaching* and *schools*. Arguments have certainly been offered, some decades ago, for questioning the usefulness of these institutions for the twenty-first century (Illich 1976: Reimer 1971). Yet the scale of the learning in which everyone needs to engage for twenty-first century living makes the idea of doing without schools look increasingly like a romantic dream. For the purposes of this chapter it will be assumed that schooling is necessary, and that professional teaching is necessary to make it work. But it will not be assumed that schooling needs to be organized as it has been in the twentieth century. On the contrary, this chapter argues that a more significant issue concerns the dominant way in which professional teaching in schools has been structured during the last century or two, and it asks how well suited that way of structuring professional teaching is for the contentious and problematic tasks which school teachers currently face. That dominant way of structuring professional teaching in schools is taken to be classroom teaching.

In raising this issue, the chapter seeks quite explicitly to challenge current suggestions that the central issues facing schooling are to be construed primarily in terms of *teachers'* skills:

> Expectations of politicians, parents and employers of what schools should accomplish in terms of student achievement, broadly conceived, have been rising for over twenty years. And they will continue to accelerate as we take further steps into the information age or the knowledge society. … It is plain that if teachers do not acquire and display the capacity to redefine their skills for the task of teaching, and if they do not model in their own conduct the very qualities – flexibility, networking, creativity – that are now key outcomes for students, then the challenge of schooling in the next millennium will not be met.
>
> (Hargreaves 1999: 122–3)

While David Hargreaves' above diagnosis of the situation must be very largely correct, the argument here is that he, together with the British government, its Teacher Training Agency and many others, is wrong to suggest that the solution can be found simply through the further development of teachers' expertise. The general thesis of this chapter is instead that, however hard teachers work, however sensitive they are to what is needed, however skilled they become, there are limits to what is possible through the classroom teaching system that we have inherited. Furthermore, we may be approaching these limits now, at a time when much more is being expected of schools; and so it is unlikely that expectations can be met except by going beyond the classroom teaching system. […]

Life in classrooms

The above subheading is borrowed from the title of a book by Philip Jackson, published in 1968. It was one of the first and most influential of the many studies which, in the last 30 years, have sought very usefully to stand back from the question, 'What ought teachers to be doing?' to ask the prior question, 'How can we best understand what teachers do?'

One of the features of classrooms that Jackson noted was that they are busy and crowded places, which led to 'four unpublicised features of school life: delay, denial, interruption, and social distraction' (Jackson 1968: 17) and imposed severe constraints upon how teachers and pupils could work. Later investigators have picked up this theme of the complexity of classroom life. It has perhaps been most fully articulated by Doyle in terms of 'six intrinsic features of the classroom environment [which] create constant pressures that shape the task of teaching' (Doyle 1986: 394–5). These he identified as:

1 *Multidimensionality*   There are not only many different people in any classroom, with different preferences, needs and abilities, but also many different tasks to which the teacher has to attend. A restricted range of resources must be used for different purposes. Many different events must be planned and implemented in

mutually complementary ways, taking account of differences among people and constantly changing circumstances. 'Records must be kept, schedules met, supplies organised and stored, and student work collected and evaluated.' Furthermore, each event has multiple possible repercussions, especially in terms of the implications of the teacher's interactions with one pupil for the work of others. Choices, therefore, are never simple.

2   *Simultaneity*   Many things happen at once in classrooms. Most simply, whatever type of activity is going on, the teacher has to attend to what all the pupils are doing. Are they engaged in appropriate activities? Are they understanding what they are doing? Are they interested? Do they need help or guidance of one sort or another? At the same time, whatever the type of activity, the teacher needs to be concerned with the passage of time, the standard of work being done, the needs of all pupils and appropriate ways of taking the learning forward. The teacher must monitor and regulate several different activities at once.

3   *Immediacy*   This refers to the rapid pace of classroom events. Teachers in practice are constantly engaged in successive, quick interactions with pupils, giving directions and explanations, questioning or answering questions, commenting, praising, or reprimanding, and all the time deciding whether to intervene in an individual or group's activities or not, whether to interrupt one conversation or activity in order to engage in another more urgent one, and with the constant need to maintain the momentum and flow of events. In most instances, therefore, teachers have little time to reflect before acting.

4   *Unpredictability*   It is difficult to predict how any activity will go on a particular day with a particular group of pupils. In addition, individual pupils have unexpected needs, and interruptions and distractions are frequent. Detailed long-term planning is counterproductive and even short-term plans need to be very flexible.

5   *Transparency*   (or 'publicness' to use Doyle's term) 'Teachers act in fishbowls, each child normally can see how the others are treated' (Lortie 1975: 70, quoted by Doyle 1986). Whatever teachers do in classrooms is observed by all the pupils, who thus learn important information about the teachers' skills and attitudes. What teachers do on any occasion can have important future repercussions.

6   *History*   When the same class meets with a teacher several times each week over many months, it establishes shared experiences, understandings and norms which inform its future activities. For example, early meetings of classes with their teachers can often shape events for the rest of the year. Planning and decision-making need to take account of a class's history.

There are of course many other complexities which teachers in specific circumstances face. For example, the tension between 'covering' a set curriculum and preparing pupils for external assessments on one hand, and trying to teach for understanding or the development of autonomy on the other, can be a major complicating factor in teachers' work. Similarly, trying to ensure thorough learning while at the same time trying to 'sell' the subject can add to the complexity. And the ever-widening range of responsibilities given to teachers, for example for identifying pupils' special needs or possible symptoms of child abuse, or checking immediately on unexplained absences, makes classroom teaching an extraordinarily complex job. [...]

Summary of the argument

Research on the nature of expert classroom teaching suggests that expert class-room teachers are highly impressive in the complexity of the information that they constructively take into account in order to achieve their purposes. Their expertise seems exceptionally well tuned to the realities of classroom teaching. It involves:

1 very sophisticated, experience-based schemata
2 highly intuitive judgements and decision-making
3 largely tacit, individual and quite private expert knowledge
4 prioritization and simplification geared to teaching purposes, for example, through

- short-term perspectives
- working within classroom walls
- simplification of differences among pupils
- practicality.

Some limitations of current classroom teaching

Having developed as a very distinctive type of expertise over the last two centuries, classroom teaching is at its best very good at doing certain kinds of things, less good at others. Of course, not all good classroom teaching is the same; most strikingly, classrooms for different age-groups tend to be very different. The early years class-room, in which the teacher is not only with the same class throughout the school day, but also aspires to concern himself with the multifaceted development of each 'whole child', is very different from the narrowly focused A-level classroom, memorably described by Stevens (1960), in which the teacher's expertise may be directed solely towards her pupils' examination success. But these are, it is claimed, variations on a central theme: classroom teaching, with one adult figure responsible for the learning of a substantial number of young people within one large room for substantial periods of time, has its distinctive strengths and limitations.

Its strengths, as already argued, are reflected in its total and virtually unchallenged dominance of schooling throughout the twentieth century. It has allowed mass schooling on an unprecedented scale not only to be possible but also to achieve enormous success; it has kept millions of young people of ever-increasing ages off the labour market and generally peaceful and law-abiding; and it has enabled most of them to be literate, numerate and to acquire diverse qualifications and knowledge which have allowed them more or less to thrive in societies that have been changing at an accelerating rate.

None the less, it is the limitations of this classroom teaching system which are most frequently commented upon. These frequent complaints are of course rarely focused on the system, but instead upon those who inhabit the system: most frequently teachers, but also teacher educators, educational researchers, school managers, parents and young people. It would be as wrong to assume that the system is inherently flawed as it is to assume that any of these different groups of people are generically incompetent or irresponsible; but it is useful to look at the nature of some of the complaints that are frequently made and to relate these to what has already been said about the nature of classroom teaching expertise.

The general thesis of this chapter is that many of the complaints made about the inadequacies of schoolteaching in recent years can best be understood as complaints about teachers' failure to take account in their teaching of various kinds of information or evidence. These complaints are therefore seen as fundamental challenges to the sophisticated kind of classroom expertise upon which teachers have learned to depend, with its emphasis on the intuitive and the tacit, on prioritization and on simplification. It is not suggested that it is impossible for classroom teachers to respond to any such demands; there is plenty of evidence that classroom teaching is, within limits, quite flexible, and that classroom teachers can, when motivated by strong convictions or pressures, adapt their teaching to take account of new kinds of information. It is suggested, however, that classroom teaching is not at all well suited as a system to meeting the demand that all these multiple kinds of information should be used by teachers. It is further suggested, therefore, that it is this unsuitability of classroom teaching as a system that has led teachers to be generally unresponsive to these demands and complaints, even though the use of each of these kinds of information can plausibly be argued to contribute to increased teaching effectiveness.

Classroom teachers characteristically make their task more manageable by prioritizing, and simplifying, the information available to them. Each of these has brought with it complaints and demands for change from critics who believe that pupils' learning could be more effectively facilitated if such prioritization and simplification were avoided. On the other hand, informed observers might reasonably argue that, unfortunate as it is that teachers do not make fuller use of the wider range of information potentially available to them, neglect of that information is a reasonable price to pay for the benefits of skilled classroom teaching. However, if it is the case that mounting complaints of diverse kinds are all to be understood as consequences of the complexity of classroom life and of teachers' best efforts to cope with it, then it might seem that the balance of the argument has swung against the classroom system, and that the costs to be paid for continuing to rely upon it are too great. The focus of the chapter now turns to five major areas of concern:

1   differentiation
2   formative assessment
3   home–school partnership
4   students' own perspectives
5   teaching as an evidence-based profession.

These will be examined in turn below.

Differentiation

It has already been noted that teachers widely depend on notions of 'general ability' in their classroom teaching. They do so in varying the materials they use, the tasks they set, the questions they ask, the explanations they offer and the standards they set, according to the perceived needs of pupils of differing abilities. Although strongly opposed by many commentators because of its oversimplifying dependence on 'general ability' (e.g. Hart 1996, 1998), such differentiation tends to be officially encouraged in the UK, both by politicians and by Her Majesty's Inspectorate, as a realistic way of taking account of differences among pupils. Alongside such encouragement, however, come repeated complaints that teachers do not differentiate adequately among their pupils.

Both inspectors and researchers have sought to judge the adequacy with which teachers vary tasks to take account of differences in ability (HMI 1978: Bennett *et al.* 1984: Simpson 1989), and have with some consistency concluded that, both for more able and for less able pupils, tasks are often poorly matched to student needs. Teachers, it appears from these studies, tend in practice to overestimate the capabilities of children whom they see as 'less able' and to underestimate the capabilities of pupils whom they see as 'more able'.

Why does this happen? The researcher who was conducting one of these studies (Simpson 1989) fed her findings back to the primary school teachers involved and asked them to comment. The teachers agreed that the tasks they set probably did over- and underestimate pupils' capabilities as the research report suggested, and commented as follows.

1   There were limits to the number of different groups or distinctive individuals with which they could cope at any one time.
2   Having a wide spread of ability in their classes was greatly preferable for both teachers and children to grouping children into classes according to ability.
3   Whereas the study had been concerned only with children's 'academic' needs, it was also important to cater for their diverse social and emotional needs.
4   They deliberately gave special attention and extra resources to the lower-ability pupils, because their need for teaching help was greater.
5   More able children in the classroom were a valuable resource in that they offered models of effective learning and problem-solving which could help the learning of the other children.
6   It was more useful for children's education to be broadened than for them to 'shoot ahead' of their peers; however, the provision of breadth depended on the availability of appropriate resources and time.
7   While the research had concentrated on number and language tasks, it was necessary to provide a wide curriculum.
8   If able children appeared to be over-practising, it was almost certainly related to the teachers' concern to ensure that the basic skills had been thoroughly mastered; the teachers had to be mindful of the prerequisites for the children's learning with the next teacher, the next stage of the curriculum, or the next school to which they were going.

The problem, these teachers suggest, is not with teachers' knowledge of the different learning needs of different children, nor even with finding ways of catering for these needs. The problem is that the careful professional prioritization which is necessary in dealing with the complexity of classroom teaching involves the simplification or neglect of much available information, with the inevitable consequence that interested parties whose priorities are different from those of the teachers will, to some extent, be disappointed. We must recognize, they are telling us, the limits of what is possible through classroom teaching.

Formative assessment

In the last few years, the concept of differentiation seems to some extent to have been replaced as a solution to the problems of classroom teaching, as offered for example in inspection reports, by that of formative assessment. Here the focus is less on stable differences among children and more on the use of information about their current individual achievements and problems, as discovered through their teachers' assessments, to guide their future learning. Unlike assessment for other purposes, for this purpose 'the aspiration is that assessment should become fully integrated with teaching and learning, and therefore part of the educational process rather than a 'bolt-on' activity' (James 1998: 172).

Formative assessment is a much less contentious idea than differentiation by ability and indeed it is difficult to find any cases of people arguing against it. It is such an obviously sensible idea that academic commentators have been queuing up for around 30 years to commend it to teachers (e.g. McIntyre 1970: Scriven 1967). It has recently been given new impetus and importance by an authoritative review of research in the field by Black and Wiliam (1998), whose main conclusion is: 'The research reported here shows conclusively that formative assessment does improve learning. The gains in achievement appear to be quite considerable ... among the largest ever reported for educational interventions.' They also report, however, that there is 'extensive evidence to show that present levels of practice in this aspect of teaching are low' (ibid.).

Why is it that, despite 30 years of propaganda, teachers appear to make little use of formative assessment in their classroom practice? Is it, as Black and Wiliam suggest, because there has not been sufficient external encouragement and support for such good practice? That may be the case but a more plausible hypothesis, derived from their own and others' conclusions, might be that regular effective formative assessment so adds to the complexity of classroom teaching as to make it an impracticable option for teachers. Black and Wiliam found from their review of classroom research that feedback or formative assessment are unlikely to have beneficial effects on performance or learning unless they meet a number of quite demanding conditions. On one hand, they conclude that the more summary kinds of feedback widely used by teachers, such as marks, grades, corrections, praise or criticism, tend to be counterproductive. On the other hand, they suggest that feedback practices guided by the following precepts are likely to promote learning (James 1998: 98–9):

- Feedback is most effective when it stimulates correction of errors through a thoughtful approach.
- Feedback should concentrate on specific errors and poor strategy and make suggestions about how to improve.
- Suggestions for improvement should act as 'scaffolding', i.e. students should be given as much help as they need to use their knowledge but they should not be given a complete solution as soon as they get stuck or they will not think things through for themselves.
- Students should be helped to find alternative solutions if a simple repetition of an explanation on the part of the teacher continues to fail.
- A focus on process goals is often more effective than a focus on product goals; and feedback on progress over a number of attempts is more effective than performance treated as isolated events.
- The quality of the dialogue in feedback is important and some research indicates that oral feedback is more effective than written feedback.
- Students need to have skills to ask for assistance and to help others.

Another recently published study of formative assessment, by Torrance and Pryor (1998: 151), concludes that the impact of formative assessment is 'complex, multi-faceted, and is not necessarily always as positive as might be intended by teachers and as some advocates of formative assessment would have us believe'. They go on to describe two ideal types of classroom assessment. *Convergent assessment*, which is 'routinely accomplished', is characterized by 'analysis of the interaction of the child and the curriculum from the point of view of the curriculum' and is close to what is done in much current classroom assessment practice.

Divergent assessment, which 'emphasises the learner's understanding rather than the agenda of the assessor', is 'aimed at prompting pupils to reflect on their own thinking (or) focusing on … aspects of learners' work which yield insights into their current understanding' and 'accepts the complexity of formative assessment'. Developed instances of divergent assessment were found to be rare, to derive from 'ideological commitments to a "child-centred approach" and [to be] not necessarily as well structured as they could and (we would argue) should be'. While Torrance and Pryor consider that both types of classroom assessment have their place, they suggest that 'divergent assessment is the more interesting approach, and the one that seems to offer more scope for positively affecting children's learning' (ibid: 154), and they go on to make more detailed suggestions about how the quality of formative assessment may be improved.

Increasingly, then, researchers seem to be able to provide teachers with detailed guidance – about how they can use formative assessment in ways that will contribute significantly to their students' effective learning. There is, however, a problem: all this advice offered by Black and Wiliam and by Torrance and Pryor to teachers seems to involve sustained, high-quality, non-routine interaction – either orally or in writing – between the teacher and either individual students or small groups. How far does this advice take account of the complexity of classroom life, and of the sophisticated ways in which expert teachers have learned to work effectively in classrooms through rigorous prioritization, simplification and intuitive decision-making? We can have a good deal of confidence in the validity of these researchers' conclusions that it is feedback from, and interaction with, teachers of the kinds they suggest which can best facilitate pupils' learning. What may well be doubted is that the current lack of frequency of such practices in classrooms is a consequence of teachers' ignorance or lack of understanding of what would be valuable, or the lack of external encouragement. On the contrary it would seem much more likely that, sensing that effective formative assessment depends on such unrealistic, high-quality engagement with individual pupils, teachers do not attempt widely to build such assessment into their classroom teaching. Current efforts to encourage and support teachers in the fuller and more effective use of formative assessment may prove this wrong, and show instead that the researchers' insights into good classroom practice are far ahead of the insights of most teachers. However, a more plausible expectation would be that the researchers' guidance will founder on their failure to take account of the real constraints imposed by classroom teaching as a system.

The point of the argument is not, of course, that we must resign ourselves to the present levels of effectiveness achieved by classroom teaching. It is instead that, if our schooling system is to become substantially more effective, through, for example, taking account of new insights into the effective use of formative assessment, this improvement may depend on a questioning of the system of classroom teaching which we have learned to take for granted. It would be wrong to leave this section without noting that James, Black and Wiliam and Torrance and Pryor offer some seeds of ideas about what such questioning might lead to, ideas to which I shall return.

Home–school partnership

British traditions of schooling have involved very limited levels of collaboration between the school and the home. Throughout the twentieth century, however, there has been a sustained critique of these traditions from progressive educational thinkers, including increasing numbers of teachers, especially in primary schools. They argue that 'meaningful' education of 'the whole child' depends, among other things, on children's experience of continuity across the home–school divide. The most important assault on the separation of schooling from home life came in the 1960s when successive studies, culminating in the Plowden Report (1967), demonstrated very clearly that children's progress and success throughout schooling were closely related to the nature of their home background. Although initially these research findings were often interpreted rather naïvely as showing a simple causal relationship between home characteristics and educational success, even this led to calls for closer home–school relationships aimed at encouraging parents to take greater interest in their children's school learning and to become more involved in the work of the school. Subsequent thinking, much influenced by the powerful theoretical contributions of Bourdieu (especially Bourdieu and Passeron 1977) and of Bernstein (1970, 1975), and by research such as that of Tizard and Hughes

(1984), has increasingly construed the problem not in terms of the deficiencies of working-class homes but as resulting from the gap between the home lives of many children and their school experiences. Accordingly it has emphasized the need for schools to work in partnership with parents, the primary educators of their children, in order to bridge that gap.

What is most needed, it has been argued, most forcibly by Atkins and Bastiani (1988), is for teachers to listen to parents. Teachers' classroom practice, it is suggested, can be made much more effective if they have the benefit of parents' authoritative insights into their children's lives away from school: their interests, their talents, their achievements, their aspirations and their learning needs. The argument is surely persuasive, since parents have much more opportunity, and generally more motivation, to understand their own children than teachers can have, especially secondary schoolteachers who are weekly teaching over a hundred students. Yet there is very little evidence of teachers being motivated to listen to such valuable information. The opportunities created for such sharing of information tend, again especially in secondary schools, to be rare and brief, and most of the talking seems generally to be done by the teachers. On the whole, parents do not complain. They have for the most part accepted the ideology of professionalism and are ready to accept that teachers know best; and so they learn not to offer their insights about their children to a system that clearly does not want to hear them.

It is very tempting to be critical of teachers because of their apparent unwillingness to work in genuine partnership with parents, and especially because of their lack of readiness to take advantage of the information that parents could provide. But classroom teachers have to select and to use the information that they find most conducive to the management of many pupils' learning activities in a classroom. The information that parents can provide, based as it is on a completely different perspective, may not be easily usable by teachers. Randell (1998), in a study of different perspectives on students' progress in their first year at secondary school, found that teachers talked about the individual students in a largely judgemental way – the two dimensions of ability and hard work/good behaviour suggested earlier – whereas parents talked predominantly about their needs. Teachers, it seemed, found it difficult, and also perhaps of questionable value, to adapt their classroom practice to take account of the distinctive needs that parents perceived their children to have.

It may thus be the case that the information which parents think they can usefully offer teachers to facilitate their children's learning cannot generally be effectively used to inform classroom teaching. The problem remains that the progress made by school systems in recent decades in serving the more socially and economically disadvantaged half of the population has been very slow; and it seems highly improbable that better progress can be made in future unless schools develop more genuine and effective ways of working in partnership with disadvantaged communities and families. It is probably unreasonable and unproductive to continue to place the major responsibility for engaging effectively in such partnerships on individual teachers working within the constraining framework of classroom teaching.

Students' own perspectives

> While teachers are for the most part supportive, stimulating and selfless in the hours they put in to help young people, the *conditions of learning* that are common across secondary schools do not adequately take account of the social maturity of young people, nor of the tensions and pressures they feel as they struggle to reconcile the demands of their social and personal lives with the development of their identity as learners.
>
> (Rudduck *et al.* 1996: 1)

That is how Rudduck and her colleagues summarize what they learned from secondary school pupils in their extensive study of pupils' own perspectives on their schooling. In introducing their book, they also quote Silberman and agree with his dictum that 'we should affirm the right of students to negotiate our purposes and demands so that the activities we undertake with them have greatest possible meaning to all' (Silberman 1971: 364). Teachers are under increasing pressure not only to take responsibility for students' attainment of learning targets but also to listen to students' voices and to take fuller account of their perspectives on their schooling. This seems to be partly in response to a view that students' rights need to be more widely respected in schools, but perhaps even more because of a recognition that improved school effectiveness will depend in large measure on the creation of conditions of learning which take fuller account of what students feel and think.

One of the major themes in the research reports from Rudduck and her colleagues concerns the significance of pupils' sense of having some control over their own learning:

> It was noticeable that when pupils spoke about work that they had designed themselves and that they felt was very much their own – whether project work in technology or work in art – they had a strong sense of purpose, strategy and goal … Clearly, the meaningfulness of particular tasks is greater when pupils have a degree of control over the planning and execution of the work: they have a greater sense of ownership.
>
> (Rudduck *et al.* 1996: 48)

However, pupils did not *expect* to have control over their learning:

> [I]t seemed that pupils did not feel that it was necessary to know, or that they had the right to know, where lessons were heading or how they fitted together. The pupils we interviewed were, in the main, prepared to live in the present and to take lessons as they came without much concern for overall sequencing in learning.
>
> (ibid: 47)

The researchers describe too 'pupils who *wanted* to learn but felt that they had little control over their own learning' (ibid: 46). Sometimes blame was attached to teachers, sometimes to pupils' own past behaviour or absences, sometimes to other (disruptive) pupils, but rarely did the pupils feel that they themselves were in a position to overcome any learning problems they had.

In classroom teaching, it is the teacher who has responsibility for determining the activities to be engaged in and the learning tasks to be undertaken. The teacher can, of course, share this responsibility with pupils or take account of pupils' interests and felt needs in deciding what to do. Cooper and McIntyre (1996) found that the teachers whom they studied always took some account of their pupils' perspectives. They characterized the teaching they observed as varying from *interactive* teaching in which pupils' contributions would be taken into account within the framework of teachers' predetermined plans, to *reactive* teaching in which teachers were willing to take more fundamental account of pupils' concerns in deciding what to do. They found reactive teaching less common, and apparently more complex, since the teachers' plans depended on finding out and using information about the different perspectives of the pupils in a class as well as about the set curriculum.

Arguments that secondary school students are not sufficiently treated as partners in their own learning are highly persuasive, both in terms of their rights to have their perspectives taken into account and also instrumentally in terms of their commitment to learning. The lack of control which students generally have over their own lives in institutions that would claim to be serving their interests can indeed be seen as quite remarkable. Within the context of classroom teaching, however, the task for the teacher of treating students as partners while continuing to take responsibility for classroom activities and outcomes cannot but be seen as adding to the complexity of the teacher's task.

Teaching as an evidence-based profession

There has been vigorous debate over recent years about the usefulness of educational research. Although the obvious target of most of the criticism has been educational researchers, a much more fundamental challenge implicit in this debate has been in relation to classroom teachers. The aspiration of the powerful groups who have been promoting this debate – that teaching should be directly informed by research evidence about the relative effectiveness of different practices – gives research an importance hitherto undreamed of, but asks teachers to transform their ways of working. It asks that teachers should somehow integrate into their subtle, complex, tacit and intuitive decision-making the very different propositional kind of knowledge offered by research results. Teaching would therefore become a less idiosyncratic craft, and instead one informed by a standard but constantly developing set of validated generalizations about the consequences of using clearly specified practices in specified types of context. The Teacher Training Agency outlines this conception of teaching and research:

> Good teachers relish the opportunity to draw upon the most up to date knowledge. They continually challenge their own practice in order to do the best for their pupils. They want to be able to examine what they do in the light of

important new knowledge, scientific investigation and evaluation, disciplined enquiry and rigorous comparison of practice in this country and in others – provided such resources are relevant to their field and accessible. Many of the resources they need to do this are, or ought to be precisely those provided by good research.

(Teacher Training Agency 1996: 2)

As yet there is a relatively modest corpus of such knowledge, especially in relation to the British context. However – and this is the complaint against educational researchers – this can in very large measure be explained by the neglect over the last 20 years by British researchers of the kinds of research which could have generated such knowledge. Although comparisons with engineering and medicine have to be treated with some scepticism, there is no reason to believe that a useful body of such knowledge could not be generated. Nor can one deny that, if the body of knowledge were sufficiently substantial and wide-ranging, as well as rigorously validated, a teaching profession guaranteed to be working consistently in accordance with such knowledge would be likely to command greater confidence from the public. Much more problematic, however, is the idea that such knowledge, if available, would be used by classroom teachers. The authors of the review of educational research commissioned in England by the Department for Education and Employment had some sense, on the basis of their assessment of current practice, that this could not be taken for granted:

> Whatever the relevance and the quality of the research and the user-friendliness of the output, its eventual impact will depend on the willingness and the capacity of policy makers and practitioners to take research into account in their decision-making and their actions. This relies on a commitment to the principle, an understanding of what research can offer, and the practical capacity to interpret research.
>
> (Hillage *et al.* 1998: 3)

It depends on all that, but in relation to classroom teaching it depends much more on how such research-based knowledge can be integrated into the kind of classroom expertise on which teachers currently rely; the two kinds of knowledge are so different that this seems highly problematic.

The idea of evidence-based teaching is not, of course, limited to the proposal that the profession should be research-based. Increasingly teachers are being asked to analyse and to plan their teaching in the light of evidence of various other kinds, such as how their pupils (and subgroups of their pupils) have performed in external examinations, in comparison to others with comparable prior attainments. The relationship of all such evidence and its use to teachers' developed classroom expertise is equally uncertain.

Summary of the argument

Having outlined the nature of the expertise which teachers have successfully developed for the distinctive task of classroom teaching, with its considerable strengths but also with some limitations, my aim in this section has been to exemplify the mounting pressure on the classroom teaching system. I have outlined five major kinds of information to which teachers are increasingly being urged to become more responsive, but there is as yet little sign of this happening. In each case, I have argued that it is not realistic to ask teachers to take account of the additional information while maintaining the kind of expertise which has made classroom teaching a viable and indeed very successful system. I have emphasized that classroom teaching has been quite flexible as a system, and that classroom teachers have shown themselves to be highly adaptable; so it may be quite possible for highly motivated teachers to incorporate any one of these five demands into their classroom expertise, or to go a little way towards absorbing all of them. None the less, I am persuaded that the classroom teaching system is near to its limits, and that it will not be able to respond adequately to the accelerating 'expectations … of what schools should accomplish' (Hargreaves 1999: 122).

The argument here has been focused on the classroom teacher's position as solely responsible for what happens in his or her classroom, on the complexity of classroom life, on the teacher's need to find special ways of handling very large amounts and diverse kinds of information, and finally on the lack of realism in asking teachers to attend carefully to an accumulation of new kinds of information traditionally neglected. That is one kind of argument for believing that classroom teaching may have served its day. But we should note briefly that there are other very good arguments which could lead us to the same conclusion. One of these is that classroom teaching seems peculiarly ill-suited to most of the more exciting possibilities for using information technology to enhance the quality of learning in schools, as seems to be reflected in the very limited impact it has had on schooling in the last quarter-century. Another might be that the very strong boundary which we have noted between classroom learning and learning in other contexts has been accepted for long enough, and that schools must, to enhance their effectiveness and usefulness, find ways of organizing learning activities so that these *normally*, not just exceptionally, relate to pupils' learning in other contexts. More pragmatic arguments might emphasize the escalating costs of provision for 'lifelong learning' and consequent pressures for greater efficiency in schooling, or the likelihood that the shortage of well-qualified subject teachers in secondary schools will be endemic. The pressures on the viability of the classroom teaching system are of many kinds.

The way ahead

To offer a clear vision of how schooling might be more effectively organized than on the classroom teaching system would be as foolhardy as it is unnecessary. There seems little doubt that change via a new system will come, but – we must hope and seek to ensure – only gradually over the next 20 years. New approaches will need to be developed, tested, modified and perfected, preferably with the help of careful research. A major constraint will be the architecture of schools, very obviously designed for classroom teaching and very badly designed for anything else. So, as new approaches are tried and found useful, they will be built into the architecture of new schools and then, one hopes, found even more useful. The change should properly be piecemeal, but it may come about in relatively efficient, rational and well-researched ways under the control of professional educators, or chaotically and through a series of reluctant and unhappy compromises to cope with external economic and political pressures. If we are clear about why change is necessary and about the principles by which the changes should be guided, the benefits can be maximized and the pain of change minimized.

What should we be seeking in a new system? Some elements of what is needed are obvious and are already apparent on a small scale in changing patterns of teachers' work. The problems of the classroom teaching system may properly be viewed as resulting from an over-dependence on certain elements which in themselves have considerable merits. The aim must be not to abandon these valuable elements, but to achieve a new balance in which dependence on their strengths does not automatically lead to problems because of their limitations. There are at least four ways in which a proper balance will require radical change:

- *Especially in secondary schools, a very different balance must be achieved between students and teachers in terms of responsibilities for generating and using information about students' achievements and needs in making decisions about their learning objectives and activities.* The research on formative assessment discussed earlier (Black and Wiliam 1998) strongly suggests that the improved learning which can come from formative assessment is most likely through students themselves gaining a thorough understanding of the criteria for effective learning, through them assessing themselves, individually and as peers, and through them having opportunities, encouragement and responsibilities for using the information from such assessment in order to improve their understanding and skills (cf James 1998, Chapter 9). Students, of course, have to learn how to do these things and how to take these responsibilities, and facilitating that learning must be an important task for schools, but while this move towards greater student responsibility is no doubt possible to some degree in classrooms, it seems much more likely to happen where the social settings more obviously reflect this shift in responsibilities.

- *A very different balance must be achieved between reliance on intuitive, tacit and private decision-making and on collaborative, explicit and evidence-based decision-making.* In all complex professional activities, as Dreyfus and Dreyfus (1986) and Schon (1983), for example, have argued, there is necessarily a heavy dependence on tacit and intuitive understanding and decision-making, just as in teaching. Classroom teaching is distinctive, however, in the scale of its dependence on such decision-making, with very little use being made traditionally of attempts to evaluate and synthesize available evidence, explicitly or rationally or collaboratively, as a basis for decision-making. The astonishingly wide acceptance of Schon's idea of reflective practice as an ideal for classroom teaching might reasonably be interpreted as a recognition of the rarity and difficulty of such explicit consideration of the evidence and of the choices to be made for important classroom decisions. The need for a change springs both from the inherent merits of rational thinking and use of evidence for the most important decisions, and also from the current state of affairs where – as has been demonstrated – even expert, intuitive classroom decision-making cannot take account of much of the evidence which could be highly relevant for facilitating learning. Already in recent years, a greater proportion of the time and professional energy of teachers has been spent on gathering information, explicitly analysing it, sharing it and discussing its implications with colleagues, and planning collaboratively for pupils' learning. The work of schoolteachers should move increasingly in this direction, with more and more decision-making being explicit, rationally justified and corporate, and with such decision-making being a larger part of teachers' work, while face-to-face teaching, though still important, will occupy less of teachers' time. As in other professions, teachers' capacities for expert intuitive decision-making must continue to be of great importance, but it should cease to be all-important. How it can best be used to complement more explicit decision-making is a matter that will require extensive research and learning from experience.

• *A very different balance must be achieved between exclusive decision-making by professional schoolteachers and shared decision-making with adults who are not professional teachers.* Schoolteachers have, and will continue to have, a crucial and distinctive kind of expertise for facilitation learning. However, partly because they have been fully occupied with classroom teaching, and partly in order to simplify their classroom teaching work, teachers have denied themselves a great deal of valuable information and insights, and have failed to develop vital shared understandings with others. A slightly greater proportion of teachers' time and professional energies seems currently to be being spent on collaborative planning with other adults who are not fellow-teachers. The work of schoolteachers should move much more in this direction, with increased consultation and joint decision-making with learning support staff, with parents, with community members, with employers and with other specialist professional workers; again, this will be possible only in so far as less time is spent in face-to-face teaching.

• *A very different balance must be achieved between the amount of pupils' learning done in classroom teaching groups and the amount done in other kinds of social groups and settings.* Individual work in resource centres, on work experience and other contexts has increased and should increase further, as should small-group work on joint projects and investigations in different contexts. Much of this work in contexts other than classrooms is likely to be related to diverse uses of computers and other modern technology. Teachers should spend much more of their time in planning and evaluating and in negotiating, with other teachers, with students and with others. However, they should continue to spend much of their time in face-to-face contact with students, individually and with groups of different sizes. Teaching – deliberately and directly facilitating learning – must continue to be their overriding responsibility.

The problem inevitably seems a good deal clearer than the solution. This chapter has aspired only to offer a tentative formulation of the problem and some very preliminary ideas towards a solution. It seems likely that the changes needed will be of different kinds and different degrees in different contexts and for different groups of pupils, for example, perhaps being much more fundamental at secondary school level than at primary. Much of the school-based research and development work of the next 20 years should be directed towards formulating and investigating possible solutions.

References

Atkins, J. and Bastiani, J. (1988) *Listening to Parents: An Approach to the Improvement of Home-School Relations*, London: Croom Helm.

Bennett, N., Desforges, C., Cockburn, A. and Wilkinson, B. (1984) *The Quality of Pupil Learning Experiences*, London: Erlbaum Associates.

Bernstein, B. (1970) 'Education cannot compensate for society' in D. Rubinstein and C. Stoneman (eds) *Education for Democracy*, 104–16, Harmondsworth: Penguin.

Bernstein, B. (1975) *Class, Codes and Control, vol. 3*, London: Routledge and Kegan Paul.

Black, P. and Wiliam, D. (1998) 'Assessment and Classroom Learning', *Assessment in Education*, 5(1).

Bourdieu, P. and Passeron, J.C. (1977) *Reproduction in Education, Society and Culture*. London–Beverly Hills: Sage.

Cooper, P. and McIntyre, D. (1996) *Effective Teaching and Learning: Teachers' and Pupils' Perspectives*, Buckingham: Open University Press.

Doyle, W. (1986) 'Classroom organisation and management' in M.C. Wittrock (ed.) *Handbook of Research on Teaching 3rd edn*, 392–431, New York: Macmillan.

Dreyfus, H.L. and Dreyfus, S.E. (1986) *Mind over Machine: The Power of Human Intuition and Expertise in the Era of the Computer*, New York: Macmillan.

Hargreaves, D.H. (1999) 'The knowledge creating school', *British Journal of Educational Studies*, 47(2): 122–44.

Hart, S. (ed.) (1996) *Differentiation and the Secondary Curriculum: Debates and Dilemmas*, London: Routledge.

Hart, S. (1998) 'A sorry tail: ability, pedagogy and educational reform' in *British Journal of Educational Studies* 46(2): 153–68.

Hillage, J., Pearson, R., Anderson, A. and Tamkin, P. (1998) *Excellence in Research on Schools*, Research Report RR74, London: Department for Education and Employment.

HMI (Her Majesty's Inspectorate) (1978) *Mixed Ability Work in Comprehensive Schools*, London: HMSO.

Illich, I. (1976) *Deschooling Society*, Harmondsworth: Penguin.

Jackson, P.M. (1968) *Life in Classrooms*, New York: Holt, Rinehart and Winston.

James, M. (1998) *Using Assessment for School Improvement*, Oxford: Heinemann.

Lortie, D.C. (1975) *Schoolteacher*, Chicago: University of Chicago Press.

McIntyre, D. (1970) 'Assessment for teaching' in D. Rubinstein and C. Stoneman (eds) *Education for Democracy*, 164–71, Harmondsworth: Penguin.

Plowden Report (1967) *Children and Their Primary Schools*, London: HMSO.

Randell, S. (1998) 'Parents, teachers, pupils: Different contributions to understanding pupils' needs?' unpublished D. Phil. diss., University of Oxford.

Reimer, E. (1971) *School is Dead*, Harmondsworth: Penguin.

Richards, M. (1996) 'Lay and professional knowledge of genetics and inheritance', *Public Understanding of Science*, 5: 217–30.

Rudduck, J., Chaplain, R. and Wallace, G. (eds) (1996) *School Improvement: What Can Pupils Tell Us?* London: David Fulton.

Schon, D.A. (1983) *The Reflective Practitioner*, London: Temple Smith.

Scriven, M. (1967) *The Methodology of Evaluation*, American Educational Research Association.

Silberman, M.L. (1971) 'Discussion' in M.L. Silberman, *The Experience of Schooling*, New York: Holt, Rinehart and Winston.

Simpson, M. (1989) *A Study of Differentiation and Learning in Schools*, Aberdeen: Northern College.

Stevens, F. (1960) *The Living Tradition*, London: n. p.

Teacher Training Agency (1996) *Teaching as a Research-based Profession*, London: Teacher Training Agency.

Tett, L. and Crowther, J. (1998) 'Families at a disadvantage: Class, culture and literacies', *British Educational Research Journal*, 24(4): 449–60.

Tizard, B. and Hughes, M. (1984) *Young Children Learning: Talking and Thinking at Home and at School*, London: Fontana.

Torrance, H. and Pryor, J. (1998) *Investigating Formative Assessment*, Buckingham: Open University Press.

14 Teaching, learning and the digital age

Jenny Leach

Introduction

Vignette 1

C.L. is sixteen and recently moved schools from an inner city comprehensive to a local sixth-form college. I asked her to represent the way she thought about Information and Communications Technologies (ICT) and gave her the following list to consider, drawn from an OECD definition of ICT (see Appendix 1, Figure 14.3): *computers and computer software; telecommunications* including cable, satellite and telephone networks; *information* such as databases, film and audio-visual products, music, photographs. Figure 14.1 shows her response. The text on the right, emanating from this self-portrait, articulates the words and ideas that came to mind as she considered the task. Her mobile phone (represented as an aerial behind her left ear) triggered the word 'RELATE'. Though switched off during college hours (a rule), she uses it several times a day to text-message close friends. She also has two e-mail accounts, one provided by college, though text messaging has largely replaced her use of these. A Nintendo 64 (represented by two function buttons on her neck, together with the words 'FUN' and 'PLAY') she bought jointly with a brother three Christmases ago. She uses it for playing adventure games, mostly with friends. The TV (reflected through her left eye – 'TRANSMISSION'; 'WATCH') she watches for a few hours each day, including one or two videos, usually as background to chat in friends' homes. Unlike most of her peers, she has no TV in her bedroom, but the music (on her lips – 'LISTEN', 'MUSIC', 'WAVES') is constantly playing there, even when she's not at home. The family PC, appearing from her right as binary code, is used for school homework. During the week in which she drew this image she created a spreadsheet for maths, used the Internet to research the risks of smoking for biology coursework, and downloaded images of Giacometti sculptures and Salvador Dali paintings from an on-line art gallery as part of an art assignment ('LEARN', 'KNOWLEDGE').

In this surreal image, influenced she says by her study of Dali in Art class, technologies represent elements of her self – her identity ('BE', 'YOU', 'ME').

Figure 14.1   ICT self-portrait

Through ICT she expresses personal preferences and feelings, learns new concepts and ideas, relates to the people she loves, cements her membership in differing groupings, delineates both the geographical and imaginary borders of her world.

Her personal selection of ICT, encapsulated through this striking image, is integral both to the individual she is and to the communities to which she belongs. Through them she reflects on fresh ideas, new people, and envisions a wider world, as, for example, she accesses medical web sites and an on-line community of painters. She is able to imagine herself in relation to what are, at present at any rate, unfamiliar adult practices, as well as participating confidently in the varied yet very familiar groups to which she belongs.

She is already keenly aware that ICT provides her with essential tools for the present – but also new contexts and future possibilities.

Throughout history the technologies of cultures and communities have always facilitated human activity and development. And be they simple telescopes or modern space probes, paint brushes and pigments or virtual design studios, they have also facilitated human creativity and inspirational leaps of imagination through the practices of, for example, science, astronomy, dance, engineering, literature, sport, music or philosophy (Leach 2001). Technologies not only encompass the *primary artefacts* controlled by our hands (the stick in the sand; wheels and levers; quills, pens, scrolls, books, notebook computers, and so forth). They also facilitate *secondary artefacts*, such as the language, symbols, and signs through which we bring ideas into being and organize thinking (Vygotsky 1962: Wertsch 1995). Consider the technologies you used in the 24 hours prior to turning this page. For me, such a list seemed endless, including mobile phone, cooker, calculator, credit card machine, bicycle, piano, lawnmower and garden spade, car, pencil, kettle, fountain pen, washing machine, tin opener, TV and radio. Whatever our setting, we make our own selections from the huge variety of technological tools available to us. They enable us both to define and carry out our day-to-day activities. They assist us in interpreting everyday experiences, solving problems and making ideas concrete. The uses we make of communications technologies, be they phone conversations, letters, web pages, faxes, posters, text messages, memos or e-mails, mediate a good deal of our day-to-day social interactions, and thus our relationships with one another.

From this perspective, as this chapter will illustrate, technologies, 'the toolkits of culture' as Bruner refers to them (Bruner 1996), are crucial for learning and learners, teaching and teachers. However, technology itself is not the point. What *is* the point are the procedures and processes for mind-using and human inquiry which they can facilitate, as well as the activities, values and outcomes which they express. Well used, they are central to the development of competent, knowledgeable, creative, thoughtful learners. They are also integral to interpretative communities and democratic cultures (Bruner 1996). Wisely selected and imaginatively used, they are also part of the toolkit of effective, creative and inspirational teachers.

Our contemporary technological context

Since technology is integral to human thought, culture and development, it is hardly surprising that the impressive leaps in new technologies, particularly ICT, over the past decade have radically transformed human activity. We can already confidently assert that Internet use and its pace of adoption has outstripped all technologies before it. The art of estimating how many people now have online access is inexact, but best estimates in June 2000 are a world total of 332.73 million (*Economist*, 2001), 147.48 million of whom were in the US and Canada, with somewhat over a quarter in Europe. Projected figures suggest 700 million users worldwide by 2001 and 2 billion by 2007 – one third of the population of the planet (Castells 2000). 49% of all adults in the UK had Internet access at home or at work in January 2001, an increase of 20% in two years (*Guardian*, 'ICM Poll', 24 Jan. 2001) and according to the UK Office of National Statistics, 82% of Internet users in the UK by that time were between 16 and 24 years old.

It is difficult to grasp that although 400 million people worldwide surfed the web's 4 billion pages during 2001, the technology that enables this is roughly where the automobile was when Henry Ford launched his Model T. Digital television products can already include web links, text files, graphics and automated marking. Broadband and communications systems are converging, with fast diminishing distinctions between web and television, whilst wireless technologies now look set to unite the two most successful communications technologies of the past decade: wireless and the Internet. Developments within the computing and telecommunications industries (OECD 1994) also enable:

- equipment which takes up less space, much of it designed to be portable;
- improvements in 'user friendliness' of computers, for example use of stylus and digitizers for controls (like using a pen to point and write) and greater use of icons in software to express emotions;
- reduction in the need for keyboard skills through improvements in speech recognition techniques, with speech input of commands and data become commonplace;
- the ability to present and manipulate 3-D images on screen;
- wireless network connections;
- Internet-enabled computing and communications platforms that run across multiple web sites, drawing information and services to combine and deliver them in customized form to any device chosen, much as a PC does at present;
- satellites enabling the distribution of TV facility across much of the earth's surface;
- optical memory cards or 'smart cards' (currently familiar to us for financial transactions, purchase of cinema or train tickets) which can be used to select education and training requirements;
- integration of video, satellite and mobile communications through integrated broadband communications;
- elimination of the division between analogue (voice) and digital (data) communication, through integrated digital networks, that enable users simultaneously to interrogate databases, whilst editing and discussing text as it appears on screen;
- expansion of the use of mobile phones capable of transmitting data, fax, video as well as voice, operating inside and out, with full interface with ISDN networks.

Such developments have led to greater *efficiency* and *extension* of working practices through, for example, sophisticated record-keeping databases, and other more powerful work tools. They have also made it possible for new, as well as established communities to develop in hitherto unimagined ways. In many workplaces in the developed world, the nature of work itself has been *transformed* (see Streibel 1993; McCormick and Scrimshaw 2001) as completely new knowledge and skills are created through new computer and telecommunication networks. Large chemical engineering companies now expect researchers to employ computers to carry out sophisticated simulations of chemical processes impossible by other means. Lawyers use computers to check the progress of a client's case or point of law, or use e-mail to contact solicitors. The drawing boards, so resonant of architectural and design n practices, have been replaced by computers that facilitate innovative design processes, whilst occupations such as accountancy, stockbroking and marketing have been significantly changed by the introduction of databases that identify patterns and problems in current practice, as well as in the quantitative aspects of future development. Medical practice is beginning to see various networks of people involved in patient care being connected to one another to deliver medicine no matter where the patient may be. Online doctors, for instance, already provide medical advice, based on standardized symptoms. Increasingly, however, remote diagnosis (telemedicine) will be based on real physiological data from the actual patient. Off-the-shelf personal data assistants, such as a palm Pilot plus mobile phone, will allow a patient's vital signs to be transmitted by telephones portable enough to be carried in a personal first aid kit. Some medical technology groups are already looking to apply telemedicine to rural care, and at least one team is investigating the use of telemedicine as a tool for disaster response – especially after an earthquake (*Economist Technology Quarterly* 2001). In many fields, then, the trend is towards global access to data and expertise through distributed human intelligence.

A new educational context

> Children cannot be effective in tomorrow's world if they are trained in yesterday's skills, nor should teachers be denied the tools that other professionals take for granted.
> (Blair 1997)

This rapidly changing technological context interacts with and impacts on the contemporary educational context. OECD (1994) figures, for example, estimate that the current installed base of personal computer systems is growing at a rate of 50,000 units per day worldwide. In 1998 there was an average of 13.3 computers in every primary school and 100.9 in every secondary school in the UK. In just two years those figures had risen to 17.8 and 112.6 respectively, whilst the percentage of computers in schools with multimedia facilities doubled (DfEE 2000). By 2001, 98 per cent of all schools in the UK were connected to the Internet. Many schools now have their own web site, whilst a growing number of schools are providing online resources to other schools, not only within the UK, but abroad (IPPR 2001). Statistics indicate that the ratio of performance of computer systems to cost is increasing at a rate of 20 per cent per annum. This means that within this decade we can expect many schoolchildren, certainly in developed countries such as the UK, to have their own PCs, with something approaching the power and facilities of today's desktop business machine (OECD 1994). It is also estimated that by 2010 at least 40 per cent of teenagers in the developed world will have 'always on' wearable terminals (*Economist* 2001).

Given such developments, it is hardly surprising that governments worldwide are keen to ensure that ICT has an impact on the work of teachers, schools and learners. In the UK the government's response to this new environment led to substantial funds being committed to digital education as a new century rolled in. £1.8bn, for example, was committed to establish a National Grid For Learning

(NGFL), most of this being spent on schools, whilst £230mn between 2000 and 2003 (from the National Lottery) has been spent on providing every primary and secondary teacher with training in the uses of ICT for subject teaching. All newly qualified teachers are now required to have basic ICT skills, as well as an understanding of how ICT can be used in the classroom. The foreword to the revised National Curriculum for 2000–2005 in England and Wales is explicit in stating that this curriculum lies at the heart of government policies to raise standards (DfEE 1999). It includes the requirement that teachers ensure pupils are 'prepared to respond as individuals, parents, workers and citizens to the rapid expansion of communication technologies' (ibid. 1999: 3). In Northern Ireland, a new strategic plan for the education service in the period 2000–2006, 'Learning for Tomorrow's World', places significant emphasis on the role of new technologies, whilst in Scotland National Guidelines ICT 5–14 have been part of a national move to encourage teachers to use ICT. Government targets for the first five years of this century included a commitment to:

- connect all schools, colleges, universities, public libraries and as many community centres as possible to the internet (and therefore the NGFL);
- ensure that serving teachers feel confident and are competent to teach using ICT within the curriculum;
- enable school leavers to have a good understanding of ICT, with measures in place for assessing their competence;
- ensure that general administrative communications between education bodies and government agencies largely cease to be paper-based;
- make Britain a centre for excellence in the development of networked software content for education and lifelong learning and a world leader in the export of learning services.

(DfEE 1997: 1998)

The digital divide

The main risk of a digital divide is the creation of a two-tier society of haves and have-nots, in which only a part of the population has access to this new technology, is comfortable using it, and can fully enjoy its benefits.

(Bangemann Report 1994)

Despite all these developments, access to ICT both within and across countries and continents, including educational institutions, is highly variable although it is largely pre-existing social contexts and relationships that shape not only access, but also the uptake and use of new technologies. As new technologies become not only integral, but indispensable, to the activities of educational communities, those denied access, by the same token, become less and less capable of participating in such activities in any meaningful way. Lack of technological access affects those in rural or poor inner urban communities, where telecommunications are non-existent, limited and or expensive.

In all countries urban communities are better served than rural areas (Kirkwood 2001), whilst in the whole of Africa there are fewer telephone lines than there are in Tokyo or New York. Statistics often mask particular gender and class inequalities. For example, a recent industry forecast in the UK predicted that by 2003 there would be internet access by personal computer in 34 per cent of households in the UK; by digital TV in 37 per cent and by WAP phone in 21 per cent. However, this accounts for only 55 per cent of UK households being reached, due to the high level of multi-device, media-rich households. An affluent minority will therefore have multiple means by which to access the Internet, whilst very many households will remain without access (Kirkwood 2001). Similarly research shows that home computers are more likely to be bought for the use of men and boys, and even when a machine is acquired as a family resource, the main users are very infrequently reported to be female.

Venezky (2000) has identified three barriers that demonstrate the complexity of a concept (see, for example, OECD 2000) that has commonly become known as the 'digital divide'. He calls these:

- the *missing link*
- the *wasteland*
- the *foreign language*.

Technological and economic solutions are required to repair the *missing link* in the sense of a lack of equipment and/or connectivity, whether at national and governmental level or at individual school level, if access is to be ensured for learners. Educational institutions, subject faculties and individual teachers need to be aware of inequalities between learners and find ways to address this, be it provision of lap-tops for home working for example, community provision, or close attention to homework policies. The second barrier, the *digital wasteland*, Venezky argues, resides in the nature of ICT itself. This barrier impacts mostly on women and girls, but also on members of some minority groups. Such groups find computers solitary, isolating and mechanical. For those experiencing the digital wasteland, the image of computer technology, the construction of appropriate software, and more imaginative approaches to the use of ICT need addressing. The third barrier, ICT *as foreign language*, affects learners who are typically but not exclusively from high-poverty homes, or who are on the periphery of society, and need guidance if they are to take advantage of the new opportunities that ICT affords. For this group the digital divide is not simply an equipment differential that can be overcome with further investment in hardware, software and connectivity. Inequality from this perspective derives from a lack of encouragement within the home environment, whatever the reason, towards self-directed school learning. Research confirms that, since networked technologies offer access to an unprecedented range of information, where home access to networked technologies is available to learners, they have the potential to develop a high degree of autonomy, since they can choose both when and what they learn (Lewis *et al.* 2000). Passey *et al.* (1997) have also linked improvements in pupil attainment to home access to ICT and parental involvement, in particular where the opportunity is provided for support of home–school electronic links.

Digitital or educational divide?

Venezky's threefold analysis is useful in providing a more nuanced approach to issues of access, of which all educators must be aware. However, the analysis does not go far enough. Castells (2000), for instance, has pointed to the implications of an 'on-connection' divide, which he argues will have significant implications for educational policy and practice. In a comprehensive research summary of domain names he has demonstrated that Internet content providers are concentrated in metropolitan areas and specific neighbourhoods with San Francisco, New York and Los Angeles currently dominating and London running in at fourth place. Those who come first, he argues, in such a potentially powerful environment shape the medium and its content. The marginalization of those for whom Internet content remains unrelated to their own purposes, experiences, language or context is inevitable. Educational projects such as the OU's DEEP (Digital Education Enhancement Project: http://www.crete-ou.org/deep) is developing country-relevant curriculum materials and ICT enhanced teaching approaches to support teachers working in economically challenged environments, such as southern Africa and Egypt. Such projects recognize that even when the technology is in place, there is a potential human, rather than technological, divide. They seek to ensure that it is not only an elite digital community that has access to relevant information, quality resources, electronic teaching and all the educational opportunities associated with such provision.

ICT and learning

Current research

Given this context, the importance of ICT within education is clear and researchers have begun to look carefully at the impact of ICT on learning. Studies have noted the importance of:

- teacher access to ICT for personal development (both at home and school) including relevant technical support and skills training;
- teacher confidence and competence in the use of ICT, including the importance of positive attitudes to innovation (including communicating value of its use to pupils and clear objective setting);
- pedagogical practices (including educational philosophy, teaching styles, strategies and classroom management).

Peha (1995) has noted that the rapid pace of technological change requires teachers continually to update their skills and knowledge. Watson (1997) and Schacter and Fagano (1999) have also argued that, unless teachers understand the philosophy of the software they are using, the effectiveness of its use with learners will be limited. Some technologies, for example, place a strong emphasis on pedagogical skills – computer conferencing, for instance, requires the teacher to act as moderator, and to be skilled in promoting discussion. Research also indicates that the success of ICT is dependent upon the way in which a variety of classroom strategies are integrated into the teacher's overall pedagogy (Wood 1998). A study by Newcastle University (Moseley *et al.* 1999) looked at specific ICT uses in a range of classrooms and concluded that successful teachers need to take account of a range of factors. These include:

- 'ensuring pupils have adequate ICT skills to achieve subject specific purposes';
- 'a planned match of pedagogy with the identified purpose of ICT activities and learning outcomes';
- 'clear identification of how ICT will be used to meet specific objectives within subjects of the curriculum to improve pupils' attainment'.

Passey (1999) suggest that educational benefits are linked to a teacher's ability to integrate networked ICT resources with other classroom resources, rather than substituting traditional methods with technology. Findings show that teachers who favour ICT use are likely to have well-developed ICT skills and to see ICT as an important tool for learning, enquiry and decision-making. Passey (2000) has also drawn attention to the way in which the boundaries of settings are changing, arguing that the home community can provide a substantial extension to the educational arena if teachers consider the appropriate approaches to be gained and the potential benefits offered. The advent of a connected learning community, he suggests, will have a direct impact on pedagogy in terms of the access it provides to knowledge beyond the classroom.

So whilst access to ICT and skills training are important, they are not the only, nor indeed the major, point. A more important question remains to be answered: in what ways can and should ICT be used in the enterprise of learning and the practice of teaching? Several reviews of the literature on technology and learning have concluded that technology has great potential to enhance student achievement, but only if used appropriately (Dede 1998). Educators need to know the precise means and processes by which technology supports learning. That in turn demands some broader understanding of the process of learning itself – a good 'theory of mind' as Bruner (1996) puts it. We now know that our physical minds, as well as individual consciousness, develop in quite phenomenal ways during our lifetime. But we also know that the interaction of mechanisms in the human brain with the external environment and our everyday experiences 'cause changes in the way neurons network together across the whole brain' (Greenfield 2000). Both brain and mind, it seems, develop in direct response to the particular purposes in which, and for which, we use them. And paradoxically, as we age and acquire ever more memories and increased understanding of the external world through the processes of *social* interaction with others, so mind becomes 'increasingly personalised and *individualised*' (Greenfield 2000). Learning then is not a discrete, abstract process of cognition, a one-way accumulation of skills and information, taking place exclusively in the mind, as commonsense views of mind would have us believe. It is a situated process: a dynamic, sometimes delicate, but always highly creative interaction between mind, body, other people – and the tools and technologies available to us.

Such insights challenge the prevalent but overly simplistic one-way models of ICT use (viz: ICT → impacts on learner → impacts on achievement). *Firstly* they require us to take account of this more subtle and sophisticated model of mind, which sees individuals as 'agentive' and mind as 'proactive, problem-oriented, selective, constructional, directed to ends' (Bruner 1996). *Secondly,* they emphasize the essentially social and situated nature of learning. Learning, from this perspective, is a process of developing *identity* – of becoming. It transforms who we are, what we can do – and what we believe we are capable of doing in the future. It entails:

- '*processes of* knowledge building'

  and

- '*places* where the interaction between experience and competence can lead to new ways of knowing' (Wenger 1999).

In the next two sections the role of new technologies in facilitating such processes and places will be addressed.

Processes of knowledge building

Tools of practice

> *Nec manus, nisi intellectus, sibi permissus, multam valent; instrumentis et auxilibus res perficitur*
> (Neither hand nor intellect by themselves serve you much: tools and aids perfect (or complete) things.)
>
> (Bacon, quoted in Vygotsky 1962 vii)

Vygotsky suggests that primary tools or artefacts are the instruments that define and shape our work and thinking even before we complete it. As Bruner (1996) puts it, the spirit-level begets the horizontal measurer, and the rebus was used for building pyramids, long before there was a theory of mechanics. The mind, to this extent, is an extension of the hands and tools that we use, as well as of the work to which we put them. Our opening vignette showed the wide range of technologies and associated skills in daily use by one teenager, creating and expressing her identity as well as enabling her to carry out some of the essential tasks of her world. Schools all too often fail to build on young people's existing knowledge and experience, still less on the toolkits of teenagers' culture. Yet an influential review of 81 studies of IT use carried out in 1994 indicated a growing body of research confirming a range of 'specific educational benefits that could be attributed to the use of IT' (NCET 1994). These included factors already known to be important for effective learning, such as increased:

- learner enthusiasm and confidence;
- concentration;
- learner autonomy, leading to improved motivation.

More recent studies have added to this list:

- critical thinking;
- information handling skills;
- higher-level conceptualization;
- better problem-solving.

Davis *et al.* (1997) found that the quality of learning can be significantly enhanced when ICT is approached and utilized as an intellectual 'multi-tool', adaptable to learners' needs and supportive of their attempts at conceptual abstracting.

Not only do schools frequently fail to build on students' existing skills and knowledge and their home use of ICT. In addition, the 'school ICT' of the formal statutory curriculum often consists of a range of institutional practices, quite divorced from ICT use beyond the classroom walls (Leach and Moon 2000). Yet as the Institute of Public Policy Research in the UK, in an open response to government policy on the digital curriculum, has argued, National Curriculums cannot be overly prescriptive if they are to encourage learners to develop the 'key skills of the global, high-tech workplace' such as creative problem-solving (IPPR 2001). Technologies have the potential to make learning practical, and when used for authentic, real-life purposes can stimulate and develop conceptual understanding.

Used for mathematical purposes, for example, ICT can enable learners to explore data, observe mathematical pattern, and visualize geometry – in other words, practise being mathematicians (see Table 14.1). Authentic mathematical activities can be developed through a range of learning technologies including calculators, spreadsheets, graphing programmes, function probes, 'mathematical supposers' for making and checking conjectures (e.g. Schwartz 1994), and modelling programmes for creating and testing models of complex phenomena (Jackson *et al.* 1996). A Middle-school Mathematics Through Applications Project (MMAP), developed at the Institute for Research on Learning, for example, has enabled learners to explore problems such as designing insulation for arctic dwellings using software tools that explored concepts in algebra (Goldman and Moschkovich 1995).

Table 14.1 could equally well have presented the very different processes supported by ICT in relation to musical activity, art, science, religious studies or drama. ICT can be used to scaffold a wide variety of concepts and disciplinary practices, such as the interpretation and composition of literary texts, historical inquiry or scientific research. Electronic writing frames, for example, can be used to support literacy activities across a variety of literary genres, much as training wheels allow young bike riders to practise cycling when they would fall without support. However, they can also move students through the complex process of becoming more competent and confident writers. Similarly text-mapping activities, using simple word-processing tools such as highlighting and italics, allow learners to carry out quite sophisticated analyses of literary texts.

Table 14.1   Opportunities for exploiting the power of ICT in mathematics

Mathematical activity	What processes will ICT enable?
Learning from feedback	The computer can provide fast and reliable feedback which is non-judgemental and impartial. This can encourage students to make their own conjectures and to test out and modify their ideas.
Observing patterns	The speed of computers and calculators enables students to produce many examples when exploring mathematical problems. This supports their observation of patterns and the making and justifying of generalizations.
Seeing connections	The computer enables formulae, tables of numbers and graphs to be linked readily. Changing one representation and seeing changes in the others helps students to understand the connections between them.
Working with dynamic images	Students can use computers to manipulate diagrams dynamically. This encourages them to visualize the geometry as they generate their own mental images.
Exploring data	Computers enable students to work with real data, which can be presented in a variety of ways. This supports interpretation and analysis.
'Teaching' the computer	When students design an algorithm (a set of instructions) to make a computer achieve a particular result, they are compelled to express their commands unambiguously and in the correct order; they make their thinking explicit as they refine their ideas.

Source: NCET 1995

Tools for collaboration

Our day-to-day human communication is an integral part of the learning process, but as Bruner indicates in his discussion of the 'interactional' tenet (see Chapter 2), our Western pedagogical tradition has to date rarely done justice to its importance. This may well change, as the knowledge and skills needed for the twenty-first century challenge the fundamental thinking of current curriculums. Today, much school learning is individually focused and sharing can be considered as cheating. But real learning processes, as we have seen, are social and this is mirrored in the world of work where learning and thinking are often developed in collaborative teams (OECD 1994). Many new technologies are interactive (Greenfield and Cocking 1996) and are already extensively and effectively being used to create and sustain collaborative processes. Research (e.g. Bereiter and Scardamalia 1993; Lavin *et al.* 2000; Leach 2000) indicates that electronic environments can enable:

- opportunities for collaborative tasks;

- discourse around a common text/resources/data;
- joint decision-making and reflection;
- the giving and receiving of feedback;
- the refining of understanding;
- more complex small-group talk;
- a shared history of learning.

Connectivity between schools and home communities is already enabling a rich medium for creating both local and global communities including teachers, students, parents, practising scientists, artists, writers and other specialists. Technologies such as e-mail, listserves and the Internet help make connections between students' in-school and out-of-school activities.

Examples include:

WORKING WITH EXPERTS

Students can be connected with working scientists or other subject experts. In some student–scientist partnerships, students collect data that are used to understand global issues; and increasingly students from geographically dispersed schools interact through the Internet. Global Lab, for example, supported an international community of student researchers from more than 200 schools in 30 countries who constructed new knowledge about their local and global environments (Tinker and Berenfeld 1993, 1994). Using shared tools, curriculums and methodologies, students collected and shared data in areas such as air and water pollution, background radiation, biodiversity and ozone depletion.

TELE-FIELD TRIPS

Teachers who take pupils to historical sites, zoos, museums, on field trips, etc., can work with students to share experiences and observations with others locally or globally. Students can collate 'visits diaries', and use others as remote researchers for their own questions. In Project Marco Polo 21 teachers and students spent three weeks on an oceanographic research ship in the Mediterranean. Marco Polo participants (aged 13–14) sent a daily journal to the internet that was read and responded to by classes from different countries.

JOINT PRODUCTS

Pupils can work on joint products. For example, The Virtual Identities Digital Arts Project involved collaboration between post-16 art and design students from schools in Kent and Liverpool. Each student was assigned a partner, with whom they exchanged and co-designed digital images. The Internet provided a medium through which they were able jointly to explore visual phenomena, experiment with visual language and extend the range of tools currently used in art, including image manipulation and layering.

Tools for reflection

Reflection, or metacognition, enables learners to think about thinking. ICT enables a range of tools that facilitate such a process, such as software tools that can be used to replay performance and try out possible improvements. Sophisticated tutoring environments that pose problems are also now available; they can give students feedback on the basis of how experts reason and organize their knowledge in physics, chemistry, algebra, computer programming, history, and economics. *The CoVis Project* developed a networked hypermedia database, called the Collaboratory Notebook, for a similar purpose. The collaboratory notebook is divided into electronic workspaces, called notebooks, that can be used by students working together on a specific investigation (Edelson *et al.* 1995). The notebook provides options for making different kinds of pages – questions, conjectures, evidence for, evidence against, plans, steps in plans, information and commentary. Using the hypermedia system, students can pose a question, then link it to competing conjectures about the questions posed by different students (perhaps from different sites) and to a plan for investigating the question. Images and documents can be electronically 'attached' to pages (Bransford *et al.* 2000).

In order to make a decision about what any specific tool is to be used for, learners also need to have a mental representation of the specific potential, as well as the 'affordances', of the technology in question. The notion of affordances is what seems to be prominent, i.e. to have salience to the learner, in a new situation. 'To be perceiving the world is to be acting in it – not in a linear input-output relation (act-observe-change)' (Clancey 1993: 95). Recent research (Somekh 2001) into children's concepts of the potential of networked technology indicates that learners often have a far richer understanding of ICT than either the researchers or teachers assumed. When concept-mapping has been used to elicit pupils' representations of ICT and reflect on its uses, in some cases they are able to depict possibilities which go beyond the current technological realities of their lives (see *Figure 14.2*).

Places for learning

Communities of practice

We learn in communities, whether they be they families, workplaces, or leisure time groups. Such 'communities of practice' (Lave and Wenger 1991; Rogoff 1994; Wenger 1999) are always small enough for members to be acquainted, although they may be dispersed over wide geographical distances and they are characterized by three essential dimensions:

- a joint enterprise – an agreed, negotiated purpose or goal with mutual accountability;
- mutual engagement – a common *activity*; participants play distinctive *roles* in this joint work;
- a shared repertoire – a distinctive *discourse* framing a shared *understanding* of *concepts, tools* and *resources* of practice.

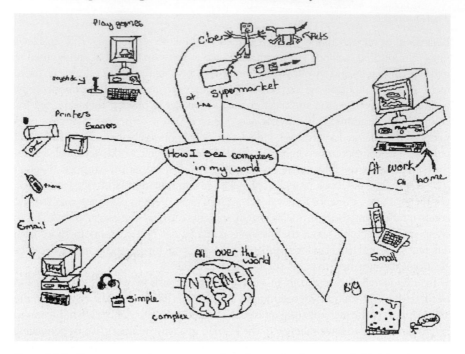

Figure 14.2 Concept-mapping as a research tool: a study of primary children's representations of Information and Communications Technologies (ICT)

Source: Matthew Pearson, University of Huddersfield and Bridget Somekh, Manchester Metropolitan University.

Classrooms themselves can be 'communities of practice'; indeed current research suggests that learning is most effective when each of these dimensions are in place. Vignette 2 describes such a community. One element of its 'shared repertoire' is a computerized database, used to develop the concepts and discourse of scientific practice, whilst encouraging intense collaboration and reflection amongst its young learners.

Vignette 2

A community of young scientists

The setting is a classroom in Ontario, Canada. A busy classroom community of nine- and ten-year-olds is immersed in a study of islands which has led them on a similar pathway of study to that which Darwin took. They have become curious as to how plant and animal species might have arrived at islands. Over a ten-week period, these young students' inquiries progress through a variety of topics such as endemic species, theories of evolution, adaptation and survival, cells, genes, systems of the human body and the Human Genome Project. Each student elects to be a member of one of five research groups focusing on a different set of research questions. In common with adult science communities they use technologies to support their research, including a database software tool called Knowledge Forum (KF).

As students log in to the KF database using name and password, a blank View, or electronic page, appears on which students post 'notes'. The 'note' function provides a framework which allows them to pose questions or problems of understanding. They can create graphics to illustrate ideas within the text, posting the notes by creating a title and clicking 'Contribute'. Customizable templates are available to scaffold the students' thinking about a problem (e.g. My theory is, I need to understand, New information, etc.). The notes appears in the View as an icon which appears with title and student's name (pink if it has been read, blue if it is unread by self). What makes Knowledge Forum different from other information storage systems is that notes and ideas contained within the database are able to communicate with each other. Although they cannot change or edit other students' notes, they can create a build-on to notes by adding new information or an opposing 'theory' or simply by asking a question. A cluster of build-on notes appears as a web on the screen. When a View in the database becomes 'hot', through some discrepancy in an explanation or opposing opinions, students are drawn to work in it.

A student who was not part of the Komodo Island Research Group posted a question to them, which ignited a discussion that continued for over three weeks (in the database and in class):

Student 1: **How did the Komodo dragon evolve?**
Well, if you look at the lizardy tongue of the Komodo dragon, and their skin type, it resembles a lot of dinosaurs, so I was thinking that maybe they were related and the Komodo evolved from a type of dinosaur. What does everyone else think?

Student 2: **(following some library research)**
Maybe they evolved from the alligator dinosaur and died out everywhere but Komodo because it had a good habitat.

Student 3: I really don't understand R's theory. It is complicated and he hasn't told us exactly what his resources are.

Student 4: If not lizards, what were they? I think that they were a type of reptile.

▤▤▤▤▤▤▤▤▤▤▤▤▤▤▤▤▤▤ ☐ Komodo – A.Z. ▤▤▤▤▤▤▤▤▤▤▤▤▤▤▤

My theory is that Komodo dragons evolved from lizards or dinosaurs.I am not sure they evolved from alligators. I think to answer this problem we have to go very deep and find stuff like the blood or skin type of the Komodo or Alligator and compare. I will do this!!

I was also wondering why Komodo dragons have not adapted to there cilmate very well? The reason I say this is Komodo dragons get to much sun and have to go inthe shade to cool off. This sounds kind of silly butif the adapted to there climate they would not have to do this.

This theory came from a paper I was reading a couple of days ago. The paper was about turtles and how they live in many places but have not adapted. Are there certain creatures they do not need to adapt? Are komodos one of those creatures?I am very interested in finding out about whee Komodos evolved from maybe they have some relation to turtles.

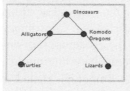

Student 5: They named dinosaurs terrible lizards because when they saw the bones they thought they were terrible because of how big they were.

▤▤▤▤▤▤▤▤▤▤▤▤▤▤▤ ☐ Dino-Sauraus – Matthew ▤▤▤▤▤▤▤▤▤▤▤▤▤

New Information The word dino is latin for terrible and the word saurus is Greek for lizard. So the word dinosaur means terrible lizard. That is why I support D.H.'s theory over Reid's it is less complicated and more accurate Reid's theory doesn't make sense to me. What I understand from Daniel is that the reptiles are a family and inside that family lizards evolved into komodo dragons and geckos and etc. Down below each graph is shown and look how less simple more accurate and easier to understand. We do not need a deep understanding on something simple. ⓐ The yellow number 1 is a link to

D.H's   graph.ⓑ if you see both you will understand.

_____

ⓐ D.H.. (Jan. 22, 2000). "My theory of evolution" [Knowledge Forum™ Note]. ICS - Island [Online]. Available: database address [date referenced].
ⓑ Reid. (Jan. 14, 2000). "Evolution: Komodo Dragon" [Knowledge Forum™ Note]. ICS - Island [Online]. Available: database address [date referenced].

The debate continues as more students join:

Student 1: What's in a name? People call whales fish when really they are mammals.

Student 4: The name dinosaurus could have been wrong. People could have just thought that a dinosaur looked like a lizard so they jumped to that conclusion. Also if the name was improper scientists have other names for dinosaurs (scientific names).

(based on Caswell 2001)

Such a community, Bruner argues, '... model(s) ways of doing and knowing, provide(s) opportunities for emulation, offer(s) running commentary, provide(s) 'scaffolding' for novices, and even provide(s) a good context for teaching deliberately. (They) even make possible that form of job-related division of labour one finds in effective work groups ... the point is for those in the group to help each other get the lay of the land and the hang of the job' (Bruner 1996: 21).

One of the greatest fallacies emerging from some of the rhetoric around ICT in the classroom is that it reduces the teacher's role. Some have argued that the computer should take the place of the teacher; others that as the learner becomes 'autonomous' and 'independent' so the teacher need only be a 'facilitator' or 'guide on the side'. But as we have seen, in order for the use of ICT to be effective, the teacher's role is central. More than ever before the teachers are needed to create 'pedagogical spaces' (Freire, *et al.* 1999), using their expertise in order to help learners pose their own problems, analyse their experiences, select and use appropriate technologies for the task in hand, and arrive at a critical understanding of the world.

Whilst we know that authentic learning is situated, as Bruner has argued, 'real' agendas, such as those addressed by students in Vignette 3, often get left out of 'school' practices. Left out, school learning 'begins to present so alien or so remote a vision of the world that many learners may find no place in it for them or their friends. This is true not just of girls, or blacks, or Latinos, or Asians, or other kids we target for special attention as potentially at risk. There are also those restless, bored kids in our sprawling suburbs who suffer the pandemic syndrome of "What am I doing here anyway?"' (Bruner 1996).

Vignette 3

DW is an RE teacher in a small city school in the UK. She used a major news story, the Kosovan refugee crisis, as a starting point with her pupils, to reflect on the 'meaning of suffering', as required by the RE curriculum. Students looked at and evaluated electronic newspapers from around the world, explored the web sites of various organizations such as Amnesty International, and used searchable databases containing religious texts. Individual students chose and researched one article each of the Universal Declaration of Human Rights, while other pupils took the opportunity to compare data between countries, researched through links to the CIA *Countries Fact Book*, and compared, for example, infant mortality rates.

(see Leach and Moon 2000)

Conclusion

> Networks may substantially change the relationship between education and
> the rest of society ... the reintegration of learning into the rest of society will
> require a redistribution of roles, a reinvention of social stuctures, and a
> rethinking of the entire learning enterprise.
>
> (Levin and Thurston 1996)

Social setting and the analysis of technology for learning are often separately considered. It is all too often assumed that the interaction of the learner with the computer
hardware and software is unrelated to the surrounding pedagogy of the classroom or
school. I have argued that simple causal models of the impact of ICT on learning are
insufficient. In addition I have suggested that increasingly the walls of educational
institutions are becoming 'transparent', as students receive information from remote
sources, learning materials from other countries, and as project work is shared
between schools (OECD 1994). The findings of a range of recent research studies on
the impact of technologies on learning (i.e. Lewin *et al.* 2000) show that ICT has a
highly positive effect on learner achievement when a number of variables come
together. New models of teaching and learning using ICT need to acknowledge a
complex set of interactions between learners, teachers, tasks and the new technologies (McCormick and Scrimshaw 2001; Leach and Moon 2000). It is not technology of itself, but a 'whole cloud of correlated variables – technology, activity, goal,
setting, teachers' role, culture – exerting their combined effect' (Salamon 1991).

McCormick and Scrimshaw (2001) have suggested that the use of ICT may
entail three levels of impact on teachers' pedagogy, namely:

- improved efficiency of conventional teaching;

This level simply entails teachers using ICT as a more effective means of promoting
a particular learning objective. The assumption is that it replaces another more
conventional resource, but that the other elements in the situation remain largely
unchanged.

- extension of the reach of teaching and learning;

This second level entails teachers using ICT to provide an extension to what can be
achieved. Here the ICT resources are different from what they replace or supplement, in ways that extend the reach of the teacher, the learners or both. The
Internet is one such example. As we have seen, it can provide a global audience or
test-bed for work normally carried out in the classroom, for example, or up-to-date
information in an easily accessible form. When students in the UK use computer
conferencing to compare life in their local community with the experiences of peers
in Cairo or South Africa, for example, they are doing more than simply learning
more efficiently about a different society.

- transformation of teachers' and learners' conceptions of the subject itself.

At this third level new technologies transform the nature of a subject at the most fundamental level.

As we have seen throughout this chapter, such transformations may well be inevitable. ICT looks set to become all-pervasive in learning, but it also looks set to transform classrooms in which hitherto the flow of knowledge and information have been controlled. 'Real agendas' will become central, and young people will need to learn how to reflect on and analyse them.

Thousands of years ago, the word used for Socrates' method of teaching was the *elenchus*, which means 'refutation'. Its intention was to destroy that elaborate edifice of internalized, taken for granted opinion, that blocks the power of authentic thinking and reflection: all the thought we have assumed and never once thought through. Plato, as a young man encountering Socrates, was changed for ever: a brilliant prospective politician under his shaping influence became the first systematic author-philosopher (Abbs 2001). Such 'refutation' by teachers in the twenty-first century will be of vital importance to learners. You will be the people with whom ideas are discussed and tested, from whom encouragement and self-discipline are obtained, and who provide feedback on progress; it will need to be you who will lead and inspire, pointing young people to future possibilities and new identities.

Appendix 1

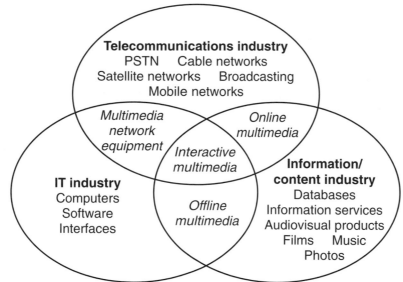

Figure 14.3 The scope of ICT

Source: OECD (2000)

References

Abbs, P. (2001) 'The Three Faces of Wisdom', inaugural address given at the University of Sussex, 29 May 2001.

Bangemann, M. (1994) Europe and the Global Information Society: recommendations to the European Council, European Union, High Level Group on the Information Society, Brussels.

Banks, F., Leach, J. and Moon, B. (1999) 'New understandings of teachers' pedagogic knowledge' in J. Leach and B. Moon (eds) *Learners and Pedagogy*, London: Paul Chapman.

Bereiter, C. and Scardamalia, M. (1991) Higher levels of agency for children in knowledge building: A challenge for the design of new knowledge media Journal of Learning Science 1: 37–68

Blair, A. (1997) Foreword to Connecting the Learning Society, DfEE 1997.

Bransford, J.D., Brown, A.L. and Cocking, R.C. (eds) (1999) *How People Learn: Brain, Mind, Experience, and School*, Committee on Developments in the Science of Learning, National Research Council, National Academic Press.

Bruner, J. (1996) *The Culture of Education*, Cambridge, Mass.: Harvard University Press.

Castells, M. (2000) Oxford Clarendon Lectures, Oxford, June 2000.

Caswell, B. (2001) 'Development of Scientific Literacy: The Evolution of Ideas in a Knowledge Building Classroom', *Education, Communication and Information*, 1(2) September 2001.

CSILE: Computer Supported Intentional Learning Environment http://csile.oise.utoronto.ca/

Davis, N. *et al.* (1997) Can Quality in Learning be enhanced through the use of ICT? In Somekh, B. and Davis, N., *Using Information Technology Effectively in Teaching and Learning*, London: Routledge.

Dede, C. (ed.) (1998) Introduction Pp v–x in Association for Supervision and Curriculum Development (ASCD) Year book: Learning with Technology, Alexandria: VA.

DfEE (1997) Connecting the Learning Society, London: DfEE.

DfEE (1998) 'Teachers Meeting The Challenge of Change', Green Paper, London: DfEE.

DfEE (1999) The National Curriculum QCA, HMSO.

DfEE (2000) *Survey of Information and Communications Technology in Schools 2000*, London: HMSO.

Economist Technology Quarterly (2001) 'The cutting edge of virtual reality – medical technology', March, 43.

Edelson, D. C., Pea, R.D. and Gomez, L. (1995) Constructivism in the collabotary in B.G. Wilson (ed.) Constructivist Learning Environments, Englewood Cliffs, NJ: Educational Technology Publications.

Freire, P. and Macedo, D. (1999) Pedagogy, Culture, Language and Race: a Dialogue in Leach, J. and Moon, B. (eds) (1999) *Learners and Pedagogy*, London: Paul Chapman.

Goldman, S. and Moschkovich, J.N. (1995) Environments for Collaborating Mathematically in Proceedings of the First International Conference on Computer Support for Collaborative Learning pp 143–6 October, Bloomington, Indiana.

Greenfield, P.M. and Cocking, R.R. (1996) Interacting with Video Norwood, NJ: Ablex.

Greenfield, S. (2000) *Brain Story*, London: BBC Publications.

IPPR (2001) *One More Push? Curriculum Online Beyond the Grid*, IPPR, London, June 2001.

Kirkwood, A. (2001) Shanty Towns and the Global Village? Reducing Distance but widening gaps with ICT in *Education, Communication and Information*, 1(2).

Lave, J. and Wenger, E. (1991) *Situated Learning*, 3–32, Cambridge: Cambridge University Press.

Leach, J. (2000) Breaking the Silence: the role of technology and community in leading professional development in Moon, B., Butcher, J. and Bird, E. (2000) *Leading Professional Development in Education*, London: Routledge.

Leach, J. (2001) One Hundred Possibilities: creativity and community and new technology in Craft, A. and Jeffreys, B. (eds) *Creativity in Education* London: Cassell.

Leach, J. and Moon, R.E. (1999) 'Recreating Pedagogy' in *Learners and Pedagogy*, London: Paul Chapman.

Leach, J. and Scrimshaw, P. (1999) 'Teaching in English' in *English: Learning Schools Programme* (to accompany CD-ROM *English)*, Open University Publications.

Leach, J. and Moon, R.E. (2000) 'Pedagogy, Information and Communication Technologies and Teacher Professional Knowledge' in *Curriculum Journal*, 11(3): 385–404.

Levin, J. and Thurston, C. (1996) Educational Electronic Networks: A review of Research and Development *Educational Leadership* 54(3): 46–50.

Lewis, C., Scrimshaw, P., Harrison, C., Somekh, B. and McFarlane, A.E. (2000) Impact 2 Preliminary Study 2 Promoting Achievement: pupils, teachers and contexts; unpublished research report, University of Nottingham.

McCormick, R. and Scrimshaw, P. (2001) 'ICT, Knowledge and Pedagogy' in *Education, Communication and Information*, 1(1) [http://www.open.ac.uk/eci]

Moseley, D., *et al.* (1999) *Ways forward with ICT: Effective Pedagogy Using ICT for Literacy and Numeracy in Primary Schools*, Newcastle: University of Newcastle.

NCET (1994) Teaching and Learning with Interactive Media. Report of the Evaluation Study http://meno.open.ac.uk/meno-ncet1.html

NCET (1995) 'Mathematics: a pupil's entitlement', Coventry, NCET.

OECD (1994) New Technology and its Impact on Classrooms in Moon, B. and Shelton-Mayes, A. *Teaching and Learning in the Secondary School*, London: Routledge.

OECD (2000) *Schooling for Tomorrow: Learning to Bridge the Digital Divide*, Paris: OECD

Office for National Statistics (2001) 'Internet Access', London: The Stationery Office.

Open University (1999) 'CD-ROM ART Learning Schools Programme', Milton Keynes: Open University and Research Machines.

Passey, D. (1999) Teachers for the 'Connected Learning Community' in Watson, D. and Downes, T. *Communication and Networking in Education*, Kleuwer: London.

Passey, D. (2000) *Developing Teaching Strategies for Distance (Out of School) Learning in Primary and Secondary Schools*, London: Educational Media International.

Rogoff, B. (1994) 'Developing understanding of the idea of communities of learners', *Mind, Culture and Activity*, 1(4): 209–29.

Rogoff, B. (1999) 'Cognitive Development Through Social Interaction: Vygostky and Piaget' in P. Murphy (ed.) *Learners, Learning and Assessment*, London: Paul Chapman.

Salamon, G., Perkins, D.N. and Globerson, T. (1991) Partners in Cognition: extending human intelligence with intelligence technologies. *Educational Researcher* 70(30): 2 –9.

Schacter, J. and Fagano, C. (1999) Does Computer Technology improve student learning and achievement? How, when and under what conditions? *Journal of Educational Computing Research* 20: 329–43.

Schwartz, J.L. (1994) The role of research in reforming mathematics education: A different approach. In *Mathematical Thinking and Problem Solving*, Schoenfeld A.H. (ed.) Hillsdale, NJ: Erlbaum.

Somekh, B. (2001) Interpreting the Externalised Images of Pupils' Conceptions of ICT: methods for the analysis of concept maps, *Computers and Education* (in press).

Streibel, M.J. (1993) Instructional Design and Human Practice: what can we learn from Grundy's interpretation of Huberman's Theory of Technical and Practical Human Interests? In Muffoletto, R. and Knupfer, N.N. (eds) *Computers in Education: Social, Political and Historical Perspectives* 114–62 Cresskill, NJ: Hampton Press.

Tinker, B. and Berenfeld, B. (1993) A Global Lab Story: A moment of glory in San Antonio Hands On! 16 (3) (Fall) 1994 Patterns of US Global Lab Adaptations Hands On! http://hou.lbl.gov

Venezky, R.L. (2000) The Digital Divide Within Formal School Education: Causes and Consequences in OECD (2000) *Schooling for Tomorrow: learning to bridge the digital divide*, OECD: Paris.

Vygotsky, L. (1962) *Thought and Language*, Cambridge, Mass.: MIT Press.

Watson, D. (ed.) (1997) *The Impact Report: An evaluation of the impact of Information Technology on children's achievements in Primary and Secondary Schools*, London: Department for Education, Kings College, London and Centre for Educational Studies.

Wenger, E. (1999) *Communities of Practice*, Cambridge: Cambridge University Press.

Wertsch, I. (1995) *Vygotsky and the Social Formation of Mind*, London: Harvard University Press.

Wood, D. (1998) *The UK ILS Evaluations: Final Report*, Coventry: BECTa.

15 Grouping by ability
What research tells us

Laura Sukhnandan and Barbara Lee

Over the past year, Ofsted reports (Ofsted 1998a, 1998b) have shown that growing numbers of schools, both secondary and primary, have begun to increase their use of setting as a system for grouping pupils. Setting can be defined as the regrouping of pupils according to their ability in a particular subject. At secondary level setting has traditionally been used to group pupils for mathematics, science and modern languages (particularly during the examination years, Years 10 and 11), but now it is being extended to a wider range of subjects and year groups. At primary level, mixed-ability grouping has been the dominant system of organizing pupils since the 1970s, but here too, the move towards grouping by ability has led to the setting of pupils in Years 5 and 6, usually for mathematics, science and English.

Why have schools started to set more often?

It has been argued that the recent shift from mixed-ability grouping to setting can be attributed to two main policy initiatives: the introduction of the National Curriculum and the move towards a market-led education system. In particular, the highly struc-tured and tiered format of the National CSurriculum has led many practitioners to believe that-mixed ability teaching is no longer feasible. In addition, the increased emphasis, in recent years, on parental choice and school league tables, and the impact of formula funding have forced schools into competition with each other.

As a consequence, research suggests that schools have begun to focus on cost-effective ways to: facilitate the teaching of the National Curriculum; attract the parents of pupils who are likely to do well in the National Curriculum assessments (NCA); and implement strategies to improve pupils' levels of achievement. One of the main approaches which schools appear to have adopted to meet these needs is the introduction or extension of setting.

This move towards more grouping by ability at school level has also been fuelled by education commentators and politicians who claim that a return to setting will help to raise educational standards.

As yet there is a limited amount of research exploring the effects of setting on teaching the National Curriculum, and how it influences parental choice of schools. However, there has been a great deal of research investigating the relation-ship between setting and achievement and pupils' experiences of learning.

What does the research on ability grouping tell us?

Since the 1920s and 1930s there have been numerous studies exploring the impact of ability grouping. Initially, studies focused on the comparative effects of grouping pupils by ability and non-grouping on pupil achievement. However, by the 1960s researchers began to explore the relationship between different forms of ability grouping and pupils' social experiences of schooling and learning.

There are studies claiming that setting has a more positive effect on pupil achievement than mixed-ability grouping and studies that state the reverse. Also, there are studies which show that setting compared with mixed-ability grouping increases pupil achievement for those of high ability but decreases levels of achievement for pupils of middle and low ability. Furthermore, there is evidence to suggest that, compared with mixed-ability grouping, setting has more positive effects on pupil achievement in subjects such as mathematics, science and modern languages. However, the only consistent finding to emerge from studies such as these is that there are no consistent findings.

As a result, some researchers have used statistical techniques known as meta-analysis to identify the main trends from the findings of numerous studies in this area. Such work reveals that setting compared with mixed-ability grouping has no statistically significant effect on the average achievement score of pupils. This finding remains consistent for pupils in both secondary and primary schools, regardless of subject areas and despite pupils levels of ability (high, middle or low).

So why are the findings inconsistent?

The findings of studies investigating the effects of different forms of ability grouping on pupil achievement are inconsistent because the impact depends on how effectively they have been implemented. For example, the main purpose of setting is to reduce the spread of ability within a class, to allow the teacher to modify the curriculum and level of instruction to match the needs of the pupils in the class, without having to do an unrealistic amount of preparation.

However, the extent to which setting can be effectively implemented is dependent upon a wide range of factors such as a school's catchment area and the way in which pupils are allocated to sets. In addition, the effective use of setting is dependent upon two factors: firstly, the extent to which teachers are willing, and able, to modify appropriately the curriculum, level of instruction and lesson pace and pitch; and secondly, the effect which setting has on perceptions, and pupils' attitudes self-esteem, expectations and level of motivation.

In contrast, however, the findings from research comparing setting with mixed-ability grouping in relation to the allocation of teachers to classes, teachers' attitudes and perceptions, and pupils' attitudes, self-esteem, level of school involvement and social characteristics, have been relatively consistent.

There is evidence that teachers who are most experienced and mostly highly qualified are more likely to be allocated to teach pupils of high ability and that teachers prefer to teach pupils of high ability rather than those of middle and low ability. The obvious consequence of this is that teachers, like pupils, find themselves placed in a hierarchy that impacts on their sense of competence and career satisfaction.

Studies also show that teachers tend to hold more positive attitudes, perceptions and expectations of high-ability pupils compared with how they react to middle- and low-ability pupils. This can have the effect of increasing high-ability pupils' levels of motivation and thus their achievement, while decreasing middle- or low-ability pupils' levels of motivation and achievement, a process which reinforces teachers' differing views of these groups of pupils' potential.

The effects of setting

This variation in teachers' orientation towards pupils of different levels of ability may contribute to the finding of many studies which reveal that setting, compared with mixed-ability grouping, has a detrimental effect on the attitudes and self-esteem of middle- and low-ability pupils. For these pupils negative attitudes and low self-esteem can lead to a decline in achievement and the creation of a vicious circle of underachievement from which it is difficult for these pupils to escape. In contrast, for pupils of high ability, setting can have the effect of artificially inflating their levels of self-esteem which may also decrease their levels of motivation and thus detrimentally affect their levels of achievement.

It has also been found that low-ability pupils who are put into sets, compared with low-ability pupils who are placed in a mixed-ability environment, participate less in school activities, experience more disciplinary problems and have higher levels of absenteeism.

Finally, there is a notable amount of research which shows that setting also has the effect of reinforcing existing social divisions in terms of social class and race, and segregating pupils in terms of gender and age (season of birth). As a result, low-ability sets often contain a disproportionately large number of pupils from working-class backgrounds, ethnic minorities, boys and summer-born children.

Drawing on the results of a wide range of research, three main findings emerge. Firstly, the evidence shows that setting, compared with mixed-ability grouping, has no significant effect, either positive or negative, on pupil achievement. Secondly, the research reveals that setting, compared with mixed-ability grouping, has detrimental effects on pupils, especially those of low or middle ability in terms of its impact on their attitudes, self-esteem, level of school involvement and opportunities to learn. Finally, the findings of studies in this area indicate that setting works to reinforce existing social divisions in terms of social class, gender, race and age.

Given the current climate of British education with its emphasis on achievement and competition and a National Curriculum with a tiered system of examination entry, the incentive for schools to organize pupils by ability is understandable. However, what is clear from the findings of the research is that a particular system of grouping pupils, on its own, is not necessarily going to:

- enable all schools to raise their achievement levels and thus their position in the league tables and presumed attractiveness to parents;
- be an appropriate method of organizing pupils across all subjects; and

- fulfil the needs of all pupils given the variations in their individual learning styles and personal/social attributes (level of ability, social class, gender, race and age).

Schools therefore need to assess their own particular needs given their local context, staff, pupils and parents when deciding on which systems or combination of systems, of pupil organization is most suitable for them. Given the rapidly changing educational climate it would also be advisable for schools to implement systems selectively and flexibly. In addition teachers should ensure that systems of pupil organization are carefully monitored and evaluated so that any negative aspects evolving out of the use of grouping can be addressed.

References

Office for Standards in Education (1998a), *Secondary Education 1993–97: a Review of Secondary Schools in England*, London: The Stationery Office.
Office for Standards in Education (1998b), *The Annual Report of Her Majesty's Chief Inspector of Schools: Standards and Quality in Education 1996/97*, London: The Stationery Office.

16 How is language used as a medium for classroom education?

Neil Mercer

Introduction

This chapter is about language as a medium for education in school. Most of its content is about spoken language, with a discussion of some aspects of written language in the later part.

Classrooms generate some typical structures of language use, patterns that reflect the nature of teaching and learning as a social, communicative process which takes place in the distinctive institutional settings of school. Some features of classroom language, described below, have been found in classrooms across the world; and to some extent at least this reflects the fact that language has a similar function in schools the world over. There are also some local, regional and national characteristics in the ways that language is used in the classroom, and different expectations are made of students in different cultures and even by different teachers within one country's education system which may also be reflected in language. Moreover, according to their out-of-school experience, students may find the language of classroom life more or less intelligible or compatible with their out-of-school life. On entering school, every student will have to engage some learning about how to use the language of the classroom. Even for students who have the classroom language as their native or first language, this will involve grasping the conventions of how spoken and written language is normally used in school, taking up the specialized vocabularies of curriculum subjects and becoming able to present ideas within the constraints of the accepted genres or discourses of spoken and written language.

Teachers have responsibility for guiding students' use of language as a social mode of thinking, and to express their understanding in the appropriate language genres or discourses. Where teachers and students are using a second or other language as the medium of classroom education, distinctive patterns of language use in the classroom are also apparent. Teachers and students may 'code-switch' between languages in class, and the content of the talk may reveal teachers' concern with the learning of a second language as well as the learning of the curriculum subject, or a teacher's concern with the enforcement of the norms of the standard, official variety of language used in school.

Function

Schools are special kinds of places, social institutions with particular purposes, conventions and traditions. There are some interesting differences in how teachers' and learners' interests interact in classrooms in different countries. But schools the world over also have much in common in how they function, and this functional similarity is reflected in the ways language is used in their classrooms.

The patterns of language use established by teachers have important consequences for how their students use language. One of the most obvious functions of spoken language in a classroom is for teachers to tell students what they are to do, how they are to do it, when to start and when to stop. Unless they resort to corporal punishment, language is the main tool of teachers' control of events in the classroom. They also assess students' learning through talk, in the familiar question-and-answer sequences of classroom life. Talk also is the means by which teachers can provide children with information, much of which it should be very hard to communicate in any other way. They tell students stories, read texts to them and describe objects, events and processes (sometimes introducing new descriptive vocabulary as they do so).

An essential element of formal education is dialogue between a teacher and a learner, an exchange of ideas which enables the learner to gain knowledge and understanding and the teacher to provide relevant guidance and evaluation. It is because we can use language to share and create knowledge and understanding that we have been able to transform the world and organize our lives in ways that are so qualitatively different from those of another species. The prime justification for setting up education systems is to enable the process of *the guided construction of knowledge* (Mercer 1995) to be carried out effectively.

Guiding students' construction of knowledge depends on the creation of shared experience and joint understanding. Day by day, in various activities and interactions, teachers and their classes generate shared experience which they use as the basis for further activity. They can talk about what they have done, what they are doing and what they will do next, so that experiences shared over long periods of time can become woven together. Each day's talk in a classroom forms part of what Janet Maybin (1994) has called the 'long conversation' between teachers and learners, a series of related dialogues that constitute the time that teachers and students spend together in school.

Throughout the process of classroom education, wherever in the world it is carried out, teachers have a special, professional responsibility for helping students achieve an understanding of a specific body of knowledge represented by 'the curriculum'. They are expected to help students understand a specific body of knowledge, and to help them acquire 'educated' ways of analysing and solving problems. They also need to help students learn to talk and write about their knowledge in appropriate varieties of language. Life in classrooms generates and sustains some distinctive ways of using language (discussed in more detail below), though this is often not well recognized by teachers because they are immersed in it, and because they take these features for granted. Even children whose mother tongue is the language used in the classroom have much to learn about how that language is used as an educational medium.

Structure

Much of the classroom talk between teachers and students is usually recognizably 'educational' in its form and content. This can be illustrated through the consideration of a particular transcribed sequence of classroom talk. Sequence 1 (below) was recorded in a secondary school in England. As part of their English curriculum, a class of 14-year-olds had taken part in an extended computer-based communication with children in a nearby primary school. Working in groups of three, the secondary students acted out the role of characters stranded in time and space. By e-mail, they explained their predicament to the primary school children, who responded with suggestions about what to do; and so the dialogue continued. In Sequence 1, the teacher is questioning one group of girls with the whole class present about their most recent e-mail interactions and their future plans.

Sequence 1

Teacher: What about the word 'dimension', because you were going to include that in our message, weren't you?

Anne: Yeh. And there's going to be – if they go in the right room, then they'll find a letter in the floor and that'll spell 'dimension'.

Teacher: What happens if they do go in the wrong room?

Emma: Well, there's no letter in the bottom, in the floor.

Teacher: Oh God! So they've got to get it right, or that's it! [*Everyone laughs.*] The adventurers are stuck there forever. And Cath can't get back to her own time. What do you mean the letters are in the room, I don't quite follow that?

Emma: On the floor, like a tile or something.

Teacher: Oh I see. Why did you choose the word 'dimension'?

Anne: Don't know.

The three students speak together, looking to each other, seeming uncertain.

Emma: It just came up. Just said, you know, 'dimension' and everyone agreed.

Sharon: Don't know.

Teacher: Right, because it seemed to fit in with, what, the fantasy flow, flavour?

Sharon: Yeh.

Teacher: OK. Why do they go through the maze rather than go back? I mean what motivation do they have for going through it in the first place?

Sharon: Um, I think that it was the king told them that Joe would be in the maze or at the end of the maze, and they didn't go back because of Joe, think it was. I'm not sure about that.

Teacher: You've really got to sort that out. It's got to be very, very clear.

(Mercer 1995: 30–1)

One noticeable feature of Sequence 1 is that all the questions were asked by the teacher. This is a common, almost universal feature of classroom talk. Teachers have good reasons for asking so many questions: they have to learn what the students have been doing, so that they can evaluate activity and provide further guidance. The questions and answers are also typical in their structural pattern. Repeatedly, the teacher elicits information from one or more student(s) and then comments on the pupil's response. So a teacher's question is followed by a student's response, followed in turn by some feedback or evaluation from the teacher. This pattern of classroom talk is first described by the British linguists Sinclair and Coulthard (1975) and is usually known as an Initiation-Response-Feedback (IRF) exchange. IRF exchanges are sometimes also called IRE sequences, where the 'E' stands for 'Evaluation'. We can separate the parts of each exchange, technically known as 'moves', as follows:

		Move
Teacher:	Why do they go through the maze rather than go back? I mean what motivation do they have for going through it in the first place?	Initiation
Sharon:	Um, I think that it was the king told them that Joe would be in the maze or at the end of the maze, and they didn't go back because of Joe, think it was. I'm not sure about that.	Response
Teacher:	You've really got to sort that out. It's got to be very, very clear.	Feedback or evaluation

Of course, other patterns of exchanges, e.g. in which students ask questions, also happen in classrooms. But although they were originally identified in the talk of rather formal British secondary classrooms, IRF exchanges are elements of the structure of classroom talk which have since been found occurring frequently in classrooms all over the world. They can be thought of as the archetypal form of interaction between a teacher and a pupil. Thus Ian Malcolm (an Australian researcher who has studied language use in Aboriginal schools) has claimed:

> This [IRF] pattern is near-universal (at least in the western world) where teachers are interacting with a class of children as a whole. It is a discourse pattern which is entailed in the social situation.
>
> (Malcolm 1982: 121)

In Sequence 1 we can also see IRF exchanges occurring as slightly more complex, linked structures. So in the following example, the teacher obtains three 'responses' to her 'initiation', and her second 'feedback' comment also functions as a further 'initiation':

		Move
Teacher:	Why did you choose the word 'dimension'?	I
Anne:	Don't know.	R

Emma:	It just came up. Just said, you know, 'dimension' and everyone agreed.	R
Sharon:	Don't know.	R
Teacher:	Right, because it seemed to fit in with, what, the fantasy flow, flavour?	F/I
Sharon:	Yeh.	R
Teacher:	OK.	F

Questions

Teachers' heavy reliance on questions has been criticized by educational researchers. For example, Dillon (1988) and Wood (1992) claim that because most teachers' questions are designed to elicit just one brief 'right answer' (which often amounts to a reiteration of information provided earlier by the teacher) this unduly limits and suppresses students' contributions to the dialogic process of teaching-and-learning. When a pupil fails to provide the only possible right answer, a teacher ignores the wrong answer which has been offered and goes on to accept a second 'bid' for an answer from a second pupil. This particular kind of use of question-and-answer by a teacher – asking 'closed' questions to which the teacher knows the answer – is the most common function of IRF exchanges in classrooms. Sequence 2 below illustrates very well how this does indeed narrowly constrain the scope that students have for making an active contribution to talk in the classroom.

Sequence 2

Teacher: Argentina, what is the capital of Argentina?
Pupil 1: Argentina city [*Some students laugh, others say 'Sir, sir' and raise their hands.*]
Teacher: [*to a pupil who has hand raised*] Brian?
Pupil 2: Buenos Aires.
Teacher: Yes, good, Buenos [*writing on board*] Aires.

Wood comments:

> If the aim of a lesson or teacher-pupil interaction is simply to establish whether or not facts have been learned and committed to memory, then talk which is rich in teacher questions and high in control will probably achieve the result intended. If, however, the aim is to discover what students think, what they want to know, or what they are prepared to share with their peers, then such lessons will prove self-defeating. If you wish to know 'where the learner is at' or where they would like to go next, then avoid frequent questions.
>
> (Wood 1992: 209)

Wood goes on to suggest that, constrained in this way, students get little opportunity to formulate knowledge and make coherent sense of what they are being taught, or to practise their own ways of using language to reason, argue and explain. There are therefore some good reasons for agreeing with such criticisms of teachers' heavy dependence on the use of IRF exchanges in which the 'I' components consist of closed questions.

However, if we look back to Sequence 1, we can see that the teacher there is not using IRFs in this way. Rather, she is asking questions to find out what the students have done and why they have done it – things that she does not know. Her questions are 'open' in that only the students know the answers. The teacher is asking students clearly to describe what they have done and to account for it, encouraging them to review their actions and plan future activities accordingly. She is using her enquiries not only to assess her students' learning, but also to guide it. Through questions like, 'Why did you choose the word "dimension"?' and, 'Why do they go through the maze rather than go back?', she directs their attention to matters requiring more thought and clarification when they return to their work. In this way, she is not only focusing their attention on how best to communicate by e-mail with the primary school children, but also shaping their own awareness and understanding of what they are doing.

The educational content and function of the teacher's questions and students' responses in Sequence 1 are therefore very different to those in Sequence 2. So, while Dillon's and Wood's critical analysis of how teachers use questions has some force, we must be aware of equating language structures with language functions. An accepted principle of discourse analysis is that particular language structures – in this case IRF exchanges – can be used for more than one purpose and function. From an educational perspective, this means that we can only understand, and evaluate, the ways in which language is used in classrooms by taking account of the *content* and *context* of any particular interaction.

We should also note that the use of IRF exchanges in classrooms depends on all the participants being familiar with the conventions of this kind of question-and-answer routine, and being willing to abide by those conventions. Research in classrooms in Britain and the USA encourages the belief that most children in those countries rapidly become familiar with the IRF structure of classroom talk, and so are able and willing to participate in it fairly readily. However, now consider Sequence 3 below which was recorded in an infant classroom in Western Australia. The children aged 5–6 were all Aboriginal Australians, and at the point the sequence begins, the teacher had read them a story in which a child finds a kitten.

Sequence 3

Teacher: How do we know she liked the kitten? How do we know she liked the kitten? [*No responses from children.*] No, you think about it, now. She got the kitten, I mean she found the kitten ... an' then she said to Mum and Dad she wanted to ... ?

Child 1: ... keep it.

Child 2:   Keep it.
Teacher: Keep it. So if she didn't want the kitten she wouldn't have kept it,
            would she? What do you think, Brenda?
Brenda: [*silence*]
Teacher: Well, you listen carefully.

(Adapted from Malcolm 1982: 129)

The researcher who recorded this sequence (Ian Malcolm) describes it as typical of interactions in Aboriginal classrooms. It appears that Aboriginal children are extremely reluctant to engage in IRF exchanges, not because of any lack of fluency in English but rather because such interactions are at odds with the conversational practices of their home culture. That is, in Aboriginal society overt interrogations and demonstrations of understanding are not considered polite.

Classroom researchers elsewhere – for example in Hawaii, and amongst Native Americans in the US and Mexico – also have reported that children from some cultural backgrounds find IRF patterns of question-and-answer alien and discomforting. But that research shows that teachers usually persist in their normal practice despite such reluctance or incomprehension. It is also reported that schools rarely make efforts to admit or incorporate the language practices which children experience in home communities if these are not part of the 'mainstream', middle class of their societies, whether they be the storytelling of Irish travellers in Britain, the 'rapping' of Afro-Caribbean teenagers, or the imaginative story-poems heard amongst young children in working-class black American communities. This problem is well elaborated by Stephen Boggs (1985), who spent more than ten years observing language use in Hawaiian communities and classrooms. He describes some of the 'oral arts' which were an important part of Hawaiian children's informal social lives and yet were completely ignored by their schools:

> The children showed very close attention to the exact pronunciation of lyrics and rhythm when learning new songs … I observed children in the third and fourth grades pronounce the lyrics of songs in Tahitian, Samoan, Maori – and even Standard English! Particular Standard English phonemes not pronounced in everyday speech would be pronounced in songs, as in names. … This … shows the close relationship between verbal learning and socially valued communication. Singing is a highly valued social activity.
>
> (Boggs 1985: 125)

Other researchers have described such divergences between the language practices children encounter in and out of school, in many parts of the English-speaking world (e.g. Heath 1983: Wells 1986), and often suggest that this is a source of educational problems. But one should perhaps be cautious in drawing the obvious conclusion that if teachers made great efforts to incorporate children's out-of-school informal language practices into the life of the classroom, this would necessarily either be welcomed by the children or be successful as a strategy for promoting educational success. One of the vital and attractive qualities of informal language practices, from a child's perspective, is that they are an integral part of life outside the classroom and are not harnessed pragmatically to the institutional purposes of school.

Cues

If a teacher asks a question and a student is unable to provide the required answer, the teacher will typically ask another student in the class, and perhaps then another, until a 'right' answer is found. If no such answer emerges, one might expect teachers simply to provide the required information. But providing answers to their own questions is one thing that teachers seem at great pains to avoid. Instead, they commonly resort to what Edwards and Mercer (1987) call *cued elicitation*. This is a way of drawing out from learners the information a teacher is seeking – the 'right' answers to their questions – by providing strong visual clues and verbal hints as to what answer is required. An example is provided by Sequence 4 below, recorded in a British primary school on an occasion when children were being taught about the science topic of 'pendulums'. The teacher introduced the topic to the children by describing Galileo sitting in church, 'very bored', when his attention was taken by a swinging incense burner:

Sequence 4

Teacher:	… and he wanted to time it, just for interest's sake, just to see how long it took to make a complete swing. Now he didn't have a watch, but he had on him something that was a very good timekeeper that he could use to hand straight away.	*Teacher begins to swing her hand back and forward in rhythm, as she talks.*
		Teacher snaps her fingers on 'straight away' and looks invitingly at students as if posing a question or inviting a response.
Teacher:	You've got it. I've got it. What is it? What could we use to count beats? What have you got? You've got it. I've got it. What is it? What could we use to count beats? What have you got?	*Teacher points on 'You've' and 'I've'. She beats her hand on the table slowly, looking around the group of students who smile and shrug.*

Teacher: You can feel it here.	*Teacher puts her fingers on her wrist.*
Students: Pulse.	*Speaking in near unison.*
Teacher: A pulse. Everybody see if you can find it.	*All copy her, feeling their wrists.*

(Mercer 1995: 26–7)

The use of cues as a teaching technique can be traced back to the Socratic dialogues constructed by the ancient Greek philosopher Plato. Why do teachers use cues so much? One likely reason is because they want learners to take an active part, however small, in the dialogue.

Sequence 4 also illustrates how the use of cues, gestures and other signs can be an important component of classroom teaching. However, the non-verbal signs used by teachers vary, sometimes considerably, between cultures. So Zukow-Goldring *et al.* (1994) observed that teachers in south California who were native Spanish speakers tended to use more gestures and physical demonstrations in their interactions with students than their Anglo (native English-speaking) colleagues, regardless of whether English or Spanish was being used at the time.

Vocabulary

As students progress through their years of schooling, they encounter an increasing number of specialized technical terms. Used effectively, the technical vocabularies of science, mathematics, art or any other subject provide clear and economical ways of describing and discussing complex and abstract issues. A shared understanding of musical vocabulary – for instance 'octave', 'bar', 'key' and so on – makes it possible for two people to discuss, in the abstract, phenomena that otherwise would have to be concretely demonstrated. However, the discourse of educated people talking about their specialism is clear only to the initiated.

Becoming familiar with the language of a subject is therefore both an important requirement for educational success, and also an important goal if students wish to enter an intellectual community of scientists, mathematicians, artists or whatever.

An important part of a teacher's job is to help students learn and understand the specialized vocabulary of curriculum subjects. Research has shown that technical language is a common source of confusion and misunderstanding amongst students. However, teachers seem often to assume that the meaning of a word will become obvious as students hear or read it repeatedly, while students are usually reluctant to reveal their ignorance by asking questions. Some technical words may be used only rarely in the wider world, but they may represent ideas that are not difficult for students to grasp, because they can easily be explained or exemplified. (A good example is 'alliteration'.) Others may be impossible to explain through a concrete set of instances. This applies to many scientific concepts describing properties of matter (like 'density') and processes (like 'evolution' and 'photosynthesis'). A consequence may be that many technical words remain for students mere jargon, and as such represent an obstacle to their developing understanding.

Many teachers and educational researchers can recount bizarre and salutary examples of how technical vocabulary has been misunderstood by students. Two such examples are of a 12-year-old who thought that 'quandary' meant a four-sided figure, and a 16-year-old who, after saying that he had never understood 'subtractions', later commented that he could do 'take-aways'. Robert Hull (1985), a British secondary teacher and researcher, discovered that some of his 14-year-old students believed that 'animals harbour insects' meant that they ate them; and that 'the lowest bridge-town' was a 'slum on a bridge'. He concluded that even terms like 'molten iron', 'physical feature', 'factor' and 'western leaders' were often insuperable obstacles to students' comprehension.

For children who are learning English as a second or other language, the vocabulary and style of technical English may pose even greater problems. And if teachers themselves are not confident users of technical English, good explanations may not be available. For example, Cleghorn *et al.* (1989) found that Kenyan teachers who were teaching science through the medium of English were often unable to explain in English the meanings of terms they were using (such as 'parasite'). They comment:

> When teachers have to search for English equivalents of what is familiar but often not conceptually the same in the local language, the actual meaning of what is being taught can be altered.
>
> (Cleghorn *et al.* 1989: 21)

Oracy

As mentioned above (see section on 'Questions') some educational researchers have argued that too much 'instructional' teacher talk in class will not achieve the important goal of encouraging students to become educated users of language. Instead it is suggested that children must have opportunities to develop and practise using language in situations that are not continuously dominated by the presence of the teacher. One outcome of such arguments was the emergence of what is sometimes called the 'oracy movement', referring to an explicit concern, amongst educationalists in the UK, Australia and some other countries, with the development of children's skills in oral language use. (The term 'oracy' was coined by the British educational researcher Andrew Wilkinson in the 1960s.) In countries where such ideas have been given some support, it has become increasingly common to set up activities in which students work and talk together without the continual presence of a teacher. There is no doubt that organizing students to work on their own in groups or pairs generates quite different patterns of talk from those that typify teacher–pupil interactions (Barnes and Todd 1995: Mercer 1995: Norman 1992).

Sequence 5 (below) is taken from a discussion between a group of 15-year-olds in a classroom in a secondary school on the edge of a large city in northern England. Their teacher had divided the class into groups of four students. Each group had some information about the setting up of the Lake District National Park in the UK and were asked to address together a set of questions about how the conservation of an area of natural beauty might be reconciled with the needs of different users of the park, such as farmers, ramblers and tourists. The sequence is the first minute or so of the discussion of one group (two girls and two boys). In the right-hand column are analytic comments about the function of the talk provided by the researchers (Barnes and Todd) who recorded the talk.

Sequence 5

Alan:	Do you think that this is a good idea for big National Parks? I think it is an excellent idea because, erm, people like us have the, erm, countryside around us, but other people in the, erm, centre of Leeds are less fortunate, and do not have, erm, centre – countryside that they can go out to within easy reach.	*Initiates discussion of the usefulness of National Parks, an issue not set on the task card.*
Bill:	Yes.	*Provides encouragement.*
Alan:	Without being polluted and, erm, chimney stacks all over the place.	*Makes the antithesis more explicit.*
Pauline:	This is all right as long as there aren't, going to be too many buildings around the place, because it's going to spoil it completely, I think. It's all right for a few like cafes or, er, camping sites, a few camping sites. That's all right, but nothing else.	*Qualifies Alan's contributions thus turning the discussion towards the set questions. She reinforces part of what Alan said, but suggests that limits need to be drawn.*
Alan:	I think this is one of the best ideas of the, erm, National Parks because they, erm, do not, don't allow buildings to be built without permissions and planning special, you know, so it blends with the countryside and not stuck out like a sore thumb.	*Accepts the qualification which leads to his extending the concept of National Parks to include the regulation of building.*
Jeanette:	Yes, but it just depends on what the ground's like, doesn't it?	*Qualifies that part of Alan's statement that refers to blending with the countryside.*

(Barnes and Todd 1995: 24–5)

Even though the students in Sequence 5 are responding to a question set by their teacher, it is apparent that the quality of their talk is quite different from that of class discussions led by a teacher. Many of the participants make quite extended contributions. They expand on each other's comments. They are willing to express uncertainty to each other, and to offer each other explanations. Talk is being used to share knowledge and construct joint understandings in ways that reflect the fact that they all have similar status in the discussion, as learners who can contribute to the discussion from the wealth of their individual experiences.

Discussion activities of this kind are only educationally valuable if they encourage students to use language as a way of thinking rationally together. The thinking and the talking in these circumstances must become inseparable, so that language is used as a *social mode of thinking* (Mercer 1995). The organization and requirements of the task should be such that students have to talk about what they are doing to collaborate successfully. The quality of students' talk is an important educational issue. Even when talking and working without a teacher, students are expected to use language in ways that are educationally appropriate. That is, when a teacher asks students to 'discuss' a topic, the teacher is usually expecting something quite specific of them – to make explicit descriptions, formulate reasons and explanations, and to agree on possible solutions to problems. One important part of becoming educated is learning how to use such 'educated' styles of language, the kinds of discursive practices which are used in cultural activities like science, law, politics and business negotiation. Research suggests that students' engagement with language-based activities can be motivated and improved by making such aims and expectations clear. But one other clear finding of classroom research is that teachers rarely do so. Similar issues arise in relation to the use of written language in school (see 'Genre' below).

Learning

Earlier parts of this chapter (see 'Structure' and 'Questions') describe ways in which teachers use language to try to direct and constrain the contributions that students make to the process of teaching and learning. The broader demands that participation in the 'official' talk of the classroom makes on students are worth careful consideration. Imagine a child, any child, starting the first day at a school. There are three kinds of learning task which that child can face, and which are crucial to their educational progress:

1   Students have to learn the special ways of using their native language that apply in school, because they are unfamiliar with educational conventions and the technical language of curriculum subjects.
2   Students have to learn to speak and write in a language that is different from the language of their home environment.
3   Students have to learn to use the standard form of their native language, because they have grown up speaking a 'non-standard' variety outside school.

In reality, the task facing any particular pupil may not neatly fit any of these three descriptions (e.g. they may be fluent speakers of a language, but not be literate in it); but this three-part distinction can nevertheless be helpful for making sense of reality in all its complexity. (See also 'Code-switching' and 'Standard' below.)

A useful and commonly encountered case for consideration is of classrooms where English is the official language of teaching-and-learning but not the native or first language of the students. The situation arises in two main forms. The first occurs in countries where English-medium education goes on, even though the mother tongue of most of the children is not English. The second is where students whose mother tongue is not English enter schools in a predominantly English-speaking country.

In any situation where English is used as a classroom language but is not the main language of children's home or community, teachers may have the multiple task of teaching

(a) the English language;
(b) the educational ground rules for using it in the classroom;
(c) any specific subject content.

An illustration is provided by research carried out by Arthur (1992) in primary school classrooms in Botswana. English was used as the medium of education, but it was not the main language of the students' local community. Arthur observed that when teachers were teaching mathematics, they commonly used question-and-answer sessions as opportunities for schooling children in the use of appropriate 'classroom English' as well as maths. For example, one primary teacher commonly insisted that students reply to questions 'in full sentences', as shown below:

Sequence 6

Teacher: How many parts are left here, [*first pupil's name*]?
First pupil: Seven parts.
Teacher: Answer fully. How many parts are there?
Pupil: There are … there are seven parts.
Teacher: How many parts are left? Sit down, my boy. You have tired. Yes, [*second pupil's name*]?
Second pupil: We are left with seven parts.
Teacher: We are left with seven parts. Say that, [*second pupil's name*].
Second pupil: We are left with seven parts.
Teacher: Good boy. We are left with seven parts.

(Arthur 1992: 7)

To make proper sense of the demands of the task they face, the Botswanan students needed to understand that their teacher was using these exchanges not only to evaluate their mathematical understanding, but also to test their fluency in spoken

English and their ability to conform to a 'ground rule' that she enforced in her class-room, viz. to 'answer in full sentences'. For students in this kind of bilingual situation, the demands of classroom communication are complicated because their teacher is attempting to get them to focus on both the medium (in this case English) and the message (mathematics).

Code-switching

In circumstances where the classroom language is not the students' first language, a teacher who is bilingual may 'code-switch' to the first language if problems of comprehension arise. Sometimes the first language may be used only for asides, for control purposes or to make personal comments. However, when code-switching amounts to translation by the teacher of the curriculum content being taught, its use as an explanatory teaching strategy is somewhat controversial. On the one hand, there are those who argue that it is a sensible, common-sense response by a teacher to the specific kind of teaching and learning situation. Thus in studying its use in English-medium classrooms in China, Lin explains a teacher's use of translation as follows:

> The teacher was anxious that her students might not understand the point clearly; she therefore sought to ensure thorough comprehension through presenting the message again in Cantonese which is the students' dominant language.
>
> (Lin 1988: 78)

Researchers of bilingual code-switching have often concluded that it is of dubious value as a teaching strategy, if one of the aims of the teaching is to improve students' competence in English. Thus Jacobson comments:

> [T]he translation into the child's vernacular of everything that is being taught may prevent him/her from ever developing the kind of English language proficiency that must be one of the objectives of a sound bilingual programme.
>
> (Jacobson 1990: 6)

It seems, however, that teachers often use code-switching in more complex ways than simply translating content directly into another language. On observing class-rooms in Hong Kong, Johnson and Lee (1987) observed that the switching strategy most commonly employed by teachers had a three-part structure as follows:

1   'key statement' of topic in English;
2   expansion, clarification or explanation in Cantonese;
3   restatement in English.

They comment that 'direct translation was comparatively rare; the general effect was of a spiralling and apparently haphazard recycling of content, which on closer examination proved to be more organised than it appeared' (ibid: 106). The implication is that teachers in those bilingual settings were pursuing the familiar task of guiding children's understanding of curriculum content through language, but using special bilingual techniques to do so. Observing teachers in Malta, Antoinette Camilleri (1994) found that code-switching was used as a teaching technique by teachers in a variety of ways. Below are two short sequences of talk of a teacher in a Maltese secondary school, during a lesson about the production and use of wool which was based on a textbook written in English. The teacher begins reading part of the text. (Talk in Maltese is italicized and the English translation is given in the right-hand column.)

Camilleri notes that the first speech passage in Sequence 7 shows the teacher using the switch from English to Maltese to amplify the point being made, rather than simply repeating it in translation. In the second extract the teacher explains the English statement in Maltese, again avoiding direct translation. Camilleri comments that the lesson therefore is a particular kind of language event, in which their are 'two parallel discourses – the written one in English, the spoken one in Maltese' (ibid: 12).

Sequence 7

Teacher:	England, Australia, New Zealand and Argentina are the best producers of wool. *Dawk, l-aktar li għandom* farms *li jrabbu n-nagħag għas-suf …*	They have the largest number of farms and the largest number of sheep for wool …
Teacher:	Wool *issa* it does not crease but it has to be washed with care *issa din importanti ma għidtil komx illi jek ikolli nara xagħra jew sufa waħda* under the microscope *ghandha qisha ħafna* scales … *tal ħuta issa jek ma nahslux semwa dawk* l-i scales *jitgħaqqdu …*	Now this is important. Didn't I tell you that if I had to look at a single hair or fibre … ? … it has many scales which if not washed properly get entangled …

(Adapted from Camilleri 1994)

Studies of code-switching in classrooms have revealed a variety of patterns of bilingual use. For example, Zentella (1981) observed and recorded events in two bilingual classes in New York schools, one first-grade class (in which the children were about 6 years old) and the other a sixth-grade (in which the average age would be about 12). The students and teachers were all native Spanish speakers, of Puerto Rican origin, but the official medium for classroom education was English. One of the focuses of her analysis of teacher–pupil interactions was IRF sequences. Both Spanish and English were actually used by teachers and students in the classes, and Zentella was able to show that there were three recurring patterns of language-switching in IRF sequences, which seemed to represent the use of certain 'ground rules' governing language choice. These are summarized below:

Table 16.1   Teachers' language choices in bilingual classrooms

Rules governing language choice	Teacher initiation	Student reply	Teacher feedback
1 Teacher and student: 'follow the leader'	English Spanish	English Spanish	English Spanish
2 Teacher: 'follow the child'	English Spanish	Spanish English	Spanish English
3 Teacher: 'include the child's choice and yours'	English Spanish	Spanish English	both languages both languages

Source: Adapted from Zentella, 1981

Distinctive patterns of language use emerge in bilingual classrooms, overlaying the familiar patterns of teacher-led IRF exchanges. The extent to which features such as 'code-switching' between English and other languages occur in any particular classroom will depend on a whole range of factors, including the degree of fluency in English that members of a particular class have achieved, the bilingual competence of teachers, the specific teaching goals of teachers, and the attitudes of both children and teachers to the other languages involved.

Policy

The use of any particular language by teachers and students in a state school system is likely to reflect, though not necessarily conform to, official educational language policy of the relevant country or region. Policy and practice in schools is often influenced by political imperatives and allegiances, as well as ideas about the supposed cognitive and social effects on children of growing up bilingual. For example, the enforcement of a severe prohibition policy on the use of a mother tongue in school was well documented in nineteenth-century Wales, where any child heard speaking Welsh on the school premises was reprimanded and made to wear round their necks a rope called the 'Welsh knot' to show that they were in disgrace. By the late 1980s, however, both Welsh and English had become officially recognized as classroom languages in Wales.

Some countries, such as Canada and various states in India, have long-standing policies of recognizing English alongside other community languages in schools. On the other hand, at the point of writing in the late 1990s, established policies of tolerance towards the use of Spanish and other languages in many state schools in the USA seem in danger of being overturned in response to a strong 'English first' campaign to establish English constitutionally as the only recognized language in schools, workplaces and public life. A specific and controversial language issue in educational policy in many parts of the world in the latter part of the twentieth century has been the choice between English (as a 'world language') and other local languages as a medium for education. English is only the obvious choice in situations where it is the only official language of a country or state and where it is spoken by the vast majority of people. Yet English has been chosen as the medium for classroom education in many countries where these conditions do not apply. Examples would be many states in India, where students receive their education in English although it is their second language. In officially bilingual countries like Canada, choices have to be made at the level of state and city about whether French or English should be used as the main language in class. In such countries, educational policy may be framed to allow parents some degree of choice of classroom language for their children. Thus in Wales, the balance of Welsh- and English-medium schools is officially monitored and is supposed to be adjusted to suit demand.

Sometimes it may seem that there is not really much choice about which language to use as a medium for education, because one language is already the dominant language in a community. However, economic and cultural factors may make such assumptions dangerous – as exemplified by the serious consideration given by the government of The Netherlands in the early 1990s to a proposal to conduct all Dutch higher education in English. If a policy choice has to be made about whether one or other language should be used as the classroom medium in a country's schools, the decision may be a matter of political controversy. As Mazrui and Mazrui (1992) put it, when discussing the use of English in African schools and other state institutions:

> Africa ... is a great battleground between Western languages and non-Western languages. English, French and Portuguese have had particularly wide-ranging influences. ... Africa's ethnic heterogeneity finds its diverse differentiation in language. *Per capita* there is a wider range of languages in Africa than in any other region of the world. By a strange twist of destiny, there are also more French-speaking, English-speaking and Portuguese-speaking countries in Africa than anywhere else in the world.
>
> (Mazrui and Mazrui 1992: 84)

Standard forms

In most countries it is normally expected that in their written work students should conform to the requirements of the standard form or variety of the official language of that country. (Standard conventions applied in schools even for one language often vary between countries, so that the Standard Englishes of the UK, USA, India and Australia show some variation, as do the standard forms of Portuguese in Portugal and Brazil.) It is also a fairly common expectation that students should use standard vocabulary and grammar in their spoken language in the formal business of the classroom – that is, when replying to teachers' questions, or making oral reports or formal presentations to an audience. In public examinations, marks may be lost if students express themselves in regional non-standard varieties. So as mentioned above (see 'Learning' and 'Policy'), students may have to learn to use Standard English, because they have grown up speaking a regional or non-British variety of English. As even the great majority of native-speakers of English use regional varieties of English – which are by definition non-standard – in their out-of-school lives, this kind of learning is faced by the majority of such students entering English-medium classrooms.

An insistence on the use of, say, the official standard variety of English in the schools of an English-speaking country may seem unsurprising, easy to justify and, at first consideration, uncontroversial. But this may become a heated and complex political issue, as has certainly been the case for many years in Britain. The more vociferous advocates of a policy which insists on the use of Standard English as a classroom language in Britain have sometimes argued that the issue is not simply one of a choice between which variety or dialect of English is most appropriate for use in the classroom, but one of maintaining standards of correctness which reflect established cultural values. Debate about these matters in the popular mass media is usually depressingly ill-informed. For example, in the British press the use by children of non-standard grammar in speech or a strong regional accent in school is often treated as part and parcel of a larger educational issue, in which perceived changes in standards of spelling, functional writing and oral communication skills amongst young people are taken to embody the moral and economic decline of society. People on both sides of this debate may take a variety of positions, but most opposition to populist enforcement of standards seems to stem from concern about the effects that any official denigration and devaluation of the local languages or non-standard varieties of communities may have on the self-esteem of students who are members of those communities.

As well as tackling the issue of the use of a standard form of a language or a particular language as a medium for classroom education, educational language policy commonly has also to deal with the issue of whether or not students should be expressly taught about other languages or varieties of a language as part of the school curriculum.

Just as one of the tasks facing all students who are being educated in English is that of learning certain educational 'ground rules' or conventions for using spoken English in the classroom (see 'Learning' above), educational success also depends on students learning to use the conventions that are used by educated writers. However, research has shown that these 'ground rules' are rarely taught explicitly by teachers. Instead, as the research of Sheeran and Barnes (1991) has shown, students are expected to infer them from whatever instructions and feedback teachers provide on the students' work. This kind of realization stimulated a group of Australian language researchers (Christie and Martin 1997) to devise a new approach to the study and teaching of writing in the classroom, based on the work of the linguist Michael Halliday, and now generally known as the 'genre approach'. One of the aims of this approach has been to focus the attention of teachers and students on how written texts in English are expected to vary according to their nature and function. The task of writing a text in any particular genre – a business letter, a report of a scientific experiment, a poem, or a short story – can be analysed in terms of the conventional expectations in any society about what such a text should look like, and what assumptions an author can reasonably make about the knowledge a reader will bring to the text. Although the genre theorists have mainly concentrated on the learning of styles of writing, their approach is also applicable to the learning of spoken genres.

One strength of the genre approach is that it offers teachers and students an analysis of how English or any other language is used in specific social contexts, and attempts to make explicit the 'ground rules' for producing socially appropriate ways of writing. The essence of most criticisms of the genre approach are set out below.

- It tends to encourage the teaching of narrowly defined models for specific kinds of texts, when 'educated' writing involves the development of a much more flexible and creative ability.
- It tends to support an uncritical view of how established, powerful groups in a society use English (or any other language).
- Learning 'powerful' ways of using a language does not necessarily gain the user access to power.

Considering the use of language in education across countries and cultures, it is apparent that the genre requirements that students encounter may vary significantly. That is, the conventional expectations amongst teachers about what constitutes a good essay, story or scientific report may be different even in countries that share the same language as a medium of education (as, say, India, Australia, the USA and the UK). It was suggested above that when children enter an English-medium classroom (having grown up speaking another language and having been educated in a country with very different cultural traditions) it may be difficult for both teachers and children to distinguish between the first two 'learning tasks' listed earlier – acquiring a basic fluency in English and learning the conventions of particular genres of English which are used in school. This variation can become a problem for students who move from one country to another. Moreover it can be difficult for a teacher to tell whether a new pupil (especially one who is not fluent in English), who appears to be having difficulties with the language demands of education, is struggling with general aspects of using English or with the 'local' ground rules for using written or spoken language in the classroom.

References

Arthur, J. (1992) 'Talking like teachers: teacher and pupil discourse in standard six Botswana classrooms', Working Paper no. 25, Centre for Language in Social Life, Lancaster University.

Barnes, D. and Todd, F. (1995) *Communication and Learning Revised*, Portsmouth, NH: Heinemann.

Boggs, S. (1985) *Speaking, Relating and Learning: a Study of Hawaiian Children at Home and in School*, Norwood, NJ: Ablex Publishing.

Camilleri, A. (1994) 'Talking bilingually, writing monolingually', paper presented at the Sociolinguistics Symposium, Lancaster University, March 1994.

Christie, F. and Martin, J. (1997) *Genre and Institutions: Social Processes in the Workplace and School*, London: Cassell.

Cleghorn, A., Merritt, M. and Obagi, J. O. (1989) 'Language policy and science instruction in Kenyan primary schools', *Comparative Education Review* 33(1): 2–39.

Dillon, J. J. (1988) (ed.) *Questioning and Discussion: a Multidisciplinary Study*, London: Croom Helm.

Edwards, D. and Mercer, N. (1987) *Common Knowledge: the Development of Understanding in the Classroom*, London: Methuen/Routledge.

Heath, S.B. (1983) *Ways with Words: Language, Life and Work in Communities and Classrooms*, Cambridge: Cambridge University Press.

Hull, R. (1985) *The Language Gap*, London: Methuen.

Jacobson, R. (1990) 'Allocating two languages as a key feature of a bilingual methodology' in R. Jacobson and C. Faltis (eds) *Language Distribution Issues in Bilingual Schooling*, Clevedon: Multilingual Matters.

Johnson, R.K. and Lee, P.L.M. (1987) 'Modes of instruction: Teaching strategies and students responses' in R. Lord and H. Cheng (eds) *Language Education in Hong Kong*, Hong Kong: The Chinese University Press.

Lin, A. (1988) 'Pedagogical and para-pedagogical levels of interaction in the classroom: a social interactional approach to the analysis of the code-switching behaviour of a bilingual teacher in English language lesson', *Working Papers in Linguistics and Language Teaching No. 11*, University of Hong Kong Language Centre.

Malcolm, I. (1982) 'Speech events of the Aboriginal classroom', *International Journal of Sociology of Language* 36: 115–34.

Maybin, J. (1994) 'Children's voices: talk, knowledge and identity' in D. Graddol, J. Maybin and B. Stierer (eds) *Researching Language and Literacy in Social Context*, Clevedon, Multilingual Matters.

Mazrui, A.M. and Mazrui, A.A. (1992) 'Language in a multicultural context: the African Experience', *Language and Education*, 6(2,3,4): 83–98.

Mercer, N. (1995) *The Guided Construction of Knowledge: Talk amongst Teachers and Learners*, Clevedon: Multilingual Matters.

Norman, K. (ed.) (1992) *Thinking Voices: the Work of the National Oracy Project*, London: Hodder & Stoughton.

Sheeran, Y. and Barnes, D. (1991) *School Writing: Discovering the Ground Rules*, Milton Keynes: Open University Press.

Sinclair, J. and Coulthard, M. (1975) *Towards an Analysis of Discourse: the English Used by Teachers and Students*, London: Oxford University Press.

Wells, G. (1986) *The Meaning Makers*, London: Hodder & Stoughton.

Wood, D. (1992) 'Teaching talk' in K. Norman (ed.) *Thinking Voices: the Work of the National Oracy Project*, London: Hodder & Stoughton.

Zentella, A.C. (1981) '*Ta bien*, you could answer me in *chalquier idioma*: Puerto Rican code-switching in bilingual classrooms' in R. Duran (ed.) *Latino Language and Communicative Behaviour*, Norwood, NJ: Ablex Publishing Corporation.

Zukow-Goldring, P., Romo, L. and Duncan, K.R. (1994) 'Gestures speak louder than words: achieving consensus in latino classrooms' in A. Alvarez and P. del Rio (eds) *Education as Cultural Construction* (Explorations in Socio-Cultural Studies, vol. 4.), Madrid, Infancia y Aprendizaje.

Section 4

Curriculum

17 Understanding the context of curriculum

Bob Moon

Whenever people join together in any form of education some notion of curriculum exists. How explicit that is depends on the formality of the setting and the influence of history and tradition. We have very detailed records of what was taught in the schools of ancient Egypt, classical Greece and Imperial Rome. In the Middle Ages the education of the elite, almost wholly in the hands of the church, was created around a curriculum that had a direct lineage to the times of Plato and Aristotle. The curriculum today reflects elements of the monastic curriculum of the *quadrium* – music, astronomy, geometry and arithmetic, and the *trivium* – grammar, rhetoric, philosophy as logic.

Over succeeding centuries new subjects were added on and a few disappeared. This was not a uniform process. Philosophy, for example, is retained in the French secondary school curriculum and features prominently in some forms of the baccalaureate examination. In Britain it has all but disappeared as a school subject. Many subjects struggled to gain inclusion in the curriculum. Historical studies now exist which analyse the ways in which English, science and geography, for example, gained a place in the secondary curriculum. In the last years of the twentieth century technology fought for a place by means not dissimilar to those deployed by scientists a century earlier.

A number of introductory comments can be made about our knowledge and understanding of curriculum. First the term is not universally used. In the Latin, southern countries of Europe, and in those parts of the world with education systems that go back to the colonizing influence of the French, Portuguese or Spanish, for example, there is no word and hence little concept of curriculum as it is understood in the northern European, North American and Australasian world. In France, the *contenu* (context), *didactique* (didactics) and *pédagogie* (pedagogy) are seen as related but separate parts of the teaching and learning process. But there is no overarching idea of curriculum. The concept of curriculum was most strongly advocated in North America in the early years of the twentieth century. In that context curriculum expressed the important connections between subjects, the choice of content, teaching methods and all aspects of schooling that impinged on successful learning. Curriculum development, therefore, was seen as a holistic process, going significantly beyond changes and reforms in subject matter.

A second point to make is that the organization of the curriculum is inextricably entwined in social, cultural and political context in which it had evolved. In

England and Wales the controversies surrounding which literacy texts should be compulsory in the National Curriculum, or which events in history should be studied or what forms of music should be taught, have all engendered profound political debate. The curriculum therefore is not above party politics or the politicking of interest groups. It is for this reason that curriculum change can be such a slow and fraught process. Over the last 50 years, for example, the primacy of classics has been slowly eroded to allow greater emphasis to the sciences. More recently technology has nudged in, just, through a transformation of what used to be termed woodwork, metalwork, home economics and some aspects of art.

A third point is to suggest that secondary schooling although currently organized around subjects need not necessarily be so. Over the last thirty or forty years there have been a number of experiments to introduce other forms of organization. An activity or project approach involving inter-disciplinary ways of working characterized many of these initiatives. Through the 1980s, for example, many secondary schools introduced what was termed the 'Technical and Vocational Initiatives' in an attempt to make teaching and learning more relevant to the lives and career aspirations of pupils. Few of these initiatives were organized around subjects.

There is a classic 1939 article on curriculum called 'the sabre-tooth curriculum'. Harold Benjamin, the author, provides a satirical account of a prehistoric tribe which decided to introduce some form of systematic education for its children. The curriculum was designed to meet particular survival needs and included subjects such as *sabre-tooth-tiger-scaring-with-fire*. But the climate of the region changes and the sabre tooth tiger perishes. Attempts to change the curriculum of the tribe's children, however, in Benjamin's satire are met with stern opposition particularly for those who see merit in the character and skill building associated with *sabre-tooth-tiger-scaring*.

The form of any curriculum therefore cannot be taken for granted. There may be many reasons why its organization is appropriate to current times. But curriculum in the broadest sense has to reflect changes in knowledge and social contexts. Inevitably curriculum becomes contested territory and change problematic.

Finally, a fourth point, curriculum in the UK and many other countries has become increasingly regulated over the past two decades. Governments of all political persuasions have seen education as a key element of social and economic prosperity. There has been an increasing reluctance to leave decisions about curriculum to teachers. The National Curriculum in England and Wales and Northern Ireland, introduced in 1988, set out the very specific regulations about the subject and the content of the curriculum.

The prescription set down then by a Conservative government was largely adopted by a succeeding Labour government. The protagonists for a National Curriculum in its early form stopped short of trying to regulate teaching methods. More recently, however, government has increasingly resorted to non-statutory guidelines, for example, in the teaching of literacy and numeracy which, although non-statutory, when backed by the powers of inspection, are difficult to disregard.

In terms of curriculum most of the UK (Scotland does not have a formal National Curriculum) is highly centralized. Such a prescription does not extend to the whole curriculum. Schools have a degree of discretion over, for example, the time allocated to different subjects (in some countries this is regulated) and whether optional subjects are provided; but in those schools where the National Curriculum has to be taught (maintained schools) it has a big impact on teaching and learning, particularly as it is backed up by national tests and, at the end of Year 11, the GCSE examinations.

Understanding the curriculum, therefore, requires historical and political knowledge as well as an appreciation of the educational issues involved. It is interesting to speculate whether the subject-based curriculum will be as durable in the twenty-first century as it has been in the twentieth. More knowledge-based forms of employment, the development of new interactive technologies and the questioning of the age-linked 'lock stop' ways of organizing schooling, might well ensure a significant shift in the form and structure of the secondary school curriculum.

18 The origins of the National Curriculum

Bob Moon

The Secretary of State's policies for the range and pattern of the 5 to 16 curriculum will not lead to national syllabuses. Diversity at local education authority and school level is healthy, accords well with the English and Welsh tradition of school education, and makes for liveliness and innovation.

(*Better Schools: a summary*, March 1985: 4)

The Government has announced its intention to legislate for a national foundation curriculum for pupils of compulsory school age in England and Wales ... Within the secular National Curriculum, the Government intends to establish essential foundation subjects – maths, English, science, foreign language, history, geography, technology in its various aspects, music, art and physical education ... the government wishes to establish programmes of study for the subjects, describing the essential content which needs to be covered to enable pupils to reach or surpass the attainment targets.

(*The National Curriculum 5–16, a consultation document*, July 1987: 35)

... In July 1988, just a year after the publication of a consultation document, the Education Reform Bill, which prescribes a National Curriculum, received Royal Assent and passed on to the statute books in the UK. Scotland does not have a National Curriculum. The curriculum clauses survived the Commons committee stages and vigorous, early-morning attacks in the House of Lords, to pass unaltered into legislation. The measures represent a remarkable political intervention to change the post-war consensus on curriculum control.

How did a centrally-prescribed National Curriculum come to be established and, moreover, how can the *volte-face* in policy represented in the change from *Better Schools* to the Education Reform Act be explained? The answer lies partly in the evolution of some recurring, even predictable, curriculum policies, but arguably more significantly in the political opportunism of those who achieved positions of power and influence prior to and shortly after the 1987 Election. This chapter, therefore, will examine these events and speculate on how the system worked to produce what a few years ago would have been unthinkable policies. [...]

Ten subjects made up the National Curriculum: English, mathematics and science, defined as *core foundation* subjects, alongside seven further *foundation* subjects: art, history, modern languages (11–16 only), music, physical education and technology. The Secretary of State is required by the 1988 Education Reform Act to establish Programmes of Study and define Attainment Targets for each of the subjects. The Attainment Targets provide the basis for national and school reported assessments at the ages of seven, eleven, fourteen and sixteen. […]

The Education Reform Act contained detail on curriculum, a point not missed in parliamentary debate, with Lord Grimond railing against legislation only being comprehensible when read with a document that was not part of it (*Hansard*, House of Lords, May 1988: 711) and Lord Kilmarnock asking for some idea of the remit given to each of the subject area working parties (ibid: 531) before making decisions about the Bill. These working parties represented a further innovative feature of the times. The Secretary of State, Kenneth Baker, set up the National Curriculum through subject working parties … and reporting direct to government … . He, and his staff, closely monitored the direction the working parties were taken. When the mathematics working party, for example, failed to achieve a model to his liking the chair was sacked and a new appointment made. At publication, therefore, the subject outlines had received informal ministerial approval. […]

In many ways the subject basis of the National Curriculum is familiar, with origins stretching back at least to the nineteenth century. The historical line is traceable and well documented in general curriculum histories. The Newcastle Report of 1861, for example, led to the 1862 Revised Code of Robert Lowe and a stress on basic subjects, age-related programmes of study, and the notorious 'payments by results' system for teachers. Three years later the Clarendon Commission investigated nine leading public schools and advocated, in addition to the central study of classics, the introduction into the curriculum of mathematics, modern languages and natural sciences. The Commission even made an attempt to assess standards, and proposed examining fifth-form boys. The replies from headteachers were terse and to the point:

> Your letter appears to be so seriously objectionable that I must beg to decline to entertain the proposal. The Dean of Westminster concurs with me.
>
> (Reverend Charles R. Scott, Westminster)

> Objectionable both in principle and detail.
>
> (Dr Elwyn, Charterhouse)

More precise objections came from Moberley of Winchester:

> We should be deeply and unnecessarily wounded by having it put on record that we had passed a bad one.

and Balsham of Eton:

> This interference with the authority of the headmaster is calculated to cause evil.
>
> (Quoted in Sherwood 1977)

In 1868 the Taunton Commission, after looking at 800 endowed grammar schools, recommended three types of school, serving three classes of society, with leaving ages of 18, 16 and 14. Each school would have a distinctive curriculum. The emphasis of the first grade school would be classics and preparation for university. In grade 2 the requirements of the army, business and the professions required a stronger emphasis on practical rather than abstract activities, whilst the sons of artisans in grade 3 schools had a less precisely prescribed curriculum, although the basics were essential.

The latter part of the nineteenth century, and the period of this century up to the Second World War, abounds with evidence of curriculum regulations.

Table 18.1   Subject regulations for 1904 and 1935

1904	1935
English language	English language
English literature	English literature
One language	One language
Geography	Geography
History	History
Mathematics	Mathematics
Science	Science
Drawing	Drawing
Due provision for manual work and physical exercises	Physical exercises and organised games
Housewifery in girls' schools	Singing [Manual instruction for boys, dramatic subjects for girls]

Note
When two languages other than English are taken, and Latin is not one of them, the 'Board' will be required to be satisfied that the omission of Latin is for the advantage of the school.

The Revised Code went through many versions, with Gladstone's fourth administration providing a significantly liberalizing influence. The 1904 Regulations for Secondary Schools included detailed syllabuses specifying the amount of time to be allocated to each subject. A senior civil servant, Robert Morant, after a meteoric rise via the Court of Siam and a private secretarial position to Permanent Secretary of the Board of Education in just eight years, drafted the regulations. A workaholic ('the day is never long enough – I must soak all the time in varied educational juices'), he is supposed to have recorded in his diary a liking for both centralized administration and for the widespread implementation in secondary schools of the classical curriculum model characteristic of the fee-paying public schools. Morant's political and bureaucratic manoeuvres succeeded on both counts, as well as markedly increasing the powers of Permanent Secretary in the revamped Board of Education. Table 18.1 of the subject regulations for 1904 and 1935 shows how successful he was and how lasting the early model was to be.

The 1935 regulations remained in force until the Butler 1944 Education Act. The elementary codes disappeared rather earlier, to be replaced by the Board of Education Blue Book, *A Handbook of Suggestions*, which went through a number of editions again until 1944.

The 1988 specification therefore looked remarkably similar to those of 1935, although planned to cover the whole rather than secondary years of compulsory schooling. What had happened in between? As far as secondary schools were concerned the pattern remained remarkably consistent. Survey after survey, culminating in the 1979 HMI Secondary School Survey, showed how lasting Morant's model was. The subjects of the National Curriculum in 1988 were the subjects of the secondary curriculum in each of the four preceding decades. The grammar school model of the 1940s was copied by the secondary moderns of the 1950s and the newly established comprehensives of the 1960s and 1970s. Some brave attempts to provide otherwise, following the Newsom Report in 1963 on the average- and below average-attaining child, and the Raising of the School Leaving Age (ROSLA) programme in 1972 were soon reformulated in a subject structure. ... In the 1980s, especially post-14, a national Technical and Vocational Educational Initiative (TVEI) funded curriculum experiments which on the whole avoided the traditional subject-based approach. The rigid implementation of the subject-based curriculum, however, as with the earlier projects, meant that little of that period survived. Today, in the early years of the new century, yet further attempts to develop a more vocational focus to the secondary curriculum are under revision.

In primary schooling the picture was more varied. The abolition of the 11+ examination helped generate a new approach to curriculum organization. Strong advocates for a more child-centred approach to teaching, such as Alec Clegg in the West Riding of Yorkshire and Edith Moorhouse in Oxfordshire, received wide publicity for the primary school reforms in their local authorities. The Plowden Report, published in 1967, gave warm approval to these new directions, and for a few years English primary schools were inundated with international visitors. More recent evidence, however, suggests that the spread of these ideas was limited. An unpublished survey commissioned for HMI in 1988 showed that, in the average primary classroom, over half the week was devoted to studying basic mathematics and English. [...]

The first indication of the form the National Curriculum would take was published within a few months of the 1987 Conservative Election victory. The red consultation document, The National Curriculum 5–16, was greeted with forceful criticism. Although the time-scale for consultation was short, two months including the summer holiday period, thousands of responses were received. Comment ranged from the right-wing Institute of Economic Affairs (IEA) arguing that the market, not government, should determine curriculum, to the National Union of Teachers' fear of uniformity and conformity. The tone of the document was strident, and made for more interesting reading than many government publications. A model curriculum was proposed for the secondary school in subject terms. There was no discussion of how the subject curriculum would apply to primary schools. The need for a ten-subject school curriculum was boldly asserted without qualification and without reference to the plethora of government and inspectorial publications that had appeared in the decade following James Callaghan's Ruskin College Speech of 1976. Ruskin is referred to in paragraph 4 of the consultation document:

> Since Sir James Callaghan's speech as Prime Minister at Ruskin College in 1976, successive Secretaries of State have aimed to achieve agreement with their partners in the education service on policies for the school curriculum.

This pointed political reference, implying a measure of cross-party support and concern, is followed by a critical passage:

> Progress has been variable, uncertain and often slow. Improvements have been made, some standards of attainment have risen. But some improvement is not enough ... the government now wishes to move ahead at a faster pace.

It is interesting to look back to 1976 and trace the curriculum events that led to a National Curriculum proposal. In the mid-1970s the signs of a breakdown in the post-war educational cohabitation between local authorities and to a lesser extent the teachers' unions were beginning to show. Political disillusion with the attempts at curriculum reform had surfaced in a confidential DES document prior to Callaghan's Ruskin speech. The widely leaked document (the Yellow Book) caused considerable consternation amongst educationalists. Callaghan commented in the speech on the interest aroused:

> There have been one or two ripples of interest in the educational world in anticipation of this visit. I hope the publicity will do Ruskin some good and I don't think it will do the world of education any harm. I must thank all those who have inundated me with advice: some helpful and others telling me less politely to keep off the grass. ... It is almost as though some people would wish that the subject matter and purpose of education should not have public attention focused on it nor that profane hands should be allowed to touch it.

He then proceeded, after a brief reference to the dedication of the teaching profession, to comment on:

> the unease felt by parents and others about the new informal methods of teaching ... the strong case for the so-called 'core curriculum' of basic knowledge ... the use of resources in order to maintain a proper national standard of performance and the need to improve relations between industry and education.

The outcome from Ruskin was a series of regional meetings (the Great Debate), usually chaired by the new Secretary of State for Education Shirley Williams, and to which a wide range of groups, including industrialists, as invited to send representatives. For a short while the DES was clearly on the offensive in orchestrating national concerns; in policy terms; however, there was little outcome. The Labour government holding power for much of the time, with a small group of Liberals, found the local authority lobby powerful in opposing central government intervention. ...

Any political momentum gained was in any case dissipated by the loss of power in the 1979 election. Ruskin did, however, represent a watershed in the post-war history of curriculum reform, and for two reasons. Firstly it brought into the open the ambitions of some DES permanent officials to increase central control over curriculum. In terms of Whitehall politics it heralded a decade of activity that many may see as one of the most significant forces in establishing a national and central curriculum. Secondly Ruskin precipitated a parallel debate amongst prominent interest groups about the way the school curriculum should be structured. Whilst the battles for control remained unresolved, a remarkable degree of unanimity began to emerge on this issue.

The consensus developed around the idea of curriculum entitlement expressed in terms of areas of curriculum experience. The influence of philosophers of education such as Paul Hirst at the London Institute and then Cambridge University, and John White also at the London Institute, was openly acknowledged. HMI were first in the field, publishing in 1977 what became known as the Red Book.

The discussion document focused on the Curriculum 11–16. After making clear that the papers included were not advocating a centrally controlled or directed curriculum, they go on to argue for a common curriculum constructed around eight areas of experience, listed they say, in alphabetical order to make clear that none should be weighted more highly than the others:

- the aesthetic and creative
- the ethical
- the linguistic
- the mathematical
- the physical
- the scientific
- the social and political
- the spiritual.

This model was soon taken up through the DES documents and, whilst it was still in existence, the publications of the Schools Council, and on the educational conference circuit. Rumours therefore of DES intervention in the late 1970s and early 1980s were associated in most people's minds with a framework based on areas of experience providing coherence and balance across the curriculum. Such a framework, it was assumed, would be interpreted according to school and local circumstances, and the publication of *Better Schools*, quoted in the introduction to this chapter, gave no reason to doubt otherwise.

At first sight therefore the presentation of a model curriculum, complete with possible percentage allocations of time, in the red 1987 consultation paper was in stark contrast to HMI's Red Book of a decade earlier. In 1977 HMI had asserted that curriculum construction through subjects was only acceptable when everyone was clear what was to be achieved through them (p. 6). The disappearance of 'areas of experience' from curriculum debate is one of the significant features of the 1987 consultation document and the debates that preceded and followed publication.

Behind this change in curriculum policy was a radical shift in the balance of power between government and the interest groups that had been so influential in building educational policy in the post-war period. It is now becoming clear that in the months immediately before and after the 1987 general election, a small group of prime ministerial advisers, including or at least influenced by the pamphleteers and polemicists of numerous right-wing 'think tanks', exerted increasing pressure on the Prime Minister. The ideas formulated, first for the Conservative Party Election Manifesto and then the consultation document, bypassed Her Majesty's Inspectorate, the Association of County Councils, the Association of Metropolitan Authorities, the teachers' unions, the Society of Education Officers, and also the Schools Curriculum Development Committee (SCDC) and Secondary Examinations Council (SEC).

Government ministers and DES officials were well aware that none of these groups could subscribe to the form and style of the 1987 Red Book proposals. It was in line with government policy to marginalize the teachers' views and those of the local authorities, but few would have predicted the ruthless exclusion of HMI or SCDC and SEC from policy formulation. This, however, represented pressure-group politics of a most active form, sustained over a significant period of time.

The way the National Curriculum finally came to occupy an important niche in the Education Reform Act, and the form in which it was expressed, can be seen to date back to Sir Keith Joseph's final years in office. ... It appears that there was impatience and disillusion within the Tory party about policy-making in the Joseph era. Despite some radical ideas (set out, for example, in his 1982 speech to the North of England Conference), he had prevaricated over many decisions, and in his clumsy handling of a teachers' industrial dispute between 1984 and 1986 he had failed to show the clear and firm resolve expected of ministers in a Thatcher government. There may also have been something of a suspicion that despite the polemic and rhetoric of the times, he had earned a grudging respect from some parts of the educational establishment. The introduction of the common 16+ GCSE examination was one major source of concern in some quarters. Rumours of his departure circulated for a long period, and Prime Minister Margaret Thatcher was said be showing an interest in education, particularly as her increasing impatience with local authority teacher unions ... was most starkly illustrated within the education service. It should also be noted that her own ministerial career, when she presided in 1970–74 over a record number of grammar school closures, was seen as hardly successful against the criteria of Thatcherism in the 1980s. This was a new opportunity to make amends.

The arguments put forward to and by her advisers were opportune and congruent with the way policy was being developed towards other parts of the Welfare State, most notably the Health Service. The polemicists of the New Right had waged a well-publicized campaign for a return to what they saw as traditional values. A number had been leading contributors to the late 1960s Black Papers, an earlier polemic against progressive and egalitarian ideas, and the prospect of a third Thatcher victory and active Prime Ministerial interest offered a unique opportunity to influence policy.

It is now widely accepted that regular informal contact was maintained between the

Prime Minister's office and leading members from pressure groups such as the Centre for Policy Studies and the Hillgate Group. In formulating the election manifesto and determining the content and style of the consultation document, this influence was highly significant. A comparison between the Hillgate Group's 1986 pamphlet *Whose Schools?* and the content of the Education Reform Act shows just how significant. In their ideas Margaret Thatcher had detected a populist appeal; in public speeches she was quick to reassert the need for traditional approaches, whilst ridiculing certain attempts to combat some of the enduring curriculum problems. In her address to the 1987 Conservative Party Conference she talked of 'children who need to be able to count and multiply learning anti-racist mathematics – whatever that might be … ', and promised her audience that the National Curriculum would comprise '… reading, writing, spelling, grammar, arithmetic, basic science and technology'. […]

The National Curriculum in the form presented surprised and offended many in the educational world. It appeared to combine the continental traditions of subject prescription and the North American predilection for testing to create a particularly powerful, and for many threatening, proposal. The level of hostility was fuelled by the scarcity of information, fears about the way the statutory orders would be produced (would the working parties be given over to Hillgate?) and rumours about the form the testing would take. It was also apparent that the measures were to be vigorously pushed through, with compromise in the climate of the late 1980s interpreted as weakness. An ambitious Secretary of State had staked his political future on the passage of the Bill.

It is difficult … to clarify the way influence was exerted and motivation tapped in establishing such a major reform of curriculum policy. A number of themes, however, in the evolution of policy generally appear to be reflected in the Education Reform Act (ERA) and the National Curriculum clauses. A brief review suggests that the events of 1987–8 were less surprising than reactions at the time suggested. Three processes in particular appear to have fused around the National Curriculum: a long-term staking-out of bureaucratic control; the drive for efficiency and accountability that had become the characteristic of government attempts to reduce public expenditure; and finally a formulation of policy that brought together competing interests among pressure groups on the right.

John Quicke (1988) has explored this final point in an interesting analysis of the politics and ideas of the 'New Right' towards education over the last decade. He points to the differences between neo-conservatives such as Roger Scruton, a member of the Hillgate Group, and neo-liberals such as Stuart Sexton, working within the Institute of Economic Affairs. Neo-conservatives, he suggests, advocate strong government and a hierarchical and disciplined view of society in which a concept of the national is central. Neo-liberals on the other hand emphasize individual freedom of choice through the free workings of the market. In terms of curriculum, therefore, the neo-conservatives appeared to have been the most influential. A central, authoritarian prescription seems incompatible with a principle that permits the market parents to determine which form of curriculum prospers. The Institute of Economic Affairs in replying to the red consultation paper was clear:

The most effective National Curriculum is that set by the market, by the consumers of the education service. This will be far more responsive to children's needs and society's demands than any centrally imposed curriculum, no matter how well meant. Attempts by Government and by Parliament to impose a curriculum, no matter how 'generally agreed' they think it to be, are a poor second best in terms of quality, flexibility and responsiveness to needs than allowing the market to decide and setting the system free to respond to the overwhelming demand for higher standards. The Government must trust market forces rather than some committee of the great and good.

The influential Institute of Economic Affairs, therefore, saw the debate over a government-imposed National Curriculum as detracting attention away from what really mattered, namely the proposals to devolve management to schools. In establishing the curriculum proposals, these two groups appear to have been in tension. Margaret Thatcher was reported as wavering over the degree of prescription required for the National Curriculum, reaching the view at one stage that English, mathematics and science should comprise the limits of regulation. Kenneth Baker, Secretary of State, is said to have convinced her of the need for more widespread control. If Baker did seek to convince in this way he may have exploited the argument of the neo-conservatives that, uncontrolled, the curriculum serves as a vehicle for the politically motivated, illiberal and indoctrinating tendencies of the left. This is a persistent theme running through both the pamphlets (such as the Hillgate Group's determined attacks on any curriculum activity described as studies – peace studies, multicultural studies) and speeches made by Margaret Thatcher and other ministers in the pre-election period.

For Quicke, therefore, the strategy of the neo-conservatives was to highlight those elements they had in common with all forms of liberal education, and to contrast the values they jointly espoused with those underpinning the radical left-of-centre ideologies said to be dominant in educational bureaucracies, particularly at the local level. Despite the failure to convince market purists at the IEA, the approach was influential with the Prime Minister and with a minister keen to enlarge the role and responsibilities of the DES. […]

A second influence on policy is the quest for measures that create accountability and efficiency within the education service. From this perspective the National Curriculum 'tidies up' the ground upon which cost and personnel divisions can be made, and testing provides a basis for valid comparative judgements about efficiency of schools and classes. Donald Naismith (1988), formerly Director of Education for Croydon, is one of the few Education Officers to have gained the respect of groups such as Hillgate. He is unequivocal in seeing managerialism and efficiency as at the core of the proposals:

The way the education service was organised after the war attached greater importance to the separation and distribution of powers and responsibilities between central and local government and schools than to bringing them together in ways which established a direct managerial link between investment in its widest sense and performance. The results were stationary or falling standards and higher costs. By reintroducing objective standards and giving schools and colleges the means to attain them the Government believes it can combine higher standards with better management of resources, particularly as a school's results will be recorded and published in uniform ways, enabling comparisons to be made between schools and local authorities not only in terms of effectiveness but, more important, efficiency, the degree of success with which a school or local authority converts what goes into it and what comes out. We are going to hear a lot about performance indicators in the future.

(1988)

It is through this perspective that the DES's preference for an objectives-led curriculum, rather than HMI's 'areas of experience', becomes clear. HMI appear to have resisted many aspects of the pressure for comprehensive testing and assessment based on objectives. They would have been aware of the unresolved technical problems and the threat posed to time-honoured styles and inspection. There would also have been concern about a change in the working relationships with teachers and schools.

The curriculum clauses of the Education Reform Act show, however, the DES in the ascendancy, a quite significant fight-back after years enduring Mrs Thatcher's reported suspicions of obstructionism and inaction. ... The ambitions of bureaucrats can develop a momentum of their own. Managerialism promotes bureaucratic activity, and the DES prospered, not least in new departmental structures and an expanded staffing.

The form in which the National Curriculum was laid down represented a victory therefore for those on the right who had seized the political agenda for reform. It also represented a significant increase in the power and importance of the central ministry, the then Department for Education and Science, and it provided a yardstick against which new and more demanding forms of accountability could be introduced. [...]

References

Naismith, D. (1988) unpublished paper, A.S.C. conference, Gateshead, April.
Quicke, J. (1988) 'The "New Right" and education', *British Journal of Educational Studies*, February.
Sherwood, T. (1977) 'Evaluating the English experience' in P.L. Houts (ed.) *The Myth of Measurability*, New York: Hart Publishing Co.

19 Planning and implementing change

Michael Fullan

[…] How can we plan and implement change more effectively? What *assumptions* about change should we note?

The assumptions we make about change are powerful and frequently subconscious sources of actions. When we begin to understand what change is as people experience it, we begin also to see clearly that assumptions made by planners of change are extremely important determinants of whether the realities of implementation get confronted or ignored. The analysis of change carried out so far leads me to identify ten 'do' and 'don't' assumptions as basic to a successful approach to educational change.

1   Do not assume that your version of what the change should be is the one that should or could be implemented. On the contrary, assume that one of the main purposes of the process of implementation is to *exchange your reality* of what should be through interaction with implementers and others concerned. Stated another way, assume that successful implementation consists of some transformation or continual development of initial ideas.
2   Assume that any significant innovation, if it is to result in change, requires individual implementers to work out their own meaning. Significant change involves a certain amount of ambiguity, ambivalence, and uncertainty for the individual about the meaning of the change. Thus, effective implementation is a *process of clarification*. It is also important not to spend too much time in the early stages on needs assessment, programme development, and problem definition activities – school staff have limited time. Clarification is likely to come in large part through reflective practice.
3   Assume that conflict and disagreement are not only inevitable but fundamental to successful change. Since any group of people possesses multiple realities, any collective change attempt will necessarily involve conflict. Assumptions 2 and 3 combine to suggest that all successful efforts of significance, no matter how well planned, will experience an implementation dip in the early stages. Smooth implementation is often a sign that not much is really changing.
4   Assume that people need pressure to change (even in directions that they desire), but it will be effective only under conditions that allow them to react, to form their own position, to interact with other implementers, to obtain

technical assistance, etc. It is all right and helpful to express what you value in the form of standards of practice and expectations of accountability, but only if coupled with capacity-building and problem-solving opportunities.

5   Assume that effective change takes time. It is a process of 'development in use'. Unrealistic or undefined time lines fail to recognize that implementation occurs developmentally. Significant change in the form of implementing specific innovations can be expected to take a minimum of 2 or 3 years; bringing about institutional reforms can take 5 or 10 years. At the same time, work on changing the infrastructure (policies, incentives, and capacity of agencies at all levels) so that valued gains can be sustained and built upon.

6   Do not assume that the reason for lack of implementation is outright rejection of the values embodied in the change, or hard-core resistance to all change. Assume that there are a number of possible reasons: value rejection, inadequate resources to support implementation, insufficient time elapsed, and the possibility that resisters have some good points to make.

7   Do not expect all or even most people or groups to change. Progress occurs when we take steps (e.g., by following the assumptions listed here) that *increase* the number of people affected. Our reach should exceed our grasp, but not by such a margin that we fall flat on our face. Instead of being discouraged by all that remains to be done, be encouraged by what has been accomplished by way of improvement resulting from your actions.

8   Assume that you will need a *plan* that is based on the above assumptions and that addresses the factors known to affect implementation. Evolutionary planning and problem-coping models based on knowledge of the change process are essential.

9   Assume that no amount of knowledge will ever make it totally clear what action should be taken. Action decisions are a combination of valid knowledge, political considerations, on-the-spot decisions, and intuition. Better knowledge of the change process will improve the mix of resources on which we draw, but it will never and should never represent the sole basis for decision.

10   Assume that changing the culture of institutions is the real agenda, not implementing single innovations. Put another way, when implementing particular innovations, we should always pay attention to whether each institution and the relationships among institutions and individuals are developing or not.

Finally, do not be seduced into looking for the silver bullet. Given the urgency of problems, there is great vulnerability to off-the-shelf solutions. But most external solutions have failed. The idea is to be a critical consumer of external ideas while working from a base of understanding and altering local context. There is no complete answer 'out there'.

The scope of change

There are many dilemmas and no clear answers to the question of where to start. The reader who by now has concluded that the theory of educational change is a theory of unanswerable questions will not be too far off the mark. Harry Truman (and later

Pierre Trudeau) said, 'We need more one-armed economists,' because they were frustrated at the advice they kept getting: 'On the one hand … on the other hand'. The same can be said about the scope of educational change efforts. No one knows for sure what is best. We are engaged in a theory of probing and understanding the meaning of multiple dilemmas in attempting to decide what to do.

Sarason (1971) identified many of the underlying issues:

> A large percentage of proposals of change are intended to affect all or most of the schools within a system. The assumption seems to be that since the change is considered as an improvement over what exists, it should be spread as wide as possible as soon as possible. The introduction of new curricula is, of course, a clear example of this. What is so strange here is that those who initiate this degree of change are quite aware of two things: that different schools in the system can be depended on differentially to respond to or implement the proposed change, and that they, the sources … do not have the time adequately to oversee this degree of change. What is strange is that awareness of these two factors seems to be unconnected with or to have no effect on thinkings about the scope of the change.
>
> (pp. 213–14)

In later work Sarason (1990) maintains that we still have not learned to focus our efforts on understanding and working with the culture of local systems:

> Ideas whose time has come are no guarantee that we know how to capitalize on the opportunities, because the process of implementation requires that you understand well the settings in which these ideas have to take root. And that understanding is frequently faulty and incomplete. Good intentions married to good ideas are necessary but not sufficient for action consistent with them.
>
> (p. 61)

Above all, planning must consider the preimplementation issues of whether and how to start, and what readiness conditions might be essential prior to commencing. Implementation planning is not a matter of establishing a logical sequence of steps deriving from the innovation or reform at hand.

Two points put the problem of scope in perspective. First, in some situations it may be more timely or compatible with our priorities to concentrate on getting a major policy 'on the books', leaving questions of implementation until later. In other words, the first priority is initiation, not implementation. Major new legislation or policies directed at important social reforms often fit this mode – for example, new legislation on desegregation, special education, or restructuring. There is no answer to the question of whether this is more effective than a more gradual approach to legislation, but it should be recognized that implementation is then an immediate problem. Sarason and Doris (1979), in commenting on special education legislation, warn us: 'To interpret a decision … as a "victory" is understandable but one should never underestimate how long it can take for the spirit of victory to become appropriately manifested in practice' (p. 358). Much social policy legislation is vague on implementation; some vagueness may be essential in order to get the policy accepted, but nonetheless it means that implementation can be easily evaded. In the face of major value or power resistance, it is probably strategically more effective in the short run to concentrate our energies on establishing new legislation, hoping that in the long run the pressure of the law, the promotion of implementation through incentives and disincentives, and the emergence of new implementers will generate results.

Second, we have reached a stage, face-to-face with urgent need, and equipped with great knowledge of the dynamics of change, where *large-scale reform* must become the agenda – reform which simultaneously focuses on local development and larger system transformation (Fullan 2000). In other words, the focus of planning has shifted in recent times, where the most advanced systems are trying to figure out how to co-ordinate state policy and local development in order to transform large numbers of schools.

We conclude, then, as Mintzberg, Ahlstrand, and Lampei (1998) have, that 'strategy formation is complex space':

> Strategy formation is judgmental designing, intuitive reasoning, and emergent learning; it is about transformation as well as perpetuation; it must involve individual cognition and social interaction, cooperation as well as conflict; it has to include analyzing before and programming after as well as negotiating during; and all of this must be in response to what can be a demanding environment. Just try to leave any of this out and watch what happens!
>
> (pp. 372–3)

[…]

References

Fullan, M. (2000) 'The return of large-scale reform', *The Journal of Educational Change*, 1(1): 1–23.

Mintzberg, H., Ahlstrand, B. and Lampei, J. (1998) *Strategy safari: A guided tour through the wilds of strategic management*, New York: Free Press.

Sarason, S. (1971) *The culture of the school and the problem of change*, Boston: Allyn & Bacon.

Sarason, S. (1990) *The predictable failure of educational reform*, San Francisco: Jossey-Bass.

Sarason, S.B. and Doris, J. (1979) *Educational handicap, public policy, and social history*, New York: Free Press.

20 Assessment
A changing practice

Sally Brown

A scenario for change

Change can be unsettling, sometimes overwhelming, but it can also be motivating and bring about real progress. In the field of assessment, a great deal of talk over the last decade has been about change and substantial attempts have been made to introduce new practices. Different practices usually reflect different ideological commitments, and one of the most salient features of the movement has been the recognition that assessment, as part of education, must be about promoting learning and opportunities, rather than about sorting people into social roles for society.

There are, of course, those who say that there has been no basic change in assessment practices, and indeed there is evidence of resistance from groups with vested interests in holding on to the past. This tendency to try to hang on to the traditional and tested methods at a time when a new philosophy and practice of assessment is being introduced has resulted, in some circumstances, in confusion and impossible demands on practitioners. However, it is important to emphasize that much valuable and ordered progress has been made in this field. Ideas about assessment are discussed and debated among policy-makers, practitioners and researchers more and more openly than in the past, and this has led to greater understanding of its role in, and effect on, the education of young people.

The traditional view of assessment

It is not so long ago that the notion of 'assessment' in schools and colleges carried with it, in the United Kingdom at least, a vision of tests or examinations, certificates and grades or lists of marks. All of these were regarded as very important and as providing objective, reliable and precise measures of achievement. The use to which such measures were put was primarily one of the *selection* of young people for such things as further study, training courses, apprenticeships or careers. This system had the great advantage of administrative simplicity: it made comparisons among individuals (norm-referencing), and everyone knew that a grade B performance was better than a grade C and a mark of 49 was less than 51. It appeared to provide an effective means of sorting out those at the 'top', the 'middle' and the 'bottom', and of directing them towards an appropriate niche in society.

The assessment itself usually was carried out in a formal atmosphere and under strictly controlled conditions. Not all of it was undertaken under the auspices of national examination boards, but schools and colleges tended to try to replicate the boards' strict examination conditions: a large hall with an invigilator, no 'cheating', examination 'papers', a fixed allocation of time for responding in writing to the questions and the whole exercise undertaken at the end of something (a course, a term, a year or a school career). Teachers in 'non-academic' areas of the school curriculum without formal examinations tended to assert that they had no assessment. In some subjects, however, it was acknowledged that skills other than those which can be manifest in written answers may be important, and efforts were made to include practical examinations in, for example, home economics, music and science. Where examination boards took such initiatives, teachers were sometimes asked to administer the practical tests, but in strict accordance with instructions prepared by the board.

There were, of course, a wide range of activities going on in which teachers were trying to find out, often in classrooms and by informal means, what pupils had learned or could do. Employers too were making judgements about what apprentices had achieved. All of this we would now include within the concept of assessment, but that has been the case only in recent years.

Over the last two decades the ideas underlying the traditional concept of assessment increasingly have been questioned, and the last ten years have seen some dramatic changes in practice.

Questioning past practice

The questioning of past assessment practice has been of several different kinds. Some of it has been concerned with technical matters and has asked: Are grades and marks reliable? Would another marker, or the same marker on another day, make the same judgement about the performance of a young person? Are the assessments valid? Do they assess all they claim to assess? Are they fair? Do they give recognition for achievement or are they more concerned with sorting people out? Perhaps the most searching questions, however, are about the purposes of assessment. Should the focus be on selection, or can it play a more constructive and educational role? If so, is the traditional form of marks and grades appropriate and adequate? And finally, there is debate about who has control of making and reporting the assessments, and of deciding which young people will have access to the benefits which any system of assessment might offer.

There has always been concern about whether tests and examinations are reliable, valid and fair. A substantial body of work of high technical quality has been undertaken, particularly in North America, which has ensured that much is now known about the conditions under which a group of items constitute a reliable test: that is, one which will give the same assessment of the performance of an individual no matter who marks it, and regardless of whether the individual takes the test this week or next. Objective tests with each item having one right answer are most likely to fill the bill; assessment instruments which have heterogeneous items, and subjective marking procedures (e.g. essays), are much less likely to do so. Indeed, measures of reliability on examination essay marking have sometimes produced results which are alarming, especially when it is remembered that the future career of a young person can depend on the outcome of an argument between two examiners about a grade. To avoid this problem, one approach has been to restrict examination questions to objectively marked items. But this may well distort the set of achievements which are assessed; some things which it is intended young people should learn or be able to do are not amenable to objective testing. The capability to create a literary idea, to understand a complex theory or to generate an imaginative artifact, may not be assessable by such means as answering a multiple-choice question, or completing a single-answer calculation.

A narrowing-down of what is assessed to that which can be accurately measured may engineer some improvement in the reliability of a test, but it is likely to endanger its validity. One may ask what use is a grade or mark which is highly reliable but does not reflect the full range of achievements for which the course or set of experiences is aiming. Where such a grade or mark is used for selecting young people, what confidence can there be in its capability to predict that they will be successful in any subsequent course or career?

At a more general level, traditional tests are seen as having substantial limitations in the extent of their sampling of the variety of competences which it is intended young people should acquire. At one level, it is clear that a three-hour examination is an inadequate means of assessing, say, the learning from a two-year course. There are, furthermore, some kinds of performance which, in principle, cannot be assessed by traditional examinations, particularly where these are restricted to written tests. The validity of marks and grades as measures of performance in any given area, therefore, has been constrained by the form the assessments have taken. In particular, the assessment of practical skills, personal development, attitudes and performance in contexts other than conventional classrooms and laboratories has been neglected.

The matter of the fairness of assessments has been a continuing and agonizing concern. Because the main aim of traditional assessments has been to spread out the performance of candidates (so that selection procedures could be carried out more efficiently), great emphasis was placed on choosing test items so as to maximize discrimination between the performance of the high achievers and those of the low achievers. This resulted in the omission of those items which everyone would get right, and so the lowest achievers were denied the opportunity to show what they were able to do. In some parts of the world this has been further exacerbated by the development of 'standardized tests'. Standardized tests are designed to spread out the performances and make no pretence to match the curriculum to which any given individual has been exposed. They are general tests within a broad area which discriminate well among the whole population of young people. High discrimination, however, is most effectively achieved by reducing the specific content of items; the greatest discrimination is to be found in those tests which closely resemble content-free IQ tests. As soon as a move is made in that direction, the validity of the test as a measure of *educational achievement* must be in doubt. A valid test of such achievement must clearly reflect all the qualities of which it claims to be a measure, and those qualities will be identified with the substance of the curriculum which has been followed.

Many of the characteristics of assessment in the past have resulted from the dominant purpose towards which it has been directed, i.e. selection. In recent years the question has been raised of whether there are not other, and more important, functions for it to fulfil. Since it is part of the educational process should it not have a more constructive role to play in teaching and learning? Should the considerable efforts which are put into making assessments not be able to produce more, and more useful, information for teachers, students and others? If other functions are to be fulfilled by assessment, then it is unlikely that the traditional form of grades or marks will be adequate. An important limitation of that form is that, while it enables comparisons to be made among the performances of individuals (norm-referenced assessment), it provides no information about *what* has been achieved. Any kind of function for assessment which aims to provide information which will help young people to learn, or teachers to teach, will require an evaluative description of what has been achieved (criterion-referenced assessment).

The question of who should carry out the assessment of young people has not been a matter for debate in the past. Most frequently it has been assumed that the teacher will be the assessor, although examination for certification (probably seen as the most important manifestation of assessment) has generally been the province of professional examiners. There are obvious constraints on the ability of a professional examiner, who under normal conditions would not see the candidate, to carry out a comprehensive assessment of that young person's capabilities in those areas where he or she has had the opportunity to learn. It has been suggested that the teacher will be in a better position than the examiner to assess, but would that hold when the young people are out of school on, say, work experience or residential courses? The way in which educational aims have changed over the last few years, so that experiences of this kind are now commonplace in the school or college curriculum, clearly has implications for who should be the assessor. Furthermore, the fact that assessments may be carried out by a variety of people, with a range of perspectives, draws attention to the question of whether it is important to have a single measure of achievement for a young person in a given area, or whether it is more rational to accept that different people assess individuals differently, and that such differences should not be concealed within some compromise overall mark or grade.

The notion of young people themselves being involved in self- or peer-assessment has not been a facet of past practice. More recently the question of whether such involvement would be of value in helping to consolidate learning and to increase self-awareness is frequently mooted. For some aspects of personal and social development, which are currently receiving substantial emphasis in curriculum planning, it might seem that the young people are in the best position to make the judgements which assessment of such qualities calls for.

This debate on the possible inadequacy of the range of qualities assessed by traditional measures, and the restrictions on who should carry out those assessments, have been accompanied by concern about the proportion of young people leaving formal education without any record of what they have achieved. The established (and academic) certificate courses were not designed for the whole population and, in any case, were unsuited to the educational aims for many young people. Educational 'qualifications', however, have become more and more important. If the curriculum is to develop in various ways to prepare everyone more effectively for their future in work and in society generally then surely, it has been argued, all should have the opportunity to work for a certificate which recognizes what has been achieved? And if everyone has the chance to earn a certificate, surely such recognition will have a motivating effect on learning and, perhaps, reduce the alienation from education characteristic of many of the low achievers?

The doubts and dissatisfactions with the traditional concept of assessment have resulted in more than academic debate. There have been substantial changes in practice, and the experience gained has led to greater understanding of the potential and the problems associated with assessment. Assessment now commands a much wider conceptualization than in the past, and tends to be seen as an important and necessary ingredient of effective teaching and learning.

Innovative themes in assessment practice

The first theme concentrates on the way in which the concept of 'assessment' has progressed from the traditional notion of 'testing' for selection purposes. Assessment is now seen as *a much broader concept and fulfilling multiple purposes*. It is considered to be closely integrated with the 'curriculum' (a concept which is itself conceived in very much broader terms than in the past) and its purposes include fostering learning, improving teaching, providing valid information about what has been done or achieved, and enabling pupils and others to make sensible and rational choices about courses, careers and other activities. Evaluation of pupils for various selection purposes will continue, but there have been major efforts to ensure that we progress from the simplistic notion that young people can be put in some kind of rank order by grades (frequently based on the results of a single examination). Assessment, therefore, now has several functions including the diagnosis of causes of young people's success or failure, the motivation of them to learn, the provision of valid and meaningful accounts of what has been achieved, and the evaluation of courses and of teaching. We are much more cautious these days about making claims for how effectively assessment in one context can predict the success of young people in other contexts at later dates. The emphasis has shifted away from assessment for summative purposes: that is, a report at the end of a course or period of study which purports to predict future performance. Much more stress is laid on assessment for formative purposes: that is, the use of the information gathered to improve the current educational process.

This multiple-purpose concept of assessment, which is closely linked to the totality of the curriculum, leads directly to the second theme. This theme is concerned with the considerable *increase in the range of qualities assessed and contexts in which that assessment takes place*. Stringent boundaries put on many assessment systems in the past are breaking down. No longer is it necessary for the qualities assessed to be 'academic' and strictly amenable to measurement. Assessment of personal, social and attitudinal characteristics is frequently under consideration, and what counts as 'achievement' within even traditional subject areas has expanded considerably. In addition, the contexts in which assessment takes place are much more diverse than in the past. No longer are examination halls the places which one immediately associates with assessment; long overdue recognition is being given to the fact that most, and the most valuable, assessment is carried out on the site where the learning takes place. Changes in the curriculum have brought about acceptance that the place of learning is no longer always the school or college. The rise of work experience and community activities, for example, have opened up the issue of assessment for school pupils in the context of the workplace.

The third theme is directed to the rise of *descriptive assessment*. Much of this has manifested itself in the form of concern for criterion-referenced approaches which replace or complement traditional norm-referenced systems. The aim has been to provide descriptions of what has (or has not) been achieved, rather than to rely on pupils' marks or grades which have little meaning other than as a comparison with the marks and grades of others. Descriptions of this kind are seen as having the potential to help us understand what, and why, children are or are not learning, and to facilitate improved learning. Such descriptions may also be able to ameliorate the disadvantages of the competitive traditional system and to promote more co-operative attitudes to learning. Perhaps the most persuasive argument, however, has related to the anticipated value of the descriptive information to teachers and young people in making rational decisions about such things as courses to be followed, curriculums to be reformed, work to be done, remediation to be carried out, and so on.

A fourth theme is concerned with the *devolution of responsibilities for assessment* to, for example, schools, teachers, work experience employers and young people themselves. Teachers have always carried out most of the assessment to which pupils and students are subjected, but traditionally the assessment which 'matters' (i.e. national certification) has been firmly in the hands of external examination boards. The recognition that at all levels internal assessment by educational institutions is of crucial importance is changing all that; but things are going further in some quarters. The concern with the assessment of a wider range of things, some of which, like work experience, happen outside the classroom, has led to the involvement of others, such as employers, in the assessment process. Furthermore, many of the arguments about the value of assessments to pupils themselves have suggested that the benefits will be greatest if the young people can be persuaded to undertake self-assessment.

A fifth and final theme focuses on assessment for certification. Much of the public debate and changes in government policy in the 1980s have supported the view that *certification should be available to a much greater proportion of the population of young people* than has been the case in the past. The nature of certification is also undergoing reform.

The innovations identified in these five themes are by no means restricted to assessment developments in the United Kingdom. Apart from the fifth theme, which reflects the substantially greater obsession with certification in this country compared with most others, there is a considerable and worldwide literature concerned with similar matters.

21 Assessment and gender

Patricia Murphy

Bias and assessment practice

Before we look at ways of interpreting gender differences in pupils' performance, let us first briefly consider bias – as a concept rather than a technical issue. There is consistency in the statements about bias in the national assessment documentation, i.e. that all efforts should be made to remove it. If assessors are to put this policy into practice, how are they to define bias? If we consider differences in group performance on an example of a reading test task (Hannon and McNally 1986), the authors report that over half of the children who had English as a second language did not select what was judged to be the correct response.

An example from the reading test

The man was very late and just managed to jump … the bus as it was pulling away from the stop.

1   at
2   up
3   on
4   by

(Hannon and McNally 1986)

To consider whether the task was biased you have to ask why these children's response was as it was. Prior to asking the question, though, the performance has to have appeared aberrant in some way. For example, was the performance atypical? If the answer is yes, you may conclude, as the authors did, that the colloquial use of the word 'jump' when literally translated makes little sense. Jumping *by* or *at* a bus makes no more sense than jumping *on* one. For certain children, the task measures their lack of knowledge of colloquialisms rather than their ability to read.

The ability to explain a group difference on an assessment item enables us to make decisions about whether that item is biased. However, more often than not, we are unable to explain why certain assessment tasks demonstrate group differences. In international surveys of secondary pupils' science performance, boys have been found to perform consistently at a higher level than girls. Tasks where girls performed at a relatively higher level were few in number and exhibited no apparent common characteristics (Humrich 1987). Consequently, they were assumed not to be biased. The overwhelming number of tasks which showed boys ahead of girls was taken as an indication of a significant difference in achievement. We tend to take a statistically significant trend in results as an indication that we are measuring something of educational significance and so we are reassured about the validity of our assessment.

Looking for atypical behaviour in assessment tasks is based on certain premises: commonly, that we expect a similar distribution of scores for groups of pupils. This interpretation is based on a norm-referenced view of the population, i.e. that some are able, others average, and half below average. The national assessment is criterion-referenced (DES 1988a). In this paradigm, it is theoretically possible for the whole population to succeed or fail on any criterion with all shades of performance possible in between.

The APU science surveys were based on one of the few existing extensive criterion-referenced assessment schemes and applied to a large proportion of the school population (DES 1989a). A review of findings for populations of 11-, 13- and 15-year-old pupils established that there was no criterion on which any group of pupils performed consistently. We have to consider, therefore, how on a criterion-referenced assessment, atypical behaviour can be identified. The premise that appears to be operating in national policy statements with regard to bias is that group scores for girls and boys, for example, are expected to be equal. Atypical behaviour is, therefore, signalled by differences between groups.

There are two further points embedded in this brief discussion which warrant consideration. We have mentioned that assessors tend to take homogeneity of group performance as indicative that the assessment is on target. Apart from the problems associated with criterion-referenced assessment, this position also needs to be challenged in terms of the values that determine what is assessed and how it assessed. The international survey results in science, referred to earlier, are a case in point. The cross-cultural uniformity of gender differences on multiple-choice tests of science achievement have been subject to numerous interpretations. For some they represent a clear measure of boys' greater scientific ability; for others they indicate that, culturally, girls are not encouraged or expected to achieve as well as boys in science; yet others use them to argue that specific cultural factors which affect girls' and boys' science achievement must be in operation across cultures. For example, Kelly (1981) identified the 'masculine' image of science, common to most countries, as a contributory factor. She argued that as girls and boys have learnt to respond to gender-appropriate situations, then a 'masculine' science will alienate girls and discourage their engagement with it. From this perspective, bias is inherent in the definition of the subject and the characterization of achievement. The trend for boys consistently to outperform girls is evidence of this.

Another way in which we imbue assessments with particular values is in the choice of modes for assessment. Changes in assessment practice such as the introduction of multiple-choice sections in public exams have affected not the numbers achieving success, but the people. In the case of multiple-choice items, girls' success was negatively influenced (Murphy 1982: Harding 1979). The introduction of continuous coursework assessment in GCSE has also led to a shift in the population achieving success which shows a marked gender difference. The pattern of performance is not uniform but there is a tendency for girls to outperform boys on coursework even in subjects where boys tend to be ahead of girls on the written exam papers (Cresswell 1990). Do we interpret these results as indications of bias or does their consistency suggest that something significant is being measured? What has to be asked, then, is whether what is being measured is what was intended and whether it is judged to be a significant element of subject achievement. At this point, our values determine our interpretations and a commonly-held view is that coursework is a 'softer' option than the more 'objective' written forms of assessment. The devaluing of aspects of a particular group's performance can also lead to bias in assessment practice.

A final point concerns the notion of *group*. We have mentioned how our lack of awareness of significant factors in tasks limits our ability to explain both typical and atypical performance. If we are of the view that assessment procedures need to be individualistic to cater for individuals' meanings and ways of making sense, then bias is not a group issue; rather it is something we have to consider in interpreting each child's response. Our understanding of the concept of bias depends on how we view the way pupils create meaning and the extent to which we give priority to their meanings in assessments of achievements that we have identified as valuable. Any selection of technical treatments of bias will be informed by these perspectives.

Interpreting gender differences in performance

The data discussed here is interpreted from a perspective that sees pupils as active participants in learning, striving to make sense of their own experiences by searching for patterns, regularity and predictability. Central to this perspective is the notion that children can understand other people's minds from a very early age because of the shared use of language. This follows because learning to use language involves understanding 'the implicit, semi-connected knowledge of the words, from which, through negotiation, people arrive at satisfactory ways of acting in given contexts' (Bruner 1986: 65). To make sense of either learning or assessment tasks, pupils have to be able to construct meaning in them. To achieve this, assessors depend on a set of shared contexts and assumptions. Pupils' inability to understand a task can be interpreted either as a failing on the behalf of the assessor to provide appropriate cues to enable pupils to access their knowledge; or as an indication that pupils have not yet achieved the criterion being assessed. We look next at these two potential interpretations in the discussion of gender differences in performance.

Differences in experience

The APU science surveys at 11 and 13 showed boys and girls performing at the same level on assessments of the use of apparatus and measuring instruments: evidence perhaps of an unbiased assessment. However, when performance on individual instruments was reviewed, girls as a group did significantly less well than boys on certain ones, e.g. microscopes, stop watches, etc. The number of instruments to show this effect increased as pupils went through school until, at 15, boys performed at a higher level overall. How do we interpret such results? Do we treat them as an indication that there are innate differences in the abilities of pupils which become more evident as the range and demands of the tasks increase? The viability of this interpretation will depend on the view we hold about the nature of individual ability and how it is distributed in the population. If, on the other hand, we assume that scores should be equal, what then? Do we statistically adjust scores to take account of this, reject certain tasks or attempt to generate others?

What was assumed in this case was that the tasks were assessing something significant. What that was had to be established before the results could be interpreted and used. Consequently, questionnaires were developed to find out what experience pupils had of the instruments outside of school that might be relevant. The results showed that boys' performance is better than girls' on precisely those instruments that they claimed to have more experience of. Thus, the assessment tasks themselves were not problematic, only the assumption that they were concerned solely with achievements acquired in school. A failure to collect such additional data would result in summative statements being misinterpreted. It would also make it difficult to meet the requirements of formative assessment which are to inform children's learning and teachers' planning. To understand and make use of assessment data, it is important that bias is considered as only one possible explanation of why responses are as they are.

If we are concerned to understand how pupils may or may not construct meaning in assessment tasks, it is important to consider the *nature* of the different experiences. Children using instruments outside of school will not only start to appreciate how to use them, but also when to use them and to what ends. An assessment task asking pupils to read off from an instrument is commonly judged to be measuring a low-level skill. Yet, such tasks assume that pupils understand: the variable being measured; the situations where the instrument is typically used; and the degree of accuracy that is appropriate. It is important to note that these assumptions cannot be overcome by minimal changes in assessment tasks such as rewording, or providing hints about instrument use.

This is a simple example of a difference in pupils' out-of-school experiences. Research studies have shown that these only account in part for the variation in scores between girls and boys (Rennie 1987). Many people concerned with bias in 16+ examinations highlight the imbalance in the use of male and female names and the stereotypical portrayal of male and female roles. Such factors do contribute to bias in tasks, but are only the tip of the iceberg. A more significant issue is raised by the monitoring sub-committee of the Mathematical Association (1990). They commented on the use of names from ethnic minority groups in GCSE papers that 'those named appear to have totally accepted the values of the host culture'. If we are concerned with bias and consider that pupils have to construct meaning in assessment tasks then we need to ask how pupils' different values might influence this. Research into gender differences has looked at the relationship between different patterns of nurturing and how people subsequently learn to relate to the world (Chodorov 1978: Harding 1985). These learnt social rules determine: what we attend to, in relationships between people and between objects, and the content of our experience; and the values that we imbue and impart in social interactions. The implications of a gendered world are that children are not only channelled into gender appropriate experiences but also into gender specific ways of experiencing. As a consequence, children may not only have different experiences, but also different expectations and approaches to learning.

Earlier we mentioned that communication depended on shared contexts and assumptions. How does a gendered world view influence what is communicated in assessment tasks? An advantage of the APU item banks is in their scale extent. A comprehensive range of scientific criteria is assessed across a wide variety of content, using different contexts and varying modes of presentation, operation and response. The results showed that across the ages, irrespective of what criterion is being assessed, questions which involve such content as health, reproduction, nutrition and domestic situations are generally answered by more girls than boys (Johnson and Murphy 1986). The girls also tend to achieve higher scores on these questions. In tasks which have a more overtly 'masculine' content, e.g. building sites, race tracks, information from spare part catalogues, or anything with an electrical content, the reverse is true.

If we are assessing pupils' ability to interpret pie charts, for example, and set a question which looks at the varying proportions of different fibres in girls' school blouses, girls achieve higher scores than boys. If, on the other hand, the focus is on the proportions of different types of cars produced by a factory at different times of the year, the situation is reversed. Pupils' experiences outside of school lead them, unconsciously, to define areas of the curriculum where they expect to be successful or, conversely, unsuccessful. Areas where they expect to succeed they approach with confidence. Areas which promise failure are avoided either on the grounds of perceived incompetence, often the case with girls, or because the pupils reject them as being unimportant or irrelevant in terms of what they have learnt to value. This latter response is more typical of boys as White has reported on in the context of writing and assessment (White 1986); and Murphy with regard to pupils' responses to practical science investigations (Murphy 1988). The performance effects found by the APU science surveys arise from the combination of avoidance by some pupils and the heightened confidence of others.

So what are such questions assessing and how should we treat them? Deciding whether the use of certain contents disadvantages either girls or boys, and therefore constitutes a source of bias, depends on whether we judge the application of the criterion in that content area to be a significant aspect of subject achievement. In other words, how are we defining mastery of the criterion? This question has to be asked whether the assessment is for formative or summative purposes. An apparently fair assessment instrument which intentionally avoids particular content areas may be an invalid representation of achievement. Unfortunately, we do not know enough about primary and secondary pupils' criterion-referenced performance to be able to answer this. Furthermore, if we regard pupils' alienation from aspects of the curriculum as an unacceptable consequence of gender differences, we need to establish its effects in order to know how to address them. 'Biased' questions are, therefore, essential in a formative assessment instrument that seeks to inform the learner and the teacher about where to go next to progress. For national assessment purposes it may be judged appropriate that assessment should concern itself only with establishing that pupils demonstrate understanding of the criterion. It follows then that girls should be assessed on girl-friendly contents and boys on boy-friendly ones, i.e. build bias in. This may seem perfectly reasonable if we only concern ourselves with gender issues but even here the problems of reinforcing and fostering gender stereotypes are self-evident. What we need to know is how the alienation of different groups and individuals is evidenced so that performance differences due to alienation are not interpreted as difference in ability. It is at the point of interpretation that bias has an effect.

Gender differences in perceptions and choices

Most researchers into gender differences argue that with an appropriate learning environment, differences between girls and boys can be ameliorated. Is this the case for assessment and what are the implications for practice?

Perceptions of success

Girls' low self-esteem in maths and science is well documented and is seen as a contributory factor in their disengagement from these subjects in school. That girls underestimate their potential as writers is less well known (DES 1985) and is more surprising as they consistently outperform boys on assessments of writing (DES 1988b). Research has suggested that perceptions of success are influenced by the feedback that pupils typically receive in school. For girls, almost all the negative commentary they receive is directed at the intellectual quality of their work and so affects their academic self-image. Boys, on the other hand, tend to receive comment on behaviour and presentation. A boy criticized for lack of effort is being encouraged to think that he can do better, irrespective of whether this is the case or not. Consequently, boys tend to overestimate their chances of success (Licht and Dweck 1983: DES 1989b). Confidence affects both pupils' ability to engage with an assessment task and the way in which they engage. For these reasons it is possible to consider some forms of *task presentation* as biased.

To enable girls to demonstrate their achievements it may be necessary to provide opportunities for them to succeed on aspects of tasks not being assessed. The actual assessment task could then be presented as a continuation of an activity in which they have already experienced success. Such a strategy would probably benefit most pupils in assessment situations. For boys, on the other hand, the need might be quite different. For example, when a class of 13-year-olds was faced with a science task involving a content already covered in class, boys were confident that they knew the answer whereas girls were anxious because they should know it (Murphy 1990). This approach favours the boys on certain types of tasks. For example, on multiple-choice items an ability to focus on the 'right' answer is an advantage. Girls tend to reflect on the ambiguities inherent in most multiple-choice distractors and so fail to find an answer or select several.

Recent innovations in assessment practice have looked at ways of assessing a broader range of achievements which probe the nature of pupils' understanding and how they apply it. Tasks to achieve this may, for example, ask pupils to provide a critique which draws on alternative viewpoints or focus on the range of observations pupils consider noteworthy in an open-ended situation. Gender differences in favour of girls on such tasks have been widely reported (DES 1988b, 1989a, 1989b). In such tasks, boys may well need additional help in understanding what constitutes an expected response. This can be addressed to an extent in the presentation of tasks. However, changes in what assessors value as achievement have to be 'learnt' by pupils. It is unlikely that such understanding can be simply transmitted.

These suggestions about assessment procedures are based on a view of assessment as a process which can only represent snatches of pupils' potential achievements. In this view, assessment procedures should aim to 'elicit the individual's best achievement' (Nuttall 1987). In the presentation of the National Tests at Key Stage 1, the help that teachers can give children is controlled as it is considered to be a potential source of both invalidity and unreliability. Here you can see how one person's procedure to ensure reliability becomes another's source of invalidity, due to the perceived potential for bias in the procedure.

Perceptions of tasks

In the last decade, assessment initiatives in the UK have attempted, with varying success, to develop procedures that reflect the principles of educational assessment, i.e. assessment that serves the learner constructively. The national assessment for England and Wales is an example of such an initiative. The national assessment tasks are intended to enable children to access their knowledge so that they can reveal what they know and can do. What would such tasks look like and how should assessors treat children's responses to be consistent with these intentions?

A consequence of pupils' differential experiences and ways of responding to the world is that girls typically tend to value the circumstances that activities are presented in and consider they give meaning to the task. They do not abstract issues from their context. Boys as a group, conversely, do consider the issues in isolation and judge the content and context to be irrelevant. How might these differences in approach affect pupils' perception of tasks?

A simple strategy for finding this out involved setting pupils open-ended design questions (Murphy 1991). Examples of tasks used involved designing a boat to go around the world; a new vehicle; a game for children; and an 'ideal' house. The tasks were given to primary and secondary pupils. The pupils' designs covered a wide range but there were striking differences between those of girls and boys. The differences reflected the different concerns that girls and boys are encouraged to attend to. The boys' boats were power boats or battleships, their vehicles army-type 'secret agent' transport or sports cars. The detail focused on included elaborate weaponry and next to no living facilities. Other features included detailed mechanisms for movement and navigation, for example. The girls' boats were generally cruisers, their vehicles agricultural machines, family cars or children's play vehicles. The girls' designs included a great deal of detail about living quarters and facilities and essential food and cleaning supplies. Very few girls included mechanistic details.

Another strategy used a similar type of task but introduced it as part of the children's classwork. For example, children exploring patterns in buildings designed their ideal house and wrote an estate agent's description to accompany it. Again, girls' houses included many embellishments, e.g. curtains, vases, gardens and flowers. Their descriptions referred to pine fittings; cupboards for saucepans, vacuum cleaners and coats; matching curtains and wallpaper, etc. The boys' houses were generally stark but all had television aerials, notably absent in the girls' pictures. Their descriptions referred to the size of the garage, the availability of television in various rooms including the bathroom, the distance away of the children's rooms and highlighted such amenities as the nearby motor racing track.

These images represent the type of detail that pupils, given an open situation, consider relevant. They help us interpret the content effects in tasks described earlier. More importantly they show the very different worlds pupils bring to assessment situations which alter what emphasis they place on assessors' cues and determine whether or not the cues provided enable them to access their knowledge. Can assessment practice deal with these differences and what are the consequences if it does not?

One important issue is that girls' attention to human concerns affects their ability to focus down on an aspect of a task. For example, moving from their boat design to investigate the load that a model boat would support made little sense to the girls as there remained other variables to consider. Even when girls focused on the narrow task, they remained committed to the original purpose for the boat, i.e. to take people around the world. Hence, they considered the stability of the boat in a range of conditions, seeking out ways to create effects, i.e. hairdryers to simulate hurricanes, watering cans for instant monsoons, spoons and buckets for creating whirlpools. In science assessments, it is common to consider girls' typical responses as inappropriate and off-task. Assessors generally look for correspondence with their world view and do not search for alternative perceptions in pupils' responses. Indeed a failure to correspond is taken as a measure of lack of achievement. Consequently, even though girls' investigative strategies represent considerable scientific achievement, it typically goes unnoticed and unremarked. Generally, girls' attention to human needs and aesthetics at best is judged to represent other subject achievement rather than science. Other interpretations are possible and potentially more damaging. In these interpretations, girls' concerns with decor, diet, hygiene, etc. are viewed as trivial. It is interpretations like this which influence teachers' judgements and their treatment of girls. The following quote about girls' performance in maths is not untypical:

> Girls' tendencies to be distracted by powerful cues or true but irrelevant facts seem to reflect the 'hesitant, dependent, anxious, unmotivated, help-searcher' learner.
>
> (Levin *et al.* 1987: 111)

If national assessment tasks, either National Tests or teachers', are open-ended, then it will be essential to look for potential alternative tasks if pupils' performance is to be interpreted in terms of their achievements. If the degree of openness is restricted to enhance the reliability of the assessments, assessors need to consider how contextual issues and out-of-school experiences and interests might prevent pupils from seeing the task in the same way as the assessor. Again, this information is essential if pupils' performance is to be interpreted appropriately.

It is a potential source of bias when certain forms of achievement are accorded more status than others. The problem for girls and boys is not that one set of concerns is more valuable than another but that not having access to both limits what they learn and the uses they can make of their knowledge. For example, the girls who designed a pram with particular safety features are not using their knowledge inappropriately, whereas the boys who computerized their pram to travel without an adult could be judged to be missing the point. In the same way Sorenson's research study of children using circuits to light a house found that girls paid attention to the details of the model house and effectively installed the circuitry. Boys, on the other hand, were content to use Lego houses. Their circuitry was also perfectly adequate, but switches for the bathroom, for example, were located on the outside of the house (Sorenson 1990). One can also see from these examples how, in subjects such as design and technology, a typical 'boy's' view of relevance may lead to lower achievement and ultimately alienation and underachievement.

Other examples of how differences in what pupils are encouraged to attend to can lead to assessment bias relating to pupils' choice of expression. The APU language surveys (DES 1988b) showed that girls choose to communicate in extended reflective composition. Boys, on the other hand, provide episodic, factual and commentative detail. Pupils' choice of expression was found to mirror their reading preferences. Depending on which subject is being assessed and the modes of expression favoured in that subject, girls' and boys' performance will create an impression of a 'good' or a 'poor' response. Presenting teachers of science and English with characteristic girls' and boys' descriptions of two butterflies showed a clear difference in what was valued. A girls' response tended to receive more credit from English teachers and a boys' from science teachers. Such interpretations help to foster images of gender-appropriate areas of the curriculum which influence teachers' expectations of pupils. The study of Goddard-Spear (1983) showed that the *same piece* of science writing when attributed to girls received lower marks from teachers than when it was attributed to boys. The attempt to move away from reporting achievement by scores to the use of more descriptive profiles will not have the beneficial effects hoped for if assessors do not disentangle features of style from the criteria they are attempting to assess.

Summary

The implications for assessment practice that might be drawn from a discussion about gender differences will depend entirely on how learners and their learning are viewed. These views will also determine whether we judge an assessment task or procedure to be biased or not. From the position argued in this article, the commonly held view that bias in assessment is signified by 'unfairness' in tasks is not a particularly helpful one. The concern is not to find 'neutral' tasks which suit most pupils as this is not judged to be possible. To be consistent with a constructivist view of learning assessment practice should rather aim to establish what the individual pupils' tasks are and to interpret their responses and their achievements in the light of these. Indeed, many children will have meanings, contexts and experiences in common but treating them as a homogeneous group is not appropriate in a constructivist paradigm. In other paradigms, where it is considered appropriate to treat children as a homogeneous group, it is odd that bias is an issue at all. On the other hand, if factors such as use of male and female names and role models are judged to affect pupils' performance then other influences that determine how they relate to the world must also matter.

If national assessment is to allow pupils to demonstrate what they know and can do then it has to consider how pupils make sense of tasks, and what purposes they might import if no purpose is presented to them or makes sense to them. How these then influence their subsequent engagement in a series of tasks also needs to be thought about. To achieve this assessment tasks need to be structured with children in mind so that they enable them to make the transition from their everyday understandings to respond to tasks in domain-specific ways. If we fail to do this, our assessments measure only our lack of understanding rather than children's lack of achievements.

References

Bruner, J.S. (1986) *Actual Minds, Possible Worlds*, Cambridge (MA): Harvard University Press.

Chodorov, N. (1978) *The Reproduction of Mothering*, Berkeley (CA): University of California Press.

Cresswell, J. (1990) 'Gender effects in GCSE – some initial analyses', paper prepared for a Nuffield Seminar, University of London.

Department of Education and Science (1985) *Language Performance in Schools – 1982 primary survey report*, London: HMSO.

Department of Education and Science (1988a) *National Curriculum Task Group on Assessment and Testing: a report*, London: HMSO.

Department of Education and Science (1988b) *Language Performance in Schools: review of APU language monitoring 1979–1985*, London: HMSO.

Department of Education and Science (1989a) *National Assessment: the APU science approach*, London: HMSO.

Department of Education and Science (1989b) *Science at Age 13: a review of APU survey findings*, London: HMSO.

Goddard-Spear, M. (1983) 'Sex bias in science teachers' ratings of work', contributions to the Second GASAT Conference, Oslo, Norway.

Hannon, P. and McNally, J. (1986) 'Children's understanding and cultural factors in reading test performance', *Educational Review*, 38(3): 237–46.

Harding, J. (1979) 'Sex differences in performance in examinations at 16+', *Physics Education*, 14: 280–4.

Harding, J. (1985) 'Values, cognitive style and the curriculum', contributions to the Third GASAT Conference 1, London, England.

Humrich, E. (1987) 'Girls in science: US and Japan', contributions to the Fourth GASAT Conference 1, Michigan, USA.

Johnson, S. and Murphy, P. (1986) *Girls and Physics: reflections on APU findings*, London: DES.

Kelly, A. (1981) 'Sex differences in science achievement' in A. Kelly (ed.) *The Missing Half*, Manchester: Manchester University Press.

Levin, T., Sabar, N. and Libman, Z. (1987) 'Girls' understanding of science: a problem of cognitive or affective readiness', contribution to the Fourth GASAT Conference, Michigan, USA.

Licht, B.G. and Dweck, C.S. (1983) 'Sex differences in achievement orientations: consequences for academic choices and attainments' in M. Marland (ed.) *Sex Differentiation and Schooling*, London: Heinemann.

Mathematical Association (1990) *Bias in GCSE Mathematics*, a report on the 1989 papers prepared by the monitoring sub-committee.

Murphy, P. (1982) 'Sex differences in objective test performance', *British Journal of Educational Psychology*, 52: 213–19.

Murphy, P. (1988) 'Insight into pupil's responses to practical investigations from the APU', *Physics Education*, 23: 330–6.

Murphy, P. (1990) 'Gender differences in pupil's reactions to practical work' in B. Woolnough (ed.) *Practical Science*, Milton Keynes: Open University Press.

Murphy, P. (1991) 'Gender and assessment practice in science' in L. Parker, L. Rennie and B. Fraser (eds) *Gender, Science and Mathematics: a way forward*, Oxford: Pergamon Press.

Nuttall, D.L. (1987) 'The validity of assessments', *European Journal of Psychology of Education*, 11(2): 109–18.

Rennie, L.J. (1987) 'Out of school science: are gender differences related to subsequent attitudes and achievements in science?', contributions to the Fourth GASAT Conference 2, Michigan, USA.

Sorenson, H. (1990) 'When girls do physics', contributions to European and Third World GASAT Conference, Jönköping, Sweden.

Times Educational Supplement (1991) 'A new flexibility and freedom', January 11: 11.

White, J. (1986) 'Writing and gender', paper presented at the *Co-ordinators Seminar, National Writing Project* (SCDC), Woolley Hall.

Section 5

Schools

22 The positive effects of schooling

Peter Mortimore

Introduction

[...] In almost all societies, attendance at school is considered essential for children between the ages of six and sixteen. In some countries, high proportions of students start school earlier and finish later. There is a widespread presumption that schooling must have a positive effect (see, for example, the six ideal types of schools recently specified by European educationalists Husen, Tuijnman and Halls 1992), although, for some children and young people, there is evidence that schooling has had a negative impact on their development. This question of the impact of school has been explored over the last twenty or so years by a series of specialist research studies. These studies have shown that the effects of schooling are differential: some schools promote positive effects, others negative ones. Furthermore, some researchers have found evidence that the same school can impact differentially on groups of students according to their gender, social class, or perceived ability.

Although the circumstances and contexts of schooling differ widely across the world, there is a fairly common view – held by governments at least – that schooling, in general, is increasing in cost and decreasing in quality. Although it is often difficult to investigate empirically the truth of these claims, they are constantly stressed by the popular media, with the result that reforms are introduced based more on ideological commitment than on research evidence. Findings from scientifically sound studies (especially where these are replicated, about the power of individual schools to promote or reduce their positive impacts are, therefore, of critical importance.

This chapter presents some of the available evidence on variations between schools with regard to four sets of outcomes: attendance, student attitudes, student behaviour and scholastic attainment. The mechanisms identified by researchers as being implicated in the differential impacts of schools will also be discussed and differences between schools in terms of their effectiveness for different groups be considered. Knowing what makes one school more effective than another (for all or some of its students), however, is not the same as knowing how to change a less effective school into a more effective one. For this reason, we will comment on the efficacy of various interventions undertaken in a number of different countries. Finally, we will consider the implications for policy-makers and practitioners of the evidence that has emerged from studies of school effectiveness and school improvement.

A major difficulty of writing a chapter like this is deciding what should and should not be included. Given the extent of the relevant literature, it will be impossible to be exhaustive. Studies have been selected, therefore, on the basis of their relevance to the argument being undertaken. Inevitably, both relevant individual works and whole categories of studies have been omitted. One example of this general omission is the category of social policy research, thus excluding from the United States the study of *High School Achievement,* focusing on public and private differences, by Coleman, Hoffer and Kligore (1982); from the United Kingdom *The Comprehensive Experiment* by Reynolds, Sullivan and Murgatroyd (1987); and from Germany the study of *The Management of Individual Differences in Single Classrooms* by Roeder and Sang (1991).

A model of school effectiveness

Studies of variations between schools exist in both simple and more sophisticated forms. The simpler studies take little or no account of differences in the characteristics of students entering and attending the schools. They also tend to focus on only one outcome measure: student scholastic achievement. The difficulties of this simple approach, as experienced teachers will recognize, is that schools do not receive uniform intakes of students. Some take high proportions of relatively advantaged students likely to do well in examinations; others (on the whole) receive high proportions of disadvantaged students who, all things considered, are less likely to do well. To compare the results of scholastic achievement tests or examinations, without taking into account these differences in the students when they enter the school, and to attribute good results to the influence of the school may, therefore, be quite misleading.

The more sophisticated form of research endeavours to overcome the problem of differential student intake by using a statistical technique to equate, as far as possible, for these differences. Ideally, the statistical technique would be replaced by a random allocation of students to schools but, in most countries, this would be considered to be an unacceptable infringement of the parental right to choose schools. Accordingly, various definitions of effectiveness have been formulated. One definition of an 'effective' school that has been used is 'one in which students progress further than might be expected from consideration of intake' (Mortimore 1991, p. 9).

Note that this definition does not assume that all students from disadvantaged backgrounds are likely to do badly in tests of scholastic attainment. Some individual students from disadvantaged backgrounds will undoubtedly do well; they will buck the trend. What the definition implies is that, all things being equal, disadvantaged students are less likely to do as well, in any assessment which is highly competitive, as those from advantaged backgrounds. Accordingly, measures of progress are needed that can take account of the students' initial starting points.

Various methods have been developed by researchers to deal with the problem of intake differences, and various statistical methods ranging from simple standardization, to multiple regression techniques, to the latest multilevel modelling, have been employed to equate for the initial differences. Regardless of the technique used, however most approaches have been based on an underlying model of school effectiveness. In this model, a series of outcomes suitable for the type of school must be identified. For an elementary school, these might include basic skills of literacy and numeracy, as well as other measures to do with the students' personal and social development. For a secondary school, the outcomes are likely to be based on achievement but may also include attendance, attitudes and behaviour.

The second stage of the usual procedure is to relate these chosen outcomes to available data on the characteristics of the students as they entered the school. Such characteristics can include earlier reading levels, former attendance rates, behaviour ratings completed by teachers in the previous phase of schooling and any available information on home background, including the occupation of the parents. Using the most sophisticated mathematical techniques available, researchers attempt to take account of this intake variation and to adjust the outcome measures accordingly to provide what is increasingly known as a value-added component. An attempt is thus made to see how the outcomes would look if all schools had received a similar intake. To use the research terminology: like is being compared with like.

At the third stage, researchers usually seek to relate the adjusted outcomes to whatever information has been collected about the life and functioning of the school. Researchers sometimes call this 'backward mapping' of outcomes to process measures. To avoid a mismatch, these previous measures must have been collected as the particular students were passing through the school. In essence, this is the model that school effectiveness researchers have been refining over the last twenty or so years as they investigated the differential effects of schools.

Methodological issues

Studies of the effects of schooling, like so many other research topics, vary a great deal in the scope of their designs and in their chosen methodologies. Some of the problems of interpretation of a number of the earlier studies have already been discussed by Rutter (1983) and by Purkey and Smith (1983). More recently, a number of articles in a special edition of the *International Journal of Educational Research* addressed this topic (Bosker and Scheerens 1989: Raudenbush 1989: Scheerens and Creemers 1989), as does a series of papers in Reynolds and Cuttance (1992). The types of issues that have been raised include:

- the need for clearer conceptualization and theory development
- the use of more sophisticated statistical techniques (such as multilevel modelling) and the inadequacy of current sampling techniques
- the choice of appropriate outcome measures
- the methods of relating outcome to process data.

On the whole, the later studies have used more sophisticated methods than the earlier ones. The improvement in methodology, however, has not been matched by similar advances in the development of theory. The need for better theory has been recognized and a number of research teams working in this area are addressing the issue.

The findings of studies into variations between schools

As noted earlier, the most common outcomes chosen by researchers have been the attendance patterns of students, their attitudes towards schooling, their behaviour, and their scholastic attainment. We will discuss each of these in turn and refer to a selection of the research studies that have been carried out.

Attendance

Attendance data have been collected by many researchers. Attendance can be defined as an outcome of schooling as well as being used as a measure of students' attitudes towards school. It can also be seen as a process variable: all things being equal, schools with high attendance rates are better able to secure scholastic achievement for their pupils than those with poorer attendance rates. Various measures of attendance have been used in studies, including one-day surveys and whole-year individual student data sets. A number of studies of the elementary years of schooling have also used this measure. In Mortimore and colleagues (1988), for instance, attendance data were collected for each student. When these were aggregated, it was found that there were systematic differences between schools. When the proportion of variance between students in their attendance was divided, however, it was found that the contribution of the school was relatively small, possibly because the overall level was so high (92 per cent), thus leaving little scope for school variation.

At secondary level, measures of attendance were used by Reynolds *et al.* (1976) in a study of nine schools in a mining community of South Wales. The researchers found that attendance data varied from a school average of 77.2 per cent to 89.1 per cent. In a study by Rutter and colleagues (1979) data on individual students in three separate age-groups were collected in each of the twelve schools in the sample. The whole-school figures revealed considerable differences. For example, out of a possible maximum of twenty attendances over two school weeks, the average for 16-year-old students varied from 12.8 in one school to 17.3 in another. Furthermore, the proportion of poor attenders in each school varied between 6 and 26 per cent.

Attendance was also addressed by Galloway *et al.* (1985) in a study of schools in the Sheffield area of England. They found clear evidence of school effects on the attendance rates. Smith and Tomlinson (1989) collected statistics of attendance in research which followed the careers of students transferring to twenty multi-ethnic secondary schools at the age of eleven, through to the end of compulsory schooling. Using a measure of the number of half-days a pupil was absent from school, they drew up a series of outcomes for each school. This measure was repeated in each of four years. On average, researchers found students to be absent about 7 per cent of the time. They found no differences between boys and girls but they did find some between students from different ethnic groups. In general, those from Caribbean ethnic backgrounds had better attendance than their British counterparts, whereas those from Asia had poorer attendance records.

Attitudes towards school

Only a few studies have used systematic measurements of attitudes to school. This is partly because the measurement of attitudes is complex and partly because the attitudes of young people tend to be less stable than those of their older counterparts. Measures have been used, however, in three studies. Mortimore and colleagues (1988) developed a set of measures to capture the feelings of young students towards their schools. A series of 'smiley' faces was used so that members of the sample were able to indicate their overall approval or disapproval of particular aspects of school life. The results showed considerable variation between schools on a range of activities. Overall, the most effective school had an average of 4 points and the least effective had an average of 2.7 out of a scale of 5. The school appeared to be a more important influence on attitudes than were the student background factors.

The same measure was adopted by Tizard and colleagues (1988) in their study of infant schools. The researchers interviewed their sample of elementary school children at the age of seven and also used the 'smiley' method to elicit feelings about mathematics, reading to the teacher, reading to themselves, writing, and going to school.

Pupil attitudes were examined in relation to secondary school students by Smith and Tomlinson (1989). They sought to investigate pupils' enthusiasm for school, as well as participation in activities within the school or organized by it. A different approach towards student attitudes was adopted by Ainley and Sherer (1992) in their Australian study of twenty-two secondary schools. These researchers sought to investigate the effectiveness of schools' 'holding power' over students. They found that some schools retained a higher percentage of students in the senior year than others, even after they had allowed for differences in the social background of students, but retention was not necessarily linked to achievement.

Behaviour of students

Like attendance and attitudes, behaviour can be viewed as an outcome of school. The rationale for such a view is that specific experiences at school, or the particular group of pupils attending it, lead to a collective style of behaviour, both within and beyond the school. Like the other variables, however, behaviour can also be viewed as part of the school processes. Other outcome measures can be influenced by the behaviour experienced within the school.

Overall, seven studies using behaviour as an outcome will be noted here. The study of student behaviour is problematic. Taking account of the impact of different teachers on different sets of students, and *vice versa*, is difficult. Bennett (1976) studied the relationship between teaching styles and pupil progress. As part of his study he sought to measure the on- and off-task behaviour in a sample of over one hundred students. He also collected measures of the level of student and teacher interactions for the same sample. In the second study, Mortimore and colleagues (1988) developed a behaviour scale which was completed by teachers. One advantage of this scale was that good as well as bad behaviour could be recorded. The results showed that the average behaviour score for a school ranged from 48 to 76 on a scale with a maximum of 135 points.

Heal (1978) studied a random sample of pupils in both elementary and secondary schools. Data from the elementary schools were used to assess their influence on subsequent behaviour of students. The measure included petty misdemeanours and more serious activities, both in and outside of school. Rutter and colleagues (1979) used a scale compiled from items from a self-report student survey, teachers' interviews, and researchers' in-school observations. In all, twenty-five items were aggregated together. Some were minor (not having a pen or pencil with which to write), but others were more important and included the serious interruption of the lesson by aggressive behaviour. The twenty-five items revealed a highly significant pattern of intercorrelations. Overall, some schools had up to five times as much good (or bad) behaviour as others. Intake differences were taken into account using the results of the 'Rutter B' behaviour scale, collected on a sample of the students during their elementary schooling.

Although the study of Reynolds et al. (1976) did not deal directly with in-school behaviour, it included a measure of delinquency. This showed that the school average ranged between 4 and 10 per cent. Delinquency data have also been used by Power and colleagues (1967) and by Cannan (1970). They used police data to examine school differences and reported considerable differences in the average delinquency rates of schools. In a study carried out in Scotland (Gray et al. 1983), over 20,000 students were tracked through the secondary school system and clear evidence of school differences was revealed.

Scholastic attainment

A great number of studies have been carried out in the United States focusing on the scholastic attainments of students (witness the 750 references in the register or the Northwest Regional Educational Laboratory synthesis [NREL 1990]). One of the first major studies was conducted in the late 1960s by Weber (1971). Four schools, considered to be 'institutionally effective', were selected for study. It was found that scholastic attainment measured by reading levels was markedly above the average for the school neighbourhood. A second study was carried out in 1974 by the New York Department of Education. Two schools, with contrasting levels of average attainment but with similar intake characteristics, were identified and studied (Edmonds 1979).

Further studies focusing on student scholastic attainment by Madden (1976), Brookover and Lezotte (1977) and Edmonds and Frederiksen (1979) reinforced the conclusion that some schools were more effective in promoting achievement than others. As a result of these pioneering studies, a number of intervention projects were inaugurated (Clark and McCarthy 1983: McCormack-Larkin and Kritek 1982: Murphy et al. 1982).

A long-term empirical investigation has been started and its early results reported (Teddlie et al. 1984, 1989). A relatively new strand of work concerns what is known as 'self-efficacy' (Wood and Bandura 1989). In this work the learners' beliefs in themselves are reinforced or reduced and the effects on achievement noted. In general, the stronger the feeling of 'self-efficacy' the better the level of achievement. Moreover, the individual's feeling is affected by the school attended. If the teachers hold positive views about ability and about their teaching skills, they are more likely to produce academic learning in their classrooms (Bandura 1992).

Bennett (1976) studied reading, writing and mathematics progress and attainment in elementary schools in the United Kingdom. Galton and Simon (1980) also studied reading attainment and progress. In addition to reading and mathematics, Mortimore and colleagues (1988) studied writing and speaking skills and, where possible, included measures of progress as well as attainment in their study of school differences. Tizard and colleagues (1988) included measures of reading, writing, mathematics attainment and progress in their study of early student attainment.

In a study of Welsh secondary schools, Reynolds *et al.* (1976) found a range of over 40 percentage points between the school with the highest and that with the lowest academic attainment. Brimer and colleagues (1978) worked with a sample of 44 secondary schools and used information on parental background to control for differences in intake in their study of examination results. Rutter and colleagues (1979a) found systematic large-scale differences between school averages when examination results were collated.

Gray, Jesson, and Sime (1990), drawing on a sample of over 20,000 Scottish students' records, found evidence of both social class and school influence on academic attainment. In their study – again focusing on examination results – Smith and Tomlinson (1989) found that school differences were stronger than differences in the ethnic background of students. Daly (1991) studied examination results in a sample of thirty secondary schools in Northern Ireland and found a complicated pattern of school differences, made more difficult to interpret by the selective school system.

Nuttall and colleagues (1989) studied the examination performance of over 30,000 students taking British school examinations over several years. They found clear evidence of school differences, as well as differences related to family background and ethnic group. Blakey and Heath (1992) have recently released preliminary findings from the Oxford University School Effectiveness Project. These findings show that, in their schools, the proportion of students obtaining high levels in five subjects in public examinations varies from 1 to 19 per cent.

Attention so far has focused on a selection of research studies carried out in the United States or in the United Kingdom. Similar studies, however, have also been undertaken in many other parts of the world. See, for instance, Fraser (1989) in Australia; Brandsma and Knuver (1989) and Creemers and Lugthart (1989) in The Netherlands; Dalin (1989) in Norway and Bashi and colleagues (1990) in Israel.

Although the studies cited vary considerably in rigour, scope and methodologies, their findings are fairly uniform: that individual schools can promote positive or student outcomes; that those outcomes can include both cognitive and social behaviours; and they are not dependent on the school receiving a favoured student intake. The fact that the studies have taken place in different phases of students' schooling and in different parts of the developed world adds considerable strength to the interpretation that schools can make a difference to the lives of their students. Although in some cases the range of attainment outcomes that can be traced directly to the influence of the school might he relatively small, it can be the difference between academic success and failure, and so can have a long-term effect on students' life chances.

It has also become apparent from these studies that there are likely to be differences in the average progress achieved by students from different schools, and that this variation is less susceptible to factors of home background than are the more usual measures or attainment at any time.

Because there have been more studies of scholastic attainment than of attendance, attitudes, or behaviour (largely confined to the UK), measures and instruments are more likely to be available for this first outcome than for the others. As a result, differential effectiveness in cognitive areas is more widely understood. The scope, however, for further development of sensitive measures of behaviour and attitudes and the opportunities for studies to use non-cognitive measures is considerable. This is especially important in view of the lack of perfect agreement between outcomes reported by Reynolds *et al.* (1976), Rutter and colleagues (1979), and Mortimore and colleagues (1988).

The studies cited here have been criticized and their methodologies dissected. (See reviews by Clark *et al.* 1984: Good and Brophy 1986: Purkey and Smith 1983: Rutter 1983.) For a detailed description of the processes involved in the public discussion of two British studies, see Mortimore (1990).

Do the positive effects of schooling vary according to time?

The evidence on whether positive effects of schooling vary over time is mixed. The earliest British studies (Reynolds *et al.* 1976: Rutter *et al.* 1979) drew on student outcomes for different years and found that in general, there was consistency over time. Two large-scale analyses, one from the Scottish data set (Willms and Raudenbush 1989) and one from the work carried out in inner London (Nuttall *et al.* 1989), revealed, however, large-scale differences in student academic outcomes over time. Unfortunately the other large-scale London-based study, by Mortimore and colleagues (1988), studied only one cohort of students over a four-year period and thus cannot contribute to this interesting debate.

The possibility of change over time should not be surprising. After all, schools take in different groups of students each year and, in some cases, change staff regularly. The question is whether the ethos of a school, once it has been established, is strong enough to resist that change. There is also the question of how rapid any change is likely to be. Gradual change in outcomes is likely if the particular ethos changes and staff are replaced. A faster rate of change would be likely if, for instance, the intake to the school varied considerably from one year to another, in terms of its social class background or its earlier performance in other phases of schooling. The school is also likely to change more rapidly as a result of some outside intervention (if a new principal is appointed or an inspection by outside experts takes place). Finally, and not surprisingly, rapid change can be expected as a result of a particular crisis in the life of the school, such as the threat of closure due to lack of students. Schools can also be conservative places, however, which seek to resist change (as the later section on interventions will demonstrate). Further work is needed to identify the most potent mechanisms for change and to investigate under what conditions they are likely to be most successfully introduced.

Do the positive effects of schooling vary according to school membership?

To answer this question, it is necessary to ask a series of related questions. First, do students with different levels of ability or with different gender, class and ethnic characteristics achieve different outcomes from the same school processes? The British evidence on this question is mixed. A large number of publications emanating from the Scottish study (Cuttance 1985: Gray *et al.* 1990: Macpherson and Willms 1987: Willms and Cuttance 1985) all suggest that schools can have differential effects according to the characteristics of their students. This actuarial approach suggests that, given the students' gender, age and social class, the likely academic outcomes can be predicted for particular schools. Further supporting evidence comes from a methodological study by Aitken and Longford (1986) which found that schools did have differential effects on the progress made by particular groups.

Against this view of differential student effect can be set the evidence from the early studies (Reynolds *et al.* 1976: Rutter *et al.* 1979) that schools that were positive were likely to have a consistent effect on all groups of students. Furthermore, Gray *et al.* (1990) reported little evidence of varied outcomes for different kinds of students.

The findings from Mortimore and colleagues (1988) were also positive on this question. In general, they found that schools that had positive effects for one group were likely to have similar positive effects for others, although these could be more or less pronounced. For example, some schools had positive effects in promoting reading progress for girls but not for boys. It is interesting, however, that in their sample of fifty schools the research team found no case where students whose parents had manual occupations performed markedly better, on average, than those from non-manual groups. Schools were not able to overcome these powerful social class effects. Students from manual groups in the most effective schools, however, sometimes outperformed those from non-manual groups in the least effective schools. The school was the unit of change rather than the class group within it. A re-analysis of the data of the School Study shows that the regression line slopes are similar for all groups of students (Sammons and Nuttall 1992). The data collected by Smith and Tomlinson (1989) showed that, although differences between ethnic groups varied between schools, much greater variations could be found in general school differences: 'The ones that are good for white people tend to be about equally good for black people' (p. 305).

Studies in the USA (Hallinger and Murphy 1987: Teddlie *et al.* 1989) have investigated this problem in a different way. By focusing on schools which, by chance, attracted different intakes and could be classified as serving low-, middle-

or upper-middle-income communities, the researchers were able to investigate whether schools that were unusually effective were similar or different in how they related to their students. They report that, in general, schools had similar characteristics regardless of the intake of students. Commonly cited correlates include a safe and orderly environment: a clear mission; capable instructional leadership; high expectations; a well co-ordinated curriculum; monitoring of student progress; and structured staff development (Hallinger and Murphy 1986: cited in Levine and Lezotte 1990: 65).

The researchers also found some differences. In the low socio-economic status (SES) schools, there was a tendency for the curriculum to focus on basic skills, and principals in low SES schools tended to be more forceful in asserting themselves and in intervening in classes. The researchers found that, in the high SES schools, principals tended to use a more collaborative style of decision-making (Hallinger and Murphy 1986).

The second related question concerns whether, if schools have different outcomes for different groups of students, this is due to policy differences in the way the students have been treated, or to differences in the reactions they have elicited from those who work in the schools. It is quite possible that a school, or an individual teacher, may have a policy of treating students equitably in terms of adult time and encouragement, and yet may end up responding to some groups of students differentially. In the London study (Mortimore *et al.* 1988), for example, classroom observations showed no evidence of inequitable attention or any obvious signs of bias. Yet the same study produced evidence of lower expectations for certain groups of students – in the main, those from Caribbean family backgrounds, or those who were chronologically young for the school year. It was not possible to explain these differences satisfactorily, but it can be speculated that a mixture of unconscious prejudice – against groups of students from a different cultural background or against children who appeared immature – and of successful student strategies, involving the elicitation of positive responses by other groups, was responsible. Those students with advantaged backgrounds, perhaps, used their advantages to get more out of their schooling experience.

In other cases, it is likely that schools will target those groups that teachers believe most to benefit. Evidence shows that, in 'tracked' selective schools, the premier group of students received a greater share of attention and resources than others and that this had a deleterious effect on all but this group (Lacey 1975). At the other extreme, Athey (1990) has shown how pre-school programmes can be targeted at the most disadvantaged students in order to lessen the gap between their achievements and those of other children. This evidence is in line with a series of studies based on other kinds of institutions, such as the work in mental hospitals which shows that differential efforts can be targeted to considerable effect (Brown and Wing 1962).

The answer to the question of whether the positive effects of schooling vary according to school membership is, therefore, complex. The evidence suggests that at the secondary stage at least, different subgroups of students may or may not benefit and, furthermore, that schools can choose to target certain groups. At the elementary stage, the evidence points to a more uniform effect. Schools that are effective are likely to be positive for all subgroups of students, although some groups may benefit to a greater extent than others. There is no evidence in either sector of schools, however, to suggest that different factors are responsible for differential effects. It is a question of which subgroup is affected, for which group are high expectations held, who is likely to be rewarded, and so forth.

Do the positive effects of schooling vary according to the particular strengths and weaknesses of schools?

It appears that, even though schools that are generally effective in one area are usually reasonably effective in others, some variation is possible. In the London study of fifty primary schools, fourteen were uniformly effective, seven were uniformly ineffective, and the rest had mixed profiles (Mortimore *et al.* 1988). The extent of this within-school variation is important and will be further investigated in a new British study of secondary schools Nuttall *et al.* (1993).

What are the mechanisms associated with differential school effectiveness?

It is seldom possible for educational researchers to impose experimental conditions on their subjects. They are generally welcomed into schools and classes, but they usually have to observe things as they are. This helps them to gain a realistic picture of school life but means that they are rarely able directly to trace causal relationships. All too frequently, researchers are limited to tracing patterns of association and the use of correlations. Nevertheless, even with such methodological limitations, researchers from different countries have reached a number of conclusions about the variables commonly associated with the functioning of more effective schools. The plausibility of these variables operating as mechanisms of school effectiveness has been increased by the frequency with which they have been replicated.

The following list of mechanisms is not intended to be comprehensive or exhaustive. It has been culled from a sample of ten reviews or studies drawn from different countries, selected because of their use of different methodologies. Because of different wording and a lack of scientifically precise language, it is not possible to compare in a highly accurate way findings from so many different studies, many of which are composite reviews of a number of individual research projects. It is possible, however, broadly to collate variables to ascertain the most common mechanisms found by researchers to be associated with effectiveness. The following list is the result of this exercise.

Strong positive leadership

Although a few studies (notably Nan de Grift 1990) have claimed that the principal has little impact or that the leadership of the school can be provided by somebody else, almost universally this mechanism was found to be important.

Different studies have drawn attention to different aspects of principals' roles, but Levine and Lezotte (1990) have provided a clear analysis of how a strong leadership can provide mechanisms to aid effectiveness. In their view, this occurs through the rigorous selection and replacement of teachers; 'buffering' the school from unhelpful external agents; frequent personal monitoring of school achievements; high expenditure of time and energy for school improvement actions; supporting teachers; and acquiring extra resources for their schools.

The British studies support this analysis but add a further, rather subtle task: that of understanding when – and not – to involve other staff in decision-making. The British studies have found evidence that both autocratic and over-democratic styles of leadership are less effective than a balanced style which depends on the crucial judgement of when, and when not, to act as decision-maker. Fullan (1992) has argued that strong leadership by itself is not sufficient in a complex, post-modern society. Instead, he argued that heads (principals) have to find appropriate leadership roles for teachers.

High expectations: an appropriate challenge for students' thinking

This mechanism was commonly cited by researchers. Despite the limitations of the original experimental work (Rosenthal and Jacobson 1968), the concept of expectations and the way these can affect the behaviour of both teachers and students have been well assimilated. Dorr-Bremme (1990), for instance, drew attention to the differing mind-sets of two groups of teachers from more, and less, effective schools. Members of the less effective group see their work one way:

> We are educators who work hard to take our students' needs into account. This means considering their total life situations and not expecting more of them than they can do.

In contrast, those in the more effective group saw their similar task in a quite different way:

> We are people who take our students' needs into account as we teach. This means we challenge our students, make them work hard and do the best that they can.
> (Levine and Lezotte 1990: 35)

The one group chose a passive role, affected by forces (the students' problems) over which they could have little control. The other group, although recognizing that problems existed, adopted a more active stance and sought to challenge the difficulties through challenging the students' thinking.

Mortimore and colleagues (1988) looked at ways in which expectations could be transmitted in the classroom. The researchers found that teachers had lower expectations for students who, for instance, were young in their year group (those with summer birthdays) or who came from lower social classes. They found that low expectations were not held in any simple way for either girls or boys *per se*, despite the fact that boys received more critical comments and girls more praise. These data were difficult to interpret and the research team drew on the findings of

Dweck and Repucci (1973) to help explain them. (Dweck and Repucci found that greater praise from male teachers to female students for less adequate work was linked to stereotyped views of female performance.)

Monitoring student progress

Although monitoring, by itself, changes little, the majority of the studies found it to be a vital procedure – as a prelude to planning instructional tactics, altering pedagogy, or increasing or decreasing workloads. They also saw it as a key message to students that the teacher was interested in their progress. Whether it is more effective for the monitoring to be carried out formally or informally cannot yet be answered and further work on the way this mechanism operates may be worthwhile.

Student responsibilities and involvement in the life of the school

The mechanism – in its various forms – of ensuring that students adopt an active role in the life of the school was also commonly found to be important. By seeking to involve students in school-oriented activities, or by allocating responsibilities to elicit a positive response from them, teachers have endeavoured to provide a sense of ownership in the school and in the students' own learning.

Although examples of talented, but alienated, students can frequently be found in literature, the general rule appears to be that learning is most likely when the students hold a positive view of the school and of their own role in it. The attitudes of students towards themselves as learners were used as a school outcome by Mortimore and colleagues (1988). The outcome consisted of a specially designed measure of self-concept. This was the mirror image of the behaviour scale completed by teachers and by students themselves. The measure revealed clear school differences. Some schools produced students who – regardless of their actual ability – felt reasonably positive about themselves; other schools produced students who were negative about themselves even when, in the judgement of the research team and according to their progress, they were performing well.

Rewards and incentives

Unlike punishments, rewards and incentives appear to act as mechanisms for eliciting positive behaviour and, in some cases, for changing students' (and at times teachers') behaviour. Thus, Purkey and Smith (1983) noted that a key cultural characteristic of effective schools is a school-wide recognition of academic success:

> publicly honouring academic achievement and stressing its importance encourages students to adopt similar norms and values.
>
> (p. 183)

Levine and Lezotte (1990) made two further points. First, that the use of rewards extends beyond academic outcomes and applies to other aspects of school life – a point supported by the British research. Second, that school-wide recognition of positive performance may be more important in urban schools, and especially those in inner cities where, because of the correlation with disadvantage, there are low-achieving students. Levine and Lezotte cited Hallinger and Murphy's (1985) study to support this argument. Hallinger and Murphy argued that one of the roles of principals in advantaged schools was to sustain existing norms, rather than create new ones:

> In low SES (disadvantaged) schools the principal must ensure that the school overcomes societal and school norms that communicate low expectations to the students ... (whereas in higher SES schools) school disciplinary and academic reward systems need not focus as much on short-term accomplishments, rely heavily on tangible reinforcers or develop elaborate linkages between the classroom and the school.
>
> (p. 3)

Finally, in one of the British studies, Mortimore and colleagues (1988) found that rewards could be given in a variety of ways, if the policy of the school was positive. In some schools, the policy was to reward individuals for good work or behaviour, whereas in others it was to focus on sport and social factors. Schools experienced the problem of trying to create a common system of incentives. This was a particular problem for schools where the age-range was wide: rewards that appealed to younger pupils sometimes lost their enchantment for older students.

Parental involvement in the life of the school

Parental involvement is possibly one of the most important issues in the current educational debate. The idea is not new and has been pioneered by a number of educational researchers in the United Kingdom and in the United States. There is also a large and rapidly growing literature on the topic. In the United Kingdom, much of the debate has been about the gains to be made from developing contact between homes and schools with regard to children's learning, as well as about ways to increase the accountability of schools to parents.

The vital role that parents can play in the intellectual development of their children has long been known, but experiments to use this resource more effectively have met with varied success. One pioneering British study (Tizard *et al.* 1982), however, demonstrated that parental involvement in reading more than equalled the benefits from the use of an extra teacher in schools.

The Head Start programmes in the United States (Lazar and Darlington 1982) have also provided evidence that the involvement of parents is an important aspect of the programmes' success. Similar programmes in England show that the gap between the achievement levels of advantaged and disadvantaged can be reduced (Athey 1990). In another British study, Mortimore and colleagues (1988) found that schools varied a great deal in their attitudes towards parents. Some schools kept parents out; others used parents as cheap labour. A few schools involved parents in school planning and sought to use their talents and abilities in both the classroom and at home. The researchers found, however, that some principals appeared to be insufficiently confident in their relationships with parents, especially in more socially advantaged areas. They found, though, that when the energy and talents of parents were harnessed, the rewards for the school were high. It is interesting that they also found Parent–Teacher Associations were not necessarily positive, in that they could form a 'clique' for particular groups of parents and thus present a barrier to the involvement of others. The range of parental involvement programmes in both elementary and secondary schooling in the United Kingdom has been summarized by Jowett and Baginsky (1991).

The ways in which parents act as a mechanism for effectiveness are not well understood. It is possible to speculate that, where both long-term and short-term objectives are shared by teachers and parents, where parents are able to offer considerable help through coaching, and where ideas generated in one area of a child's life can be rehearsed and expanded in another, learning will be helped. Stevenson and Shin-Ying's (1990) study of three cities (Taipei in Taiwan; Sendai in Japan; Minneapolis in the United States) illustrates the lengths to which oriental families will go to involve not just parents, but other relations, in coaching their children. Stevenson and Shin-Ying showed that a belief in the supremacy of hard work over natural ability and the willingness to be critical, when combined with expectations, can provide powerful support for learning. Parental involvement, however, is not without difficulties and those responsible for school programmes need to have clear policies in place before embarking on this potentially valuable strategy (Mortimore and Mortimore 1984).

Joint planning and consistent approaches towards students

The efficacy of joint planning and consistent approaches have been clearly recognized by many research studies. Levine and Lezotte (1990) argued that, almost by definition, faculty members committed to a school-wide mission focusing on academic improvement for all students tend to exemplify greater cohesiveness and consensus regarding central organizational goals than do faculty members at less effective schools (p.12).

Levine and Lezotte maintained that cohesion and consensus are especially important to schools rather than other institutions because schools set teachers a number of difficult and sometimes conflicting goals. Teachers must respond to the individual needs of students while emphasizing the requirements of the whole class. They have to be fair to the group but take account of individual circumstances. It is thus easy for what Levine and Lezotte call 'goal clarity' to be reduced and for improvement efforts to be fragmented. Where students are subject to conflicting expectations and demands and, as a result, become less confident, they often take time to learn the ways of each new teacher. This exercise may provide a helpful pointer to the ways of adults, but it is clearly not a useful mechanism for a school.

The involvement of faculty members in joint decisions relates to the strength of leadership of the institution. There is clear evidence that when teachers and others in authority (including the assistant principal) are given a role to play, they – in the best management tradition – will be far more likely to feel ownership of the institution and, as a result, offer greater commitment to it.

Academic emphasis and a focus on learning

There has been much research on this topic. Some of it has been concerned with the question of time-on-task (see, for example, Sizemore 1987). A number of research studies have drawn attention to the waste of time in the school day, particularly at the start of classes, through poor administration and lack of preparation (Blum 1984). Rutter and colleagues (1979) found evidence of time wasted at the end of classes. The researchers described the chaotic situation that could develop when a high proportion of classes in the school finished before the scheduled time. The problem, therefore, is not simply about time: it is about the use of time. Mortimore and colleagues (1988) noted that, although some schools in their sample programmed extra time (some twenty minutes per day) for classes, a straightforward correlation with effectiveness was not found. The value of time appeared to depend greatly on how it was used.

Emphasizing the learning of core skills has also been cited as an important aspect of this mechanism. In the United States, this has sometimes been associated with experiments in mastery learning (Gregory and Mueller 1980). Levine and Lezotte (1990) argued, however, that in some cases the original concept of Bloom-type mastery learning has been mis-implemented and cannot fairly be judged. In Britain, a Department of Education and Science (DES) discussion paper (Alexander *et al.* 1992) has drawn attention to the danger that elementary schools can lose sight of the central focus on student learning and dissipate the energies of teachers in an unproductive way.

These were the most commonly cited mechanisms arising from the research literature. As noted earlier, however, other factors have frequently been studied and may also be of considerable importance for particular schools at particular times. Thus, if schools receive students of a certain background, if the community is subject to particular experiences, or if the school authorities involve a specific series of reforms, other mechanisms for coping with change will come into play. These may act as mediating influences and, as a result, distract the attention of teachers and principals. They should never supplant the prime focus of school – the learning of pupils.

How successful have preventative interventions been?

This question is difficult to answer. It requires a clear definition of preventative interventions and in view of the most recent history of schooling in many parts of the world such a definition is not easy to formulate. Straightforward application of the knowledge and understanding of, for instance, school effectiveness, by those involved in school improvement programmes, represents one kind of intervention. Complex governmental initiatives, for what have previously been considered fairly autonomous school systems, are another. Both may be found in some school systems.

In reality, school effectiveness and school improvement are very different phenomena. As Clark *et al.* (1984) have argued so clearly, researchers pursuing these two lines of enquiry pursue different questions (about what affects student outcomes and about how schools change) and use different outcome measures (student achievement and the level of innovation). What the two approaches share is their interest in schools. The contrast between school effectiveness and school improvement is illustrated by a comparison of the work of Rutter and colleagues (1979), seeking explanations for poor student outcomes in one geographical area with the International School Improvement Study's (ISIS) endeavours, operating in fourteen countries to describe and, where appropriate, to change various school processes (Bollen and Hopkins 1987).

A different kind of initiative is a government-sponsored project, such as that on the school development plans of the (then) English Department of Education and Science (now the Department for Education). This project was designed to promote concepts, culled from research, on the necessity of systematic planning (Hargreaves and Hopkins 1989: DES 1991).

Different again are the programmes of school restructuring and school reforms that have been introduced in the United States and the United Kingdom. In the case of school restructuring, a variety of different interest groups have expressed their fears about aspects of American schooling and, in line with political policy, have been encouraged to put thinking into practice (Murphy 1991). In Chicago, for instance, a parents' collective alliance has been established to oversee the restructuring of the city's education system (Hess 1992). In New York, critics such as Domanico and Cenn (1992) have argued that curtailment of the city's power over education is essential to enable parents and others – using public money – to run their own schools.

In the United Kingdom, a series of legislative changes has dominated recent educational events. Among other actions, the 1988 Education Reform Act established a National Curriculum and its associated testing at the ages of seven, eleven, fourteen and sixteen; it introduced a system of parental choice based on open enrolment; and it delegated financial decision-making to the school principal and the governors (a small group representing the interests of teachers, the local education authority and – where appropriate – the wider community).

The 1992 Education Act created a new form of privatized school inspections, whereby appropriately qualified and trained inspectors can compete for contracts to inspect schools as part of a four-year cycle. Among the proposals of recent British legislation are the establishment of 'education associations' to take over the management of failing schools and a further loosening of local government powers over schooling.

These developments in the United States and the United Kingdom have led to different kinds of interventions, designed by researchers and practitioners, with different patterns of outcomes. The American situation has been summarized in a briefing report to the House of Representatives by the United States General Accounting Office (GAO 1989). This shows that, in the last year for which full data were available, approximately 41 per cent (6,500) of US districts representing over 38,000 schools were involved in various forms of interventions, and that a further 17 per cent of districts were planning to implement such programmes during the next couple of years. Based on published accounts, Levine and Lezotte (1990) have drawn up a list of the most promising interventions. Practices studied by researchers include the following 14 types of intervention:

- Establishment and facilitation of an informal group of participating principals who regularly meet and work together
- Provision of parallel and co-ordinated training for administrators
- Sponsorship of individual schools' audits
- Establishment of principals' academies
- Redesign and utilization of personnel evaluation instruments
- Assignment of new principals to a programme of shadowing
- Selection of faculty at poorly functioning schools for a tailored programme of improvement
- Training of future administrators
- Establishment of a central office intervention team to work with schools
- Establishment of paid link teachers between individual schools and central office
- Assignment of former principals to serve as mentors
- Accelerated learning programmes for students
- Development of auditing and other technical assistance teams
- Establishment of mentor teachers to staff other than the principal.

The UK has had fewer interventions by researchers and practitioners, but more government-generated initiatives. Reynolds (1992) has summarized those that have taken place. In particular, he has drawn attention to the following developments:

- Teacher-researcher movement's focus on improvement in the 1970s
- Self-evaluation and review programmes of the 1980s
- Local Education Authorities' own initiatives (such as the Hargreaves and the Thomas Reports, Inner London Education Authority [ILEA], 1984 and 1985 respectively)
- Schools' Council's Guidelines for Review and Institutional Development (GRIDS) scheme.

To this list should be added the recent work on school development planning (Beresford *et al.* 1992) and government-sponsored activities. The work on school planning shows that almost all LEAs have encouraged their schools to adopt school development plans and that many authorities are now using these as a basis for their own support and interventions in schools.

By seeking to create a market in which parents can choose schools to suit their children, the UK government has striven to induce competitive conditions which, it hopes, will improve the effectiveness of schools. In particular, by enabling school communities to opt out of their school districts and to manage themselves, it has sought to encourage principals to take initiatives otherwise denied them. It is as yet too early to report systematically on the outcome of this experiment, but it is already possible to see both encouraging and worrying signs in those schools that have taken advantage of opting out. Encouraging signs can be detected in the increasing self-confidence of staff and in the benefits of local, rather than area-based, decision-making mechanisms. (The schools have also benefited from increased funding.) The worrying signs are that, rather than parents choosing schools, the schools appear to be choosing the students, and, because of a legislative requirement to publish examination results, pupils with special needs, or those who are likely to be low-achieving, are less likely to be chosen than are their more able, less problematic, peers. If this trend develops, the low achievers will be clustered in those schools (with fewer resources) that have not opted out and the vital ingredient of effectiveness – a balanced intake – identified by Rutter and colleagues (1979) will be stymied. This situation needs to be monitored closely.

Table 22.1 shows the range of interventions that take place. This list is not intended to be exhaustive. Interventions have been included simply to illustrate the available range of activities. Two dimensions have been identified, focus and scope. The *focus* varies from specific to general. The *scope* includes single schools, groups of schools, the local system, and national categories.

In terms of success, most of the preventative interventions cited have achieved something. None, however, has been hailed as a panacea for all the ills of schooling. Each has a range of costs and benefits. Some initiatives, such as the Reading Recovery Project (Clay 1985), are still the subject of critical evaluation (for example Glyn *et al.* 1989) but have been hailed as being of direct value in other countries and other systems. Others, such as the Comer Programme (Comer 1991)

Table 22.1 Interventions classified according to their focus and scope

	Single school
Specific	US High School Academies of enriched schooling (Archer and Montesano 1990) Changing an English Disruptive School (Badger 1992)
General	The Baz Attack – Canada (Toews and Murray-Barker 1985) Enrichment for pre-school students (Athey 1990)
	Group of schools
Specific	The Comer New Haven Programme (Comer 1991) Cognitive Interactions in Primary Schooling in Germany (Einsiedler 1992)
General	The London Study (Maughan *et al.* 1990) The Israeli Study (Bashi *et al.* 1990)
	Local systems
Specific	Sheffield Early Literacy Programme (Hannon *et al.* 1991) Academic Feedback in Northern Ireland (FitzGibbon 1991)
General	The Halton Growth Plan (Stoll and Fink 1989) The Calgary Plan (Waldron 1983)
	National systems
Specific	Norwegian Ministry of Education anti-Bullying Programme (Olweus 1991) Reading Recovery in New Zealand, the US and the UK (Clay 1985)
General	What Works? (US Dept. of Education 1987) The Australian Project (McGaw *et al.* 1991)

and the Olweus (1991) project, have been recognized nationally as being capable of supporting young people and their schools, particularly in urban areas. The London study (Maughan *et al.* 1990: Ouston *et al.* 1991) revealed much information about whether – and how – schools can change their practices and their outcomes, although the changes were not brought about as a direct result of the intervention. More work needs to be done in order to exploit fully the knowledge that now exists about the potential positive effects of schools.

The Olweus intervention (one of the 'national systems') is interesting in view of its long time-scale and its complex research design. Its major goals were to limit, as much as possible, the number of incidents of bullying and to prevent development of new bully and victim problems. The intervention programme included the development of better information for teachers and school administrators about bullying and what they could do to counteract it. Information about bullying was also provided to parents of all children in the Norwegian school system. A cassette showing episodes of bullying was produced and made available for schools to rent or borrow. Finally, a questionnaire was designed to elicit information about all aspects of the bully and victim problem in schools. This was completed anonymously by individual students in school time.

About 2,500 students drawn from 42 schools in Bergen were followed up over a period of two-and-a-half years. This student sample was divided into four cohorts and a series of measurements was collected from before the initiation of the anti-bullying programme until several years after it had been completed. The research team used time-lagged contrasts between different cohorts to investigate whether there were genuine changes in behaviour over this period. A series of outcome variables based on the reported accounts of being bullied or of taking part in bullying incidents were developed from a questionnaire completed by the students. The research team concluded that reductions in bully and victim problems had taken place and that these were likely to be the result of the intervention programme rather than other factors.

What are the implications of this work for policy and practice?

There are numerous possible implications stemming from the work carried out over the last twenty or so years on the positive effects of schooling. Perhaps the most important is an implication for those involved closely with schools – the confirmation of the potential power of schools to affect the life chances of their students. Although the difference in scholastic attainment likely to be achieved by the same student in contrasting schools is unlikely to be great, in many instances it represents the difference between success and failure and operates as a facilitating or inhibiting factor in higher education. When coupled with the promotion of other pro-social attitudes and behaviours, and the inculcation of a positive self-image, the potential of the school to improve the life chances of students is considerable.

The second major implication of this work relates to governments. Legislation can provide a helpful framework for achieving an education system of high quality, but this can only be guaranteed by the conscious strategies of teachers and administrators, and the purposeful commitment of students. Excellence cannot be mandated by politicians or bureaucrats. Governments, central or local, would do well to realize this and ensure that any legislative framework that is created is likely to stim-ulate and elicit from those most involved ownership, commitment and dedication – rather than learned helplessness and resentment.

The third major implication relates to practitioners. A critical body of knowledge – replicated, in many cases, over time and in many different settings – has been established. This knowledge needs to be drawn upon more frequently in the quest for better schools. Some practitioners complain that information drawn from research studies is seldom made accessible or disseminated widely. This criticism undoubtedly has some validity: research journals seldom make compulsive reading for busy practitioners. It is not true, however, that efforts to disseminate widely the findings reported here have been half-hearted. Many conferences and meetings of principals' associations in many different countries have featured presentations on this topic. The work needs to continue. All those involved in trying to improve schools need to recognize the potential – not just in terms of specific actions by principals or teachers that may or may nor be related to the rest of their way of working – for describing, analysing and evaluating effectiveness.

The fourth and final implication concerns the work of researchers. The literature on school effectiveness is now enormous. There are vast numbers of books, journal articles, chapters in edited collections, and conference papers on this topic. There are, however, relatively fewer detailed empirical studies than there are critiques and commentaries. If the field is to flourish, more empirical work is needed. Further studies extending the focus from schools to other educational institutions would help to broaden still further the knowledge base. Possibly even more important is the need for careful experimental work that tests the mainly correlational findings of the early studies. This, coupled with a compilation of an adequate theory both of what makes schools effective and of how to make them more so, would be of great value to the educational community. Some work on the theoretical underpinning of the topic has been undertaken, as the very careful synthesis of research on educational change illustrates (Fullan 1991), but more is needed.

In conclusion, therefore, it can be stated that the positive effects of schooling have been well documented by a number of research studies carried out in different coun-tries at different times. The mechanisms associated with these effects are also well known and are, to a large extent, common to the studies. The effects vary, however, according to a number of different variables and more work is needed to disentangle the influence of student characteristics from school effects. Justified by the ground-breaking early research, a number of intervention studies have been carried out, but the outcomes of such work have, in general, proved less than hoped for. The difficul-ties of integrating such interventions – based on sound research findings – with those dictated by the political concerns of governments remain. Finally, a number of impli-cations for different groups, stemming from this work, still need to be addressed.

[…]

References

Ainley, J. and Sheret, M. (1992) 'Effectiveness of high schools in Australia: Holding power and achievement', paper presented to the International Congress for School Effectiveness and Improvement, Victoria, British Columbia.

Aitken, M. and Longford, N. (1986) 'Statistical modelling issues in school effectiveness studies', *Journal of the Royal Statistical Society* (Series A) 149(1): 1–43.

Alexander, R., Rose, J. and Woodhead, C. (1992) *Curriculum Organisation and Classroom Practice in Primary Schools: A Discussion Paper*, London: Department of Education and Science.

Archer, E. and Montesano, P. (1990) 'High school academies: Engaging students in school and work', *Equity and Choice* (Special Report), Winter: 16–17.

Athey, C. (1990) *Extending Thought in Young Children*, London: Paul Chapman Publishing.

Badger, B. (1992) 'Changing a destructive school' in D. Reynolds and P. Cuttance (eds) *School Effectiveness: Research, Policy and Practice*, 134–53, London: Cassell.

Bandura, A. (1992) 'Perceived self-efficacy in cognitive development and functioning', paper presented to the American Educational Research Association, San Francisco.

Bashi, J., Sass, Z., Katzir, R. and Margolin, I. (1990) *Effective Schools – From Theory to Practice: An Implementation Model and Its Outcomes*, Jerusalem: Van Leer Institute.

Bennett, S.N. (1976) *Teaching Styles and Pupil Progress*, London: Open Books.

Beresford, C., Mortimore, P., MacGilchrist, B. and Savage, J. (1992) 'School development planning matters in the UK', *Unicorn* 18 (2): 12–16.

Blakey, L. and Heath, A. (1992) 'Differences between comprehensive schools: Some preliminary findings' in D. Reynolds and P. Cuttance (eds) *School Effectiveness: Research, Policy and Practice*, 1221–33, London: Cassell.

Blum, R. (1984) *Onward to Excellence: Making Schools More Effective*, Portland, OR: Northwest Regional Educational Laboratory.

Bollen, R. and Hopkins, D. (1987) *School Based Research: Towards a Praxis*, Leuven, Belgium: Academic Publishing Company (ACCO).

Bosker, R. and Scheerens, J. (1989) 'Issues and interpretations of the results of school effectiveness research', *International Journal of Educational Research* 13 (7): 41–52.

Brandsma, H.P. and Knuver, J.W. (1989) 'Effects of school and classroom characteristics on pupil progress in language and arithmetic', *International Journal of Educational Research* (Special Issue, *Developments in School Effectiveness Research*) 13 (7): 777–88.

Brimer, A., Madaus, C., Chapman, B., Kellaghan, T. and Wood, D. (1978) *Sources of Difference in School Achievement*, Slough, Buckinghamshire: National Foundation for Educational Research.

Brookover, W. and Lezotte, L. (1977) *Changes in School Characteristics Co-incident with Changes in Student Achievement*, Michigan: East Lansing Institute for Research on Teaching, Michigan State University.

Brown, C. and Wing, J. (1962) 'A comparative clinical and social survey of three mental hospitals', *Sociological Review Monograph* 5: 145–71.

Cannan, C. (1970) 'Schools for delinquency', *New Society* 427: 1004.

Clark, D., Lotto, L. and Astuto, T. (1984) 'Effective schools and school improvement: A comparative analysis of two lines of enquiry', *Educational Administration Quarterly* 20(3): 41–68.

Clark, T. and McCarthy, D. (1983) 'School improvement in New York: The evolution of a project', *Educational Researcher* 12(4): 17–24.

Clay, M. (1985) *The Early Detection of Reading Difficulties*, London: Heinemann.

Coleman, J., Hoffer, I. and Kilgore, S. (1982) *High School Achievement*, New York: Basic Books.

Comer, J.P. (1991) 'The Comer school development program', *Urban Education* 26 (1): 56–82.

Creemers, B. and Lugthart, E. (1989) 'School effectiveness and improvement in The Netherlands' in D. Reynolds, B. Creemers and T. Peters (eds) *School Effectiveness and Improvement: Proceedings of the First International Congress, London 1988*, 89–103. Groningen: RION Institute for Educational Research/Cardiff: School of Education, University of Wales.

Cuttance, P. (1985) 'Methodological issues in the statistical analysis of data on the effectiveness of schooling', *British Educational Review Journal* 11(2): 163–79.

Dalin, P. (1989) 'Reconceptualising the school improvement process: Charting a paradigm shift' in D. Reynolds, B. Creemers and T. Peters (eds) *School Effectiveness and Improvement, Proceedings of the First International Congress, London 1988*, 30–45, Groningen: RION Institute for Educational Research/ Cardiff: School of Education, University of Wales.

Daly, P. (1991) *How Large Are Secondary School Effects in Northern Ireland?* Belfast: School of Education, Queen's University.

Department of Education and Science (1991) *Development Planning: A Practical Guide*, School Development Plans Project 2, London: DES.

Domanico, R. and Cenn, C. (1992) 'Creating the context for improvement in New York City's public schools', paper presented to the Quality of Life in London/New York Conference, London.

Dorr-Bremme, D. (1990) 'Culture, practice and change: School effectiveness reconsidered' in D. Levine and L. Lezotte (eds) *Unusually Effective Schools: A Review of Research and Practice*, Madison, WI: National Center for Effective Schools Research and Development.

Dweck, C. and Repucci, N. (1973) 'Learned helplessness and reinforcement responsibility in children', *Journal of Personality and Social Psychology* 25(1): 109–16.

Edmonds, R. (1979) 'Effective schools for the urban poor', *Educational Leadership* 37(1): 15–27.

Edmonds, R. and Frederiksen, J. (1979) *'Search for Effective Schools: The Identification and Analysis of City Schools that are Instructionally Effective for Poor Children'*, ERIC Document Reproduction Service No. ED 170 396, Cambridge, MA: Graduate School of Education, Center for Urban Studies.

Einsiedler, W. (1992) 'The effects of teaching methods, class methods and patterns of cognitive teacher–pupil interactions in an experimental study in primary school classes', paper presented to the International Congress for School Effectiveness and School Improvement, Victoria, British Columbia.

FitzGibbon, C. (1991) 'A-levels: Corrective comparisons', *Managing Schools Today* 1(2): 44–5.

Fraser, B. (1989) 'Research synthesis on school and instructional effectiveness', *International Journal of Educational Research* 13(7): 707–20.

Fullan, M. (1991) *The New Meaning of Educational Change*, London: Cassell.

Fullan, M. (1992) 'The evolution of change and the new work of the educational leader', paper presented at the Regional Conference of the Commonwealth Council for Education Administration, Hong Kong.

Galloway, D., Martin, R. and Willcox, B. (1985) 'Persistent absence from school and exclusions from school', *British Educational Research Journal* 11(2): 51–61.

Galton, M. and Simon, B. (1980) *Progress and Performance in the Primary Classroom*, London: Routledge and Kegan Paul.

General Accounting Office of the United States (GAO) (1989) *Effective School Programs: Their Extent and Characteristics*, Washington, DC: GAO.

Glyn, T., Crooks, T., Bethune, N., Ballard, K. and Smith, J. (1989) *Reading Recovery in Context*, Wellington, New Zealand: Department of Education.

Good, J. and Brophy, J. (1986) 'Social and institutional context of teaching: School effects', in *Third Handbook of Research on Teaching*, New York: Macmillan.

Gray, J., Jesson, D. and Sime, N. (1990) 'Estimating differences in the examination performance of secondary schools in six LEAS: A multilevel approach to school effectiveness', *Oxford Review of Education* 16(2): 137–58.

Gray, J., McPherson, A. and Raffe, D. (1983) *Reconstructions of Secondary Education: Theory, Myth and Practice Since the War*, London: Routledge and Kegan Paul.

Gregory, K. and Mueller, S. (1980) 'Leif Ericson Elementary School, Chicago' in W. Duckett (ed.) *Why Do Some Urban Schools Succeed?*, 60–74, Bloomington, IN: Phi Delta Kappa.

Hallinger, P. and Murphy, J. (1985) Instructional leadership and school socio-economic status: A preliminary investigation. *Administrator's notebook* 31(5): 1–4.

Hallinger, P. and Murphy, J. (1986) 'The social context of effective schools', *American Journal of Education* 94(3): 328–54.

Hallinger, P. and Murphy, J. (1987) 'Instructional leadership in the school context' in W. Greenfield (ed.) *Instructional Leadership*, 179–202. Boston, MA: Allyn and Bacon.

Hannon, P., Weinberger, J. and Nutbrown, C. (1991) 'A study of work with parents to promote early literacy development', *Research Papers in Education* 6(2): 77–98.

Hargreaves, D. and Hopkins, D. (1989) *School Development Plans Project: Planning for School Development*, London: Department for Education and Science.

Heal, K. (1978) 'Misbehaviour among school children', *Policy and Politics* 6: 321–32.

Hess, J. (1992) *School Restructuring, Chicago Style: A Midway Report*, Chicago, IL: The Chicago Panel on Public School Policy and Finance.

Husen, T., Tuijnman, A. and Halls, W. (1992) *Schooling in Modern European Society*, Oxford: Pergamon Press.

Inner London Education Authority (1984) *Improving Secondary Schools* (The Hargreaves Report), London: ILEA.

Inner London Education Authority (1985) *Improving Primary Schools* (The Thomas Report), London: ILEA.

Jowett, S. and Baginsky, M., with MacDonald, M. (1991) *Building Bridges: Parental Involvement in Schools*, Windsor: NFER/Nelson.

Lacey, C. (1970) *Hightown Grammar: The School as a Social System*, Manchester: Manchester University Press.

Lacey, C. (1974) 'Destreaming in a "pressurised" academic environment' in J. Eggleston (ed.) *Contemporary Research in the Sociology of Education*, pp. 148–66, London: Methuen.

Lazar, I. and Darlington, R. (1982) 'Lasting effects of early education: A report from the consortium for longitudinal studies', *Monographs of the Society for Research in Child Development* 195: 47.

Levine, D. and Lezotte, L. (1990) *Unusually Effective Schools: A Review and Analysis of Research and Practice*, Madison, WI: National Center for Effective Schools Research and Development.

McCormack-Larkin, M. and Kritek, W. (1982) 'Milwaukee's project RISE', *Educational Leadership* 40(3): 16–21.

McGaw, B., Banks, D. and Piper, K. (1991) *Effective Schools: Schools that Make a Difference*. Hawthorn, Victoria: Australian Council for Educational Research.

MacPherson, A. and Willms, D. (1987) 'Equalisation and improvement: Some effects of comprehensive reorganisation in Scotland', paper presented at the annual meeting of the American Educational Research Association.

Madden, J. (1976) cited in R. Edmonds, 'Effective schools for the urban poor', *Educational Leadership* 37(1): 15–27.

Maughan, B., Pickles, A., Rutter, M. and Ouston, J. (1990), 'Can schools change I? Outcomes at six London secondary schools', *School Effectiveness and School Improvement* 1(3): 188–210.

Mortimore, J. and Mortimore, P. (1984) 'Parents and schools', *Education* 164, Special Report 5 October.

Mortimore, P. (1990) The front page or yesterday's news: The reception of educational research, in G. Welford (ed.) *Doing Educational Research* 210–33, London: Routledge.

Mortimore, P. (1991) 'The nature and findings of research on school effectiveness in the primary sector' in S. Riddell and S. Brown (eds) *School Effectiveness Research: Its Messages for School Improvement*, 9–19, Edinburgh: HMSO.

Mortimore, P., Sammons, P., Stoll, L., Lewis, D. and Ecob, R. (1988) *School Matters: The Junior Years*, Wells, Somerset, Open Books. Reprinted 1995, London: Paul Chapman Publishing.

Murphy, J. (1991) *Restructuring Schools: Capturing and Assessing the Phenomena*, New York: Teachers' College Press.

Murphy, J., Weil, M., Hallinger, P. and Mitman, A. (1982) Academic press: Translating high expectations into school policies and classroom practices', *Educational Leadership* 40(3): 22–6.

Northwest Regional Educational Laboratory (NREL) (1990) *Effective Schooling Practices Update*, Portland, OR: Northwest Regional Educational Laboratory.

Nuttall, D.L., Goldstein, H., Prosser, R. and Rasbash, J. (1989) 'Differential school effectiveness' in *International Journal of Education Research, Special Issue: Developments in School Effectiveness Research* 13(7): 769–76.

Nuttall, D.L., Sammons, P. and Thomas, S. (1993) personal communication.

Olweus, D. (1991) 'Bully/victim problems among school children: Basic facts and effects of a school-based intervention programme' in D. Pepler and K. Rubin (eds) *The Development and Treatment of Childhood Aggression*, 411–88, Hove and London: Erlbaum.

Ouston, J., Maughan, B. and Rutter, M. (1991) 'Can schools change? II: Practice in six London secondary schools', *School Effectiveness and School Improvement* 2(l): 3–13.

Power, M., Alderson, M., Phillipson, C., Schoenberg, E. and Morris, J. (1967) 'Delinquent schools?', *New Society* 264: 542–3.

Purkey, S. and Smith, M. (1983) 'Effective schools: A review', *Elementary School Journal* 83(4): 427–52.

Raudenbush, S. (1989) 'The analysis of longitudinal, multilevel data', *International Journal of Educational Research, Special Issue: Developments in School Effectiveness Research* 13(7): 721–40.

Reynolds, D. (1976) 'The delinquent school' in M. Hammersley and P. Woods (eds) *The Process of Schooling*, 217–29, London: Routledge and Kegan Paul.

Reynolds, D. (1992) 'School effectiveness and school improvement: An updated review of the British literature' in D. Reynolds and P. Cuttance (eds) *School Effectiveness Research, Policy and Practice*, 1–24, London: Cassell.

Reynolds, D. and Cuttance, P. (eds) (1992) *School Effectiveness: Research, Policy and Practice*, London: Cassell.

Reynolds, D., Jones, D. and St. Leger, S. (1976) 'Schools do make a difference', *New Society* 37(721): 223–5.

Reynolds, D., Sullivan, M. and Murgatroyd, S. (1987) *The Comprehensive Experiment*, Lewes: Falmer Press.

Roeder, P. and Sang, F. (1991) 'Über die institutionelle Verarbeitung von Leistungsunterschieden', *Zeitschrift f. Entwicklungspsychologie u. Pädagogische Psychologie* 23(2): 159–70.

Rosenthal, R. and Jacobson, L. (1968) *Pygmalion in the Classroom: Teacher Expectations and Pupils' Intellectual Development*, New York: Holt Rinehart and Winston.

Rutter, M. (1983) 'School effects on pupil progress: Research findings and policy implications', *Child Development* 54: 1–29.

Rutter, M., Maughan, B., Mortimore, P. and Ouston, J. (1979) *Fifteen Thousand Hours; Secondary Schools and Their Effects on Children,* London: Open Books. Reprinted 1995, Paul Chapman Publishing.

Sammons, P. and Nuttall, D.L. (1992) 'Differential school effectiveness', paper presented to the British Educational Research Association Conference, Stirling.

Scheerens, J. and Creemers, B. (1989) (eds) 'Conceptualizing school effectiveness', *International Journal of Educational Research* 13: 691–706.

Scheerens, J. and Creemers, B. (1989) (eds) 'Developments in school effectiveness research', *International Journal of Educational Research* 13: 7.

Sizemore, B. (1987) 'The effective African American elementary school', in G. Noblit and W. Pink (eds) *Context: Qualitative Studies,* 175–202, Norwood, NJ: Ablex.

Smith, D. and Tomlinson, S. (1989) *The School Effect,* London: Policy Studies Institute.

Stevenson, M. and Shin-Ying, L. (1990) 'Contexts of achievement: A study of American, Chinese and Japanese children', *Monographs of the Society for Research in Child Development,* 221: 55.

Stoll, L. and Fink, D. (1989) 'An effective schools project: The Halton approach' in D. Reynolds, D. Creemers and T. Peters (eds.) *School Effectiveness and Improvement: Proceedings of the First International Congress, London 1988,* 286–99. Groningen, The Netherlands:, RION Institute for Educational Research/Cardiff: School of Education, University of Wales.

Teddlie, C., Falkowski, C., Stringfield, S., Deselle, S. and Garvue, R. (1984) *The Education School Effectiveness Study, Phase 2,* Louisiana: Louisiana State Department of Education.

Teddlie, C., Kirby, P. and Stringfield, S. (1989) 'Effective versus ineffective schools: Observable differences in the classroom', *American Journal of Education.*

Tizard, B., Blatchford, P., Burke, J., Farquhar, C. and Plewis, I. (1988) *Young Children at School in the Inner City,* Hove: Erlbaum.

Tizzard, J., Schofield, W. and Hewison, J. (1982) 'Symposium: Reading – collaboration between teachers and parents in assisting children's reading', *British Journal of Educational Psychology* 52: 1–15.

Toews, J. and Murray-Barker, D. (1985) *The Baz Attack: The School Improvement Experience Utilising Effective Schools Research, 1981–85,* Calgary, Alberta: Bazalgette Junior High School.

US Department of Education (1987) *What Works?* Washington, DC, US Department of Education.

Van de Grift, W. (1990) 'Educational leadership and academic achievement in elementary education', *School Effectiveness and School Improvement* 1: 26–40.

Waldron, P. (1983) *Towards a More Effective School,* Banff, Alberta: Canadian Education Association.

Weber, G. (1971) *Inner-city Children Can Be Taught to Read: Four Successful Schools,* Washington, DC: Council for Basic Education.

Willms, J. and Cuttance, R. (1985) 'School effects in Scottish secondary schools', *British Journal of Sociology of Education* 6(3): 287–306.

Willms, J. and Raudenbush, S. (1989) 'A longitudinal hierarchical linear model for estimating school effects and their stability, *Journal of Educational Measurement* 26(3): 209–32.

Wood, R. and Bandura, A. (1989) 'Impact of conceptions of ability on self-regulating mechanisms and complex decision-making', *Journal of Personality and Social Psychology* 56: 407–15.

23 Transitions between primary and secondary schools

Hilary Burgess

Introduction

The age of transfer from primary to secondary school and issues surrounding it have been the subject of debate and research for the past fifty years in the UK. This chapter seeks to explore pupil transition between Key Stage 2 and Key Stage 3 and pupil experiences of transitions as they change year groups in the secondary school. A brief look at the historical background will provide a context for issues of continuity and progression following transition.

In the 1950s, most educational policy-makers were convinced that a change of school around the age of eleven was desirable. This supported the vision of secondary education as a tripartite system of grammar schools for the most academic pupils, technical schools for those with an aptitude for craft and technology and secondary modern schools for the remaining majority of pupils. However, much controversy surrounded the selection processes for secondary education. It was no surprise, therefore, when the Labour government of that time requested local authorities to produce schemes for reorganization for a comprehensive education (Circular 10/65, DES 1965). The request was not mandatory and therefore some local education authorities continued with the tripartite system, thus increasing transitional problems for pupils who had to relocate when they changed schools because of the geographic mobility of their parents.

Difficulties associated with transition were apparent in one of the earliest large-scale studies to examine transfer and performance (Nisbet and Entwistle 1969). This study found that the academically less motivated and working-class pupils had difficulty adjusting to a new school and were less successful in their homework.

In the primary sector, the Plowden Report (CACE 1967) was particularly influential in encouraging the development of middle schools. The committee recommended:

(a) part-time nursery experience for those whose parents wish it;
(b) a three-year course in the first (at present the infant) school with one annual intake in September at a median age of five years six months;

(c)   the first school should be followed by a four-year course in a middle (at present the junior) school with a median age range from eight years six months to twelve years six months.

(CACE 1967: para. 386: 146)

Several local education authorities introduced middle schools following the advocacy of Plowden and, in some areas such as Northumberland and Leicestershire, they became well established. The growth of middle schools was based on the philosophy that the middle years of schooling were particularly important and a distinctive school with its own identity was required for children of this age. Middle schools would provide the bridge between the separate primary and secondary school sectors thus allowing smooth transition between these stages. They were intended to be a 'zone of transition' where children would gradually move from the generalist class teacher environment of the primary school to the secondary subject specialist curriculum of the secondary school (Hargreaves 1986: 5). However, with the introduction of National Curriculum Key Stages, a break at the age of eleven for the end of Key Stage 2 was re-emphasized, and the continued viability of middle schools became questionable. Official support for middle schools has been ambivalent and in education directories and statistical returns to the DfE, middle schools are deemed to be either primary or secondary. In some areas such as Dorset and Milton Keynes, first and middle schools are linked under one headteacher and known as combined schools. Transfer to a new school environment, therefore, occurs at different ages and stages of a pupil's career depending upon locality and the organization of schools.

There have been a number of research studies that have looked at transfer issues, most of which have focused on the pupil experience and the personal, social and emotional aspects of transfer. The pupil perspective and the development of identities was analysed by Measor and Woods (1984) while other studies (Benyon 1985) have focused on the relationships between teachers and pupils and the way in which pupils become labelled by teachers. Impact of transfer upon academic progress was the main area of research in the ORACLE (Observation Research and Classroom Learning Evaluation) study which followed primary school pupils through five years of primary education and a year after transfer to secondary schools. There has been only one major study on transition (Rudduck *et al.* 1996) and this argues that the earlier focus upon the social aspects of transfer and induction programmes for pupils has neglected the impact of transfer upon academic learning. They suggest that at the time of transfer, pupils need induction into the social life of their new school and help in developing a routine for managing their learning if they are to maintain academic progress. What is the evidence to support this suggestion?

Evidence on the effects of transition

How do transition and transfer affect pupil progress and what is the evidence to demonstrate that changing classes and schools has an impact on pupil learning? With the introduction of the National Curriculum it was hoped that improved curriculum continuity would ease the difficulties pupils faced in managing learning across transitional phases. However, it has been argued (Gorwood 1994) that transfer between primary and secondary schools continues to have a major impact upon pupil learning because of the different philosophies that underpin the teaching of the curriculum. In primary schools, the emphasis upon skills, attitudes and values leads to a more thematic approach to teaching than the subject-based curriculum in the secondary school. The National Curriculum, therefore, aids continuity in terms of teaching content but the different pedagogical approaches and organization of the classes are barriers to smooth transition and pupil progress (Nicholls and Gardner 1999).

The range and diversity of secondary schools and the increasing numbers of specialist schools, such as technology colleges, create many transitional challenges for teachers and pupils. Other reforms that have affected the management and organization of schools and hence pupil transition, have emerged from the principle of parental choice. Until 1998, schools had the option to take up grant maintained status and, therefore, were able to become independent of LEAs and their cluster arrangements designed to promote effective transition. Open enrolment has also allowed parents to select a secondary school that is not in their neighbourhood. This has resulted in some secondary schools having a large number of feeder primary schools making the tracking of individual pupil progression much more difficult.

Further evidence on the problems pupils face at transitional stages is available in Ofsted reviews and reports of inspections. A review of science inspection findings during 1993–4 Ofsted suggested that teaching at Key Stage 3 'seldom takes sufficient account of pupils' capabilities and previous learning' (Ofsted 1995 11(4)). Later evidence from the reports of the Chief Inspector (Ofsted 1998, 1999) demonstrates that there is a very noticeable drop in pupil performance around the age of transfer from primary to secondary school. A steep rise was noted, by the inspectors, between the end of Key Stage 2 and the early stages of Year 7 in proportions of schools where pupil attainment was judged to be unsatisfactory by Ofsted inspectors (Ofsted 1998). This may, however, be linked to the fact that different groups of primary and secondary Ofsted inspectors were making judgements about pupils at those two points in time (Galton, Gray and Rudduck 1999). The data from Ofsted in 1999 illustrates that transfer to another school is not the only occasion that pupil performance varies. Indeed, pupils are judged to be making good or very good progress in 45 per cent of lessons in both Year 6 and Year 7. This drops to 42 per cent in Year 8 lessons; while in only 40 per cent of Year 9 lessons are pupils judged to be achieving good or very good progress. Year 10 shows an improvement in pupil performance with 44 per cent of lessons regarded as helping pupils to make good or very good progress. The evidence suggests that transitions within phases as well as between phases have an effect upon pupil learning and attainment.

Research undertaken by the NFER (National Foundation for Educational Research) has examined continuity and progression across the 5–16 age range (Lee *et al.* 1995). However, as the fieldwork for this research was carried out in 1993, before the full national testing system was in place, it was not at that time clear how testing at Key Stage 2 would be taken into account at the point of transfer to another school. Later NFER research by Schagen and Kerr (1999) focused on the impact of

Key Stage 1 and 2 tests on curriculum continuity and pupil progression at the point of transfer. They argue that schools have made considerable efforts to smooth the process of transfer for pupils with induction meetings and activities that have done much to allay the fears of pupils. However, they suggest that the National Curriculum has not had the expected positive impact on curriculum continuity and individual progression as many secondary schools adopt a 'fresh start' approach to pupil learning in Year 7 rather than plan learning programmes based on the results of Key Stage 2 tests.

All the evidence suggests that there are several transitional stages in pupils' school careers that teachers need to focus upon. Transfer between primary and secondary school appears to create the most transitional problems for pupils but there are also issues in terms of pupil learning that need to be addressed around Year 8 and Year 9. What have pupils had to say about transitions between schools and different classes?

Pupil perceptions of transitions

Pupils have proved to be immensely capable and perceptive in commenting upon their own experiences of transfer (Brown and Armstrong 1986). Their accounts illustrate how adaptable children can be as well as the deep and lasting impression some experiences can have on their future progress through school.

Research from the ORACLE project (Galton and Willcocks 1983) presented data on two anxieties that pupils had about moving to a new school. The first was about being separated from their old friends and not being able to find new ones, and the second anxiety related to bullying. Both boys and girls worried about friendship. An interview between two boys, Josh and Luke, and an interview researcher revealed:

> They had been very worried about finding new friends here and were very scared that they would not make friends easily and get very left out. ... They both admitted that once they arrived here they did in fact make friends quickly.
>
> (Galton and Willcocks 1983: 137)

However, they found that where pupils moved schools with their friends such worries did not exist.

Bullying in the new school was an even greater concern to many pupils and could affect the way they behaved even where there was little real evidence of bullying behaviour. Two girls, Jasmine and Lavinia, spoke to an ORACLE researcher who commented:

> The main information which these two girls had got from their siblings was to expect bullying. They had been told that the third years often pick on you. When I asked them if this had in fact happened to them they said no it had not. They have been very careful to avoid it, and they very rarely went out at break time or lunchtime so they would not have any trouble. They said they had seen

some of the boys being bullied. Jasmine explained that some of the big lads came up and half strangled them. Nobody came to help. 'They daren't.'

(Galton and Willcocks 1983: 143)

Later studies (Brown and Armstrong 1986) revealed a variety of concerns pupils in the last year of their junior school held about transfer. The comments relate to organizational aspects of the new secondary school as well as very personal issues. For example,

I am scared about the size of the school, because it's very big and some of the places in the school, I don't know where they are.

What happens if nobody likes me?

The one thing I'm not looking forward to is the showers because when I came to visit there weren't any curtains for them.

(Brown and Armstrong 1986: 34)

Rudduck (1996) interviewed pupils at the start of Year 8 and reported some similar experiences. A sense of loss about leaving the security of the primary school and the overwhelming size of the secondary school were two of the main feelings described by pupils. The hall was a feature of the primary school that several pupils missed as meeting together gave a sense of community which pupils felt was lacking in their secondary school. Myths pupils encounter linked to transition about laboratory rats, terrifying teachers, five-mile runs, violent gangs or lavatory/shower myths (Delamont 1989) allowed pupils to cope with aspects of transition, although some new activities, such as using a bunsen burner, may be unexpected. Looking after personal property was also an issue, as pupils commented:

… our old school … it wasn't a small school but you still, like, in some ways you knew your name and there was no, I mean, there was no troubles, with not really people stealing anything. Just like some people took things out of lunch boxes, like a chocolate biscuit. (Y8, F)

And that used to be a really major thing but here you can't even leave your coat or bag in the cloakroom without it getting nicked. (Y8, F)

(Rudduck 1996: 20)

Pupils were anxious about new activities and also about doing the right thing so that they were not embarrassed, for example, at the first school disco.

We ended up wearing jeans and a nice top and we wore high heels. And everyone else was in like trainers and shell suits and I just felt so out of place. (Y8, F)

(Rudduck 1996: 21)

Even from the distance of Year 8, these pupils clearly remember episodes from their early days in a secondary school and the embarrassment or worry caused by incidents.

However, many pupils described advantages, benefits and variety, for example in extra-curricular activities that had not occurred to them at the time of changing schools.

> If there's a teacher you don't like you're not stuck with them for every single lesson every day of the year. (Y8, F)

> After school there's trampolining, badminton, football and things like that. (Y8, M)

> 'Cos at primary school we started at quarter to nine and finished at half past three and now we start at nine and end at quarter to four. So we can stay in bed a bit longer. (Y8, F)

> (Rudduck 1996: 22–3)

It has been assumed in earlier research studies (Delamont and Galton 1986) that after the first year at secondary school, pupils quickly become caught up in the normal routines of school life. New research (Rudduck *et al.* 1996) suggests that this is only part of the story, and learning to manage homework and organisation of personal time outside school play a major part in the academic success of pupils at transitional stages.

They argue that in Year 10 pupils are confronted with the realities of work experience and the implications of not gaining qualifications and, therefore, begin to value good work habits and continuity in their learning. This conclusion would also appear to be supported by the Ofsted evidence discussed earlier in this chapter.

Curriculum subjects and transition

The practice of going over the basics in the first year of secondary school is a traditional feature that has become built into curriculum planning and teaching. Since the introduction of the National Curriculum, teachers have continued to believe it important for cross-phase liaison to take place as, while the content of learning should be more consistent in their feeder schools, the methodology may vary. However, the gap between primary and secondary in the teaching of the core subjects is still considered to be an issue by secondary teachers (Schagen and Kerr 1999). Doubts about the texts children may have used and the topics they may have covered are their major concerns. Sequencing of topics, in science for example, can vary in primary schools. Where pupils have studied an aspect of the curriculum in Year 5 rather than Year 6 their memory of the work covered may be sketchy by the time they transfer into Year 7. Thus, secondary school teachers may feel it necessary to repeat primary school topics as revealed in the NFER study:

> For some pupils the work in the first six weeks of Year 7 is repetition of what they already know, while for others it is obviously new. I see the repetition as reinforcement for these pupils. Reinforcement is not a bad thing as it boosts

pupils' confidence in what they can do in their new surroundings. However, the important thing is that the work provides the same basic foundation for every pupil. This will hold them in good stead as they move on from Year 7 to GCSE and, hopefully, beyond.

(Comment from a Head of Science, Schagen and Kerr 1999: 38)

Knowledge of Key Stage 2 Programmes of Study is important if curriculum continuity is to be effective. In the NFER (Schagen and Kerr 1999) study, secondary teachers' responses to questions about Key Stage 2 revealed that few could provide examples of how information about Key Stage 2 had influenced their approach to Key Stage 3. Trust in primary teaching was also an issue, as one mathematics teacher commented:

It's useful to know what pupils have supposedly covered, but you cannot take this at face value.

(Schagen and Kerr 1999: 39)

Such repetition is often picked up by both pupils and parents and more regularly occurs in mathematics and science where the curriculum content is defined very specifically. The potential, therefore, for revisiting a particular topic is high (Nicholls and Gardner 1999).

Some subjects may be particularly vulnerable to acquiring a negative image as pupils move through transitional phases. For example, there is evidence that pupils' lack of interest in science may begin as early as Year 5 (Galton *et al.* 1999). They argue that particular attention should be paid to the middle years of schooling to encourage interest and enthusiasm in science as a subject. It has also been suggested that English is vulnerable because of the different emphasis placed on writing, speaking, and listening in primary and secondary schools. Secondary teachers focus more closely on a response to literature and therefore writing and talk arise from reading. In primary schools, the focus is on literacy skills and comprehension. Poor readers, therefore, find it more difficult to cope with the secondary approach to the teaching of English and may begin to lose interest in the subject (Marshall and Brindley 1998).

In mathematics it has been noted that most teachers prefer to start with a clean slate approach (Suffolk LEA 1997: Schlagen and Kerr 1999). Obviously, some pupils will have gaps in their mathematics knowledge as they enter Year 7 and this can be damaging to future progress if pupils fail to grasp fundamental concepts such as number theory. However, a consequence of revisiting material is that lower attaining pupils may become confused through attempts to relearn a topic using different methods while more able pupils may become bored.

Science lessons described in several studies (cf. Delamont and Galton 1986) have required pupils to perform at a lower level than that achieved in Key Stage 2 tests. Early science lessons have mainly been concerned with safety when using the bunsen burner and measuring and filtering instruments. However, it appears that only rarely are the development of these skills situated in the wider context of an investigation which would stimulate pupil curiosity as well as achieve the aim of learning to use equipment safely. After transfer to a secondary school, less time is spent in discussion and this is matched by an increase in the time spent listening to the teacher (Galton *et al.*1999).

Discontinuities in curriculum content and different methodologies used in teaching clearly have an impact as pupils' transfer from Key Stage 2 to Key Stage 3. Is this a necessary part of pupil progression that cannot be avoided? Standards for 11–14-year-olds have been criticized by the Secretary of State as 'not nearly high enough' (Blunkett, March 2000) who suggests that secondary schools do not build on the enormous progress made by primary schools. The fallback in performance at the start of secondary education, the impact of disaffection on pupil performance and the quality of teaching in Key Stage 3 are all issues that he argues need to be addressed. One initiative to raise achievement at Key Stage 3 is the focus on the teaching of literacy and numeracy so that the work begun in the primary school continues. Summer programmes of courses on literacy and numeracy, teaching packs in mathematics to support primary–secondary transfer and numeracy and literacy frameworks for Year 7 have all been introduced to promote an improvement in standards and the quality of teaching at Key Stage 3. If these new initiatives are to be carried out effectively a deeper understanding of the priorities and strategies of primary and secondary school teachers needs to be shared so that transitional disruption is lessened.

What can teachers do?

A number of concerns for teachers have been raised in this chapter and this final section will suggest some ways in which transitions between schools and year groups may be assisted. At the point of transfer from one school to another, all the evidence points to teachers needing to have an in-depth understanding not only of the National Curriculum Programmes of Study but also the different methodologies employed by teachers. The need for liaison between primary and secondary schools is not lessened, therefore, because of the introduction of the National Curriculum. It will be important for secondary teachers to find out how the subject orders have been implemented and talk with primary colleagues about their different approaches to teaching. Liaison activities, where clearly defined, can help to create a meaningful dialogue between primary and secondary teachers.

Dialogue about learning is also an important issue for pupils as they attempt to understand the long-term implications of what they do in school and begin to understand themselves as learners. Making time to talk and discuss work in lessons at transitional stages may be of great benefit to pupils.

Evidence discussed in this chapter demonstrates that Year 8 and Year 9 is a period when pupil work can take a dip as the newness of being a pupil in Year 7 fades and the greater responsibilities of Year 10 have not begun to be thought about. Transition into and through these middle years of the secondary school may be particularly important in terms of confirming work habits. How pupils can continue to develop learning-oriented habits in this phase is a particular challenge to teachers. Visits to enhance curricular activities and special responsibilities or privileges may all help to enhance pupil performance and attitude towards learning.

Finding ways to encourage pupils to manage their homework time may assist considerably with continuity as they come to see the value and gains in learning that can be made through keeping up with their studies. If good homework practices are not established in the early years of the secondary school the pupils may find it very difficult to cope with the demands of later examination syllabuses and lose both interest and motivation. Data from the research studies suggests that teachers can also be unreliable in setting homework that has a clear purpose and explaining how it links to the work that pupils have covered in school. Returning marked homework with helpful comments is not always promptly carried out by some teachers (Rudduck 1996).

Schools need to be highly organized places and it is tempting to allow the daily chores and immediate demands of teaching to take priority. It can appear easier to lead a lesson rather than allow time for pupils to discuss and to listen to their views and comments. However, the pupil voice about what it is like to be a pupil moving through transition is powerful and disturbing. It needs to be listened to by both primary and secondary teachers if we are to improve the social and intellectual experiences of pupils at points of transfer and transition in school.

References

Benyon, J. (1985) *Initial Encounters in the Secondary School*, Lewes: Falmer Press.

Blunkett, D. (2000) 'Transforming Secondary Education', keynote speech delivered on 15 March 2000.

Brown, J.M. and Armstrong, P. (1986) 'Transfer from junior. to secondary: the child's perspective' in M.B. Youngman (ed.) *Mid-schooling Transfer: Problems and Proposals*, Windsor: NFER Nelson.

CACE (Central Advisory Council for Education) (1967) *Children and their Primary Schools*, (The Plowden Report), London: HMSO.

DES (1965) *The Organisation of Secondary Education*, (Circular 10/65), London: HMSO.

Delamont, S. and Galton, M. (1986) *Inside the Secondary Classroom*, London: Routledge and Kegan Paul.

Delamont, S. (1989) 'the Nun in the toilet: urban legends and educational research', *International Journal of Qualitative Studies in Education* 2(3): 191–202.

Galton, M., Gray, J. and Rudduck, J. (1999) *The Impact of School Transitions and Transfers on Pupil Progress and Attainment*, London: DfEE.

Galton, M. and Willcocks, J. (1983) *Moving from the Primary Classroom*, London: Routledge and Kegan Paul.

Gorwood, B. (1986) *School Transfer and Curriculum Continuity*, London: Croom Helm.

Gorwood, B. (1994) 'Primary-secondary transfer after the National Curriculum' in B. Moon and A. Shelton-Mayes (eds) *Teaching and Learning in the Secondary School*, London: Routledge.

Hargreaves, A. (1986) *Two Cultures of Schooling: The Case of Middle Schools*, Lewes: Falmer Press.

Lee, B., Harris, S. and Dickson, P. (1995) *Continuity and Progression 5–16: Developments in School*, Slough: NFER.

Marshall, B. and Brindley, S. (1998) 'Cross-phase or just a lack of communication: models of English at key stage 2 and 3 and their possible effects on pupil transfer', *Changing English*, 5(2): 123–33.

Measor, L. and Woods, P. (1984) *Changing Schools: Pupil Perspectives on Transfer to a Comprehensive*, Milton Keynes: Open University Press.

Nicholls, G. and Gardner, J. (1999) *Pupils in Transition: Moving between Key Stages*, London: Routledge.

Nisbet, J.D. and Entwistle, N.J. (1969) *The Transition to Secondary School*, London: London University Press.

Ofsted (1995) *Science: A Review of Inspection Findings 1993/94*, London: HMSO.

Ofsted (1998) *Standards and Quality in Schools 1996/97* (Annual Report of the Chief Inspector of Schools), London: HMSO.

Ofsted (1999) *Standards and Quality in Schools 1997/98* (Annual Report of the Chief Inspector of Schools), London: HMSO.

Rudduck, J. (1996) 'Going to "the big school": the turbulence of transition' in J. Rudduck, L.R. Chaplain and G. Wallace (eds) *School Improvement: What Can Pupils Tell Us?* London: David Fulton.

Rudduck, J., Chaplain, R. and Wallace, G. (1996) (eds) *School Improvement: What Can Pupils Tell Us?* London: David Fulton.

Schagen, S. and Kerr, D. (1999) *Bridging the gap? The National Curriculum and progression from primary to secondary school*, Slough: NFER.

Suffolk LEA (1997) *A Report on an Investigation into what happens when Pupils Transfer into their next School at the Ages of 9, 11, and 13*, Ipswich: Inspection and Advice Division, Suffolk Education Department.

24 The intelligent school

John MacBeath[1]

First of all I would like to consider the past before turning to the future. Before we face the future we have to lay the three ghosts of the millennium past. These are

1 the universal product;
2 the tyranny of time;
3 the mythology of measurement.

The universal product

In his book *The Seven Cultures of Capitalism*, Charles Hampden Turner looks at and compares seven different cultures. The USA, he says, has been brilliant at giving us the universal product. It has given us the paradigmatic hamburger, Coca-Cola, Levi Jeans. You probably won't know the difference between a Burger King and a McDonald's, or a Coke and a Pepsi, or even between Levi's and other jeans. Hampden Turner's point is that we have got from the USA this notion of the universal product which is not just about hamburgers or cola, but is symptomatic of a deep way of thinking about the world.

It is also a deeply rooted way of thinking about schools and the curriculum, teaching and leadership. If you take the notion of the perfect product and apply it to schools, you join the search for the effective school, the excellent leader, the perfect teacher, the National Curriculum.

A French philosopher said the best was the enemy of the good. There is something profound in that. Hampden Turner quotes the Passchendaele slaughter which was the absolutely perfect plan, devised by generals far from the front line.

The danger of universalism is a constant quest for the right answer, the exemplary set of rules, the perfect plan.

The tyranny of time

The second ghost of the millennium past is the tyranny of time. Time has become a universal commodity as well. We can measure time and time is valuable. We talk about the race against time and everybody values time and knows it is limited.

I was reminded of a quote by Bernard Berenson:

> If only I could stand at the street corner with my hat in hand asking people to donate their unused minutes.

It says something about the inner quality of time, but also the tremendous pressure we are under to use and to seek out more time.

Interestingly one of the measures of the effective school and the effective teacher that researchers constantly refer to and measure is time 'on task'. That is a very useful measure and one that teachers need to look at.

But when we look at the emerging research, we discover that one of the best indicators is actually time '*off* task', when children have time to stop what they are doing and reflect, to think, to change activity, to listen to music or become involved in drama or movement. This involves the use of a different kind of intelligence – kinaesthetic intelligence.

Time 'off task' is absolutely critical, and I am only learning in my late fifties that when I sit down and work at my computer I must stop after 20 to 25 minutes and go and take a walk or do something different because that will actually increase my brain power. When I come back to the task I will be much more productive.

Measuring what?

Then there is a mythology of measurement. I think we've become obsessed with the measurement industry. It has become a huge industry: measuring, measuring, and schools are spending huge amounts of money on more and more measurement. Therein lies the danger, because it reifies this notion of measurement, and quantitative measurement in particular. Going back to Hampden Turner:

> We now have the technology to split two athletes crossing the tape by a microsecond so that an athlete can win by a literal fingernail.

But he adds:

> Why do we want to know that? Why do we want to have a winner and a loser when in the world of natural intelligence these two people look as if they've crossed the line together? Why do we do it?

We do it because we have the technology, because we can measure and we are dominated by it. Henry Mintzberg, whose heretical book *The Rise and Fall of Strategic Planning*, a wonderful book which demythologizes strategic planning, says:

> The danger is that hard data drives out soft data but that soft data is what organisations use to actually grow and change.

In other words, it is people's perceptions, it is listening to the day-to-day conversation, that counts. He says the complaint from one customer may be more valuable to an organization than all the data that it has.

The well-known plea that we must learn to measure what we can value rather than valuing what we can measure could not be more appropriate. I think that is one of the things we need to pay careful attention to, trying to get a more accurate measurement for what we, as teachers, headteachers, authorities or whoever, actually value.

So looking to the future it seems to me there are three things to consider for the new century. We have to think about the learning profession more than the teaching profession.

We're told there is something called the intensification of teaching. This means doing more and more as a teacher because we are pushed and pressured to spend less and less time on the things that matter, such as the time to reflect on the value and quality of what we are doing.

Robert Ornstein, the neuro-scientist who discovered the functions of the right brain, talks about the stressed-out salmon. As salmon fight their way up river they produce cortisol, because fighting your way against the current is a highly stressful activity. By the time they get to the top of the river, they die of stress from cortisol overproduction. Exactly the same process occurs in human beings.

Intensification of teaching

Steven Covey, who wrote *The Seven Habits of Highly Effective People,* tells the story of coming across a man who is sawing down a tree. He says: 'How long have you been at that?' The man says: 'Hours and hours, and it's really hard work.' And he says to him: 'Have you thought about stopping to sharpen the saw?' 'Oh no, I'm far too busy sawing,' the man replies.

The moral is that we *have* to have time to sharpen the saw. Covey defines sanity as continuing to do the same thing again and again but expecting different results.

We will not get different results from intensifying teaching by extending the curriculum, by making the school day longer. That is insanity – to think that if children aren't achieving we need to look towards the Pacific Rim or elsewhere and extend the school day and the curriculum. This is to give them more of the same. In fact countries in the Pacific Rim are looking to cut down the curriculum. In Singapore, a 30 per cent reduction is being proposed, an acknowledgement that they over-teach.

Knowledge about learning

In the knowledge revolution there is a huge amount happening. Something like 85 per cent of what we know about learning has been discovered in the last 10 to 15 years, because of advances in neuro-psychology and neuro-science. There is an explosion of knowledge, and teaching as a learning profession needs to have time to deal with it.

I quote Roland Barthes' metaphor of the aircraft steward who says: 'When the oxygen mask falls down, put the mask on your own face first before putting the child's mask on' – an absolutely critical piece of advice for leadership, for authorities and policy-making. Children cannot have self-esteem, take responsibility, feel good about what they're doing if their teachers don't have self-esteem and high morale as well.

Time 'off task' is absolutely critical for the learner. Time 'off task' is absolutely critical for teachers as well because it means renewal, time to reflect and absorb that information that we now have which is at the forefront of knowledge about learning.

School self-evaluation

The thinking school is one in which we start from a position of self-evaluation. I am totally 100 per cent committed to the notion of self-evaluation. 'What am I good at? What could I get better at? Who could help me?' are three questions which apply to children at the age of five. 'What am I good at? What could I get better at?' apply equally to teacher and organization.

The 'thinking school' says: 'What are we good at in this school?', 'What could we be better at?' and 'Who can give us help?' The answer is that schools need friends. Schools don't need critics, they need critical friends. There is not a single piece of research worldwide that says there is such a thing as the 'self-improving school'. Schools need networking. They need friends. They need people who can give them an outside perspective, who can offer a challenge. The challenge, however, comes on the basis of what the school has done itself in terms of its own self-evaluation.

In Scotland, we are hopefully moving away from the 'big bang' school audit which was where we started when we began school self-evaluation. We have moved more to the question of 'How do we learn as a school?' and 'How do we change?' Two of my favourite writers on the subject, Argyris and Schon, write:

> There are too many cases where schools know less than their members.

There are even cases where schools cannot seem to learn what everybody knows. The knowledge is in the organization, in teachers, pupils, parents. If you find the tools to unlock what the school knows, it becomes a much more reflective, thinking organization.

But it needs the tools to do that, to be self-evaluating and to do that with the support of critical friends.

Organizational learning difficulties

One of things we are looking at in our current research is 'organizational learning disabilties'. That is, if you look at an organization, how is it disabled from learning? One of the ways is that it becomes more dependent on what people outside tell it about itself.

Ornstein has a wonderful metaphor of the pathetic cat, which sits by the bowl looking pathetic until it gets fed. He found (because he's a neurological researcher) that wild cats are 30 per cent more intelligent than domesticated cats because they retain a bit of creativity, self-initiative and drive.

Daniel Goleman talks about the 'MacBroom Syndrome' in his book *Emotional Intelligence*. MacBroom was an American pilot who crashed a plane because his two co-pilots, who saw something was wrong, were too afraid to confront MacBroom and tell him he was heading for a crash. I was told by someone who worked in NASA that there were people in NASA who knew that the Challenger was going to crash. People on the shop floor said there was a deep flaw in the craft, but the people at the top of the organization did not want to hear.

The issue is how we create organizations which can confront their own learning disabilities and are able to ask those kind of critical questions.

The intelligent society

Lastly, let's consider the intelligent society. If we have more thinking and more self-evaluating schools we are much more likely to move towards the intelligent society, the society marked by learnable intelligence.

What is striking about the new literature coming from biologists, neuroscientists, linguists, inter-disciplinary fields, is that intelligence can be greatly enhanced. There was recently a staggering programme on autism on television. An autistic child was written off with an IQ of 40. We saw that child graduating from Harvard because they had found a way of dealing with that child's learnable intelligence.

If you read David Perkins and Sternberg and Feuerstein and others who are writing about intelligence, they say forget the bell curve, forget the g-factor, forget those things you've been told in the past.

One of the things I constantly fail to understand is the notion of the mixed-ability group. What is a mixed-ability group? Isn't any group of people a mixed-ability group? Howard Gardner has written about *Seven Intelligences* and now says there are eight and a half. Charles Handy says there are eleven! Robert Sternberg says there are three! But whatever the final count, we have been fixated with this notion of the single thing called 'intelligence'. We have to think much more widely about that. That is borderless thinking.

You have probably seen the small test where you have to join up the dots for four lines and not take your pen off the paper. People can struggle with this, but the only way is to go outside the dots. Why is it we create for ourselves a border around our thinking which is not actually there? When we have tried this with young children, they are better at it because they have not yet put these borders on their own thinking.

As we grow older and go through school, we are more inclined to accept the borders. We think less in borderless terms and less in terms of partnership. I think that is where my last word is. In terms of moving forward in the intelligente society we have to create our own 'future history'.

It was Muhammad Ali who coined the term 'future history'. He used to say about his opponent, 'In the fifth round he's going to fall!'. What he did was to talk about how a person creates history in the future. At the centre of future history lie teachers, the partnerships, the partnerships with business, the partnerships with universities, the partnerships with authorities and government. At the centre of those partnerships lie teachers. They are at the epicentre of new partnerships in the intelligent society.

We are going to see massive changes in the next five to ten years. People are questioning schools, the role of schools, the central place of schools. The danger is that we begin to expect too much.

We must ask ourselves, 'What is the relationship between teaching and learning?' We have to be aggressively curious and healthily sceptical in pursuing the connections. The more we begin to explore them the more we will begin to escape from the mythology that has been created and is continuously being re-created around the relationship between teaching and learning.

It is a problematic relationship. It is one that good teachers are always exploring, finding new ways of doing the job and doing the job better. I can't understand education which isn't child-centred; I can't understand the concept of education that does not start with the individual child or with the individual person or the individual teacher.

Valued – and valuable

I was at a conference of primary headteachers in Glasgow recently and I asked them to spend a little time looking at what things in their primary schools they valued: fun, colour, variety, responsibility, praise, humour, partnerships, music and movement. We discussed how all these things are now emerging in research as incredibly important in learning.

We haven't even begun to explore musical intelligence and kinaesthetic intelligence which come through music and movement. If you want to get examples of those look at what is happening in the 'University of the First Age' and elsewhere where they are using musical intelligence to raise literacy standards and to raise maths standards.

We call it education

You don't raise standards simply by focusing on the technical skills of literacy and numeracy. These things are improved because you explore other ways of enhancing children's self-esteem and repertoire of abilities.

There are so many examples. Chess is one. There has been much research on chess. If you want to raise literacy and numeracy, introduce chess for everyone. It stimulates right and left brain functions. It requires you to examine the overall picture (right brain), then to look carefully at the detail (left brain).

We constantly need to explore and look at new ways of helping young people, teachers and organizations to become more intelligent. In that way we will develop the learning profession, the thinking school and the intelligent society.

Note

1   This chapter is based on my presentation to the National Union of Teachers/*Times Educational Supplement* Conference held on 16 September 1997.

25 Equal opportunities and educational performance

Gender, race and class

Madeleine Arnot

It is one of the paradoxes of the Education Reform Act 1988 that even though it was assumed that 'the pursuit of egalitarianism is now over' (Kenneth Baker, then Secretary of State for Education), the effect of the legislation has been to promote greater public concern about the unequal performance of different groups of children in the school system and onwards. Social inequalities now receive considerable public exposure from the publication of school performance tables, the breakdown of National Test results into gender categories and, for example, the publication of Ofsted reviews such as that by Gillborn and Gipps (1996) and Gillborn and Mirze (2000) on the achievement of ethnic minority pupils, and Arnot *et al.* (1998) on recent research on gender and educational performance.

Although the level of support offered to schools from LEA advisers and specialist teachers on equal opportunities, financial assistance and networking between schools has declined in many areas of the country in the last fifteen years (Arnot *et al.* 1996), there were signs in 1995 of a 'third wave' of interest in gender-equality issues, particularly in the rural shires. The increased attention given to differences in academic performance in the standardized tests and in the GCSE results, especially by Ofsted inspectors, highlighted for schools the importance of monitoring and reducing gender inequalities in outcomes (ibid). The new debate about girls' and boys' schooling is therefore directly related to issues of standards and performance rather than to the more general concerns of gender equality and social justice (Arnot *et al.* 1999).

In contrast, the issue of ethnicity has had a far more chequered career in the last decade. In 1985, the Swann Committee (1985) in its investigation of the achievement levels of ethnic minority children, endorsed the concept of multiculturalism (which it called *Education for All*). Nevertheless, the Education Reform Act 1988 made only passing references to the need for schools to promote cultural diversity within existing Programmes of Study and as part of one of the cross-curricular 'dimensions' identified by the National Curriculum Council. No official guidance was published. By the 1990s, the use of targeted funding through what used to be known as Section 11 grants (since April 1999 renamed the Ethnic Minority Achievement Grant [EMAG]) was tightly focused upon helping students with difficulties in English. Thus, little support was offered (either financial or advisory) on how to tackle racism within schooling. Sociological research continued, nevertheless, to point to racial harassment and race attacks in schools and communities, to experiences of black pupils in secondary schools which negatively affected their identities as learners, and to their perceptions about how their communities were regarded by white pupils (see Gillborn 1995: Troyna and Hatcher 1992: Connolly 1998: Wright *et al.* 1998).

Support for multicultural education and initiatives to combat racism in education regained political currency again in 1998 after the Gillborn and Gipps (1996) review, *Recent Research on the Achievements of Ethnic Minority Pupils*, documented the extensive differences in achievement between ethnic groups in a range of different localities. Although schools collect their own ethnic data, no national statistics are available. LEA data, however, indicate the continuing inequalities in achievement between white and ethnic minority communities, and the alarmingly high rate of expulsion of some black children. Black African–Caribbean pupils have been found to be between three and six times more likely to be excluded from schools, and the proportion of black boys has been found to be over-represented by a factor of up to eight (ibid). Government concern about such forms of institutional racism in schools was raised in a very direct fashion by the report of Sir William McPherson (1999) on the murder of Stephen Lawrence. This report drew the government's and the public's attention to the importance of schools promoting racial tolerance through multiculturalism and developing new strategies to combat racism. These renewed concerns are directly linked to the promotion of citizenship education for all pupils.

Gillborn and Gipps' review of research also revealed the extent to which ethnic minority communities such as the Bangladeshi community in the East End of London were *improving* their educational qualifications. Furthermore, statistics and case studies suggest that certain patterns of positive achievement (rather than failure) by particular groups of ethnic minority pupils, e.g. Indian pupils, and by ethnic minority girls, e.g. African-Caribbean and Muslim girls, should be recognized if black pupils are not to continue to be collectively stigmatized as 'a problem' and as failures. Teachers had been found to have unrealistically low expectations of African-Caribbean pupils in particular, and to find explanations for the low academic achievement of certain black pupils by stereotyping their communities and their homes. More recognition is now needed of the value which the great majority of ethnic minority communities place on schooling (Basit 1997: Mirza 1992) and the importance of working collaboratively with such communities (e.g. Bastiani 1997).

The boys' achievement debate

The interest in gender and race issues often comes together in discussions about boys' educational experiences. The relatively low academic performance of male pupils, especially of both black and white working-class boys, has become a matter of great concern for schools attempting to improve their literacy levels and overall performance. The press has called the relative underachievement of boys a 'crisis in masculinity'. Various chapters in the Epstein *et al.* collection *Failing Boys?* (1998) suggest how and why this debate has developed in the 1990s in the UK (in much the same way as it has developed in Australia – see Gilbert and Gillbert 1998). Two key gender gaps in performance were identified by the recent Ofsted review (Arnot *et al.* 1998): first, the literacy gap, and second, the different pattern of male and female success in achieving five or more higher grade GCSEs. The gap between boys and girls in terms of literacy is already established by the age of 7 and, as recent evidence shows, remains sizeable as pupils progress through schooling. Boys also lag behind girls in their performance in modern foreign languages. This difference in male and female performance is especially significant because not only have girls kept their advantage in such conventionally 'female' subjects but they have, with the support of teachers and schools, substantially reduced boys' traditional advantage in terms of entry into, and performance in, 'male' subjects such as mathematics, chemistry and physics (Arnot *et al.* 1996, 1998: Kenway and Willis 1998).

By the mid-1990s, only 80 boys compared to every 100 girls were achieving five higher grade GCSEs, compared with over 90 boys in the mid-1970s. This pattern has since remained relatively stable. To some extent the comparatively slow progress of boys in improving their qualifications is associated with the increase in numbers of pupils entering for GCSE – especially after the introduction of the National Curriculum and the changed patterns of subject entry which followed. Boys and girls are now expected to succeed in subjects which traditionally they avoided. Many other theories have been put forward to explain why boys have failed to match the substantial improvement in girls' performance. Attention has, for example, been focused on boys' 'laddish' culture, which represents schooling – and especially 'feminized' subjects such as English and literacy – as 'not cool'. Commentators also point to the collapse of traditional male transitions from school to work because of the decline in manufacturing industry and the associated loss of traditional male apprenticeships. These cultural and economic factors suggest that many boys, who traditionally used to 'pick up' in terms of academic achievement in secondary schools, may have lost motivation and, especially by Years 8 and 9, have, in some cases, become disaffected from schooling.

The levels of disaffection amongst boys has been noted by researchers in a range of different studies (see Arnot *et al.* 1998 and MacDonald *et al.* 1999). The evidence is interesting but remains inconclusive. Far more attention, however, has been paid to boys' learning preferences and the reasons why boys report lower levels of enjoyment at school. There is interest in whether boys and girls prefer different subjects, and whether they respond differently to, for example, coursework/project work, extended writing, factual teaching, and also whether they are motivated differently in relation to the same subject. Research has also encouraged an interest in whether boys and girls are equally comfortable with different styles of assessment: for example, is their performance affected by the choice of items for assessment, terminal examinations, multiple choice versus coursework, etc? The Ofsted review on gender research (Arnot *et al.* 1998) offered the following summary of research findings:

- Girls are more attentive in class and more willing to learn. They do better on sustained tasks that are open-ended, process-based, relate to realistic situations and require thinking for oneself. Girls may over-rate the difficulty of particular subjects. Girls find timed end-of-course examinations less congenial. Teachers believe that coursework favours girls, but other factors (including syllabus selection) may be more important.

- Boys show greater adaptability to traditional approaches which require memorizing abstract, unambiguous facts which have to be acquired quickly. They are more willing to sacrifice deep understanding for correct answers achieved at speed. Boys do better on multiple-choice papers, whatever the subject.

Research on teaching and learning differences between girls and boys has been identified as an important area for raising teacher awareness, encouraging the view that gender blindness (treating all pupils alike) may no longer be helpful. Investigating the similarities and differences in learning styles of boys and girls is likely to be more fruitful for identifying appropriate strategies.

At the same time, a number of other gender issues in schooling are being brought into focus. Of central importance are teachers' gender values, especially in relation to their pupils' concepts of masculinity and femininity – and the effect such values might have on pupils' learning experiences. Gender values can affect how teachers deal with, for example, male and female pupils' anxieties, their motivation to learn, their choices of subjects to study, their work experience placements and the careers advice they receive at school. In certain contexts, teachers can encourage rather than discourage male disaffection. Increasingly, researchers (cf. Arnot *et al.* 1998 for references) are highlighting the following:

- Images of masculinity being legitimated by the school (through the hidden curriculum) and by teachers' interactions with boys. There is evidence from research of conflict between male and female teachers and boys, especially over overtly 'masculine' behaviour (Abraham 1995: Sewell 1997: Mac an Ghaill 1994).
- Teacher expectations about boys' abilities insofar as they affect, for example, the diagnosis of special needs (especially behavioural and emotional difficulties), learning support provision, and disciplining strategies (expulsions, suspensions). Boys are over-represented in all these categories.
- The levels of bullying reported by pupils in the UK raise concern about teachers' responses to such incidents, especially when they involve boys. If teachers' responses are considered unfair or not sufficiently protective by pupils, then they may contribute to the lower levels of male enjoyment and engagement with schooling (Chaplain 1996).

Which girls, which boys?

There is a concern that the strong level of interest in boys' underachievement will ignore not just their successes, but also will fail to engage with the continuing problem of girls' lesser involvement in science. The statistics of male and female achievement reveal not only that boys do better at A level, even in female subjects such as English, but that they are far more likely to study the sciences, technology and computing at this level than girls. Despite girls' success in performing comparably in the sciences and mathematics in primary and secondary schools, boys gain a slight advantage as they progress through school, and many more boys than girls sit single-science GCSEs in physics and chemistry (Arnot *et al.* 1998). At A level these subjects are getting more rather than less 'masculinized', with the statistics of further and higher education also demonstrating the low proportions of girls going on after school to study science or science-related courses/degrees. Vocational courses are also still strongly sex stereotyped, with young women opting for traditional female training courses for work in the service sectors (e.g. hairdressing, beauty care, caring courses or social studies). In this respect, they continue to make 'poor choices' in terms of post-16 training and careers, since such courses have low economic benefits. Gender stereotyping by pupils (and possibly teachers) therefore remains an ongoing issue for schools. It also remains the case that women still experience what is called a 'glass ceiling' in relation to advancement in top jobs. The Equal Opportunities Commission's (EOC) report (Rolfe 1999) argues that the careers service and school-based careers education programmes should take responsibility for promoting equal opportunities, but that this should not be interpreted solely as 'promoting entry into non-traditional areas, but focus on equal access and achievement at all levels, including in management and the professions' (p. xi).

Statistical data on achievement also suggest that the extraordinary success of girls in raising their achievement of five higher grade GCSEs may mainly apply to white girls. Data presented by Gillborn and Gipps (1996) suggest that the interconnections between gender, ethnicity, and class patterns of achievement can differ substantially in different localities. Some groups of Asian boys, for example, may perform better than equivalent groups of Asian girls, whilst both African-Caribbean boys and girls might do less well than white male and female pupils (Gillborn 1997). Research has shown that gender never works in isolation; it affects and is affected by ethnic patterns of performance. Many schools recognize the need to break down performance data into ethnic subgroups, and some local education authorities provide excellent databases which allow schools to target particular groups of underachieving pupils. Also, as indicated earlier, teachers are becoming more aware of the importance of not sustaining the notion of the 'failing black pupil', for example by recognizing patterns of improved or high levels of ethnic minority performance (see Channer 1995).

Describing social class differences is notoriously problematic and schools find it difficult to identify indices to highlight the effects of socio-economic background on pupils' performance. Often, free school meals are used as rough indicators of low income and of class status. Such indicators are unsatisfactory, but the attempt to assess the impact of class background is, nevertheless, essential since social class repeatedly has been found to be strongly associated with academic progress. The National Commission on Education (1993) reminded us that:

> Children from social classes I and II do better, on average, in examinations at 16, are more likely to stay on longer in full time education and are more likely to go to university than those in social classes III to V. There has been little change over the years in the proportion of entrants to higher education who come from working class families.

Evidence from a major Australian study *Who Wins at School?* (Teese *et al.* 1995) found not only that working-class girls had higher rates of failure in some subjects than other girls (for example, in English) but that working-class boys were more likely to depress the overall scores for boys in literacy, and in language more generally. Gender differences appeared narrowest where students have the greatest cultural and material advantages and sharpest where their parents were more socially disadvantaged. The lower the social status of girls, the less likely they were to take mathematics and the more likely they were to fail when they did. Working-class boys in contrast over-enrolled in mathematics and physics, and were more likely to play truant in classes in literature, history or modern languages. Unfortunately there is no comparable study in the UK.

Whilst one should not adopt too deterministic a view about the effects of social class, it is nevertheless essential to recognize that family background and the nature of the locality can still be a critical influence on pupils' achievement. The considerable increase in the proportion of all pupils achieving higher grades in GCSE masks the serious effects of unemployment and poverty in certain parts of the UK and in particular communities – where a high proportion of single-parent families lives close to the poverty line and there are few local employment opportunities for young people. Each year more than 10,000 pupils are excluded from schools as a result of disaffection and conflicts in school. The loss of traditional transitions from school to work challenges secondary schools in particular to find new ways of motivating pupils to 'stay on' and to become more flexible in their life choices. In such areas, teachers attempt a range of strategies: for example, working more closely with the community, encouraging parents to express their values and needs in relation to their children's schooling, signing up parents to contracts over homework, and becoming involved in pupil mentoring and setting homework targets. Concern about social inequality encourages schools to engage more actively with their local community.

School equality strategies

Various agencies (e.g. the Qualifications, Curriculum and Assessment Authority, the Equal Opportunities Commission, the Secondary Heads Association, and Ofsted) have now entered the fray, with suggestions about how teachers might improve pupils' academic performance. In 1999, the Schools Standards minister, Stephen Byers, made the gender gap a matter of national concern, when he publicly encouraged each local education authority and every school to develop its own plans to tackle the differences between male and female examination performance. Improved overall school performance was seen as dependent upon such efforts. He warned that a new trend has been identified for a minority of boys who are disaffected with school, quoting figures which showed that 83 per cent of permanent exclusions are of boys and that 7,000 more boys than girls left school at 16 with no qualifications. He argued that the 'laddish anti-learning culture' which has been allowed to develop over recent years should be challenged and that we should not simply 'accept with a shrug of our shoulders that boys will be boys'. He commented:

> Failure to raise the educational achievement of boys will mean that thousands of young men will face a bleak future in which a lack of qualifications and basic skills will mean unemployment and little hope of finding work.

At the same time, he argued it was vital that 'policies aimed at disaffected boys are not introduced at the expense of girls whose improvement over recent years has been a real success story'. Despite such concerns about girls, many more recent projects have focused on how to raise boys' academic achievement, with noticeably less attention and funding being devoted to girls and science/mathematics after 16.

The Ofsted review's conclusion that 'there are no simple explanations for gender differences in performances: in any one context several factors are likely to have an influence' (Arnot *et al.* 1998) is reflected in the range of school approaches to gender equality developed in the UK. Macdonald *et al.*'s (1999) report on boys' achievement suggested that schools should take a whole-school approach to gender issues, putting into place a range of departmental strategies and management techniques, one of which is the annual monitoring of gender performance (SATs, GCSEs and measures of value-added performance), or the targeting of particular pupils – particularly in Years 8 or 9. Short-term single-sex learning groups have been tried in mixed secondary schools in order to explore gender stereotypes about learning and to offer 'safe' contexts to review pupils' preferences and attitudes (e.g. in English). More opportunities have been provided in different subjects for boys and girls to explore their interests. Some schools have given more recognition to the need to work directly with boys and to build their confidence in themselves and their abilities. Teachers are now called upon to research for themselves how gender works within the culture and structure of the school, in relation, for example, to male and female responses to different teaching styles and learning demands, to different modes of assessment, and to various types of classroom organization (see Arnot and Gibb 2001).

Blair *et al.* (1998), having investigated a number of successful multi-ethnic primary and secondary schools, found that what had made them effective was that they were 'listening schools'. These were schools that:

> ... took time to talk with students and parents: schools which were prepared to consider and debate values as well as strategies: schools which took seriously the views students and parents offered and their own interpretations of school processes, and schools which used this learning to reappraise, and where necessary, change their practices and to build a more inclusive curriculum. These schools did not assume the existence of ethnic stereotypes or indeed of fixed ethnic identities, but recognised the shared experiences of students in their evolving, culturally diverse communities. In this way, they were able to incorporate not only a respect for individuals but also for the collective or group identities to which students and their parents, in their own local context, had a sense of belonging. (p. 2)

The Ofsted (1999) report on school strategies in relation to ethnicity also picked up this theme, arguing that the most successful school approaches were associated with senior management making clear that the under-performance of any groups was not acceptable, that evidence was gathered systematically and that teachers and departments were challenged to 'spell out what they intend to do to improve the situation':

The schools where minority ethnic pupils flourish understand the hostility these pupils often face…. These schools have developed successful strategies for countering stereotyping which have not only had a tangible impact on the pupils' confidence and self-esteem, but have also influenced the attitudes of the majority …

An important feature of successful race relations work is a school ethos which is open and vigilant, in which pupils can talk about their concerns and share in the development of strategies for their resolution.

(Ofsted 1999: 7–8)

As a result of the MacPherson inquiry (1999) into the murder of Stephen Lawrence, schools are also being encouraged to ensure that they have clear policies for dealing with racial harassment. The police inspectorate has produced videos to help schools tackle racial incidents in schools, to help parents and carers of children who are experiencing racial harassment at schools, and to set up parent support groups.

Schools are aware of the controversies over, for example, the ways pupils are grouped (setting, streaming, banding and mixed-ability teaching) and the need to encourage a learning culture in the school among all pupils. There are still many more debates to be had over the most appropriate organization of pupils, in order to ensure genuinely 'inclusive education' which allows each pupil to develop his or her abilities to the full. Other discussions are likely to focus on effective teaching approaches of successful black teachers (cf. Callender 1997) in multi-racial schools. Discussions about both inclusive education and 'teaching for diversity' are especially relevant in a government climate which seeks to promote greater social cohesion as well as higher educational performances in schools. New ways of involving all pupils in learning are being sought therefore – not just in the new arenas of 'education action zones' but also by teachers keen to think creatively about the challenges schools are faced with today.

Improving the effectiveness of schools in relation to all their pupils is a task engaging teachers in a range of 'egalitarian' initiatives which involve thinking critically and constructively about gender, ethnic and social class patterns as part of the professional ethos and practice of teaching.

References

Abraham, J. (1995) *Divide and School: Gender and Class Dynamics in Comprehensive Education*, London: Falmer Press.

Arnot, M. and Gibb, J. (2001) *Adding Value to Boys' and Girls' Education*, Chichester: West Sussex County Council.

Arnot, M., David, M. and Weiner, G. (1996) *Educational Reforms and Gender Equality in Schools*, Manchester: Equal Opportunities Commission.

Arnot, M., Gray, J., James, M. and Rudduck, J. (1998) *Recent Research on Gender and Educational Performance*, London: Ofsted/The Stationery Office.

Arnot, M., David, M. and Weiner, G. (1999) *Closing the Gender Gap: Post-war Social and Educational Change*, Oxford: Polity Press.

Basit, T.B. (1997) *Eastern Values, Western Milieu: Identities and Aspirations of Adolescent Muslim Girls*, Aldershot: Ashgate.

Bastiani, J. (1997) *Home and School in Multicultural Settings: A Working Alliance*, London: David Fulton.

Blair, M. and Bourne, J. with Coffin, C., Creese, A. and Kenner, C. (1998) *Making the Difference: Teaching and Learning Strategies in Successful Multi-ethnic Schools*, Sudbury: DfEE Publications.

Bleach, K. (ed.) (1998) *Raising Boys' Achievement in Schools*, Stoke-on-Trent, Trentham Books.

Bray, R., Downes, P., Gardner, C., Hannan, G. and Parsons, N. (1997) *Can Boys Do Better?* Leicester: Secondary Heads Association.

Callender, C. (1997) *Education and Empowerment: The Practice and Philosophies of Black Teachers*, Stoke-on-Trent: Trentham Books.

Channer, Y. (1995) *I am a Promise, The School Achievement of British African Caribbeans*, Stoke-on-Trent: Trentham Books.

Chaplain, R. (1996) 'Making a strategic withdrawal: disengagement and self-worth protection in male pupils' in J. Rudduck, R. Chaplain and G. Wallace (eds) *School Improvement: What Can Pupils Tell Us?* London: David Fulton.

Connolly, P. (1998) *Racism, Gender Identities and Young Children: Social Relations in a Multi-ethnic Inner-city Primary School*, London: Routledge.

Epstein, D., Elwood, J., Hey, V. and Maw, J. (eds) (1998) *Failing Boys? Issues in Gender and Achievement*, Buckingham: Open University.

Gilbert, R. and Gilbert, P. (1998) *Masculinity Goes to School*, London: Routledge.

Gillborn, D. (1995) *Racism and Anti-racism in Real Schools*, Buckingham: Open University Press.

Gillborn, D. (1997) 'Young black and failed by school: the market, education reform and black students', *International Journal of Inclusive Education*, 1(1): 65–87.

Gillborn, D. and Gipps, C. (1996) *Recent Research on the Achievements of Ethnic Minority Pupils*, London: Ofsted/HMSO.

Gillborn, D. and Mirze, H. (2000) *Educational inequality: Mapping race, class and gender*, London: Ofsted.

Kenway, J. and Willis, S. (1998) *Answering Back: Girls, Boys and Feminism in Schools*, London: Routledge.

Mac an Ghaill, M. (1994) *The Making of Men: Masculinities, Sexualities and Schooling*, Buckingham: Open University Press.

MacDonald, A., Saunders, L. and Benfield, P. (1999) *Boys' Achievement: Progress, Motivation and Participation. Issues Raised by the Recent Literature*, Slough: NFER.

MacPherson, Sir William (1999) *The Stephen Lawrence Inquiry. Report of an Inquiry*, London: The Stationery Office.

Mirza, H.S. (1992) *Young, Female and Black*, London: Routledge.

National Commission on Education (1993) *Learning to Succeed: A Radical Look at Education Today and a Strategy for the Future*, London: Heinemann.

Office for Standards in Education (1999) *Raising the Attainment of Minority Ethnic Pupils: School and LEA Responses*, London: Ofsted.

Rolfe, H. (1999) *Gender Equality and the Careers Service*, Manchester: Equal Opportunities Commission.

Runnymede Trust (1998) (with Weekes, D. and Wright, C.) *Improving Practice: A Whole School Approach to Raising the Achievement of African Caribbean Youth*, London: Runnymede Trust.

Sewell, T. (1997) *Black Masculinities and Schooling*, Stoke-on-Trent: Trentham Books.

Swann, Lord (1985) *Education for All: Final Report of the Committee of Inquiry into the Education of Children from Ethnic Minority Groups*, Cmnd 9453, London: HMSO.

Teese, R., Davies, M., Charlton, M. and Polesel, J. (1995) *Who Wins at School? Boys and Girls in Australian Secondary Education*, Melbourne: Department of Education, Policy and Management, University of Melbourne.

Troyna, B. and Hatcher, R. (1992) *Racism in Children's Lives*, London: Routledge.

Wright, C., Weekes, D., McLaughlin, A. and Webb, D. (1998) 'Masculinised discourses within education and the construction of black male identities amongst African Caribbean youths', *British Journal of Sociology of Education*, 19(1): 75–87.

26 Home–school links

Sally Tomlinson

> The case for involving parents in their children's development and education has been established by innumerable studies and many schools are now committed to pursuing home–school links.
>
> (Wolfendale 1989: ix)

This chapter is largely about the development of links between homes and schools which create a partnership. For most of the twentieth century education has been equated with schooling, teachers have defended their professional territory and there has been a separation of home and school. Now, there are increasingly moves to reverse this situation and to recognize that children's school performance and their personal and social development are most successful when a partnership is established between home and school. Home–school relations figure prominently on the agendas of politicians, professionals and parents, although from different perspectives, but there is a widespread acceptance that 'good' relations include effective communication and information-giving, accountability of schools to parents, encouraging parents to support children's learning and development and creating a sense of shared purpose and identity between parents, pupils and teachers. However, there is currently a political divide as to the form parental involvement should take. The Conservative government, via the 1986, 1988 and 1993 Education Acts, has encouraged parents to regard themselves as consumers in an educational market and as managers via representation on governing bodies. Parental choices of schools are intended to promote competition between schools and to help close ineffective ones. Whether the role of parent as a consumer and agent of competition will actually improve children's educational performance and enhance their personal and social development is debatable.

This chapter briefly reviews home–school contacts in Britain up to the present, noting that much of the literature on home–school relations has used a simplistic social class model in which 'working-class' homes have been regarded as deficient and less likely to care about children's achievements or pastoral needs. The chapter also covers problems inherent in creating partnerships, especially with ethnic-minority parents and parents of children with special educational needs, the experiences of other European countries, and policies for closer home, school and community co-operation.

Home–school contacts

Home–school contacts have never figured large as a priority in English education, and up to the 1970s talk of partnership in education usually referred to that between central and local education authorities. Within the Department for Education the responsibility for overseeing home–school relationships is still relatively a minor chore. The social history of parent–school contacts indicates that – in the State system – relations have often been marked by tension and sometimes overt conflict. Willard Waller, an American sociologist, wrote in the 1930s that 'parents and teachers usually live in conditions of mutual mistrust and enmity'(Waller 1932). In the Victorian era, and particularly from 1870 when mass elementary education was introduced, it was easy to see why this should be the case. Apart from removing potential wage-earning children into school, the type of education offered was rigid, inflexible and authoritarian teachers were enjoined to 'civilise and control' their pupils (Grace 1978), a task which involved not only harsh discipline for pupils but also the denigration of homes and parental values. Many teachers came to see themselves as compensating for the deficiencies of homes – a view that lived on in the 1990s – and teachers felt free to criticize parents, especially mothers, for perceived inadequacies. Staffrooms have always been familiar with the theme of, 'What can we do with Johnny, have you *seen* his mother?' (Tomlinson 1988).

Literature discussing the relationship between school attainments, personal and social behaviour and homes has always worked to the disadvantage of working-class homes and parents. On measures of achievement, children from manual workers' homes and those with unemployed parents have tended on average to do less well, and it has usually been children from the lower socio-economic groups who have acquired the labels and reputation for being 'troublesome'. Explanations for this have, over the past hundred years, run a gamut from Victorian beliefs in the genetic inferiority of the 'lower classes' (Tredgold 1908) through material and social disadvantage, cultural and linguistic deprivation, apathetic parenting and ineffective homes (Rutter and Madge 1976). The misuse of Basil Bernstein's 1960s work on language codes (Bernstein 1973) reinforced teachers' views that working-class speech was 'deficient'. Many teachers came to believe that school influence was marginal when set against a 'poor' home background, and held low expectations of large groups of children. This included, from the 1960s, pupils from ethnic minorities who were also subject to stereotyped beliefs about their culture, language and potentialities.

The middle–working-class divide appearing in much of the literature undoubtedly led some teachers to underestimate the ambitions and capabilities of working-class and minority parents and their children, and many of the perceived problems in home–school contacts do have a class and a racial dimension. Research during the 1980s demonstrated that working-class and minority parents actually have very positive attitudes to education but lack the knowledge and information about the education system, and how to 'manage' it, that middle-class parents usually have (Roberts 1984: Tomlinson 1984, 1991: Gewirtz, Ball and Bowe 1992). It has become a truism that it has always been the more informed and articulate parents who can obtain most from the education system.

Over the past twenty years major efforts have been made to improve home–school contacts and more information has become available on parental views. As the authors of the Royal Society of Arts Home–School project recently wrote:

> Among parents there has been a slow but definite shift in attitudes away from deference, puzzlement and helplessness, clearly documented in the 1960s and 1970s, towards a general recognition that parents do have a formal right to information and access concerning their children's schooling, and to a share in the decisions regarding this.
>
> (Jones *et al.* 1992: 13)

Home–school links

The Plowden Report (Plowden 1967) proved to be a watershed in helping schools to understand why closer home–school links were desirable, although Edwards and Redfern (1988) have pointed out that, ironically, the underlying message from the Plowden committee was similar to traditional views that poor educational performance and unacceptable social behaviour were likely to emanate from 'deficient' homes. Whilst it is undoubtedly true that there are some children whose home backgrounds are such that they need special pastoral care and attention, this is not necessarily linked to socio-economic status.

The Plowden committee did, however, set out a minimum programme by which schools could inform parents and encourage home–school links. This included welcome to school, open days, regular reports and written information, and meetings with teachers. By the 1980s the extent of home–school links in a majority of schools had gone beyond this minimum programme. Visits of teachers to homes, and parents to school, letters, circulars, pupil reports and records of achievement, governors' reports, school prospectuses and education–employer–parent compacts all constituted very direct forms of communication and linkage. Parental involvement in day-to-day activities as classroom helpers, translators, materials-makers, assistants on outings, and in home–school reading, maths and homework schemes, and involvement via parent–teacher and other associations had also become more commonplace.

Parental partnerships and home–school links have been furthered, to some extent, by the existence of parents' voluntary organizations. The Home–School Council, founded in 1930, and the National Confederation of Parent–Teacher Associations, founded in 1956, have acted as pressure groups on government to improve home–school links, as have more radical groups such as the Campaign for State Education (1962), The National Association for Governors and Managers (1970) and local groups such as the All London Parents Action Group, and the Haringey and Brent Black Parents Associations. The only national parental advisory service, ACE (Advisory Centre for Education, 1962) is currently encouraging the creation of local advisory services, to help give parents a local powerbase from which to influence schools and government policies.

Legislation in the 1980s gave parents far more rights to information about schools, access to curriculum documents, governors and HMI reports, and equal representation on government bodies. From 1988 parents were, however, encouraged to 'choose' between schools rather than opt for a local neighbourhood school, and to vote in ballots for their children's school to opt out of local authority control and become grant-maintained by central government. A Parents' Charter published in 1991 set out existing parental rights and promised a variety of new rights but devoted only a short section to the notion of parents as partners. While this legislation and approach placed a premium on home–school links best described as customer–provider, and actively *discouraged* parents from supporting local schools in their local community, there has also been, over the past ten years particularly, a countervailing movement. There has in practice been an expansion of many different kinds of home–school links which indicate an increasing desire on the part of teachers and parents to work together. The most up-to-date (to 1992) record of such links is contained in a *Directory of Home–School Initiatives in the UK* compiled by John Bastiani at Nottingham University (Bastiani and Bailey 1992). Some of the initiatives described are Lewisham's development of a code of practice on home–school links, an advice service to parents with independent advocacy, a project to improve school–community practices in seven primary schools and funding for a project on 'Raising pupil standards in the inner city'. In rural Devon the LEA has a policy of developing family education through schools and works with the Devon Federation of Home and School to produce materials.

There is also an advisory teacher on family initiatives, home–school files and workshops for parent-governors. Cleveland has a team of home–school liaison teachers, City Challenge-funded home–school link projects and a focus on parents of special educational needs pupils.

The most comprehensive project in England to date, exploring expanded partnerships in education, was set up in 1989 by the Royal Society of Arts and the National Association of Headteachers. This project was initially based in twenty schools around Britain, the schools being selected on the basis of an interest in developing home–school relations. The essence of the project was that it set out to:

- consider changing legal and contractual requirements to develop effective partnerships between schools and homes. This means that partnership will be not an optional extra but an essential requirement, and will include all parents, not just the 'active and unrepresentative' ones;
- develop whole-school approaches to policy and practice – reviewing existing home–school relations, developing home–school contracts or signed understandings, and planning, organizing and evaluating home–school activities.

This project, which included a strong European dimension, is described in Tomlinson (1991) and Jones *et al.* (1992).

Parents as partners

Whatever the political context and desires of government, home–school links cannot be forced. Contacts take different forms and are at different levels, most parents initially becoming involved in school activities to improve the progress and well-being of their own child. From this point parents may become involved at whole-class and whole-school level, but only a few go on to influence school policies via governance and management. There are, as a wide variety of studies testify, different dimensions and kinds of parental involvement and there are also parents who choose not to be involved with schools (see Cunningham and Davis 1985: Pugh and De'Ath 1989: Wolfendale 1989). A major obstacle to the creation of partnerships has been that many teachers have embraced a notion of professionalism that excluded parents, and needed to be persuaded that professional teaching does recognize the integral role of parents in education. Macbeth (1989) suggested that there were four stages of progression in the growth of home–school partnerships which depended on a developing teacher and school acceptance of a new professionalism:

- *The self-contained school* is characterized by teacher autonomy, limited and formalized contacts with parents, little parental choice or consultation, a denial of access to school records, and with curriculum and teaching methods regarded as the teacher's domain.
- *Professional uncertainty* is characterized by tentative experiment with home–school liaison and participation but teachers still restricting consultation and blaming homes for low pupil attainment.
- *Growing commitment* is the stage at which the school leadership encourages liaison and consultation with parents, recognizes the value of home teaching, encourages parents onto governing bodies, and generally begins to adapt the school system to include parents.
- *The school and family concordat* represents the ultimate stage in the attempt to involve all families in formal schooling, recognizing that home learning is part of education and the role of parents is crucial in this, and emphasizing the obligation of parents to be involved and to co-operate with schools.

Schools in Britain could certainly be rated along this continuum with many being at stages one or two. On the parental side, many parents are still reluctant to become involved in their children's formal education, lacking confidence and knowledge, or regarding classroom affairs as the teacher's domain. Asking teachers to incorporate a 'practice' of home–school contacts into their professional activity, to accept criticism of their practice and to accept parents as equal partners requires justification. Teachers must be convinced that it is in their interests, as well as the interests of parents and children, to regard parents as integral to the whole process of education and training from pre-school to post-16. They will also have to work out the different kinds of partnership required as children progress through school.

New requirements for teacher training, however, do not encourage student-teachers to think of parents as partners, but as consumers to be informed of their children's comparative achievements *vis-à-vis* other children's. The Council for the Accreditation of Teacher Education published new guidelines for teacher trainers in November 1992 which noted that, as the Parents' Charter requires teachers to report comparative information about pupils in relation to others in schools ... it is expected that students will be given some opportunity to demonstrate ability in reporting and discussing pupil progress with parents.

(CATE 1992: 11)

It would be unfortunate if teacher–parent relationships were to be confined to such a narrow professional–client role, as there are compelling reasons why a partnership model is to be preferred. One reason is *legality*. Parents are the primary educators of their children and are responsible in law for their education up to 16. The United Nations Declaration of the Rights of the Child also places the final responsibility for the education and guidance of their children on parents. A legal framework is in place to enhance the teacher–parent link. Another compelling reason is adherence to democracy. In a democracy parents have a right to be involved in decisions which affect the education, development and future of their children beyond merely receiving reports and 'discussing' them.

There are other problems inherent in the notion of partnership – particularly from the parents' side. Parents, for example, have no distinctive power-base. There is a plethora of local and national groups but no single group that the government could negotiate with or fund. Parents' organizations may influence policy on single issues but are not regarded at national, local or school level as integral to decision-making. Parent-governors still have limited influence, especially given the historically dominant position of headteachers in England.

Parents often find the language of education difficult, particularly as the educational reforms have introduced a whole new curriculum and assessment language, and initials and acronyms abound. In addition, many aspects of school are beyond actual parental influence. Inadequate resourcing and poor teachers are two issues which worry parents but which are difficult to address, particularly if parents are regarded simply as clients and consumers.

Ethnic minority parents

A group of parents who have particular problems with the notion of partnership are ethnic minority parents. The involvement of ethnic minority parents as partners in the education process is more difficult to achieve than with white parents, given that the majority of teachers are from the white, majority culture. Over the past thirty years, minority home–school encounters have perforce taken place in a society marked by racial antagonisms and intercultural tensions. Teachers, having not been equipped during their training to deal with minority parents, have often clung to negative, stereotyping and patronizing views. The research literature into the 1990s still indicated that minority parents were perceived as a problem for schools rather than as equal partners (Brar 1991: Tomlinson 1993).

There has long been a mismatch of expectations between what minority parents expected of education and what teachers felt they could offer. Minority parents – Afro-Caribbean, Indian, Pakistani, Bangladeshi, Chinese and others – have all indicated that they not only want their children equipped with the credentials and skills on a par with white pupils, but they also want their backgrounds and cultures taken seriously in schools, and they want racism and racial harassment eradicated. While some schools and local authorities have always taken these issues seriously, others have found it more difficult. The insensitive treatment of the parents of Ahmed Ullah, the boy murdered at Burnage School, Manchester in 1986, received wide publicity (MacDonald 1989), and research by Brar in Birmingham has demonstrated that stereotyped ideas of minority families and communities continue to be held. He found that teachers' knowledge of the 'black community' in Handsworth was based on 'common sense, or racist media distortion' (Brar 1991: 33). The Handsworth community was presumed to be all-black, all-working-class and often all-male. Teachers continued to stereotype parents as uninterested in their children's education and perpetuated a blame-the-parents syndrome which 'has often been the excuse for schools to sit back and avoid developing school–community consultation' (p. 34).

During the 1980s, ethnic minority parents, in common with other parents, did benefit from improved home–school contacts and from legal requirements to pass over more information to homes. Some urban schools in areas of high minority settlement have been in the forefront of pioneering imaginative contacts and developing LEA and school policies on multicultural and anti-racist education, although it does remain the case that minority parents are less likely than white parents to be involved in day-to-day school activities or represented on governing bodies (National Consumer Council 1990).

White parental antagonism to the education of their children alongside minorities, a feature of our multi-racial society since the 1960s, has become more vocal and open since the 1988 Education Act. During the passage of the Bill through Parliament in 1987, opposition peers in the House of Lords moved an amendment to remove the duty on LEAs to comply with parental preference for choice of school if it was believed to be on racial grounds. The amendment was withdrawn after a government minister gave assurances that it was unlikely that white parents would openly use racial reasons for choice of school. This had, in fact, already happened in Cleveland, where a white parent had requested her child be transferred to a majority white school on what were deemed to be racial grounds (Commission for Racial Equality 1989). There are now legal dilemmas over the precedence given to educational and to race relations legislation, and white parents have also been using the clauses in the 1988 Act requiring religious education to be 'predominantly Christian' as a way of moving their children away from multi-racial schools (CRE 1989).

Special educational needs

A second, and often overlapping, group of parents who have particular problems in creating partnerships with schools are the parents of those children designated as having special educational needs. Over the past twenty years there has been an increasing emphasis on involving the parents of these children in assessment discussions, but evidence continues to suggest that many parents, particularly minority parents, feel uninvolved or inadequately consulted in decisions about the assessment of their children, and uninformed, misinformed or overwhelmed by professional expertise once the children are actually in a special education programme (Tomlinson 1982: Chaudhury 1990). This is perhaps unsurprising, as the fact that their children are regarded in a negative light, as 'disabled', 'incapable' and so on, makes it less likely that parental views will be taken seriously, or the notion of partnership be considered. The parents of children with special educational needs have, historically, been subject to more strategies of persuasion and coercion than any other parents, and it still remains the case that there are legal sanctions against parents who refuse to accept final placement decisions.

There has been rhetoric about parental partnership in the special education area which has never quite coincided with reality. The Warnock committee, reporting in 1978 on *Special Educational Needs*, wrote that

> we have insisted throughout our report that the successful education of children with special needs is dependent on the full involvement of their parents. Indeed, unless parents are seen as equal partners in the educative process the purpose of our report will be frustrated.
>
> (Warnock Report 1978: 150)

However, research during the 1980s has continued to demonstrate that, while ostensibly committed to parental involvement, teachers and other professionals still expect parents to be passive partners, accepting professional decisions without questions. In a study following the assessment of thirty children as 'emotionally and behaviourally disturbed' (Galloway *et al.* 1993), the professionals claimed that their overriding concern was to act in the interests of the children and involve parents at the centre of decision-making, but parents felt they were listened to only when they were confirming professional views, and that ultimately the professionals knew that, in any conflict of interest, they had the sanction of coercion against uncooperative parents.

One way in which parents are becoming more involved in special education is through litigation, which does not encourage the formation of partnerships. There is a growing consciousness amongst some parents, particularly articulate and knowledgeable ones, that their rights under the 1981 Special Education Act are not being respected, as during the 1980s local education authorities, with budgets reduced by central government, have sought to minimize spending on special educational needs. The production of inadequate statements and the failure to specify resources has resulted in more legal challenges from parents (Audit Commission 1991: Pyke 1993).

European policies

It is useful to consider some other European home–school policies and learn from positive developments. An EEC-funded project in the early 1980s, 'The school and family in the European Community', suggested that politicians, educators and parents themselves often assumed that home–school partnerships could be achieved by simple strategies (Macbeth 1989). An EEC conference held in Luxembourg in 1983 noted that 'there is widespread recognition that parents and teachers should be partners in educating children but there are difficulties in putting this ideal into practice'. However, it is possible that Europe-wide parental initiatives are now in advance of governmental or educationalists' thinking. The European Parents Association – and a more recent French initiative, le Centre Européen des Parents de l'Ecole Publique (CEPEP) – aim to work out joint goals for the future of publicly-funded education in Europe which will include parental partnership. CEPEP has representation from parents' organizations in France, England (via Parents Initiative), Eire, Italy, Germany, Spain, Portugal and Belgium, and interest expressed by groups in Holland, Denmark, Greece, Austria and Luxembourg. This group has set in train discussion of a common educational philosophy for EEC countries and has suggested that national education systems should all include a home–school association in every school, government-funded parent associations, home–school links to be compulsory study in teacher training, and parents to be represented at all local and national levels where educational policies are formulated.

In France the schooling is secular and centralized, teachers are civil servants and there is a National Curriculum. However, dialogue with parents has been a feature of the education system for some time. The Ministry of Education publishes material explaining the education system and a bulletin, 'A letter to parents'. All French primary schools are required by law to have a joint committee of teachers and parents and parents are consulted over the choice of books and materials for schools.

In Italy co-operation with parents has been included in Ministerial decrees since 1955, and the *decreti delegati* in 1974 introduced an elaborate system of councils which were intended to involve parents and local communities in all aspects and levels of education. The complexity of the pyramid of councils – school class, school, district, provincial, and a national council – and the elaborate system of representation has not notably included parents in actual decision-making but the councils have reduced mutual mistrust between parents and teachers, given parents better information and encouraged parents to regard education as a joint home–school process.

In Germany the post-war Federal Basic Law laid down broad guidelines for the control and administration of education in (West) Germany which is undertaken by the eleven provinces (Länder). The Basic Law incorporated principles of parental rights and responsibilities for their children's education and all the provincial constitutions require co-operation between schools and families, although each province varies in the details of its written requirements. The Bavarian constitution, for example, notes that 'The common educational task which confronts school and parents requires co-operation carried out in mutual trust'. In Rhineland-Palatinate, 'parents have the right and duty to co-operate with schools in the education of their children'.

All provinces have legal requirements for parents' councils at different levels of education. In Baden-Württemberg, for example, there are school class councils chaired by a parent, school, district and provincial councils. The provincial parents' council offers advice to the Minister of Education and must be kept informed by the Ministry.

The Danish school system is rooted in the notion of community education and gives more legal recognition and informed support to partnership between the family and the school than any other country. The Danish Basic School Law of 1975 reads:

> The task of the Basic School is, in co-operation with parents, to offer possibilities for pupils to acquire knowledge, skills, working methods and forms of expression which will contribute to each individual's development.
>
> (Macbeth 1989: 174)

The Danish approach recognizes that schools can do no more than make facilities available; they cannot, unaided, educate the 'whole child' and make no claims to this. Pupils attend the basic school (*Folkeskole*) for a minimum of nine years, and the class teacher moves with the pupils accentuating the possibilities of partnership with families. Municipal committees oversee the Folkeskoles and there is parental representation on these committees. Each school board comprises parents with voting rights, teachers and pupils in its participants. Within schools, class associations of parents, teachers and pupils have developed, and the Education Ministry publishes a guide to co-operation between homes and schools. The national parents' organization *Skole og Samfund* incorporates all school boards and voluntary parental associations. Danish parents are recognized in law and in practice as sharing partnership rights and responsibilities at all levels of schooling.

In Spain one approach to parental involvement has been to recognize that parental involvement means educating parents in school and educational matters in ways not hitherto envisaged. At the University of Navarre 'schools for parents' have been devised, working on a modular basis with university staff and parent co-ordinators. Sexton, who learned about this development at a European Parents Association Conference in Italy, was so impressed by the way such courses improved parental participation in education that he has introduced pilot 'schools for parents' in the UK (Sexton 1992).

New policies

In considering new policies which will improve home–school links and create genuine partnerships, it has to be recognized that it will not be easy to work out a practice of education based on the reversal of a 150-year-old process. Educational policies have until the 1980s sought to *reduce* the impact of parents on their children's education, since mass schooling had been created partly because parents in the nineteenth century could not communicate the knowledge and skills required for an industrial society. Policies were geared to *replace* parental influence. Now it has become apparent that schools on their own cannot communicate the knowledge and skills required for an advanced technological society or the moral, social and political skills for living in such a society. Schools must now reorient their work to collaborate with parents as an educational force.

New legislation which requires schools to pass over much more information to parents is to be welcomed, although presenting information in the form of league tables (of exam results, attendance figures, post-16 destinations, etc.) without close parental involvement in the life of the school may be more a recipe for conflict and alienation than closer co-operation.

Offering a wide range of information to parents, in conjunction with 'schools for parents', perhaps as suggested by Stuart Sexton (1992), constitutes one policy for improving home–school links. It has already been noted that particular groups – ethnic minority parents and the parents of those with special educational needs – will require particular attention.

A second and crucial policy which could easily be implemented and which would go a long way towards including *all* parents in home–school co-operation would be a new legal requirement that all schools should set up a home–school association, open to *all* parents, teachers and representative pupils. Given the history of parent associations in England, such associations, if voluntary, might be dominated by white middle-class parents. If associations have a statutory base, all parents being automatic members when their child joins a school, this objection would be overcome.

The associations would:

- not principally be concerned with fund-raising or social activities. They would be a forum for passing over knowledge and information about formal schooling to parents, and the passing of information on home learning to teachers;
- discuss matters relating to children's learning, progress and achievement, debate matters related to curriculum, assessment, recording teaching methods, behaviour in schools and school organization;
- include class associations as the main way to bring teachers and parents together. Parents would work with teachers to involve those parents who, for practical or other reasons, find it difficult to involve themselves with school. (This would help remove the teacher complaint that 'the parents we really want to see never come'.);
- inform themselves of the professional services teachers offer, their rights, their conditions of service and their needs as a professional body;
- be statutorily consulted at local level when important decisions were being made on education, and representatives would be similarly consulted at national level. The associations would liaise with, but not replace, governing bodies.

The associations would organize home–school communications, make arrangements for obligatory consultation about individual children, co-ordinate home–school learning schemes and homework arrangements and arrange parental involvement in day-to-day school activities.

Given the interest in written home–school educational agreements (contracts) pioneered in the RSA home–school project, the development of such agreements within the framework of a home–school association could be explored.

Conclusion

This chapter started from the premise that improving children's educational performance, enhancing their personal and social development and creating genuine home–school links could happen only if the current stress on parents as consumers of education and agents of competition gave way to a belief that parents must be partners in the educative process.

If we are really concerned to raise educational standards and improve the quality of education, a convergence of home and school and a partnership between parents and teachers is a necessity. Policies must be geared to the understanding that schools and homes are joint producers of education and that in future parents will need to be more centrally involved in the process of schooling.

Any government which is seriously concerned about raising standards and offering an improved education to all pupils will concentrate on enhancing parental support, involvement and obligation to participate in formal education. It will also recognize that a more equal relationship between parents and teachers will require a different legislative framework to the present one. The legal framework will need to include more rights to information, for parent education, for parents to be involved in their children's day-to-day schooling, to be automatically members of a home–school association and to make an educational agreement with the school.

Home–school partnerships can remain empty rhetoric, be a cover for enhancing professional powers or become another mechanism for 'policing' pupils. We need open and equal relationships between schools and homes to contribute to better understandings, higher standards and an improved quality of education.

References

Audit Commission (1991) *Getting in on the Act: Provision for Pupils with Special Educational Needs*, London: HMSO.

Bastiani, J. and Bailey, G. (1992) *Directory of Home–School Initiatives in the UK*, London: Royal Society of Arts and National Association of Headteachers.

Bernstein, B. (1973) *Class Codes and Control*, 1, London: Routledge.

Brar, H.S. (1991) Teaching, professionalism and home–school links, *Multicultural Teaching*, 9(1): 32–5.

Chaudhury, A. (1990) 'Problems for parents: experiences in Tower Hamlets' in C. Orton (ed.) *Asian Children and Special Educational Needs*, London: Advisory Centre for Education.

Commission for Racial Equality (1989) *Racial Segregation in Education: Report of a Formal Investigation into Cleveland LEA*, London: CRE.

Council for the Accreditation of Teacher Education (1992) *The Accreditation of Initial Teacher Training Index, Circulars 9/92 and 35/92, A Note of Guidance*, London: CATE.

Cunningham, C. and Davis, H. (1985) *Working with Parents: Frameworks for Collaboration*, Milton Keynes: Open University Press.

Edwards, V. and Redfern, A. (1988) *At Home in School*, London: Routledge.

Galloway, D., Armstrong, D. and Tomlinson, S. (1993) *Whose Special Educational Needs?* London: Longman.

Gewirtz, S., Ball, S. and Bowe, R. (1992) 'Parents, privilege and the education market place', paper to the British Educational Research Association, Stirling: Scotland, August.

Grace, G. (1978) *Education Ideology and Social Control*, London: Routledge.

Jones, G., Bastiani, J., Bell, G. and Chapman, C. (1992) *A Willing Partnership: Project Study of the Home–School Contract of Partnership*, London: Royal Society of Arts.

Macbeth, A. (1989) *Involving Parents*, Oxford: Heinemann.

MacDonald, I. (1989) *Murder in the Playground*, Manchester: Longsight Press.

National Consumer Council (1990) *Minority Ethnic Communities and School Governing Bodies*, London: NCC.

Parents' Charter (1991) *You and Your Child's Education*, London: DES.

Plowden Report (1967) *Children and Their Primary Schools*, London: HMSO (2 vols).

Pugh, G. and De'Ath, E. (1989) *Parents, Professionals and Partnership: Rhetoric or Reality*, London: National Children's Bureau.

Pyke, N. (1993) 'Parents take to High Court', *Times Educational Supplement*, 15 January.

Roberts, K. (1984) *School Leavers and Their Prospects*, Milton Keynes: Open University Press.

Rutter, M. and Madge, N. (1976) *Cycles of Disadvantage*, London: Heinemann.

Sexton, S. (1992) 'Parents can be teachers too', *The Times*, 3 November.

Tomlinson, S. (1982) *A Sociology of Special Education*, London: Routledge.

Tomlinson, S. (1984) *Home and School in Multicultural Britain*, London: Batsford.

Tomlinson, S. (1988) 'Why Johnny can't read: critical theory and special education', *European Journal of Special Needs Education*, 3(l): 45–58.

Tomlinson, S. (1991) 'Home–School partnerships' in *Teachers and Parents*, Education and Training paper no. 7, 1–18, London: Institute for Public Policy Research.

Tomlinson, S. (1993) 'Ethnic minorities: involved partners or problem parents' in P. Munn (ed.) *Parents and Schools: Customers, Managers or Partners*, London: Routledge.

Tredgold, A.E. (1908) *Mental Deficiency*, London: Baillière, Tindall and Cox.

Waller, W. (1932) *The Sociology of Teaching*, New York: Wiley.

Warnock Report (1978) *Special Educational Needs*, London: HMSO.

Wolfendale, S. (1989) *Parental Involvement: Developing Networks between Home, School and Community*, London: Cassell.

27 Policy alternatives to exclusion from school

Pamela Munn, Gwynedd Lloyd and
Mairi Ann Cullen

Explanations of disaffected behaviour

Underpinning policy and practice on exclusion from school are explanations of the causes of disaffected behaviour and hence of the appropriate response to it. Broadly speaking explanations fall into two categories, those which locate 'causes' within the individual child and family and those which locate 'causes' in society in general and in schools as organizations. In the past most explanations were rooted in the individual child who was seen as either 'mad' or 'bad' and so requiring either sustained medical or psychiatrically based intervention or punishment (Bridgeland 1971). Often the best that could be done was to provide some form of containment. As Sandow (1994: 2) makes clear, 'The implication of such a view is that education for the affected child is impossible and may be almost sacrilegious: "flying in the face of nature."' Contemporary explanations include the neo-biological, used for example to explain the behaviour of children who show an apparently abnormal incapacity for sustained attention. Labels like attention deficit and hyperactivity disorder are increasingly used by teachers and psychologists to explain problem behaviour (Armstrong and Galloway 1994: Ferguson *et al.* 1997). Thus one strand of response to disaffected behaviour is to 'do something' about the individual young person. Interventions range from drug therapy for Attention Deficit Hyperactivity Disorder to psychological and psychiatric treatments.

A wide range of research studies has pointed to the influence of school effects on behaviour. Such studies include the large-scale and statistically robust research on school effectiveness (e.g. Rutter *et al.* 1979: Reynolds 1997: Sammons *et al.* 1997) as well as in-depth qualitative studies of small numbers of schools and pupils (e.g. Hargreaves *et al.* 1975: Munn *et al.* 1992a, 1992b: Jones and Jones 1992: Ruddock *et al.* 1996). These studies show that schools (and departments and teachers) make a difference. Schools with pupils from similar backgrounds can vary in their effectiveness in terms of pupils' behaviour, achievement and attendance, and much else besides. These studies attempt to identify the various aspects of schools which, taken together, make a difference. They include:

- the physical environment being made welcoming and comfortable
- pupils' work valued through regular displays which are updated regularly

- positive teacher–pupil relationships incorporating high teacher expectations of pupils' academic and other achievements
- personal and social development given a high priority
- homework set and marked regularly
- active leadership and a shared vision of what the school is aiming to do
- pupil participation in decision-making about school and classroom life.

Taken together, these elements are generally regarded as a school's *ethos* or culture. These studies, therefore, suggest that there are things schools can do to influence the behaviour of pupils.

Cooper and Upton (1991); Upton and Cooper (1990); Cooper *et al.* (1996) highlight the usefulness of the 'ecosystemic approach' with young people exhibiting emotional and behavioural difficulties. As the label suggests, the approach focuses on systems at school and in the environment of the young person in ways which 'are compatible with the humanistic aims of education, which are to facilitate the development of autonomy and self-direction in students, and in ways that do not appear to shift the blame for emotional and behavioural difficulties from pupils to their teachers and parents' (Cooper and Upton 1991: 22).

Policy and guidance on school exclusion reveal the tensions in the explanations for disaffection. These include the individualization of reasons for challenging behaviour and the consequent need for interventions or treatment targeted at the individual young people. Within this research literature there have also been attempts to categorize more precisely than hitherto the diverse nature of social, emotional and behavioural difficulties exhibited by pupils. These challenge the usefulness of social, emotional and behavioural difficulties as a category. This has resulted in some authors suggesting that some categories of pupils with social, emotional and behavioural difficulties are authors of their own misfortune and therefore deserve punishment, while others have intrinsic social, emotional and behavioural difficulties which deserve therapy or other forms of treatment. The tension between punishment and treatment is evident in exclusions legislation as we shall see below. Policy and guidance also include the encouragement to schools to work with other agencies to support young people in trouble and for schools to develop a more positive and caring ethos.

Avoiding inappropriate blame

It is all too easy to blame schools, social work services or psychological services for failing young people. It is equally easy for schools and the like to blame the individual young person for anti-social behaviour. This individualization process, whether to institutions or people, diverts attention from structural inequalities in terms of wealth, and so of housing, health and educational opportunity. When Halsey was writing in 1972 about the introduction of Educational Priority Areas, he argued that we should avoid treating education as a waste-paper basket of social policy, as a way of dealing with social problems where there seem to be no solutions.

Similarly Hopmann and Konzuli (1997), reflecting on schooling in Sweden but conscious of its similarities to many other Western countries, claim that common social problems which are difficult to resolve have come to be blamed on schools with little thought about what is appropriate or realistic to expect of schools, or the purposes for which schools are actually resourced.

Current policies to tackle social exclusion seem to recognize that schools are only part of the jigsaw, albeit an important one in developing a more inclusive society. As subsequent chapters reveal, there is a great deal that schools are already doing to provide good-quality alternatives to exclusion. The broader approach under the banner of tackling social exclusion is untested, but it is an overdue and welcome recognition of the need for school policy to be integrated into broader social policy development. [...]

Dilemmas of policy and practice

... School is the place where decisions are taken to exclude a young person and so an exploration of some of the dilemmas facing schools is an important starting point in considering the extent to which local and national policies to reduce exclusion will take root.

Schools may be understood as institutions driven by diverse and contested purposes, by the values of those who go there and by the practices which may or may not reflect purposes and values. Thus when it comes to decisions on exclusion, competing claims have to be weighed and compromises reached. Few people involved in exclusion from school, at whatever level, see it as straightforward and unproblematic. Four main dilemmas are highlighted by way of illustrating one part of the terrain in which a policy to tackle exclusion will operate.

Conflicting goals

School discipline has always served two purposes. Good discipline is a *means to an end*, the end being to create the conditions for pupils to learn. It is fairly self-evident that pupils cannot learn in a disorderly and unsafe classroom or school. Of course we are not suggesting here that good discipline guarantees effective learning; many factors contribute to this, including pupils' motivation, their previous learning, the resources available and so on. Nevertheless good classroom and school discipline are important ingredients in the factors affecting learning. Good discipline, however, is also *an end in itself*. Schools play an inescapable role in the socialization of pupils. This has been so for as long as schools have been in existence. Thus in the early seventeenth century, for example:

> The 1675 Synod of Aberdeen asked its presbyteries only to demand three questions of the school master: whether he makes the bairns learn the catechism, whether he teaches them prayers for morning and evening and grace for meals

and whether 'he chastise them for cursing, swearing, lying, speaking profanietie, for disobedience to parents and what vices that appears in them'.

(Simpson, quoted in Smout 1969: 84)

More recently Barber (1996: 187–8) comments:

> If we want young people to learn the rules of living and working in communities – how to solve differences of opinion, how to respect a variety of beliefs ... then these must feature in the curriculum of schools.

The inherent dilemmas for schools of pursuing these twin purposes are evident in the current policy context. On the one hand the importance of discipline as a means to an end can be seen in the drive to raise standards of pupils' attainment as measured in national tests, public examination results and international comparisons. Furthermore, the publication of school performance tables, giving details of the relative attainments of pupils in schools across the UK, provides a very clear mechanism of public accountability for schools. It therefore seems entirely logical for schools to seek to maximize their position on such tables, especially when a further mechanism of public accountability is the right for parents to choose the schools their children will attend. On the other hand, schools are being discouraged from excluding pupils, pupils who might well be seen as threatening attainment targets because of disruptive behaviour in classrooms. The resolution of this dilemma might be the greater use of internal exclusion which camouflages the extent of disaffection and also raises questions about the quality of schooling on offer.

Similarly schools are being given mixed messages about how they should view pupils. The Children's Act (1989) and the Children (Scotland) Act (1995) stress a welfare principle, the best interests of the child, and delineate children's rights to be consulted about and participate in decisions which directly affect them. Education legislation carries no such imperatives (Parsons 1999). As Parsons further points out (1999: 7):

> Childhood activity, and roles proper for it, are social constructions, varying across national cultures and history. We see child workers in the Indian subcontinent and gun-toting 12-year-olds in Africa. In the UK, probably more than other countries in the 'developed' west, children have no legitimate voice.

It is noteworthy, for instance, that in recent legislation such as the 1997 Education Act and the 1998 School Standards and Framework Act 'the quantity of text ... devoted to regulating the process of exclusion and establishing judicial and ever more complex procedures for appeal, overshadowed any text relating to the needs of the child or the child's access to full-time education' (Parsons 1999: 108). We contend that this approach differs from that adopted in Scotland where there has been no flurry of legislation relating to exclusion, and national guidance on exclusion (Scottish Office 1998) is congruent with the child welfare emphasis underpinning the Scottish approach to youth offending.

Collective and individual welfare

There are, furthermore, the competing claims of the rights of the individual disruptive child or young person to schooling weighed against the claims of the majority of pupils to enjoy a safe and secure educational environment and not to be distracted from work by disruptive behaviour. Teachers and others are aware of the time and effort which can be devoted to a small number of disaffected pupils, time which is, therefore, being denied the majority. The competing claims of individual and collective welfare rights are beginning to be tackled in cases of young people with special educational needs. In the past it was rare for these young people to be educated in mainstream schools; they were typically educated in specialist day or residential provision or in special units attached to mainstream schools. That situation is gradually changing and there is now a more varied population of children with special needs in both mainstream and special schools (Allan *et al.* 1995), although the figure of 1.2 per cent of all school pupils educated in special schools has changed little over the years (Cross 1997). In contrast, the special school population declined in England in 1996 to 1.4 per cent of all 5–15-year-olds, the lowest ever percentage for England (Norwich 1997), although there are wide variations across local education authorities in the percentages of pupils they place in special schools. Norwich (1997) identifies a range from 0.32 per cent in Newham to 2.31 per cent in Hackney.

The practice of assessing and recording or statementing children with special educational needs is now well established although problematic in practice (Thomson *et al.* 1996). Yet recording/statementing remains an important vehicle promoting entitlement to specialist provision for young people in need. The more recent adoption of Individual Education Plans (IEPs) and the current advocacy of Personal Learning Plans (PLPs) for all children (Scottish Office 1999) may be a useful way of a) encouraging teachers to see children with behavioural difficulties as having special needs and worthy of support in much the same way as other children with special needs and b) identifying the specialist help and other resources needed to meet their needs. This approach, however, is not without its problems. Petrie and Shaw (1998: 123) confirm that the needs-based approach reduces whole groups of people:

> to bundles of need – deficit individuals requiring help without anything to offer – objects rather than active subjects.

Writing about the struggle for inclusion they contend that professionals can conceptualize their role as a series of technical challenges to overcome barriers to the inclusion of those with special needs. Rather, the concern should be 'to shift the discourse of disability from one of "in-person" deficiency to one of discrimination and rights' (Petrie and Shaw 1998: 124). Many schools have begun to shift from individual deficit explanations as the only way of understanding challenging behaviour. We are, however, still far away from establishing a rights agenda for pupils who are excluded from school, although recent Scottish guidance on exclusion mentioned above (Scottish Office 1998) signals such a move. Even if teachers can be encouraged to see troubled and troublesome youngsters as having special needs, however, there remains the question of where these needs might be met and also who should do so.

Even if headteachers do not massage the figures a low exclusion rate may conceal poor-quality provision for pupils in trouble, such as sitting in corridors or other forms of 'internal exclusion'. Thus ways of affirming the broad range of the purposes of schooling need to be found in addition to performance management systems. More fundamentally, however, the aspects of schooling concerned with pupils' cognitive attainments, as certificated by public examinations, confer distinct advantages to those possessing such certificates over those who do not possess them. Public examination certificates are the gateway to further and higher education and to the labour market. Access to these opportunities is competitive. Thus things which stand in the way of pupils maximizing their chances of securing good examination results are bound to be resisted by pupils themselves and especially parents, who are aware of the advantages good results can bring. Schools can be under significant pressure from parents to exclude children who are perceived as threatening the opportunity of other children to succeed, as well as their safety and general welfare. Thus schools wanting to reduce or eliminate exclusions face very real dilemmas about the balance of effort devoted to individual as opposed to collective welfare. In matters of safety and well-being, collective welfare will always take precedence over individual welfare.

Professional autonomy

A third dilemma concerns the professional autonomy of teachers and headteachers. A consistent approach to classroom discipline across a range of subjects and staff in a large secondary school is no easy matter even where staff are inclined to adopt such an approach. The private nature of teaching, the professional autonomy of the individual teacher in the day-to-day management of the classroom and the context-specific nature of discipline, all make consistency a goal which has to be continually reaffirmed. Many schools are adopting policies highlighting praise and reward for good behaviour which can open up discussion among staff and pupils about what counts as good behaviour and about how to promote positive relationships between staff and pupils. This kind of approach, as well as staff analysing patterns of 'referral' and exclusion of pupils, is beginning to show some positive results (Munn 1999). Yet the private nature of much teaching can make it difficult for headteachers to be seen to be fair to both staff and pupils in using exclusion as a sanction. It is noteworthy that almost all excluded pupils interviewed in research studies say that they have been treated unfairly. 'They would say that, wouldn't they?' is an easy reaction from stressed or cynical staff. Yet sufficient is known about the negative effects of labelling pupils as disruptive to raise questions about consistency and justice in the use of exclusions.

National and local policy can help put structures in place to promote justice. Local authorities, for instance, can require a series of steps to be taken before exclusion, such as consultation with and the provision of reports from educational psychologists, which constrain the power of a headteacher to exclude a child for more than three days. Headteachers themselves may draw up procedures to discourage staff from using exclusion, such as meetings with guidance staff, social workers and others to assess the needs of the child and determine ways of meeting these. Structures and procedures alone, however, are insufficient. The nature of teacher and of headteacher autonomy means that procedures and structures can be subverted, sometimes in a bid to access scarce resources, sometimes as a way of obtaining respite from a difficult pupil. Policies, structures and procedures need to be underpinned by a sense of belief and support for their aims. Caught up as they are with the day-to-day realities of teaching and managing schools, it can be difficult for teachers and headteachers to remind themselves of the broader social functions of schooling, the successes which the school system has delivered in terms of rising numbers of pupils achieving passes in public examinations. It is this kind of awareness that needs to be encouraged in initial teacher education and continued professional development programmes if the spirit as well as the letter of exclusion policy and guidelines are to be followed.

[...]

References

Allan, J., Brown, S. and Riddell, S. (1995) *Special Educational Needs Provision in Mainstream and Special Schools in Scotland*, University of Stirling.

Armstrong, D. and Galloway, D. (1994) 'Special educational needs and problem behaviour, making policy in the classroom' in S. Riddell and S. Brown (eds) *Special Educational Needs Policy in the 90s*, London: Routledge.

Barber, M. (1996) *The Learning Game, Arguments for an Education Revolution*, London: Victor Gollancz.

Bridgeland, M. (1971) *Pioneer Work with Maladjusted Children*, London: Staples.

Cross, A. (1997) 'Special educational provision' in M.M. Clark and P. Munn (eds) *Education in Scotland, Policy and Practice from Pre-school to Secondary*, London: Routledge.

Cooper, P. and Upton, G. (1991) 'Controlling the urge to control: An ecosystemic approach to problem behaviour in schools', *Support for Learning*, 6(1): 22–6.

Cooper, P., Smith, C. and Upton, G. (1996) *Emotional and Behavioural Difficulties – Theory to Practice*, London: Routledge.

Ferguson, R., Lloyd, G. and Reid, G. (1997) *Attention Deficit and Hyperactivity Disorder: A Literature Review*, Edinburgh: Moray House Publications.

Hargreaves, D.H., Hester, J.K. and Mellor, F.J. (1975) *Deviance in Classrooms*, London: Routledge and Kegan Paul.

Hopmann, S. and Konzuli, R. (1997) 'Close our schools! Against trends in policy-making, educational theory and curriculum studies', *Journal of Curriculum Studies*, 29(3): 259–66.

Jones, N. and Jones, E. (eds) (1992) *Learning to Behave*, London: Kogan Page.

Munn, P. (ed.) (1999) *Promoting Positive Discipline in Scottish Schools, Whole School Approaches to Tackling Low-Level Disruption*, Edinburgh: Faculty of Education.

Munn, P. and Lloyd, G. (forthcoming) *Indiscipline in Schools: A Review of Extent, 'Causes' and 'Cures'*, Edinburgh: Scottish Council for Research in Education.

Munn, P., Johnstone, M. and Chalmers, V. (1992a) *Effective Discipline in Secondary Schools and Classrooms*, London: Paul Chapman.

Munn, P., Johnstone, M. and Chalmers, V. (1992b) *Effective Discipline in Primary Schools and Classrooms*, London: Paul Chapman.

Norwich, B. (1997) A *Trend Towards Inclusion, Statistics on Special School Placements and Pupils with Statements in Ordinary Schools, England 1992–96*, London: Centre for Studies on Inclusive Education.

Parsons, C. (1999) *Education, Exclusion and Citizenship*, London: Routledge.

Petrie, M. and Shaw, M. (1998) 'The disability movement and the struggle for inclusion' in J. Crowther, I. Martin and M. Shaw (eds) *Popular Education and Social Movements in Scotland Today*, Leicester: National Institute for Adult and Continuing Education.

Reynolds, D. (1997) 'School effectiveness, retrospect and prospect', *Scottish Educational Review*, 29(2): 97–113.

Ruddock, J., Chaplain, R. and Wallace, G. (1996) *School Improvement, What Can Pupils Tell Us?*, London: David Fulton.

Rutter, M., Maughan, B., Mortimore, P. and Ouston, J. (1979) *Fifteen Thousand Hours, Secondary Schools and Their Effects on Children*, London: Paul Chapman.

Sammons, P., Thomas, S. and Mortimore, P. (1997) *Forging Links, Effective Schools and Effective Departments*, London: Paul Chapman.

Sandow, S. (1994) 'More ways than one, models of special needs' in S. Sandow (ed.) *Whose Special Need?*, London: Paul Chapman.

Scottish Office (1998) *Guidance on Issues Concerning Exclusion from School*, Circular No. 2/98, Edinburgh: Scottish Office.

Scottish Office (1999) *New Community Schools Prospectus*, Edinburgh: Scottish Office.

Smout, T.C. (1969) *A History of the Scottish People 1560–1830*, Glasgow: Fontana.

Thomson, G., Stewart, M. and Ward, K. (1996) *Criteria for Opening Records of Needs*, Edinburgh: Interchange 40, Scottish Office.

Upton, G. and Cooper, P. (1990) 'A new perspective on behaviour problems in schools, the ecosystemic approach', *Maladjustment and Therapeutic Education*, 8(1): 3–18.

Index